Mental Health and Higher Education in Australia

Abraham P. Francis · Margaret Anne Carter
Editors

Mental Health and Higher Education in Australia

Springer

Editors
Abraham P. Francis
College of Arts, Society, and Education
James Cook University
Townsville, QLD, Australia

Margaret Anne Carter
Australian College of Applied Professions
Brisbane, QLD, Australia

ISBN 978-981-16-8039-7 ISBN 978-981-16-8040-3 (eBook)
https://doi.org/10.1007/978-981-16-8040-3

This Springer imprint is published by the registered company Springer Nature Singapore Pte Ltd.
The registered company address is: 152 Beach Road, #21-01/04 Gateway East, Singapore 189721, Singapore

Dedicated to 'our fellow authors and to our families'

Foreword

I have had the privilege of working with this book's editors, Professor Margaret Carter and Associate Professor Abraham Francis, over a number of years. We first met in 2016, in the lead-up to the inaugural Australian Mental Health in Higher Education Conference (AMHHEC). These two clever and kind academics conceived the Conference together, up in the furthest reach of the Australian continent. At that stage, I had only recently published my Churchill Fellowship report and was honoured to be invited as a keynote speaker to present my findings on 'The Wicked Problem of University Student Mental Health'. Townsville seemed an unlikely venue for such a meeting—in fact, when Abraham first approached me at a conference in Melbourne with a smile on his face and a flyer in hand, I was a little sceptical that they could pull it off—but it went brilliantly. Now, half a decade on, AMHHEC has become a fixture in the Australian higher education calendar. Or at least it had, until the novel coronavirus pandemic hit in early 2020.

Just as it has made an indelible mark on all our lives, so has the pandemic influenced this book. It is appropriate that COVID 19 features prominently, given its impact on higher education. Education was Australia's fourth largest export prior to the pandemic[1]; closing our borders has threatened this. Universities were essentially excluded from the 'JobKeeper' income support package and thus job insecurity for academics worsened, with many positions now gone. Students also lost jobs, and not all were eligible for compensatory government support. Social distancing meant everyone was suddenly learning and teaching remotely, increasing lecturer and tutor workloads, and affecting the learning experience and socialisation opportunities. Several of the book chapters address the pandemic explicitly, focusing, for example, on the impact that COVID-19 has had on international students who were already studying far from home but were suddenly even more disconnected from their families. Elsewhere, the text reminds us of the importance of the broader context of the higher education institution itself, and the role that mentally healthy cities play in supporting healthy places of learning, and vice versa.

---

[1] https://www.rba.gov.au/publications/bulletin/2020/dec/pdf/the-covid-19-outbreak-and-australias-education-and-tourism-exports.pdf.

Reflecting the same spirit with which the co-editors established AMHHEC, this book is ambitious. It seeks to weave together many threads of thought, penned by a diverse group of thinkers. The authors range from researchers at the beginning of their doctorates to very senior academics and in one case, even a former federal member of parliament. Lived experience makes a welcome contribution, as does the inclusion of a sprinkle of international voices from the United Kingdom.

During the five years, I have known and worked with the editors, my primary focus has been on my clinical responsibilities and studies as a medical doctor, sub-specialising in child and adolescent psychiatry. Now at the end of my training, I find myself working in infant mental health. Between this and the fact I am frequently guilty of procrastination, which often feels maladaptive, my interest was particularly piqued by Kaz Mitchell's chapter on perfectionism, procrastination and attachment. My current clinical work with young children reflects my desire to see a greater emphasis in early—as opposed to late—intervention, and so it is pleasing to see this concept explored in the higher education literature. It challenges my own thinking, as when I undertook my Churchill Fellowship I must admit that I considered 'early intervention' to be the freshman year. Of course, our earliest attachment bonds cast a long shadow, which is reflected in the chapter on relationship issues. These are very important for students, yet frequently overlooked, and tend to arise during undergraduate education because of such study's coincident timing with the 'intimacy vs. isolation' stage in Erik Erikson's theory of psychological development. That they are discussed in this book reflects the editors' own broad and thoughtful approach to their work.

In a similar spirit, I was pleased to see the editors follow a bio-psycho-social-cultural recipe in the making of this book. Neuroscience and psychology certainly feature, but they are matched by a welcome emphasis on social, cultural and even spiritual aspects of higher education and how these mediate mental health. The chapters generally privilege the experience of students, but they do not omit that of the academics, whose mental health is also important, both independently and because of its interplay with that of their pupils. Where specific disciplines are considered, the scope is also wide, encompassing not just the usual suspects of medicine and law, but in multiple chapters, the visual and creative arts. Building of the 'Enhancing Student Wellbeing' program of work led by Associate Professor Chi Baik in Melbourne, this book also discusses the role of curricula as both an undue contributor to student stress and a tool with which healthy learning environments may be curated.

I congratulate all of the authors whose work is proudly featured in this eclectic and significant contribution to our understanding of what it means to seek to build more resilient communities and positive cultures in higher education. These aims are important not only for the sustainability of the sector, but also because of the scale of impact that the sector has on modern society. At time of writing, the Australian Bureau of Statistics is still crunching the numbers on the 2021 Census, but data from 2016[2] show that about four million Australians held a bachelor's or postgraduate degree.

---

[2] https://www.abs.gov.au/AUSSTATS/abs@.nsf/mediareleasesbyReleaseDate/1533FE5A8541D66CCA2581BF00362D1D.

The trajectory is up, and over time, the moral imperative to positively influence the mental health of all those who come into contact with our institutions of higher learning will likewise only increase. My hope is that the type of lessons found inside this book are heeded, trialled and improved upon with the degree of emphasis and support they deserve.

September 2021

Dr. Benjamin Veness
Churchill Fellow and Child
and Adolescent Psychiatry Registrar
Melbourne, Australia

Dr. Benjamin Veness is a medical doctor in Melbourne, Australia, with sub-specialist training in child and adolescent psychiatry. In 2013, he was awarded the Monash University Churchill Fellowship to explore innovative prevention and early intervention strategies to improve the mental health of university students. His Fellowship involved travel to the United States, Canada, the United Kingdom, Switzerland, China and Singapore, and culminated in the publication of his report, 'The Wicked Problem of University Student Mental Health'. Subsequently, both the Federal Government and the universities' sector have shown significantly increased interest in the topic, and he has been invited to share his expertise with a variety of institutions.

In addition to a medical degree, he holds Master's degrees in Psychiatry and Public Health, and a Bachelor's degree in Accounting. Prior to studying medicine, he worked in the corporate sector, predominantly in banking strategy. He has extensive advocacy experience gained through various roles, including as President of the Australian Medical Students' Association, which involved representing 17,000 medical students across the country. He was awarded the Edmund Barton Medal by the University of Sydney and acquired governance experience in tertiary education by virtue of serving two terms as an elected Fellow of Senate of the University of Sydney.

Declarations

This book is conceived and edited by Abraham P. Francis and Margaret Anne Carter. They have had extensive discussions with the authors of this book at every stage of the production. It is a work that has involved many authors from various contexts and professional backgrounds. The focus of the book is about mental health in higher education. The ideas, concepts, and research and practice experiences discussed in this book are useful in any social contexts. Our efforts have been to support authors to present their ideas and research outcomes with a view to retain their style, research focus, and voices to reflect the collaborative nature of this book. The editors are responsible for the ideological framework, identifying the authors for this book, providing an overall structure and presentation of this book, while the individual author/authors are responsible for the key ideas presented in their respective chapters. Some of the chapters are based on research studies and others are views, experiences, and reflections of the authors engaged in this area of research, practice, and engagement.

Acknowledgements

It is with a great sense of hope, excitement and accomplishment that we would like to present this book to the readers. There have been several people who have been instrumental in supporting us achieve our dream of a Mental Health Book in Higher Education becoming a reality. We would like to acknowledge and thank them for their support and contributions.

We would like to acknowledge the loving providence of God, who protected us, and blessed us with fantastic colleagues and friends to work with on this project. Likewise, support and assistance have come from many corners for which we are indebted and grateful. We thank all our chapter contributors for their excellent contribution to this book. Very sincerely we thank Dr. Benjamin Veness, Churchill Fellow who presents regularly on the topic of university students' mental health at conferences and other events around Australia. He is also an advocate for doctors' and medical students' mental health, and during the COVID-19 pandemic has been campaigning for improvements in all healthcare workers' occupational health and safety.

We are grateful for the tremendous support and encouragement we have received from Dr. Mark David Chong, Dr. Beryl Buckby, Dr. Simone Ross, A/P David Lindsay, Claire Ovaska and Jeremy Audas. Our colleagues at James Cook University, the Australian College of Applied Professions, and the wider community have been instrumental in this project.

Our profound gratitude goes to our peer reviewers—Professor Debra Miles, A/Professor Nonie Harris, Dr. Hyacinth Udah, and Dr. Frank Baffour (James Cook University), Dr. Obed Adonteng-Kissi, (Australian Catholic University), Dr. Kalpana Goel (University of South Australia), Dr. Venkat Pulla (Charles Sturt University), Dr. Jeanette Ninnis (Charles Sturt University), Dr. Ndungi wa Mungai (Charles Sturt University). Dr Isaac Yeboah (University of Professional Studies, Ghana), Emmanuel Adomako (University of Ghana), Dr. Matthew Mabefam (University of Melbourne), Prof. Sanjai Bhatt (Delhi University), Dr. Naveen Kumar (Delhi University), Dr. Rajeev S. P. (Rajagiri College of Social Sciences, Kerala), Dr. Teddy Andrews (Manipal University), Dr. Elsa Mary Jacob (M. G. University), Dr. Bhavna Mehta (The Maharaja Sayajirao University of Baroda), Dr. Purnima Venkat (TAPMI Centre for Inclusive Growth & Competitiveness T A Pai Management Institute), Dr. Sheeja

Karalam, Christ University, Bangalore, Dr. Nevashnee Perumal (Nelson Mandela University,) who took time from their busy schedules to offer constructive criticisms and suggestions to the individual authors in this book.

During this project, we have encountered many scholars hailing from different walks of life and working in many different professional fields. Some scholars have contributed chapters, while offer have offered their time deliberating with us in both the formulation and implementation of this project. We thank them for their generosity of spirit.

On the production side, we wish to thank Grace Ma, publishing editor for Springer Education books, and the Production team for their professional support, comments, suggestions, and commitment to seeing this work being published.

As you can imagine, this has been a long and passionate journey for us and our families. We thank our families for their belief in us and the project, their patience, and their care.

Abraham P. Francis
Margaret Anne Carter

About This Book

This book interrogates the landscape of mental health within higher education and the specifics of creating and sustaining a more resilient culture within higher education and the community. This is the first Australian publication targeting the complexities of building a more resilient community by working within the higher education landscape. Focusing on creating a brighter future for staff, students and local communities, the contributors who are leading scholars, researchers and practitioners in higher education and mental health contribute to the discussion on community resilience and well-being in higher education. All these authors come together with a united voice, interrogating the complexities of mental health and ill health for the intentional purpose of promoting a more resilient culture within higher education and the community. While there are similar titles on mental health contribute in higher education, this current title is context and content-specific in its orientation. The Australian focused content is an original contribution to the mental health field. The content goes beyond the practical application of mental health policy analysis and strategies in higher education and purposefully explores the conundrum of establishing and nurturing a more robust culture within higher education with industry leaders and communities. The contemporary content presented in this book offers a multidisciplinary perspective encompassing a shared vision of mental health supports and services. The book responds to the question—how can we build more resilient communities and nurture a positive culture within the higher education sector?

Contents

About the Editors

Abraham P. Francis is an Associate Professor and the Head of Academic Group in Social Work and Human Services at James Cook University, Australia. He has worked with government, non-government and corporate sector and has developed many international partnerships. He taught social work at the Delhi University in India and worked as a senior mental health social worker with Country Health South Australia before moving to Townsville to join James Cook University. Dr. Francis has established many international partnerships and research collaborations with universities and non-government organisations.

He has extensively contributed to the literature on social work practice in mental health through his publications, convening conferences, establishing research networks and by developing consortiums. His other research interests are in the field of communities, criminal justice, international social work and gerontological social work. His excellence in teaching has been recognised on a number of occasions. For example, in 2010, he was a recipient of James Cook University's Inclusive Practice Award for his 'exceptional support for students with a disability'. In 2016, he received the university's 'Citation for Outstanding Contributions to Student Learning' for his 'leadership and expertise in social work education in mental health that inspires and nurtures students to be competent, confident and compassionate practitioners'.

Dr. Francis was one of the finalists at the 2018 India Australia Business and Community Awards in the category of Community Services Excellence Award and Business Leader/Professional of the Year. In 2018, Dr. Francis received the NAPSWI (National Association of Professional Association Social Workers in India) Life Time Achievement Award for his outstanding contribution to social work education.

For more details: https://research.jcu.edu.au/portfolio/abraham.francis/.

Margaret Anne Carter's career in higher education, both in Singapore and in Australia, includes teaching, academic leadership, community service and research. In 2017, Margaret Anne was awarded the National Citation for Outstanding Contribution to Student Learning. Her strong research interests provide a solid foundation for the integration of expert theory and quality practice to promote academic excellence and high levels of student engagement, productivity and wellbeing. Contributing to a sense of social consciousness, Margaret Anne's research continues to generate new knowledge and insight to enhance student learning and experiences. Margaret Anne publishes in areas including teaching and learning in higher education, resilience, mental health and wellbeing, preventing cyber bullying, young children's social behaviour and character education in early childhood.

An Evolving Higher Education Landscape in Australia Including Institutional and Curriculum Responses

Introduction

Margaret Anne Carter and Abraham P. Francis

Abstract Welcome to our editorial, introducing the broad expanse of mental health and well-being and the higher education world. This multidisciplinary book is an eclectic mix of chapters. The authors bring to life diverse challenges, endeavours and best practice responses to mental health and well-being in higher education and the broader community. We invite you to explore the impact of mental health and well-being issues in higher education and enjoy the discoveries, curiosities, interventions, interventions, and implications discussed by our authors.

Keywords Well-being · Mental health · Higher education · University · Student · Staff · Community

The Context and the Background

Notwithstanding the efforts made by higher education institutions, governments, and nongovernment organisations in promoting well-being, mental health issues continue to rise. Recently, the Productivity Commission (2020) reported that mental health complications among university students are increasing at an exponential rate compared to the general population. This position confirms Larcombe et al.'s. (2016) earlier study that employed the 21-item depression, anxiety, and scale to measure over 5000 Australian students' mental well-being. Twenty-two percent of the students reported moderate symptoms of psychological distress, 18% experienced severe symptoms of anxiety disorder, and 13% reported severe depressive symptoms. Reportedly, this finding was higher when compared to the mental health disorders (5%) among the similar age groups in the general population (Larcombe et al., 2016).

M. A. Carter (✉)
Australian College of Applied Professions, Sydney, Australia
e-mail: Margaret.Carter@acap.edu.au

A. P. Francis
James Cook University, Townsville, Australia
e-mail: Abraham.framcis@jcu.edu.au

A. P. Francis and M. A. Carter (eds.), *Mental Health and Higher Education in Australia*,
https://doi.org/10.1007/978-981-16-8040-3_1

The National Union of Students and Headspace (2016) collected data from 3303 students from 40 Australian universities and 30 TAFEs and found similar results. This study grouped student participants into two categories—students 16–25 years of age (2637) as young adults and students 26–50 or above years of age (652) as mature adults. Results indicated that 67% of the students whose age was between 16 and 25 rated their well-being as poor or fair and 65% reported high psychological and emotional distresses. Among this category of students (young adults), 1.6% reported no incident of mental health issues. With the second student participant group (matured adults), 3.4% reported no symptoms of mental health issues, while 53% reported high emotional or psychological distresses and 59% rated their well-being as fair or poor.

Accessing sufficient well-being initiatives and mental health support services is not as simple as it might sound. Studies on students' mental health in Australia have reported that the demand for mental health support among higher education students exceeds available resources (see Auerbach et al., 2018; Beasy et al., 2019; Productivity Commission, 2020). One recent study conducted with a regional Australian University suggested that even though a significant number of the students were experiencing mental health challenges, access to institutional support and services for students experiencing mental ill health was limited (Beasy et al., 2019; Productivity Commission, 2020). Similar concerns have been raised by institutions themselves and by Orygen (2020) in the Australian University Mental Health Framework report (Lyons et al., 2020). Within this context, it is important to recognise that many students who experience mental ill health do not always seek professional support for themselves (Gomes, 2020).

Studying in higher education can be challenging for students and for staff, and the institutions themselves need to respond to these challenges with diverse fit for purpose well-being policies, support services, systems and services. Our authors suggest the need for higher education institutions to promote evidence-based partnerships and leaderships that will facilitate the design and implementation of sustainable whole-of-institution fit for purpose well-being cultures, policies, programs, systems, and practices responsive to the needs of diverse students and staff.

In June 2015, the International Conference on Health Promoting Universities and Colleges was adopted by over 40 countries including Australia. The outcome of this conference was the development of the Okanagan Charter (2015). The Okanagan Charter (2015) advocates that.

> Health promoting universities and colleges infuse health into everyday operations, business practices and academic mandates. By doing so, health promoting universities and colleges enhance the success of our institutions; create campus cultures of compassion, well-being, equity and social justice; improve the health of the people who will live, learn, work, play and love on our campuses; and strengthen the ecological, social and economic sustainability of our communities and wider society (p. 2).

Universities in Canada such as the University of British Colombia, Memorial University of the Newfoundland, Simon Fraser University, to name a few, have adopted the principles of the Okanagan Charter, as well as institutions in Latin America (The University of British Colombia, 2016). Moreover, the Tertiary

Well-being Aotearoa New Zealand (TWANZ) was established on the principles of Okanagan Charter. The TWANZ version of student well-being is emulating due to how it embedded the New Zealand Maori culture to the Okanagan Charter's university well-being principles (Waterworth & Thorpe, 2017). Waterworth and Thorpe (2017) reported that the cultural sensitivity nature of the TWANZ makes the Charter relevant and effective when utilised with peoples from diverse cultures.

The direction for promoting higher education mentally healthy well-being cultures is guided by the Australian University Mental Health Framework (Orygen, 2020) and the Framework for Promoting Student Mental Well-being in universities (Baik et al., 2017). Some institutions have embraced the Okanagan Charter (An International Charter for Health Promoting Universities and Colleges). The University of New South Wales (University of New South Wales, 2020), through the recommendation of the Scientia Education Academy (a university-based department tasked to promote students' and staff well-being), adopted the Healthy University Initiative towards achieving whole-of-university well-being culture. Institutions such as the University of Sydney, Victoria University, and University of Melbourne have revised their well-being policies in response to the challenges presented by the COVID-19 pandemic. These universities have drafted fit for purpose policies and systems that seek to promote whole-of-university well-being through the development of a student-driven curriculum aimed at achieving students' academic and career successes.

Taylor et al. (2019) argue that Australian universities require leadership and commitment to whole-of-institution well-being cultures to be able to fully adopt and implement the principles of the Okanagan Charter. This warrants the need for research to better understand how the principles of the Okanagan Charter be adopted to meet the multicultural needs of the Australian higher education sector.

Encouragingly, a scan through the Websites of universities in Australia has indicated that some universities are making strides towards the promotion of healthy well-being environments. The University of New South Wales, University of Melbourne, Victoria University, University of Sydney, Royal Melbourne Institute of Technology (RMIT), La Trobe University, University of the Sunshine Coast, and Queensland University of Technology (Baik et al., 2017; University of New South Wales, 2020; University of Sunshine Coast, n.d.) are examples of institutions who have adopted and enacted comprehensive health promotion policies. Furthermore, government and nongovernmental organisations such as the Productivity Commission, Universities Australia, and Orygen have provided health promoting policy and system directions to higher education institutions in Australia.

The level of leadership, partnership, and commitment to higher education well-being research has varied across Australian with some wonderful examples of promoting higher education well-being fit for purpose environments during and beyond the COVID-19 pandemic (e.g. Victoria University and University of New South Wales). Nevertheless, recent reports on students' well-being in Australia suggest that the higher education sector designs, develops, implements, and monitors fit for purpose frameworks within their institutions and the mental health sector (Orygen, 2020; Productivity Commission, 2020). We concur with Hampole et al. (2019) that 'universities must optimise outreach and mental health services for different ethnic groups to improve campus experience around mental health conditions' (p. 66).

Introduction to the Book

The scope of this book is broad, and the authors represent a diversity of perspectives on the reality and rhetoric of mental health and well-being in higher education and the broader community. Including different voices and perspectives in this book is intentional as the editors believe it is not one voice, but many voices, that represents the road map forward for quality mental health and well-being in higher education and the community. The content contributes to the wider conversations on mental health and well-being, serving as a reference point for planning, promoting, and nurturing student and staff mental health and well-being in higher education and the wider community.

This is a resource for anyone working or interested in the potential integration of mental health and well-being practices and processes in higher education with community mental health services in Australia. It has relevance for students and academics working in higher education as well as community mental health services and practitioners striving to understand how to develop and maintain cross-sector collaborative approaches to mental health and well-being, so all sectors work productively, harmoniously, and collaboratively.

The book is divided into three parts:

Part One—An evolving higher education landscape in Australia including institutional and curriculum responses.
Part Two—Interdisciplinary research initiatives.
Part Three—Community initiatives, responses, and ways forward.

Part 1—An evolving higher education landscape in Australia including institutional and curriculum responses

Vivienne Browne and Penny Carlson start our journey with their chapter "Developing a University Mental Health Framework for Australia", setting the scene of the evolving landscape of mental health in higher education. In 2018, the Australian Government funded Orygen to engage in national consultation with students, universities, health providers, and mental health organisations to develop a whole-of-university strength-based Mental Health Framework. These authors provide a succinct overview of the Australian University Mental Health Framework (2020) designed to support Australian universities establish learning environments conducive to mental health and well-being and positive education outcomes and fortify associations between universities and community mental health services.

The impact of the COVID-19 pandemic on academics' mental health and well-being and the need for creating a mentally healthy workplace are discussed in their chapter "COVID-19 and the Changing Higher Education Landscape: The Impact on

Academics and their Well-being". **Margaret-Anne Carter, Vicki Hutton, Hyacinth Udah and Abraham Francis** discuss how academics from various universities have contributed to this discussion through their recent publications and other presentations in *The Conversation* media outlet. These authors employ qualitative content analysis to identify the emergent issues among higher education academics and the need to create mentally healthy workplaces. Results indicate that many academics feel overworked, stressed, socially isolated and disconnected, with a flow-on effect to reduced mental health. Acknowledging that while these sentiments are not a new phenomenon in academia, the authors explain that the COVID-19 pandemic has added a layer of complexity to the issue.

Narayan Gopalkrishnan and Hurriyet Babacan consider cultural partnership practice and mental health in higher education in chapter "Cultural Partnership Practice and Mental Health in Higher Education". Foregrounding this chapter with an acknowledgment that the higher education sector is principally impacted by the opportunities and issues of cultural diversity, these authors examine the ways in which the needs of First Nations students and faculty can be met in teaching and learning-supportive environments where histories of colonisation and oppression have left their scars. Grounded in this reality they consider relevant elements of cultural diversity within higher education, focusing on constructive responses to the challenges and opportunities of cultural diversity. Recommendations for sustainable higher education cultural partnership practices and mental health for students and staff are identified.

"Investigating Whether Law Schools in the UK and Australia are Workplaces That Support the Wellbeing of Law Teachers" by **Rachael Field, Caroline Strevens, and Colin James** presents the qualitative results of national surveys of UK and Australian legal academics conducted in 2017 and 2020 exploring law teachers' perceptions of the quality of working life in their law school. The authors consider actions law school managers and leaders are taking to support their academics address the downward trend of well-being for law students during their first year of legal education. Some major challenges experienced by law academics are studied with numerous constructive recommendations which may support law school managers and leaders in endorsing structural and cultural change in support of the well*being of legal academics are recounted.

In response to the impact of neoliberalism across higher education, authors **Mark David Chong, Abraham P. Francis, Margaret Anne Carter, and Frank Darkwa Baffour**, in their chapter "Employing Humanistic Teaching Approaches to Promote Student Wellbeing in Higher Education", challenge educators to enact humanistic teaching philosophies within a caring environment. These authors maintain that these nurturing and supportive practices are well suited to address the effects of neoliberalism throughout the higher education sector. Advocating for mutually respectful student–faculty partnerships, the authors present evidence informed practice for initiating humanistic pedagogical approaches that focus on well-being and mental health to learning and teaching in social work higher education.

In the chapter "Student Support in Rural Medical Education: What Does Evidence-Based Practice Look Like?", **Anna Kokavec, Jane Harte, and Simone**

Ross contemplate student support in rural medical higher education courses and ask the provocative question: what does evidence-based practice look like? The authors explain that annually a small number of medical students 'fail to thrive' (for several reasons) and need to repeat the academic year. Due to the high cost of academic failure, medical schools must be proactive in identifying and supporting at-risk students before failure occurs. The conundrum is knowing the best approach for medical schools to adopt, ensuring the approach is financially affordable, accessible, and valued by students. The authors provide an overview of how student support can be provided to medical students by using the James Cook University Medicine Student Risk Management Model.

Part 2 Interdisciplinary research initiatives

Eileen Siddins's research discussed in the chapter "Exploring Visual Art Students' Wellbeing: A Multi-level Research Approach" focuses on optimising the curriculum environment so visual art students' well-being can be enhanced in Australian higher education institutions. The author interrogates the lived experience of Australian visual art students' experiences to examine their perspectives of student well-being during their courses of study. Presenting the voices of an underrepresented student group in higher education, the author's research findings identify generic and discipline specific evidence to improve students' creative learning experiences within their academic studies, career, and personal lives.

Surveying recent research literature relevant to artists and mental health, **Ryan Daniel** identifies several implications for higher education courses in the arts in the chapter "Reimagining Higher Education Curricula for Creative and Performing Artists: Creating More Resilient and Industry-Ready Graduates". Explaining that creative and performing artists graduates enter a sector which offers challenges, the author advocates for reimagining higher education curricula for creative and performing artists for the purpose of graduating more resilient and industry-ready alumni. The author provides rich evidence for teaching academics in higher education to pursue so that creative and performing artists graduates are better equipped to sustain themselves cope with the realities of their practice.

The chapter "Embedding an Aboriginal Well-being Intervention in Australian Social Work Curriculum" discusses the outcome on student mental health when embedding Aboriginal well-being empowerment course work material in a foundational first year subject of an Australian social work curriculum. Explaining the rationale, authors **Fiona Gardner, Mary Whiteside, and Rachael Sanders** present a curriculum-based response to student well-being in relation to Aboriginal Family Well-being. These authors introduce their pilot research on the impact of the curricula, emphasising its application for enhancing student well-being, foundational social work skill development, and student's capacity to manage an increasingly complex and changing world.

The conundrum of promoting the mental well-being of law students through the curriculum and communities of practice is reviewed by **Ozlem Susler and Alperhan Babacan** in their chapter "Promoting the Mental Wellbeing of Law Students Through the Curriculum and Communities of Practice". Recognising the evidence-based practice literature, the authors report on the psychological distress reported amongst law students in Australia, including the factors contributing to these elevated levels. This sets the scene for reimaging legal education curriculum through the enhancement of mindfulness and resilience and the adoption of a transformative approach to learning and teaching, grounded in a sense of community and belonging.

Kaz Michell's informative literature review "How Perfectionism, Procrastination and Parenting Styles Impact Students Mental Health and How Mindfulness and Self--Compassion May be the Antidote"—deals with the practice of supporting students' well-being and mental health in higher through the exploration of student exam and assessment stress. The author examines links between perfectionism, panic attacks, and attachment bonds through a well-being and mental health lens. Explaining that when students stress levels are elevated their cognitive function is impacted, the author identifies practical interventions to support the student including the practice of mindfulness and self-compassion. Leading to better mental health, these practices are offered as tools to regulate emotions and soothe the autonomic nervous system.

Drawing on research studies across five countries, **Saradamoyee Chatterjee's** chapter "The Higher Education Experience of Students During COVID-19 Pandemic and the Impact on Mental Well-being: A Review of the Literature" evaluates the impact of the COVID-19 pandemic on the virtual transformation of higher education on students. With findings showing students benefited from the flexibility and autonomy of online learning, the author reports potential drawbacks of online learning that adversely affected students learning experience and their mental health. These shortcomings included inaccessibility to appropriate digital technology and devices, an absence of face-to-face social interactions with teachers and peers, and prolonged screen time. Further research is interrogated to understand the mental health challenges and coping strategies adopted by students during the pandemic.

Raquel Peel and Natalie Ward investigate the role of intimate relationships as potential root causes of mental health challenges experienced by students studying in higher education in their chapter "The Impact of Relationship Issues on the Mental Health of Students in Higher Education". The authors present a theoretical discussion of the literature, highlighting the significance of recognising and understanding intimate relationships in the context of higher education. They focus the negative relations and relationship breakdowns as the backdrop for identifying the mental health of individuals impacted by these intimate relationships. Investigating issues including conflict, lack of relationship skills, and self-sabotage, the authors uncover implications for research and practices specific to intimate relationships and mental health in higher education.

Ross Prior advocates for using creativity, more specifically expressive arts practice, to enhance the well-being of students in higher education, in his chapter "Detoxing University Through Creative Engagement". The author takes the reader on a philosophical journey of higher education practice that includes a purposeful emphasis on using creativity to engage students, both in and outside of formal classes, to improve well-being. This author offers hope in how creative activity might bring about essential change to combat a corporate hardening that has in recent times usurped the love of learning and of enabling others. Reporting on an initiative where artistic processes have been used as an antidote to the toxic university, the author presents actions for positive change for students and staff.

The chapter "Art, Truth and Beauty in the Classroom: Individual Creativity, Knowledge and the Natural Emergent Properties of a Self-Organising System" delves into the potential benefits of approaching education and learning from perspectives that seem outside the practical and pragmatic constructs of the current education system. Working with the lenses of *art truth* and *beauty,* **Richard Hill** reveals how methods of teaching and learning can emerge that are individually and/or context driven. Setting the scene by re-counting the historic and current expressions of these qualities, the author connects with neuroscience research, discussing diversions from the generalised dimension of education towards a universally flexible and/or individually relevant process of education.

Part Three—Community initiatives, responses, and ways forward

Working within the context of the COVID-19 pandemonic, **Venkat Pulla, Elizabeth Carter, and Abraham P. Francis** identify issues in their chapter "Australian International Border Closures: Impact on International Student Well-being", that significantly impacted the international student community. These issues involve loss of jobs and income, COVID-19 lockdown, and restriction rules including international border closure, and for many, an overnight shift to online education. These authors scrutinise the international student community debate that followed with academic commentators, the response of the Australian universities, the federal and the state governments, and the broader Australian society.

The chapter "COVID-19 and Mental Health and Well-being of Higher Education International Students" highlights the role of higher education institutions in supporting and sustaining international student's academic performance and general well-being. Drawing upon findings from an ongoing research project into the experiences of international students in North Queensland, Australia, during the COVID-19, **Hyacinth Udah and Abraham P. Francis** advocate that mental health and well-being strongly correlate with an international student's academic performance and general overseas experience. Focusing on practice-based evidence to improve students education outcomes and well-being, the authors clarify the role higher education institutions have in providing mentally healthy needs-based teaching and learning spaces and places for international students.

The chapter "Mental Health in Higher Education and the Community–Building Capability, Sharing Experience" **by Jeremy Audas** is a timely reminder that a positive focus on well-being and mental health cannot be the jurisdiction of the local social and community service community organisations or higher education institution. Advocating for partnerships focusing on well-being and mental health, the author recognises shared objectives and opportunities for collaboration between community organisations and higher education institutions. Resulting in better mental health outcomes and increased connectivity, possibilities for forming this collaboration are named through a range of associations within social and community services.

The chapter "Interprofessional Collaboration in Promoting Well-being in the Higher Education Sector: The AMHHEC Experience" presents **Beryl Buckby's** interdisciplinary initiative working collaboratively with higher education and the community in promoting well-being in the higher education sector. Outlining the purpose, scope and reach of the Australasian Mental Health and Higher Education Conference, the authors explores this initiative in promoting mental health both in higher education and within the community. The author challenges faculty and leadership to consider lessons learned, to reflect on missed opportunities and to embrace potential opportunities for collaborating across disciplines on well-being and mental health initiatives in the higher education environment and within the broader community.

Our final chapter "Mentally Healthy City Townsville: Promoting Wellbeing in Communities", authors **Sue McGinty, Cathy Day, Cathy O'Toole, Kathryn Montafia, Anneliese Young, and Zoltan Sarnyai**, tells the story of the implementation and outcomes of a the Mentally Healthy City Townsville program, a person-centred and coordinated evidence-based, staged approach to supporting and maintaining positive mental wellness outcomes for individual community members who experience mental ill health. Based on two international programs, the European Alliance against Depression and the model adopted by the Mentally Healthy Cities Alliance, the authors discuss the Mentally Healthy City Townsville program, in enabling people with mental ill health continue to participate in the local community.

The chapters in this book contribute to some of the drivers which have placed mental health and well-being in higher education and the broader community on the national agenda, including policy movement, research, pedagogical practices, workload, and graduate employability. All drivers are central to the conundrum of mental health and well-being in this complex and challenging landscape. Today's challenging global environment demands the continuous acquisition and development of new knowledge and skills required for academics and students to succeed in higher education environments.

When mental health and well-being is prioritised and focuses on common goals that confront shared social, economic, demographic, and educational issues, higher education and community sectors will be more strategic in their responses to the escalating numbers of individuals experiencing mental ill health. Only then will the mental health and well-being of academics and students in higher education become an agenda item worthy of action, at the national, institutional, and community levels, moving away from rhetoric towards reality.

Keep safe and well.

References

Auerbach, R. P., Mortier, P., Bruffaerts, R., Alonso, J., Benjet, C., Cuijpers, P., Demyttenaere, K., Ebert, D. D., Green, J. G., Hasking, P., Murray, E., Nock, M. K., Pinder-Amaker, S., Sampson, N. A., Stein, D. J., Vilagut, G., Zaslavsky, A. M., Kessler, R. C., & WHOWMH-ICS Collaborators.

(2018). WHO world mental health surveys international college student project: Prevalence and distribution of mental disorders. *Journal of Abnormal Psychology, 127*(7), 623–638.

Baik, C., Larcombe, W., Brooker, A., Wyn, J., Allen, L., Brett, M., Field, R., & James, R. (2017). *Enhancing students mental wellbeing: A handbook for academic educators*. https://www.melbourne-cshe.unimelb.edu.au/_data/assets/pdf

Beasy, K., Emery, S., & Crawford, J. (2019). Drowning in the shallows: An Australian study of the PhD experience of wellbeing. *Teaching in Higher Education*, 1–17. https://doi.org/10.1080/13562517.2019.1669014

Okanagan Charter: An International Charter for Health Promoting Universities and Colleges. (2015). *An outcome of the 2015 international conference on health promoting universities and colleges/VII International Congress*. https://www.open.library.ubc.ca/clRcle/collections/53926/items/1.0132754

Gomes, C. (2020). Outside the classroom: The language of English and its impact on international student mental wellbeing in Australia. *Journal of International Students, 10*(4), 934–953.

Hampole, S. R., Nguyen, S. H. S., & Woodhead, E. L. (2019). Experience disclosing mental health conditions among college students from different ethnic background. *Building Health Academic Communities Journal, 3*(2), 66–72.

Larcombe, W., Finch, S., Sore, R., Murray, C. M., Kentish, S., Mulder, R. A., Lee-Stecum, P., Baik, C., Tokatlidis, O., & Williams, D. A. (2016). Prevalence and socio-demographic correlates of psychological distress among students at an Australian university. *Studies in Higher Education*, 41(6), 1074–1091.

Lyons, Z., Wilcox, H., Leung, L., & Dearsley, O. (2020). COVID-19 and the mental well-being of Australian medical students: Impact, concerns and coping strategies used. *Australian Psychiatry, 28*(6), 649–652. https://doi.org/10.1177/1039856220947945

Orygen, The National Centre of Excellence in Youth Mental Health. (2020). *Australian university mental health framework*. Orygen. https://www.orygen.org.au

Productivity Commission. (2020). *Mental health* (Report no. 95, Issue). https://www.pc.gov.au/inquiries/completed/mental-health#report

Taylor, P., Saheb, R., & Howse, E. (2019). Creating healthier graduates, campuses and communities: Why Australia needs to invest in health promoting universities. *Health Promotion Journal of Australia, 30*(2), 285–289.

The University of British Colombia. (2016). *Six Canadian universities partner on ground breaking health promotion movement*, [press release]. The University of British Columbia. https://www.wellbeing.ubc.ca

Universities Australia. (2019). *Data snapshot, 2019: Australia has one of the best higher education systems in the world*. https://www.universitiesaustralia.edu.au/wp-content/uploads/2019/06/data-snapshot-2019-FINAL.pdf

University of New South Wales. (2020). *UNSW healthy university initiative*. https://www.teaching.unsw.edu.au/healthyuni-main

Waterworth, C., & Thorpe, A. (2017). Applying the okanagan charter in aotearoa New Zealand. *JANZSSA – Journal of the Australian and New Zealand Student Services Association, 25*(1). https://www.janzssa.scholasticahq.com/article/1338

Margaret Anne Carter's career in higher education, both in Singapore and Australia, includes teaching, academic leadership, community service and research. In 2017 Margaret Anne was awarded the National Citation for Outstanding Contribution to Student Learning. Her strong research interests provide a solid foundation for the integration of expert theory and quality practice to promote academic excellence and high levels of student engagement, productivity and wellbeing. Contributing to a sense hatof social consciousness, Margaret Anne's research continues to generate new knowledge and insight to enhance student learning and experiences. Margaret Anne publishes in areas including teaching and learning in higher education, resilience, mental health and well-being, preventing cyber bullying, young children's social behaviour and character education in early childhood.

Abraham P. Francis is an Associate Professor, and currently the Head of Academic Group in Social Work and Human Services at James Cook University, Australia. He has worked with Government, Non-government and corporate sector, and has developed many international partnerships. He taught social work at the Delhi University in India and worked as a senior mental health social worker with Country Health South Australia before moving to Townsville to join James Cook University. Dr. Francis has established many international partnerships and research collaborations with universities and non-government organizations.

He has extensively contributed to the literature on Social Work practice in mental health through his publications, convening conferences, establishing research networks and by developing consortiums. His other research interests are in the field of communities, criminal justice, international social work, and gerontological social work. His excellence in teaching has been recognised on a number of occasions. For example, in 2010, he was a recipient of James Cook University's Inclusive Practice Award for his "exceptional support for students with a disability". In 2016, he received the university's '**Citation for Outstanding Contributions to Student Learning**' for his "leadership and expertise in social work education in mental health that inspires and nurtures students to be competent, confident and compassionate practitioners".

Dr. Francis was one of the finalists at the 2018 India ***Australia business and community awards*** in the category of Community Services Excellence Award and Business Leader/Professional of the year. In 2018, Dr. Francis received the NAPASWI (National Association of Professional Association Social Workers in India) lifetime achievement for his outstanding contribution to social work Education.

For more details—https://research.jcu.edu.au/portfolio/abraham.francis/

Developing a University Mental Health Framework for Australia

Vivienne Browne and Penny Carlson

Abstract In September 2018, the Australian Government announced that funding would be provided to Orygen to develop an Australian University Mental Health Framework. The project was initiated to provide guidelines to: support Australian universities to create positive learning environments which prevent mental health issues and poor education outcomes and strengthen connections between universities and community mental health services in relation to care and treatment for students who do experience mental ill-health. The framework has been developed through national consultation with students, universities, health providers, and mental health organisations. This process aimed to: identify evidence-informed practices; consider the current experiences; and ensure that the final framework meets the needs of the Australian context. The framework was launched in December 2020. It takes a whole-of-university, settings-based approach focused on the creation of learning environments conducive to good mental health and wellbeing. A coordinated, joined-up response, delivered through appropriate partnerships, is required to provide effective support for students. Consequently, the mental health sector is encouraged to work in partnership with universities to provide expertise and facilitate pathways to care. This chapter will provide an overview on the process and progress of developing the framework, with consideration given to the challenges of developing a cross-sector approach. It will present the key areas of action included in the framework and highlight key findings from extensive consultations across the university and mental health sectors and, importantly, with students.

Keywords Mental health · University · Framework · Guidance · Wellbeing · Student

---

V. Browne (✉) · P. Carlson
Orygen, the National Centre of Excellence in Youth Mental Health, Melbourne, Australia
e-mail: Vivienne.Browne@orygen.org.au

P. Carlson
e-mail: penny.carlson@orygen.org.au

A. P. Francis and M. A. Carter (eds.), *Mental Health and Higher Education in Australia*,
https://doi.org/10.1007/978-981-16-8040-3_2

Background

In 2017, Orygen released the report *Under the radar: The mental health of Australian university students* (Orygen, 2017). At the time, the paucity of relevant research and data made it difficult to estimate the prevalence of mental health concerns among university student populations in Australia. However, some of the available research suggested that university students were experiencing increasing levels of psychological distress (Headspace & National Union of Students, 2017, Stallman, 2008, 2010; Stallman & Shochet, 2009).

University counselling service managers had also noted an increase in demand, complexity, and severity of mental health presentations. The Heads of Counselling Services (HOCS) Benchmarking survey undertaken in 2013 with participants from 29 Australian and two New Zealand universities found 64% of HOCS reported that they could not respond to all requests for the service within two weeks (Andrews, 2016). A follow-up survey conducted in 2018, with 27 responders from Australia and six responders from New Zealand, found that more than 60% of HOCS reported an increase in demand for the counselling service in their institution. All respondents agreed, or strongly agreed, that there had been a steady increase in the complexity and severity of student mental health presentations and an increase in the proportion of students affected by mental ill-health over the past decade (Andrews, 2019).

Experiences of poor mental health or mental ill-health can have a significant impact on educational attainment and retention and, as a result, can alter or limit intended career pathways and future economic participation. National data collected annually on student experiences through the Quality Indicators for Learning and Teaching Survey indicates a 20% increase over the past five years in the numbers of students considering an early exit from their course due to health and stress. In 2016, this was the reason selected by 41% of students considering an early course exit (QILT Social Research Centre, 2017) increasing to 50% in 2020 (QILT Social Research Centre, 2021). The increase could be partially attributed to the COVID-19 pandemic which significantly disrupted business and life on many university campuses during 2020 and resulted in increased levels of anxiety and stress for both students and staff (Dodd et al., 2021; Fruehwirth et al., 2021; Spalek, 2021). However, it is worth noting that even prior to the pandemic, health and stress were increasingly cited a reason for considering early course exit year after year.

Not only does mental ill-health increase the likelihood of early course exit or academic slumps mid-year (Jevons & Lindsay, 2018), but struggling or failing academically may also exacerbate or extend experiences of mental health issues. Analysing ABS data, the Grattan institute found individuals with an incomplete university degree were twice as likely to report long-term mental ill-health that those who had not dropped out (Norton, 2018).

Under the Radar recommended the development of national guidance for universities to respond to student mental health and for all universities to have a mental health strategy (Orygen, 2017). An earlier report, *The Wicked Problem of University Student Mental Health*, similarly called for greater leadership and a ‘tone from the top' to systemically address mental health issues throughout the university (Veness, 2016).

In September 2018, the Australian Government announced that funding would be provided to Orygen to develop an Australian University Mental Health Framework. Orygen is Australia's national centre of excellence in youth mental health and has extensive experience in translating evidence-based research into guidance, technical advice, workforce development activities, and clinical care.

The framework would aim to assist universities to create positive, healthy learning environments, and prevent mental health issues and poor education outcomes. The framework would also aim to build stronger connections between universities and mental health services, so they can better support students experiencing mental ill-health to access the care they need (Minister for Health, 2018).

International Context

A number of other countries have progressed a similar approach to guidance and standards for mental health supports in universities and higher education. Building on its 2015 *Student Mental Wellbeing in Higher Education Good Practice Guide* (Universities UK & Mental Wellbeing in Higher Education Group, 2015), Universities UK (UUK) released the *Stepchange framework* in 2017 (Universities UK, 2017). The *Stepchange framework* was further revised and adapted in 2020 (Universities UK, 2020) a process that occurred in conjunction with the development of the Student Minds University Mental Health Charter (Student Minds, 2019).

In Canada, the Mental Health Commission of Canada (MHCC) built on the previous guidance *Post-Secondary Student Mental Health: Guide to a Systemic Approach* (CACUSS & CMHA, 2013) and developed a *Standard on Psychological Health and Safety for Post-Secondary Students*. The standard was released in 2020 (Mental Health Commission of Canada, 2020) and complements a previously developed standard for Canada's workplace psychological health and safety.

Universitas 21 (U21) Declaration

The U21 is a network of 27 member universities across 18 countries that aims to facilitate and empower members to share excellence, collaborate, and exchange knowledge globally. It consists of a number of networking groups across: leadership; specific areas of focus (such as educational innovation and student experience); and collaborative groups. One of the collaborative groups is the Health Sciences Group.

The 2018 U21 Health Sciences Group Annual Meeting included a theme on mental health and student wellbeing. At the conclusion of the student wellbeing session, the idea of a declaration for supporting mental health in U21 universities was presented to attendees as a potential platform for international cooperation, data collection, and sharing and reporting on activities and actions. A subgroup was established to progress this work during 2019, and following endorsement by the U21 Presidents, the *U21 University Mental Health Declaration* was officially launched on 28 August 2020. The Five Principles of the Declaration (Universitas 21 Health Sciences Group, 2020) are as follows:

Principle 1: The university and everyone in its community commit to its role in creating, promoting, and sustaining a positive environment for optimal mental health and wellbeing among its staff and students.

Principle 2: Students and staff are at the heart of our concern. Therefore, all discussions and delivery of improved services around mental health will consult and engage with the community it aims to serve.

Principle 3: The university commits to its role in linking staff and students who require additional support for their mental health to professional and evidence-based mental health supports either on-campus or off-campus.

Principle 4: The university will facilitate the building of an evidence base through monitoring and evaluating the need for, and outcome and effectiveness of, all mental health and wellbeing policies, programs, and services delivered by the university.

Principle 5: The university takes seriously and will address promptly, prejudice related to mental ill-health and will endeavour to foster a stigma-free environment of support and understanding.

Process for Developing the Australian Framework

This section provides an overview of the consultation approach for the development of the framework and a summary of the key themes, challenges, and opportunities that emerged.

Consultation

Effective and extensive consultation with students, university staff, and mental health organisations was considered to be the most critical factor in achieving a final product which would have impact and acceptance across both the university and the mental health sectors.

To achieve this, key stakeholder engagement mechanisms were established to provide direction and expert guidance to inform development of the framework. These were as follows:

- **An Advisory Group** which comprised of senior executives and individual experts across the mental health sector, the university sector, and university student representative bodies and organisations. The group met quarterly to provide guidance and advice particularly in relation to the content of the framework.
- **Four Expert Working Groups** comprised of individual experts and university/organisational representatives who were asked to contribute their expertise and experience via online surveys and follow-up discussions with the framework project team where required. The four working groups were as follows:
  - Student mental health supports and services.
  - Mentally healthy universities—a whole university community approach focused on harm minimisation, mental health promotion, and preventative actions.
  - Evidence-based responses—what was known and what was not about what approaches, programs, and interventions were effective with university student populations.
  - Enhancing collaboration between universities and the mental health sector and between students and staff.

Wider consultation was then undertaken through a variety of mechanisms with both a national and international focus. The project team frequently attended conferences and workshops where there was an opportunity to share progress, build momentum, and provide avenues for input and feedback. Over 400 stakeholders were engaged through these events.

Focus groups with university students were also facilitated to provide insight into student needs and preferences in relation to mental health and wellbeing. A total of 93 participants attended eight focus groups across five states. Participants were selected to reflect the diversity of the university student population across: ages; stages and areas of study; metropolitan and regional areas; and specific groups identified in the literature as being of high risk/high need in relation to mental health.

In February 2020, a symposium was held with key stakeholders who had engaged in the process to date including members of the working groups. The aim of the symposium was three fold: to present the findings from the consultations; to seek input into the development of a draft framework; and to position the work within an international context. To achieve the latter, the symposium included keynotes from John DePury, Director Policy, Universities UK, and Sandra Koppert, Director, Mental Health, Mental Health Commission of Canada, who had led the work on the development of similar guidance for supporting mental health in post-secondary education settings in their countries and presented on the progress and lessons learned and future opportunities.

A draft of the framework was released for consultation in late April 2020, and the university and mental health sector were again invited to provide their feedback and input via an online consultation.

Key Themes Emerging Through the Consultations

Consider the Context

Initial conversations identified a number of contextual factors to be recognised and appropriately responded to from the outset of the framework's development. These included.

- The student population is not homogenous, and as such, the framework would need to include and recognise the unique experiences and attributes of a number of student cohorts, including those who were at greater risk of experiencing mental ill-health; different age groups; cultural diversity (including the needs of international students); and students studying remotely vs on-campus.
- That universities are diverse and independent institutions. While nationally consistent guidance was seen as providing a valuable foundation, the framework needed to be flexible enough to adapt to different university contexts, resources, and needs. Should the actions and activities within the Framework be too specific, instructive or take a tone of setting 'standards' there would be a risk that it would not be accepted.

Thematic Content

As the consultation approach broadened to the working groups, presentations, forums, and events, feedback increasingly represented the diversity of voices within and between the university workforce, students, and the mental health sector. Six consistent themes emerged. These were as follows:

- **The whole university was responsible**. This meant that the framework needed to provide guidance for building leadership and governance; developing an institution mental health strategy; incorporating workplace mental health activities; and building the skills, mental health literacy, and capacity of the broader university workforce.
- **Students should be at the centre of mental health and wellbeing responses**. This included not only building student's skills and literacy in mental health but also co-designing university mental health and wellbeing policies, strategies, activities, and programs with students from the outset.
- **Supports and services needed to be appropriate, acceptable, inclusive, and accessible to students**. There was an appetite for the framework to provide guidance (where evidence existed) on new and innovative models of supports including integrated service centres, using digital interventions and building a peer support workforce.
- **The university environment and culture needed to be conducive to good mental health and wellbeing**. The university was seen to have an important role

to play in the prevention of mental ill-health, in promoting healthy behaviours, addressing stigma and discrimination, and creating a supportive, inclusive, and connected community both within the institution and in the community.

- **An increased understanding of the prevalence, experience of mental ill-health, or poor wellbeing among university students was required.** This would assist in the development of programs, services, and initiatives that meet student needs, as well as, monitor, and evaluate what works to build the evidence base.
- **A collaborative approach to student mental health within and beyond the university would drive action and improvement.** This included collaboration between faculties, services, and functions of the university, between universities (to develop and share knowledge and practice), and between universities and the mental health sector—locally, regionally and nationally.

Tone and Design

Considerable feedback was also provided relating to the tone and design of the framework. The language used in the framework needed to be accessible to both sectors. As the project was being led by a mental health organisation, stakeholders warned against the use of technical and medicalised language. In addition, stakeholders suggested that the framework's language should convey a positive tone and recognise existing efforts, rather than focussing on deficits.

Stakeholders also wanted the framework to be aspirational, to celebrate current good practice while striving for continual improvement and tapping into the research ethos of universities to inspire and drive innovation. Acknowledging that the framework would represent a 'point in time', stakeholders suggested that there may be a need to iteratively revise and update the guidance into the future, adapting new evidence as it emerges.

Stakeholders emphasised the need for the framework to adopt the tone of a holistic and systems-based approach to mental health and wellbeing in universities, building the narrative and case for change beyond addressing student mental ill-health to one which encapsulated the interconnections between wellbeing, good mental health, and student's success both educationally and in their future careers.

Themes from Students

Students sought a humanitarian underpinning to the framework and hoped it would emphasise the need for empathy, connection, and supportive communities within universities.

Students also described practical programmatic, policy, and service responses they believed would assist in identifying risk and responding early to experiences of mental ill-health. These included

- consistent promotional and preventative activities spread throughout the year, augmenting current activities which peak around exam and assessment periods;
- increased availability of mental health services and increased accessibility of services;
- an integrated triage system for mental health services within a 'service hub';
- the continuation and expansion of initiatives targeting holistic development outside of traditionally clinical mental health services;
- the creation and maintenance of safe spaces, both physically and within learning environments;
- increased mental health literacy among both students and staff; and
- mentoring opportunities, including academic and non-academic supports (Orygen, 2020c).

Divergent Views and Perspectives

Given the breadth and reach of the consultation process for the framework's development and the diversity of stakeholders involved, it is unsurprising that points of difference or contestability emerged. In some instances, but not all, these were able to be resolved within the final framework.

Some of these related to document format, structure, and language. There were preferences for both: (a) the final framework to be a detailed document, providing evidence, examples, and resources; and (b) a simpler, shorter, and more accessible document. The team attempted to address this by producing a high-level framework describing the key principles and actions which was then supported by a number of additional outputs including a detailed report (which included an evidence summary and links to further resources); case studies; videos; and a 2-page summary.

In addition, there were differing opinions regarding the language used with some stakeholders seeking a more directive, authoritative approach to set expectations, while others believed this would convey a lack of understanding and respect for the significant efforts, work, and good practice that was already occurring to support student wellbeing.

The discussions and feedback regularly returned to the issue of assigning roles and responsibilities for student mental health between universities and the mental health sector. Some stakeholders believed that the framework should not be prescriptive and allow individual institutions to decide what services they will provide, while others were seeking the framework to articulate a clear demarcation of what was in the remit and duty of care of universities and what was the mental health sectors' responsibility—this was particularly evident when discussing direct service provision.

Finally, there were a range of perspectives regarding accountability with some stakeholders of the view that accountability and reporting against activities and action in student mental health and wellbeing should be determined by the individual institution, while others were supportive of a publicly transparent line of accountability to a government agency or statutory body, such as the Tertiary Education and Quality Skills Authority or the Department of Education. Direction or resolution of this issue was beyond the scope of this project.

Overview of the Final Framework

The Australian University Mental Health Framework (Orygen, 2020a) provides guidance to support universities and their communities to create a mentally healthy university setting which provides the best opportunities for students to thrive, educationally and personally.

The framework aims to

- promote mental health and wellbeing and prevent mental ill-health for university students;
- provide effective support for those experiencing mental ill-health to enable them to actively participate in education and society; and
- create healthy university settings which are conducive to providing protective factors for students' mental health and wellbeing.

The framework is structured around six principles and provides illustrations on what each principle might look like in practice. The principles and a highlighted selection of practice examples are described below.

Principle 1. The student experience is enhanced through mental health and wellbeing approaches that are informed by students' needs, perspectives, and the reality of their experiences. In practice, this could look like

- Actively consulting with students and seeking information from them to inform actions, reviews, and evaluations of mental health responses in the university.
- Co-designing activities, programs, and services with students (including those with a lived experience of mental ill-health).
- Creating peer support opportunities to enable students to share experiences and feel more connected with their university.

Principle 2. All members of the university community contribute to learning environments that enhance student mental health and wellbeing. In practice, this could look like

- Leaders demonstrate that mental health is the core business of the university and enable the development of whole-of-university mental health strategies which are co-ordinated and integrated across all business areas, including teaching and learning activities.
- Staff in student-facing roles are supported to know what to do, within the scope of their role, to assist students with mental health and wellbeing.
- A mentally healthy workplace is maintained by complementary student and staff wellbeing initiatives.

Principle 3. Mentally healthy university communities encourage participation; foster a diverse, inclusive environment; promote connectedness; and support academic and personal achievement. In practice, this could look like

- A focus on enhancing student connectedness and participation more broadly in university life.
- Clear demonstration that diverse student cultures and identities are valued and visible across the university community.
- Physical and digital spaces in the university environment which enhance mental health and wellbeing.

Principle 4. The response to mental health and wellbeing is strengthened through collaboration and coordinated actions. In practice, this could look like

- Universities and the mental health services in their region developing joined-up mental health service and support approach to student mental health and wellbeing.
- The university sector sharing good practice and resources within and between institutions.
- The mental health sector actively engaging with universities to tap into their research and development expertise to assist in mental health service planning in local and regional areas.

Principle 5. Students are able to access appropriate, effective, timely services, and supports to meet their mental health and wellbeing needs. In practice, this could look like

- Providing services and supports that are appropriate and accessible for a diverse student population.
- Integrating services to assist students to access the right level and type of support, including for more complex issues, in a seamless way.
- Incorporating digital approaches as part of actions to support student mental health and wellbeing.

Principle 6. Continuous improvement and innovation is informed by evidence and helps build an understanding of what works for student mental health and wellbeing. In practice, this could look like

- Ensuring initiatives, programs, and activities are evaluated, and outcomes/evidence is shared.
- Building accessible data sources including (but not limited to) information related to mental health, wellbeing, mental ill-health, students lived experiences, stories of hope and recovery, student perceptions, impact of initiatives and services, challenge or stress points for individuals and systems, and implementation of the framework.

Towards Implementation

Where university mental health frameworks and strategies have previously been developed in Australia and internationally, a lack of investment and accountability in their implementation has resulted in mixed success in achieving systemic change or intended impact (Orygen, 2017).

To address framework implementation challenges in Canada, the MHCC developed a 'starter kit' to assist institutions to take the initial steps towards implementing the mental health guidance and standards developed for post-secondary education.

UUK have also continued to focus on implementation. In the past few years, UUK have released a self-assessment tool for universities, piloted the framework with universities, developed aligned frameworks on suicide prevention, developed a process for establishing partnerships between universities and the National Health Service, and held a leadership learning collaborative to further develop ideas.

While implementation support was out of scope for the framework project, questions and concerns regarding the practicalities of how implementation would occur and be resourced was raised at every phase of consultation. Stakeholders identified a number of potential opportunities including creating greater accountability through external oversight and reporting on progress and action and/or incentivising, recognising, and actively promoting good practice. The 'carrot or the stick' metaphor was a feature of many conversations during consultation and engagement for the framework.

There remain a number of key drivers that will support future take-up and implementation of the principles and practices described in the framework. These include

Policies and strategies drivers: The Final Report of the Australian Government's Productivity Commission into Mental Health (Productivity Commission, 2020) recognised the development and (then) upcoming release of the University Mental Health Framework and further recommended instating a requirement for institutions to have a mental health and wellbeing strategy (Action 6.3). Prior to this, the Final Report from the Higher Education Standards Panel, *Improving retention, completion and success in higher education*, made a specific recommendation (Recommendation 8) that every institution should have an institution-wide mental health strategy and implementation plan to assist students with mental illness (Department of Education & Training, 2017). In 2018, the Education Minister endorsed this recommendation (Department of Education Skills & Employment, 2018); however, it was noted in the consultations that there had been variable adaption of this recommendation, that it was still difficult to access many university strategies and implementation plans online and that, once the strategy had been submitted to the government, there was little in the way of a follow-up response. Therefore, while policy drivers are important, they also require mechanisms for implementation, accountability, and review in order to understand their efficacy and impact.

Access to data and the evidence base as it develops: The lack of available and nationally consistent datasets to understand the prevalence and experience of mental ill-health among university students remains a key gap to be addressed. The Productivity Commission also recognised that there were significant gaps in the availability and dissemination of evidence for effective mental health interventions in these education settings which needed to be addressed—both in the university sector and higher education more broadly (Productivity Commission, 2020). Increasing the collection and monitoring of data and evidence is therefore required to demonstrate need, gaps in current approaches, and effectiveness of interventions and inform decisions regarding allocation of resources to mental health and wellbeing supports and services.

Adequate funding: Stakeholders acknowledged that current efforts to support students experiencing mental ill-health were restricted due to funding and resourcing limitations. Many support services within universities indicated they were not resourced at levels to meet demand, and there is a broader, well documented, shortfall in resourcing in mental health services which has led to long waiting lists and the 'missing middle' (Orygen, 2020b) hampering efforts by university staff to successfully refer students into community-based services.

Workforce capacity: The limitations in funding and resourcing have a flow on impact on workforce capacity. This includes challenges in recruitment and retention of the mental health workforce both within and outside universities. However, it also includes challenges in building mental health skill sets and literacy of all staff and students, particularly when they are already experiencing pressures within the roles they are primarily employed for, whether it be in teaching, administration, or leadership positions, or within their field of academic study. In implementing the Framework, universities are encouraged to consider how they could best incentivise skill and knowledge development in relation to student wellbeing and mental health across such a broad and diverse workforce.

Conclusion

The *Australian University Mental Health Framework* was developed through more than two years of extensive and productive stakeholder engagement. Throughout the process, it was clear that all those involved were strongly committed to supporting students to achieve the best possible outcomes for both their mental health and their educational pathways. While the release marked the end of this phase of work, the framework will only result in a positive impact on student mental health and wellbeing when universities and the mental health sector make concerted efforts towards its implementation and translate the principles and practices into action. As the framework reflects the good practice and evidence available at the time of its development, it will also be critical for this work to be continually revisited, refined, and redeveloped as new research, data, and innovative practice continue to emerge.

References

Andrews, A. (2016). ANZSSA heads of counselling services benchmarking survey 2013 summary report. *Journal of the Australian and New Zealand Student Services Association, 47*, 96–105.

Andrews, A. (2019). ANZSSA heads of counselling services HOCS benchmarking survey: 2018 summary report. *Journal of the Australian and New Zealand Student Services Association, 27*(1), 67–171.

CACUSS and CMHA. (2013). *Post-secondary student mental health: Guide to a systemic approach*. Retrieved from Vancouver, BC.

Department of Education and Training. (2017). *Higher education standards panel: Final report—Improving retention, completion and success in higher education*. Retrieved from Canberra.

Department of Education Skills and Employment. (2018). *Response to recommendations: HESP final report—Improving retention, completion and success in higher education*. Retrieved from Online: https://www.dese.gov.au/higher-education-funding/resources/response-recommendations-hesp-final-report-improving-retention-completion-and-success-higher

Dodd, R. H., Dadaczynski, K., Okan, O., McCaffery, K. J., & Pickles, K. (2021). Psychological wellbeing and academic experience of University Students in Australia during COVID-19. *International Journal of Environmental Research and Public Health, 18*(3). https://doi.org/10.3390/ijerph18030866

Fruehwirth, J. C., Biswas, S., & Perreira, K. M. (2021). The Covid-19 pandemic and mental health of first-year college students: Examining the effect of Covid-19 stressors using longitudinal data. *PLoS ONE, 16*(3), e0247999. https://doi.org/10.1371/journal.pone.0247999

Headspace, & National Union of Students. (2017). *National tertiary student wellbeing survey 2016*. Retrieved from https://www.headspace.org.au/news/national-student-wellbeing-survey-report/

Jevons, C., & Lindsay, S. (2018). The middle years slump: Addressing student-reported barriers to academic progress. *Higher Education Research & Development, 37*(6), 1156–1170. https://doi.org/10.1080/07294360.2018.1462305

Mental Health Commission of Canada. (2020). *Standard on psychological health and safety for post-secondary students*. Retrieved from https://www.mentalhealthcommission.ca/English/studentstandard

Minister for Health. (2018). *$9 million boost for youth mental health* [*Press release*]. Retrieved from https://www.health.gov.au/ministers/the-hon-greg-hunt-mp/media/9-million-boost-for-youth-mental-health

Norton, A., Cherastidtham, I., & Mackey, W. (2018). Dropping out: the benefits and costs of trying university. Retrieved from Victoria: https://grattan.edu.au/wp-content/uploads/2018/04/904-dropping-out-the-benefits-and-costs-of-trying-university.pdf

Orygen. (2017). *Under the radar: The mental health of Australian University students*. Retrieved from Parkville, Victoria: https://www.orygen.org.au/Policy/Policy-Reports/Under-the-radar

Orygen. (2020a). *Australian University mental health framework*. Retrieved from Melbourne: https://www.orygen.org.au/Policy/University-Mental-Health-Framework

Orygen. (2020b). *Defining the 'missing middle'*. Retrieved from Melbourne: https://www.orygen.org.au/Policy/Policy-Areas/Government-policy-service-delivery-and-workforce/Service-delivery/Defining-the-missing-middle/orygen-defining-the-missing-middle-pdf.aspx?ext=

Orygen. (2020c). *University mental health framework report*. Retrieved from Parkville: https://www.orygen.org.au/Policy/University-Mental-Health-Framework/Framework/University-Mental-Health-Framework-full-report.aspx

Productivity Commission. (2020). *Mental health* (Report no. 95). Retrieved from Canberra.

QILT Social Research Centre. (2017). *2016 student experience survey national report*. Retrieved from https://www.qilt.edu.au/qilt-surveys/student-experience

QILT Social Research Centre. (2021). *2020 student experience survey*. Retrieved from Canberra: https://www.qilt.edu.au/qilt-surveys/student-experience

Spalek, B. (2021). *The forgotten mental health crisis: Pressures on staff*. University World News. https://www.universityworldnews.com/post.php?story=20210111140929866

Stallman, H. M. (2008). Prevalence of psychological distress in university students–implications for service delivery. *Australian Family Physician, 37*(8), 673–677.

Stallman, H. M. (2010). Psychological distress in university students: A comparison with general population data. *Australian Psychologist, 45*(4), 249–257. https://doi.org/10.1080/00050067.2010.482109

Stallman, H. M., & Shochet, I. (2009). Prevalence of mental health problems in Australian university health services. *Australian Psychologist, 44*(2), 122–127.

Student Minds. (2019). *University mental health charter*. Retrieved from United Kingdom: https://www.studentminds.org.uk/uploads/3/7/8/4/3784584/191208_umhc_artwork.pdf

Universitas 21 Health Sciences Group. (2020). *U21 university mental health declaration*. Retrieved from https://universitas21.com/what-we-do/u21-university-mental-health-declaration

Universities UK, & Mental Wellbeing in Higher Education Group. (2015). *Student mental wellbeing in higher education. Good practice guide*. Retrieved from London: https://www.universitiesuk.ac.uk/policy-and-analysis/reports/Documents/2015/student-mental-wellbeing-in-he.pdf

Universities UK. (2017). *New framework for universities to help improve student mental health [Press release]*. Retrieved from https://www.universitiesuk.ac.uk/news/Pages/New-framework-for-universities-to-help-improve-student-mental-health.aspx

Universities UK. (2020). *Stepchange: Mentally healthy universities*. Retrieved from London: https://www.universitiesuk.ac.uk/policy-and-analysis/reports/Documents/2020/uuk-stepchange-mhu.pdf

Veness, B. (2016). *The wicked problem of university student mental health*. Retrieved from https://benveness.com/churchill-report/

Vivienne Browne is the Associate Director, Government Relations and Policy at Orygen, Australia's centre of excellence in youth mental health. Vivienne has worked for over 15 years in policy development, project management and program delivery in state government, local government and the community sector. In her current role at Orygen, Vivienne is responsible for the development, coordination and delivery of Orygen's policy, government relations and advocacy strategies. She has authored a number of policy reports and briefings across a range of issues including: trauma and young people, self-harm, youth suicide prevention and eating disorders.

In particular, Vivienne authored Orygen's policy report *Under the radar: the mental health of Australian university students*. As a result of this work, and ongoing advocacy to progress the report's recommendations, the Australian Government funded Orygen to develop a National University Mental Health Framework to provide universities with guidance on implementing a 'whole of university' response to this issue.

Penny Carlson is a Senior Policy Officer at the Department of Education and Training, Victorian Government. Prior to this she was the Senior Education Sector Project Manager at Orygen, with a special interest in cross-sector collaboration and advocating for change to improve health and wellbeing outcomes for students. At Orygen, she led development of the Australian University Mental Health Framework and has established the groundwork for implementation of the framework across sectors. Penny is experienced in managing national policy and program development, and strategically engaging stakeholders to facilitate change. Her background includes a range of roles focused on supporting students to be healthy, happy and to reach their potential.

COVID-19 and the Changing Higher Education Landscape: The Impact on Academics and Their Well-Being

Margaret Anne Carter, Vicki Hutton, Hyacinth Udah, and Abraham Francis

Abstract Workers' well-being in the workplace is attributed to productivity, workplace culture, job satisfaction, and work–life balance. The higher education work context is no different, with some evidence that academic staff experience higher levels of occupational stress, mental health issues, and work-related pressures. COVID-19 has added another layer to existing pressure for academic staff. The chapter builds on the ongoing discussion of higher education academics' about the impact of the COVID-19 pandemic on their health and well-being and discusses the need for creating mentally healthy work environments. Adopting a qualitative content analysis method the chapter examines how academics from various universities have contributed to this discussion through their recent publications in *The Conversation* media outlet. These academics' voices present emergent issues and strategic directions in response to the changing higher education landscape and the impacts of the COVID-19 pandemic. The chapter concludes with a rationale for a longitudinal study of the mental health and well-being of academics, providing rich material to influence the development of mentally healthy, supportive, and inclusive working environments.

Keywords Mental health · COVID-19 · Well-being · Higher education

---

M. A. Carter (✉)
Australian College of Applied Professions Brisbane, Brisbane, Australia
e-mail: Margaret.Carter@acap.edu.au

V. Hutton
Australian College of Applied Professions, Melbourne, Australia
e-mail: Vicki.Hutton@acap.edu.au

H. Udah · A. Francis
James Cook University, Townsville, Australia
e-mail: hyacinth.udah@jcu.edu.au

A. Francis
e-mail: Abraham.framcis@jcu.edu.au

A. P. Francis and M. A. Carter (eds.), *Mental Health and Higher Education in Australia*,
https://doi.org/10.1007/978-981-16-8040-3_3

Introduction

The potential for COVID-19, or coronavirus, to impact overall health and well-being was recognised early in the pandemic (World Health Organisation [WHO], 2020a). In addition to concerns about contracting the virus, unprecedented social isolation and safety measures implemented to curb transmission of the virus have negatively impacted mental health (WHO, 2020b) at an individual and community level. Sudden localised restrictions and lockdowns have resulted in university campus closures, loss of social interaction, economic downturns, financial hardship, lack of job security, and sudden loss of employment (Harris et al., 2020; Lee et al., 2021; Rakhmani et al., 2021).

All Australian higher education institutions suspended face-to-face teaching, switched to fully online delivery for part of the 2020 academic year, and were at different stages of readiness to embrace this change. For many academics, the rapid onset of COVID-19 meant upskilling and adjusting to different forms of remote teaching and learning arrangements and new modes of learning and teaching and researching (Lee et al., 2021; Rakhmani et al., 2021). With the consolidation of virtual teaching and online learning models as long-term viable options, many academics experienced changed work conditions and, in some cases, uncertain job security (Frantz et al., 2020; Lee et al., 2021). These changes have not only added to existing academic challenges but had ramifications for academics and their mental health and well-being (Lee et al., 2021).

For some academics, meeting the challenges of such a rapid shift also became a struggle for personal and professional survival as many higher education institutions began more stringent levels of managerial control and rounds of cost cutting to remain viable (Rakhmani et al., 2021). Throughout this period of uncertainty, anecdotal evidence suggests academics responded on a continuum ranging from heightened distress to pragmatic acceptance, to the enthusiastic embracing of strategies and new skillsets relevant to the changing landscape of higher education.

The chapter discusses the impact of the COVID-19 pandemic and explores the need to pay a higher level of attention than ever before to academics' mental health and well-being. A qualitative content analysis of *The Conversation Australia/New Zealand* articles are written by academics from 26 higher education institutions between 2013 and 2021 used as the data source for this chapter. Data prior to the peak of COVID-19 2020–2021 is included to contextualise the pre-existing stresses academics experiences and how these stresses have been magnified for academics as they adjust to the complexities of the pandemic. The perspectives of these academics are reported through the lens of mental health, the key driver of academic engagement, productivity, and participation in higher education. Key insights and strategic directions are identified and considered. The chapter concludes with a rationale for a longitudinal study of the mental health and well-being of academics, providing rich material to influence the development of mentally healthy, supportive, and inclusive working environments.

The authors align with PricewaterhoseCoopers' (2014) definition of mentally healthy workplaces and spaces as places that support everyone in the workplace to identify and manage potential risks to mental well-being, foster a culture of inclusion by addressing mental health stigma, prejudice, and discrimination, take mutually effective actions in response to mental health issues, and support people with mental ill health. These work environments purposefully invest in mental health and well-being responsive to individual and collective well-being needs, enhancing overall productivity and work performance.

Methods and Procedures

The Conversation Australia/New Zealand, with a monthly readership of 8.9 million, seeks to 'democratise knowledge and work with academic experts to inject evidence into public debate' (The Conversation, 2010–2021). Since its inception in 2010, over 17,200 academics have published articles on *The Conversation*. Its readership of 85% non-academic readers supports the publication's vision of sharing academic knowledge direct with the public. *The Conversation* has become recognised as a platform for people to produce content on potentially important topics such as mental health that is easy to read and free to access, thus directly and indirectly influencing others.

The Conversation articles written by higher education academics between 2013 and 2021 were used as the data source for this qualitative content analysis. A search of articles using the keywords 'higher education', 'universities', 'COVID-19', 'academics', 'mental health', and 'well-being' yielded the selected articles from which to identify themes related to the mental health and well-being of higher education academics during this time frame.

Qualitative content analysis relies on the subjective interpretation of the selected content through systematic coding and identifying patterns (Hsieh & Shannon, 2005), thereby making it possible to draw some interpretations of the results (Bengtsson, 2016). This method was identified as appropriate for the inductive approach required to examine the emergent issues among higher education academics and the need to create mentally healthy workplaces. Acknowledging that any qualitative coding is a subjective process, researchers' subjectivity in this study was of relevance given that the four authors are themselves immersed in the environment of interest. The authors, therefore, adopted a reflexive stance that allowed for reflection on how their assumptions might shape and limit the analysis (Braun & Clarke, 2021).

Data Description

Based on the keywords listed above, 18 units of analysis (articles) written by academics were identified. Nine were published between 2013 and 2019, and the

Table 1 Regions and Universities

Region	University
Australia	Australian National University Bond University Charles Sturt University Griffith University Macquarie University Melbourne University Monash University Queensland University of Technology RMIT University Southern Cross University Swinburne University of Technology University of Queensland University of Newcastle
United Kingdom	Coventry University University of Bath University of Brighton University of London University of Portsmouth University of Surrey
South Africa	University of the Western Cape University of Pretoria
Indonesia	Universitas Indonesia Universitas Negeri Semarang
Malaysia and SE Asia	Taylor's University
New Zealand	Massey University
United States	University of California

remaining nine were published in 2020 and 2021, perhaps indicative of the increased interest in mental health during the COVID-19 pandemic. Five of the nine 2020/2021 articles directly referred to the impact of COVID-19, supporting this observation. The latent content, or underlying meaning of each entire article (Bengtsson, 2016), formed the basis of the analysis.

The voices of academics (see Table 1) from 13 Australian universities as well as academics from six United Kingdom universities, two South African universities, two Indonesian universities, one Malaysia and South-East Asia university, one New Zealand university, and one US university are represented in this sample.

Data Analysis

De-contextualisation and re-contextualisation of data were undertaken in this qualitative content analysis. De-contextualisation required breaking the article latent content into meaning units and condensing and coding those units (Lindgren et al., 2020). The complexity of the phenomena articulated in these articles required an increased level of abstraction and interpretation when considering the emotions and latent meanings expressed, as well as rigorous monitoring of the authors' subjectivity given their positioning within the environment under discussion. Re-contextualisation required combining these meaning units into themes to allow a deeper understanding of the area of interest and discussing the results within the context of current research (Lindgren et al., 2020). During the de-contextualisation stage of condensing and coding units, we searched for keywords and metaphors to support analysis and interpretation. This process helped to identify and produce a concise matrix of key meaning units that were then combined into the following five themes:

1. Unhealthy workplace environment
2. Higher education as a stressful occupation
3. Performativity and increased metrics in higher education
4. Intersectionality and gendered inequalities in higher education
5. Feelings of dependency and vulnerability.

Table 2 provides a brief summary of each theme and lists the articles informing those themes.

Results

Results from this content analysis of *The Conversation* articles highlight important issue facing academics in the higher education sector. The results indicate that many academics feel overworked, stressed, and isolated, with a flow-on effect to reduced mental health and well-being. Results also indicate that while this is not a new phenomenon in academia, the COVID-19 pandemic has added another layer of complexity to the issue. The themes listed above are described and discussed in more depth next.

1. ***Unhealthy workplace environment***

Five articles identified increased workplace stressors such as harassment, bullying, and job insecurity that were preventing the development and maintenance of mentally healthy workplaces.

For over a decade, research has suggested that there is a strong link between workers' well-being and performance (Blustein, 2008). In mentally healthy organisational environments, workers' productivity is high. However, research shows that some Australian workplaces may not be creating and/or sustaining mentally healthy workplace environments free from work-related stressors (Hannan, 2013). Workplace stress is leading to lower levels of workplace well-being and job satisfaction, posing a risk to both workers and employers. For workers, the impact of workplace stress can include reduced productivity, incidental sick leave, or increased mental health days (Hannan, 2013). On the more severe end, workplace stress

Table 2 Themes and articles

Theme	Description	Articles
1. Unhealthy workplace environment	Increased workplace stressors are preventing the development and maintenance of mentally healthy workplaces	Erickson, M., Walker, C., & Hanna, P. (2020, February 29). Survey of academics finds widespread feelings of stress and overwork Hannan, T. (2013, November 11). Australian workplaces failing to create a healthy environment Hil, R., & Lyons, K. (2016, September 20). Academics are unhappy – it's time to transform our troubled university system Kupe, T., & Wangenge-Ouma, G. (2020, November 15). Post COVID-19: opportunity for universities to have a rethink Page, K. (2020, December 12). Managing stress and mental illness in the workplace

(continued)

Table 2 (continued)

Theme	Description	Articles
2. Higher education as a stressful occupation	The academic role has become a stressful occupation associated with feelings of decreased control and loneliness	Bone, K. (2019, July 18). Dependent and vulnerable: the experiences of academics on casual and insecure contracts Frantz, J., Munnik, E., & Smith, M. (2020, May 19). How academics in health sciences cope with stress Gorczynski, P. (2018, February 22). More academics and students have mental health problems than ever before Lee, M., Nasrawi, D., Hutchinson, M., & Lakeman, R. (2021, July 19). Our uni teachers were already among the world's most stressed. COVID and student feedback have just made things worse Morini, L. (2019, March 27). Universities: increasingly stressful environments taking psychological toll – here's what needs to change Sibai, O., Figueiredo, B., & Ferreira, M. (2019, January 29). Overworked and isolated: the rising epidemic of loneliness in academia Sullivan, N. (2013, May 6). Uni cuts will lead to health problems for academics

(continued)

Table 2 (continued)

Theme	Description	Articles
3. Performativity and increased metrics in higher education	Pressure to meet increasing metrics in performance, productivity, and quality is having a serious impact *on academics' mental health and well-being*	Allen, K., Donoghue, G., Hattie, J., Pahlevansharif, S., & Jimerson, S. (2021, February 3, 2021). Journal *papers, grants, jobs … as rejections pile up, it's not* enough to tell academics to 'suck it up.' Gorczynski, P. (2018, February 22). More academics and students have mental health problems than ever before Morini, L. (2019, March 27). Universities: Increasingly stressful environments taking psychological toll – here's what needs to change Watermeyer, R. (2016, August 1). Stress put on academics by the REF recognised in Stern review
4. Intersectionality and gendered inequalities in higher education	Some academics faced additional stressors within the higher education workplace due to intersectionality and gendered inequalities	Frantz, J., Munnik, E., & Smith, M. (2020, May 19). How academics in health sciences cope with stress Rakhmani, I., Eliyanah, E., & Sakhiyya, Z. (2021, February 15). Research: Indonesian female academics bear the brunt of the pandemic

(continued)

Table 2 (continued)

Theme	Description	Articles
5. Feelings of dependency and vulnerability	Academics expressed feelings of dependency and vulnerability related to poor job security, funding cuts, and casualisation of higher education workforces	Bone, K. (2019, July 18). Dependent and vulnerable: the experiences of academics on casual and insecure contracts Harris, J., Smithers, K., & Spina, N. (2020, May 15). More than 70% of academics at some universities are casuals. They are losing work and are cut out of JobKeeper Morini, L. (2019, March 27). Universities: increasingly stressful environments taking psychological toll – here's what needs to change Shepherd, S. (2020, November 16). How to support junior staff in a time of turmoil for universities Wright, B., & Winslade, M. (2018, August 21). University staff and students are at high risk of ill health. Here's how to make sure they can cope

can lead to extended time off work, workers compensation claims, and permanent disability (Page, 2020). For workers, the main workplace stress and pressures relate to coping with poor managerial control and workplace practices, excessive workloads, little control over their work, demands to do more with less, and interpersonal conflict (Hannan, 2013; Page, 2020). Among academics, especially early career academics, workplace stressors are impacting mental health and well-being with reports of harassment, bullying, and widespread job insecurity (Erickson et al., 2020). Two articles—one pre-COVID-19 and one during COVID-19—call on universities to transform the 'troubled university system' (Hil & Lyons, 2016) and use the changes forced on higher education during COVID-19 to rethink the system (Kupe & Wangenge-Ouma, 2020).

2. ***Higher education as a stressful occupation***

The academic role as a stressful occupation was the focus of seven articles, with negative factors such as unmanageable workloads, feelings of decreased control, tighter managerial control and greater surveillance, casualisation of the workforce, loneliness, and change contributing to this perception.

Research indicates that higher education is increasingly becoming a stressful occupation (Frantz et al., 2020; Lee et al., 2021; Morini, 2019; Sullivan, 2013). The top three stressors identified in higher education are unmanageable workloads, the interface and imbalance between work and home, and general work stress (Frantz et al., 2020). However, many university academics, especially in health professions including psychology, physiotherapy, occupational therapy, and social work, experience additional sources of stress related to clinical training (Frantz et al., 2020; Lee et al., 2021). The changes in higher education that draw attention to increased focus on research and social responsibility have also expanded the stress academics experience (Bone, 2019; Lee et al., 2021). Thus, data suggests that the modern higher education system is having extreme impacts on the health and well-being of many academics. Many academics in Australia and New Zealand are suffering high levels of occupational stress (Lee et al., 2021), insomnia and disorientation, as well as physical and psychological illnesses related to workplace stress (Sullivan, 2013). What is more, neoliberal policies across the higher education sector present manifold risks to the welfare of academics (Morini, 2019; Sullivan, 2013). Neoliberal policies have led to academics experiencing 'ever-increasing workloads, ever-decreasing control in the workplace, diminished job security, increased casualisation, expanding surveillance and performance measures, the fragmentation of collegiality, and the associated rise of a culture of competition and permanent distrust' (Sullivan, 2013, para 5). The success of neoliberal policies across the higher education sector is believed to be the production of what education researchers Bronwyn Davies and Peter Bansel refer to as the 'new enterprise individual'—the individual who embodies and reproduces, whether knowingly or not—the logic of market fundamentalism (Sullivan, 2013).

Driven by neoliberal technologies of massification, marketisation, and new public managerialism, the enterprise university has led to a deep affective somatic crisis (Lee et al., 2021; Sullivan, 2013). As such, academic survival in the modern higher education system requires that academics, to varying degrees, become individuals and take individual responsibility for their work, health, and well-being. Simultaneously, it inhabits an ethos in which there is no space for legitimate debate and where critique is treated as seditious, turning academics into their own worst enemies.

Loneliness adds another layer of distress for academics, as reported in Sibai et al.'s (2019) article. Many academics feel overworked and lonely at work. Social isolation is particularly common among early career academics whose jobs are not secure and who often have very heavy teaching workloads (Sibai et al., 2019). For example, 40% of academics, and more than half below the age of 35, view isolation at work as the main factor affecting their mental health (Sibai et al., 2019). Often, this is related to the pressure to perform. This pressure to perform can contribute to academics disengaging from relationships with colleagues and friends to avoid damaging their productivity or preventing them from reaching their goals (Sibai et al., 2019). In universities, isolation can push academics into distress, with many abandoning their research careers.

3. ***Performativity and increased metrics in higher education***

Four articles raised concerns that the pressure to meet increasing metrics in performance, productivity, and quality was having a serious impact on academics' mental health and well-being.

There was a pervasive discontent and low job satisfaction among academics who felt pressured to meet increasing metrics that had generated an audit culture where many things are measured, but few things are valued. In addition, the pursuit of excellence and public money by universities put further stress on academics (Gorczynski, 2018; Watermeyer, 2016). For example, given the increased workloads of academics and demands to publish and obtain external revenue, many academics exhibit symptoms of at least a mild mental disorder and report nearly twice the prevalence of mental disorders compared to the general population (Gorczynski, 2018). In addition, an institutional policy of cherry-picking 'the best' researchers for competitive Excellence in Research Awards (ERA) or Research Excellence Framework (REF) submission can have a devastating impact on morale, self-worth, and trust among academics (Gorczynski, 2018; Watermeyer, 2016). Similarly, performance indicators across the higher education sector can have serious impacts on academics' mental health and well-being as these indicators become increasingly 'gamified' with points and rankings and winners and losers (Morini, 2019). Without doubt, making knowledge production into a game, and driven by neoliberal policies, puts academics in competition with each other, as research is being measured mainly by who publishes first and in the best journals, thus slowing the progress and sharing of knowledge (Morini, 2019).

Also, given that academics' careers are strongly linked to their success in publishing and funding applications, rejection can have serious implications for mental health and well-being. It is not enough to tell academics to suck it up as rejections pile up (Allen et al. 2021). Rejection culture, together with excessive workloads, contributes to stress and anxiety among academics. The culture of rejection neither helps academics to function at their best nor benefits society. Rather, it impedes academics' pursuit and dissemination of new knowledge (Allen et al., 2021).

4. ***Intersectionality and gendered inequalities in higher education***

Gendered inequalities and intersectionality were cited as additional stressors within the higher education workplace in two articles.

Frantz et al. (2020) and Rakhmani et al. (2021) show that women and minority groups experience more stress in higher education. While it is not uncommon for minority groups to experience high levels of stress related to job security, women report higher rates of work-related stress, vulnerability, and mental ill health associated with discrimination in the workplace, caregiving responsibilities, work disruptions, financial worries, and job security (Frantz et al., 2020). This is supported by evidence that during the COVID-19 pandemic, female academics carried a larger burden associated with heavy teaching loads, the pressure of balancing family responsibilities, and work demands for increased productivity (Frantz et al., 2020; Rakhmani et al., 2021). This resulted in increased levels of stress, low job satisfaction, and relatively little time for research and publication compared to their male colleagues.

5. ***Feelings of dependency and vulnerability***

Five articles alluded to academics' feelings of dependency and vulnerability related to poor job security, funding cuts, and casualisation of higher education workforces.

Research indicates that university academics are at risk of high levels of stress due to poor job security, low income, and job pressures (Morini, 2019; Wright & Winslade, 2018). Ongoing university funding cuts, performance management, and casualisation of the workforce have contributed to an environment of insecurity, psychological distress, and feelings of job dissatisfaction among many academics (Wright & Winslade, 2018). There is evidence that the COVID-19 pandemic has amplified academic staff vulnerabilities, thus contributing to the maintenance or exacerbation of existing mental health issues (Harris et al., 2020). With casual positions often perceived as more exploitative and insecure, and more than 70% of academics at some universities being in casual positions, casual and contract academics are increasingly vulnerable in their pursuit for a permanent position in academia (Harris et al., 2020). They are precariously employed and vulnerable to imminent job losses, increasing workloads and expectations, potential exploitation, and burnout (Harris et al., 2020; Shepherd, 2020). It is not surprising that reports indicate academics on precarious employment or casual contracts feel vulnerable, dependent, and of lower status than permanent academics (Bone, 2019). Feeling continually at risk of being excluded from the university makes these academics particularly anxious and causes high levels of stress and pressure to perform and impress their supervisors (Bone, 2019). In addition, when compounded by a culture of silence and stigma around mental health issues within university environments and a corresponding lack of services, few academics staff disclose a mental health condition resulting from reduced professional autonomy and increased demand for performance and productivity (Gorczynski, 2018).

Discussion

The relatively poor health outcomes of academics as reported in this content analysis significantly impact academics work satisfaction, productivity, and general well-being (Frantz et al., 2020; Morini, 2019; Plotnikoff et al., 2015; Sibai et al., 2019). With an increased number of academics experiencing distress and mental health issues, which COVID-19 has exacerbated, mental health has become a serious workplace issue that can no longer be the elephant in the room. Acknowledging higher education environments as stressful workplaces is, therefore, important.

Within the landscape of neoliberal ideology and economically rational policies (Connell, 2013; Hil & Lyons, 2016), the results of this *The Conversation* content analysis identify academics as susceptible to work-related stress, increased job pressures and workloads, exhaustion, burnout, reduced enthusiasm for teaching and research, and general psychological distress (Gorczynski, 2018; Jansson & Gunnarsson, 2018; Kupe & Wangenge-Ouma, 2020; Lee et al., 2021; Morini, 2019; Sibai et al., 2019; Stapleton, 2019; Wright & Winslade, 2018).

Prior to the COVID-19 pandemic, academics working in Australian higher education institutions were reported to be in a state of transition, moving from traditional teaching, research, management, and service commitment responsibilities to more differentiated duties such as management of casual staff, accreditation, and administration tasks. This shift was because of the cuts to higher education institution funding and casualisation of the higher education institution workforce (Bennett et al., 2018; Carter & Goldie, 2018). These cuts and casualisation of the workforce have resulted in high levels of psychological distress and feelings of vulnerability and job dissatisfaction among many academics (Wright & Winslade, 2018). While the COVID-19 pandemic has exacerbated and amplified the vulnerabilities of academics, more must be done to address the poor mental health of academics so they are supported to function at their best (Allen et al., 2021; Carter et al., 2017; Orman, 2017; Sullivan, 2013; Veness, 2016, 2017). If things are left the way they are, there will be a rise in absenteeism, presenteeism, burnout and reduced enthusiasm, and worker's compensation claims (Hannan, 2013; Lee et al., 2021; Sullivan, 2013).

The identification of workplace stress as the common reason for disengagement and reduced enthusiasm and work performance among academics is concerning and calls for higher education institutions to address the state of mental health among academics. Universities need to recognise the impacts of overworking, changes in technology, reduced professional autonomy, micro-managing, and demands for increased performance and productivity on academic well-being. With academics at the forefront of the education system and vital to supporting student success, poor mental health may undermine their capacity to promote well-being in students which will have serious consequences in terms of the future of higher education institutions (Erickson et al., 2020; Sibai et al., 2019; Wright & Winslade, 2018).

The COVID-19 pandemic forced a shift from face-to-face learning and teaching to online teaching and learning, with countless academics forced to rapidly learn and apply different pedagogical content knowledge and digital technologies, so they could design distinctive online learning environments. For many academics who had minimal experience with online learning, this meant longer work hours, developing new skillsets, procuring tools, and mastering software applications so they could redesign and facilitate curriculum content and assessments in response to the new teaching and learning landscape (Rakhmani et al., 2021). These changes in expectations and duties have added to the workloads and distress experienced by academics' (Frantz et al., 2020), already struggling with balancing their teaching, research, and service engagement and with work–life balance (Houlden & Veletsianos, 2020).

The lack of social interaction and communication during COVID-19 social distancing restrictions and lockdowns has also contributed to a sense of isolation and social disconnectedness. For many academics, social isolation has been a source of loneliness and distress, with significantly reduced personal and professional interactions with colleagues. Set against this background, subjective perceptions of loneliness have compounded existing workload stresses and resulted in many academics putting their research on hold. Without ongoing research ideas and projects, higher education institutions will innovate less (Sibai et al., 2019). To maximise the benefits to society from the pursuit of research and dissemination of new knowledge, there is a need to address the underlying sources of anxiety, stress, exploitation, and isolation among academics. This could mean setting up informal communication channels to encourage conversations between academics so they feel less alone and more supported, adopting a more coordinated and comprehensive approach to promoting and sustaining the health and well-being of academics (Wright & Winslade, 2018), cultivating collegiality, collaboration, and a more inclusive environment (Hil & Lyons, 2016), and creating systems for assessing collective rather than individual performance (Sibai et al., 2019).

Acknowledging individuals have a duty to take responsibility for their mental health and well-being and not adversely impact others' mental health and safety, Hickie (2018) names mental health awareness, self-management competency, personal responsibility, and organisational planning, policy, and action, identifying more personalised staged care regimes through designated services (e.g. headspace) and evidence informed e-health platforms (e.g. mood gym; head the health) as the pathway forward for individuals and institutions towards growing mental health. This implies the need for meaningful structural changes to the university environment to support behaviour change and address the underlying factors such as job security, workload and pay associated with academics' low productivity, high absenteeism, and presenteeism so that academics are empowered to perform at their optimal level while at work (Gorczynski, 2018).

Prioritising the mental health of academics at an institutional level will lessen the impact of the performance and rejection culture and gender inequalities in higher education. It is important for higher education institutions to consider performance in writing and research—independent of publication metrics—ideally without any time-consuming application process (Allen et al., 2021). It is also important for universities to recognise the impacts of student feedback on academic well-being and reputation. Many academics report post-traumatic stress disorder (PTSD) after receiving comments that are distressing, offensive, or disrespectful from unfiltered anonymous feedback from student surveys (Lee et al., 2021). This involves creating a positive environment for academics—a mentally healthy workplace—through supportive leadership and positive team management processes (Hannan, 2013). While creating a mentally healthy work environment will not eliminate all the impacts of the performance and rejection culture and gender inequalities, including overworking, tighter managerial control and greater surveillance (Lee et al., 2021) impacting academics, especially academic women, in higher education, it is an initial but important step in reducing the prevalence of workplace-related stress (Hannan, 2013).

Therefore, higher education institutions are challenged to articulate, address, and enact family-friendly work environments in response to the conundrum experienced by academics—mainly academic women—balancing working hours to accommodate caring responsibilities, including home-schooling, while working from home (Nash & Churchill, 2020; Rakhmani et al., 2021). Understanding the interplay between institutional gender equality, socio-demographic variables, workplace-related distress, and emotional intelligence is key to developing and managing appropriate provisions of mental health care and support (Frantz et al., 2020; Nash & Churchill, 2020).

According to Safe Work Australia (2018), an Australian Government statutory agency, a best practice systematic approach to developing and sustaining a mentally healthy workplace focuses on 'mental illness prevention and mental health promotion' (p. 22). This is because fostering a people-oriented culture through supportive management can aid in the prevention of harm, early identification and intervention, and management of mental health conditions and recovery in the workplace (Safe Work Australia, 2018).

This approach is in line with the 2017 Australian government response to the Higher Education Standards Panel (2017, p. 7) final report—*Improving retention, completion, and success in higher education*—that 'every institution should have an institution-wide mental health strategy and implementation plan'. Institutional-level health promotion initiatives, such as work–life balance policies, health promotion interventions, peer support groups, counselling, coaching, career planning, and reducing overtime are possible actions towards harm prevention, early intervention, and stress management in higher education workplaces (Bhui et al., 2016).

Furthermore, improving mental health literacy (MHL) among academics has been hailed as an effective strategy to support academics' mental health and well-being (Gorczynski, 2018). Improving MHL among academics—including symptom identification, self-care practices, and knowing where to seek support—is one action to potentially influence and change academics' attitudes towards conversations on mental ill health and help-seeking behaviours. Like the work being done with students, academics need information about mental health and help to change their attitudes towards seeking care (Gorczynski, 2018). The four dimensions comprising MHL include understanding how to obtain and sustain mental health; understanding mental ill health and interventions and treatments; decreasing stigma and discrimination against mental ill health; and enhancing help-seeking behaviour (Wei et al., 2015). However, MHL must not be seen as a panacea. This is because one-off MHL professional development sessions or short-term MHL professional development courses need to be taught alongside long-term, campus-based, large-scale programs if individuals are to build and apply MHL knowledge, attitudes, and behaviours (Sontag-Padilla et al., 2018).

Sustainable mental health promoting cultures in higher education institutions need to incorporate everyone—government, higher education institutions, health professionals, community, and individuals (Carter & Goldie, 2018; Hickie, 2018). Available evidence shows a holistic approach to building cultures that enhance health and well-being on university campuses promote the mental health and well-being of academics, as well as students (Newton et al., 2016). The Healthy Universities framework is one example of a holistic approach higher education institutions could use to address the risk factors common among academics and students. Instead of having a range of separate programs that focus on specific areas of health, a 'healthy university' takes a whole-of-institution approach to creating a supportive environment for everyone who works and studies in higher education institutions (Newton et al., 2016; Wright & Winslade, 2018).

The Australian University Mental Health Framework, launched in 2020 by Orygen, Australia's centre of excellence for youth mental health, while voluntary, provides evidence informed guidelines and standards for Australian universities to follow and develop mentally healthy university settings, partnering the mental health sector with universities. The framework is built on six guiding principles (see Table 3), with higher education institutions and the community mental health sector collaboratively committing to actions to advance mental health and well-being supports. This holistic approach is grounded in building and sustaining a culture where students and academics experience a sense of belonging, energy, and engagement (Wright & Winslade, 2018).

Table 3 Australian University Mental Health Framework (Orygen, 2020)

Principles	Actions
Principle 1	The student experience is enhanced through mental health and well-being approaches that are informed by students' needs, perspectives, and the reality of their experiences
Principle 2	All members of the university community contribute to learning environments that enhance student mental health and well-being
Principle 3	Mentally healthy university communities encourage participation; foster a diverse, inclusive environment; promote connectedness; and support academic and personal achievement
Principle 4	The response to mental health and well-being is strengthened through collaboration and coordinated actions
Principle 5	Students are able to access appropriate, effective, and timely services and supports to meet their mental health and well-being needs
Principle 6	Continuous improvement and innovation is informed by evidence and helps build an understanding of what works for student mental health and well-being

Conclusion and Ways Forward

The qualitative content analysis in this chapter provides some insight into commentary from academics who chose *The Conversation* as a respected common platform to articulate their thoughts and emotions prior to and during the 2020 COVID-19 pandemic crisis period. With the data limited to only those academics who self-selected to express their feelings and experiences in this public forum, this study is not an endpoint. As the higher education sector moves to rebuild and restructure in a post-COVID world, academics will continue to be confronted with a changing landscape. Results from our study provide a rationale for the importance of adopting a longitudinal approach to explore these emergent issues in the higher education sector.

We acknowledge that prior to the pandemic academics have been experiencing changing and escalating work pressures. Drawing from, and building on, the knowledge gained from this content analysis, we propose a longitudinal study be undertaken to explore the mental health and well-being of higher education academics as they settle into the changed teaching and learning environment of post-COVID-19. In particular, we would examine (1) whether rebuilding and reshaping are proving harder than surviving for some members of this group (academics); (2) if any sub-groups within academia have fallen through the cracks as rebuilding, micro-managing, and reshaping gain momentum; and (3) what are the strategies to develop sustainable working practices to create a mentally healthy workplace. This would involve administering a brief survey among higher education academics on an annual or biennial basis to explore their well-being. The survey would include a self-report measure, such as the personal well-being index (International Well-being Group, 2013) that assesses subjective well-being and can also be compared to general population normative data to position the well-being of academics within the broader population. An open question related to strategies used to maintain health and well-being during and post-COVID would be included to contribute towards the development and the necessity of building a mentally healthy, supportive, and inclusive working environment where academics can work productively and safely.

References

Allen, K., Donoghue, G., Hattie, J., Pahlevansharif, S., & Jimerson, S. (2021, February 3). Journal papers, grants, jobs ... as rejections pile up, it's not enough to tell academics to 'suck it up.' *The Conversation*. https://theconversation.com/journal-papers-grants-jobs-as-rejections-pile-up-its-not-enough-to-tell-academics-to-suck-it-up-153886

Bengtsson, M. (2016). How to plan and perform a qualitative study using content analysis. *NursingPlus Open, 2*, 8–14.

Bennett, D., Roberts, L., Ananthram, S., & Broughton, M. (2018). What is required to develop career pathways for teaching academics? *Higher Education, 75*(2), 271–286. https://doi.org/10.1007/s10734-017-0138-9

Bhui, K., Dinos, S., Galant-Miecznikowska, M., de Jongh, B., & Stansfeld, S. (2016). Perceptions of work stress causes and effective interventions in employees working in public, private and non-governmental organisations: A qualitative study. *Bjpsych Bulletin, 40*(6), 318–325. https://doi.org/10.1192/pb.bp.115.050823

Blustein, D. L. (2008). The role of work in psychological health and well-being: A conceptual, historical, and public policy perspective. *American Psychologist, 63*(4), 228–240. https://doi.org/10.1037/0003-066X.63.4.228

Bone, K. (2019, July 18). Dependent and vulnerable: the experiences of academics on casual and insecure contracts. *The Conversation*. https://theconversation.com/dependent-and-vulnerable-the-experiences-of-academics-on-casual-and-insecure-contracts-118608

Braun, V., & Clarke, V. (2021). Can I use TA? Should I use TA? Should I *not* use TA? Comparing reflexive thematic analysis and other pattern-based qualitative analytic approaches. *Counselling and Psychotherapy Research, 21*, 37–47.

Carter, M., & Goldie, D. (2018). Potential enablers of mental health and wellness for those teaching in tertiary education. *International Journal of Innovation, Creativity and Change, 4*(3), 3–20.

Carter, M., Pagliano, P., Francis, A., & Thorne, M. (2017). Australian university students and Mental Health: Viewpoints form the literature. *International Journal of Innovation, Creativity and Change, 3*(3), 1–25.

Connell, R. (2013). The neoliberal cascade and education: An essay on the market agenda and its consequences. *Critical Studies in Education, 54*(2), 99–112.

Erickson, M., Walker, C., & Hanna, P. (2020, February 29). Survey of academics finds widespread feelings of stress and overwork. *The Conversation*. https://theconversation.com/survey-of-academics-finds-widespread-feelings-of-stress-and-overwork-130715

Frantz, J., Munnik, E., & Smith, M. (2020, May 19). How academics in health sciences cope with stress. *The Conversation*. https://theconversation.com/how-academics-in-health-sciences-cope-with-stress-138031

Gorczynski, P. (2018, February 22). More academics and students have mental health problems than ever before. *The Conversation*. https://theconversation.com/more-academics-and-students-have-mental-health-problems-than-ever-before-90339

Hannan, T. (2013, November 11). Australian workplaces failing to create a healthy environment. *The Conversation*. https://theconversation.com/australian-workplaces-failing-to-create-a-healthy-environment-19986

Harris, J., Smithers, K., & Spina, N. (2020, May 15). More than 70% of academics at some universities are casuals. They are losing work and are cut out of JobKeeper. *The Conversation*. https://theconversation.com/more-than-70-of-academics-at-some-universities-are-casuals-theyre-losing-work-and-are-cut-out-of-jobkeeper-137778

Hickie, I. (2018). *Developing the 'mental wealth' of Australian youth attending higher education settings*. Paper presented at the Australasian Mental Health and Higher Education Conference, Townsville, Queensland, Australia.

Higher Education Standards Panel. (2017). *Improving retention, completion, and success in higher education report*. Australian Government.

Hil, R., & Lyons, K. (2016, September 20). Academics are unhappy—It's time to transform our troubled university system. *The Conversation*. https://theconversation.com/academics-are-unhappy-its-time-to-transform-our-troubled-university-system-62682

Houlden, S., & Veletsianos, S. (2020, March 12). Coronavirus pushes universities to switch to online classes—But are they ready? *The Conversation*. https://theconversation.com/coronavirus-pushes-universities-to-switch-to-online-classes-but-are-they-ready-132728. Accessed July 25, 2021

Hsieh, H., & Shannon, S. (2005). Three approaches to qualitative content analysis. *Qualitative Health Research, 15*(9), 1277–1288.

Jansson, I., & Gunnarsson, A. (2018). Employers' views of the impact of mental health problems on the ability to work. *Work—A Journal of Prevention Assessment & Rehabilitation, 59*(4), 585–598. https://doi.org/10.3233/WOR-182700

Kupe, T., & Wangenge-Ouma, G. (2020, November 15). Post COVID-19: Opportunity for universities to have a rethink. *The Conversation*. https://theconversation.com/post-covid-19-opportunity-for-universities-to-have-a-rethink-149474

Lee, M., Nasrawi, D., Hutchinson, M., & Lakeman, R (2021, July 19). Our uni teachers were already among the world's most stressed. COVID and student feedback have just made things worse. *The Conversation*. https://theconversation.com/our-uni-teachers-were-already-among-the-worlds-most-stressed-covid-and-student-feedback-have-just-made-things-worse-162612

Lindgren, B.-M., Lundman, B., & Graneheim, U. (2020). Abstraction and interpretation during the qualitative content analysis process. *International Journal of Nursing Studies, 108*, 1–6.

Morini, L. (2019, March 27). Universities: Increasingly stressful environments taking psychological toll—Here's what needs to change. *The Conversation*. https://theconversation.com/universities-increasingly-stressful-environments-taking-psychological-toll-heres-what-needs-to-change-97045

Nash, M., & Churchill, B. (2020). Caring during COVID-19: A gendered analysis of Australian university responses to managing remote working and caring responsibilities. *Gender, Work, and Organisation, 27*(5), 833–846. https://doi.org/10.1111/gwao.12484.

Newton, J., Dooris, M., & Wills, J. (2016). Healthy universities: An example of a whole-system health-promoting setting. *Global Health Promotion, 23*(1), 57–65.

Orman, J. (2017, 30 June–1 July). *Mental health on campus—Practical ways to help*. PowerPoint presented at the Inaugural Australasian Mental Health and Higher Education Conference Townsville, QLD, Australia.

Orygen. (2020). Australian University Mental Health Framework Report. Orygen.

Page, K. (2020, December 12). Managing stress and mental illness in the workplace. *The Conversation*. https://theconversation.com/managing-stress-and-mental-illness-in-the-workplace-19647

Plotnikoff, R., Costigan, S., Williams, R., Hutchesson, M., Kennedy, S., Robards, S., & Germov, J. (2015). Effectiveness of interventions targeting physical activity, nutrition and healthy weight for university and college students: A systematic review and meta-analysis. *The International Journal of Behavioral Nutrition and Physical Activity, 12*(1), 45. https://doi.org/10.1186/s12966-015-0203-7

PricewaterhouseCoopers. (2018). *Creating a mentally healthy workplace: Return on investment final report for beyondblue, the National Mental Health Commission, and the Mentally Healthy Workplace Alliance*. https://www.qhrc.qld.gov.au/__data/assets/pdf_file/0008/20150/PwC-report.pdf

Rakhmani, I., Eliyanah, E., & Sakhiyya, Z. (2021, February 15). Research: Indonesian female academics bear the brunt of the pandemic. *The Conversation*. https://theconversation.com/research-indonesian-female-academics-bear-the-brunt-of-the-pandemic-154487

Safe Work Australia. (2018). *Work-related psychological health and safety: A systematic approach to meeting your duties*. http://www.safeworkaustralia.gov.au/doc/work-related-psychological-health-and-safety-systematic-approach-meeting-your-duties

Shepherd, S. (2020, November 16). How to support junior staff in a time of turmoil for universities. *The Conversation*. https://theconversation.com/how-to-support-junior-staff-in-a-time-of-turmoil-for-universities-148917

Sibai, O., Figueiredo, B., & Ferreira, M. (2019, January 29). Overworked and isolated: the rising epidemic of loneliness in academia. *The Conversation*. https://theconversation.com/overworked-and-isolated-the-rising-epidemic-of-loneliness-in-academia-110009

Sontag-Padilla, L., Dunbar, S., Ye, F., Kase, C., Fein, R., Abelson, S., & Stein, B. (2018). Strengthening college students' mental health knowledge, awareness, and helping behaviors: The impact of active minds, a peer mental health organization. *Journal of the American Academy of Child & Adolescent Psychiatry, 57*(7), 500–507. https://doi.org/10.1016/j.jaac.2018.03.019

Stapleton, P. (2019, June 7). Teachers are more depressed and anxious than the average Australian. *The Conversation*. https://theconversation.com/teachers-are-more-depressed-and-anxious-than-the-average-australian-117267

Sullivan, N. (2013, May 6). Uni cuts will lead to health problems for academics. *The Conversation*. https://theconversation.com/uni-cuts-will-lead-to-health-problems-for-academics-13875

Veness, B. (2016). *The wicked problem of university student mental health*. Monash University Churchill Fellowship. https://www.churchilltrust.com.au/media/fellows/Veness_B_2013_The_wicked_problem_of_university_student_mental_health.pdf

Veness, B. (2017, 30 June–1 July). *The wicked problem of university student mental health*. PowerPoint presented at the Inaugural Australasian Mental Health and Higher O'Hagan Education Conference Townsville, QLD, Australia. https://www.jcu.edu.au/__data/assets/pdf_file/0007/517633/Dr-Ben-Veness.pdf

Watermeyer, R. (2016, August 1). Stress put on academics by the REF recognised in Stern review. *The Conversation*. https://theconversation.com/stress-put-on-academics-by-the-ref-recognised-in-stern-review-63237

Wei, Y., McGrath, P. J., Hayden, J., & Kutcher, S. (2015). Mental health literacy measures: Evaluating knowledge, attitudes and help-seeking: A scoping review. *BMC Psychiatry, 15*(1), 1–20. https://doi.org/10.1186/s12888-015-0681-9

World Health Organisation. (2020a). *Substantial investment needed to avert mental health crisis*. https://www.who.int/news/item/14-05-2020-substantial-investment-needed-to-avert-mental-health-crisis

World Health Organisation. (2020b). *Mental health and COVID-19*. https://www.who.int/teams/mental-health-and-substance-use/covid-19

Wright, B., & Winslade, M. (2018, August 21). University staff and students are at high risk of ill health. Here's how to make sure they can cope. *The Conversation*. https://theconversation.com/university-staff-and-students-are-at-high-risk-of-ill-health-heres-how-to-make-sure-they-can-cope-101070

Margaret Anne Carter's career in higher education, both in Singapore and Australia, includes teaching, academic leadership, community service and research. In 2017 Margaret Anne was awarded the National Citation for Outstanding Contribution to Student Learning. Her strong research interests provide a solid foundation for the integration of expert theory and quality practice to promote academic excellence and high levels of student engagement, productivity and wellbeing. Contributing to a sense hatof social consciousness, Margaret Anne's research continues to generate new knowledge and insight to enhance student learning and experiences. Margaret Anne publishes in areas including teaching and learning in higher education, resilience, mental health and wellbeing, preventing cyber bullying, young children's social behaviour and character education in early childhood.

Vicki Hutton is Associate Professor in the Discipline of Counselling at the Australian College of Applied Professions. After working in the health and community sectors as a counsellor and group facilitator specialising in trauma, family violence, carer support and crisis counselling, Vicki moved into teaching and research at Monash University (Australia) where she completed her PhD in Applied Psychology.

An important part of Vicki's role in higher education teaching and learning relates to developing and promoting ethical sensitivity and cultural responsiveness among students as they prepare to enter a culturally diverse society. She believes curricula should engage students at a cognitive, affective and behavioural level in order to foster the understanding and skills required to be responsive to the worldview of others. Vicki is also passionate about animal ethics and the relationship between human and non-human animals.

Vicki's research interests include mental health and wellbeing, diversity, stigma, and human-animal studies, with a particular focus on subjective wellbeing, HIV and AIDS, sexual orientation and gender identity, community-connectedness, compassion fatigue and the human-animal relationship.

Hyacinth Udah is a Senior Lecturer in Social Work and Human Services at the James Cook University. He holds Doctorate and Master's Degrees in Social Work from Griffith University, and the Australian Catholic University, respectively. He also has a First-Class Honours Degree in Theology and Philosophy. His doctoral study explored the African immigrant experiences, and his recent research publications are extending his interests in immigrant experiences, coloniality and decoloniality, community development, mental health and wellbeing, social work ethics, values, education, research, and practice.

Abraham P. Francis is an Associate Professor, and currently the Head of Academic Group in Social Work and Human Services at James Cook University, Australia. He has worked with Government, Non-government and corporate sector, and has developed many international partnerships. He taught social work at the Delhi University in India and worked as a senior mental health social worker with Country Health South Australia before moving to Townsville to join James Cook University. Dr. Francis has established many international partnerships and research collaborations with universities and non-government organizations.

He has extensively contributed to the literature on Social Work practice in mental health through his publications, convening conferences, establishing research networks and by developing consortiums. His other research interests are in the field of communities, criminal justice, international social work, and gerontological social work. His excellence in teaching has been recognised on a number of occasions. For example, in 2010, he was a recipient of James Cook University's Inclusive Practice Award for his "exceptional support for students with a disability". In 2016, he received the university's "***Citation for Outstanding Contributions to Student Learning***" for his "leadership and expertise in social work education in mental health that inspires and nurtures students to be competent, confident and compassionate practitioners".

Dr. Francis was one of the finalists at the 2018 India ***Australia business and community awards*** in the category of Community Services Excellence Award and Business Leader/ Professional of the Year. In 2018, Dr. Francis received the NAPASWI (National Association of Professional Association Social Workers in India) lifetime achievement for his outstanding contribution to social work Education.

Cultural Partnership Practice and Mental Health in Higher Education

Narayan Gopalkrishnan and Hurriyet Babacan

Abstract We live in a world that is increasingly interconnected through the processes of globalization and where diverse cultures interact with each other in complex ways. The higher education sector is particularly impacted on by the opportunities and issues of cultural diversity, with students and staff of culturally and linguistically diverse backgrounds. Further, in many high-income countries (HICs), the higher education sector has also to consider the ways in which the needs of First Nations students and staff can be met in contexts where histories of colonization and oppression have left their scars. This chapter explores some of the critical elements of mental health and cultural diversity within higher education and excavates the protective and risk factors that exist in the present context. It goes on to highlight the positive ways in which higher education institutions have responded to the challenges and opportunities of mental health and cultural diversity and posits some strategies for the future.

Keywords Culture · Higher education · Mental health · Cultural competency · Cultural partnerships · Globalization

Context

Culture is a very broad term that incorporates notions of shared values and group identity across a range of descriptors (Spencer-Oatey, 2008). In this chapter, the term is used in the context of ethnic identity, with a focus on identity that is shared around factors such as language, historical origin, religion and socially constructed notions of race. Another related term is "cultural diversity" which refers to the fact that there are diverse cultural groups within the population in question, and where the same cultural values and identity are not shared by everyone in the population.

N. Gopalkrishnan (✉) · H. Babacan
James Cook University, Townsville, Australia
e-mail: narayan.gopalkrishnan@jcu.edu.au

H. Babacan
e-mail: hurriyet.babacan@jcu.edu.au

A. P. Francis and M. A. Carter (eds.), *Mental Health and Higher Education in Australia*,
https://doi.org/10.1007/978-981-16-8040-3_4

Several factors play a part in terms of the levels of cultural diversity in any country, especially in the high-income countries (HICs) like Australia, New Zealand, the United States, and Canada, factors that also play a part in the cultural diversity of higher education in these countries.

The first of these relates to the Indigenous or First Nations peoples of these countries. There are between 370 and 500 million indigenous peoples globally, though the true numbers are often obscured by the lack of disaggregated data (UN, 2019; WB, 2021; WHO, 2007). The data is a bit clearer in the HICs with histories of colonization, where indigenous peoples are more clearly identified. In Australia, for example, the 2016 Census identified around 649,000 Aboriginal and Torres Strait Islander people in the population, approximately 2.8% of the population (ABS, 2017). The United States recognizes over 2 million people among the 565 federally designated tribal nations, and Canada recognizes over 1.2 million people as indigenous (Gone, 2013). Indigenous populations in these countries have a history of trauma, dispossession and oppression that have major implications for their mental health (Nelson & Wilson, 2017). The terms "Historical Trauma" and "Inter-generational Trauma" are increasingly gaining acceptance to represent the complex, cumulative and inter-generational impacts of the processes of colonization (Gone, 2013). Nelson and Wilson (2017) describe this as First Nations people bearing a disproportionate burden of mental and physical illness. This issue is also negatively impacted by the fact that mental health professionals may be perceived with suspicion by students of First Nations backgrounds, as they could be seen as implicated in the historic oppression of their people (Bessarab & Crawford, 2013). These factors can lead to reduced utilization of health systems as well as later and more acute presentations when they do occur. This utilization of mental health services is also impacted on by issues of *discrimination* that can reduce indigenous peoples' access to appropriate mental health services, especially in no-indigenous health service settings (Boksa et al., 2015).

The second major factor in changing demographics and rates of cultural diversity relates to migration. The processes of globalization are compressing the boundaries of time and space and play an important role in the increasing levels of migration and the complex and nuanced "super-diversity" that emerges from migration (Vertovec, 2007). The estimated number of international migrants globally was estimated to be over 272 million (3.5% of global population) in 2020 and had been consistently climbing until the impacts of the COVID-19 pandemic began to be felt (IOM, 2020). This is of particular relevance in HICs where migration is responsible for two-thirds of the population growth (Bélanger et al., 2019). In addition to the skilled migration and family reunion visa streams, many of these countries also take in significant numbers of refugees as humanitarian entrants, all of whom add to the cultural diversity of the host country (IOM, 2020; UNHCR, 2017). Many migrants take up citizenship of the host country, and they and their subsequent generations do not reflect in the figures of international migrants just cited. Countries like Australia have a long history of immigration flows that make up the culturally diverse population of the present day. By the 2016 Census, 49% of Australians identified as either been born overseas or having one or more parents who had been born overseas (ABS, 2017). Further, increasing percentages of these overseas born were from countries like India and China as against the traditional flows from England and New Zealand.

Migration patterns have a major impact on the ways in which migrants can access mental health systems. Many of the migrants and refugees who settle in HICs often end up in lower paying jobs with higher levels of casualization as compared to the general population, thereby experiencing levels of inequality that can impact adversely on their mental health (Luiking et al., 2019; Vertovec, 2007). Further, migrants can face significant challenges in terms of accessing appropriate health care because they may have limited or no access to the healthcare systems that are available to the host population (Luiking et al., 2019). They may only be able to access healthcare systems under the terms of the health insurance policies that they have taken up prior to entering their host country. This can place them at a disadvantage in terms of accessing appropriate mental health support and seeking preventative health interventions.

The process of migration can itself involve s*tages of settlement* that have mental health implications. When people move to another country through a process of migration, they go through a period of settlement into the new context, where they establish themselves economically, socially and culturally. This process can involve several stages that have been described by the author in an earlier report for the Queensland Government in Australia (Gopalkrishnan, 2001). These stages are also applicable to the experience of international students who may have an expectation of settling into the new country where they are studying. The first stage, usually referred to as the honeymoon stage, is the period when people have just arrived in the new country, and everything appears new and full of possibilities. The complexities and the problems of the new context are not yet known or understood. The length of this phase varies from individual to individual depending on factors such as pre-migration experiences and cultural differences. Generally, this phase is shorter than the later ones. The second stage, frustration, begins as migrants interact with the complexity of living in a new environment, speaking a new language (or dealing with accent differences even while speaking the same language), dealing with cultural differences and cultural conflicts and working their ways through unfamiliar institutional frameworks. This can be a period of intense distress and can be a phase where migrants seek mental health support. The experience of racism and discrimination can also play a part in exacerbating this situation especially in the case of refugees who may have prior experience of trauma (Babacan & Gopalkrishnan, 2005). The third stage is the coping stage where migrants begin to develop trust in the host society and to develop strategies to cope with many of the challenges involved in living in the new country. The level of anger and frustration begins to lessen, and the person is in a better place to deal with the challenges that they face. Finally, they enter the adjustment phase where they are comfortable in the new context, have developed a sense of clarity in a new bi-cultural identity and are able to interact with confidence with systems and people (Gopalkrishnan, 2001).

Similar to the discussion of the settlement journey, Bhugra and Becker (2005) discuss three aspects of culture that link migration and mental health. The first is *cultural bereavement*, which describes the distress caused by the loss of language, connections and other forms of social capital. When this distress is so severe that it causes functional impairment, it becomes a mental health issue. The second is *cultural identity,* which relates to the individual's sense of self in a cultural context, and the loss of which can cause stress and distress. Processes of acculturation and assimilation that take place during migration can also have significant effects on the levels of distress experienced by the migrant. The third is *cultural congruity,* which relates to the sense of belonging and comfort that a migrant can feel if s/he is surrounded by people of the same culture. On the other hand, being alone among others who do not share one's culture can lead to a sense of alienation and attendant distress. Knowledge of these stages and an understanding of where people are in their settlement journey are useful to support migrants in terms of enabling them to flourish in their endeavors.

These discussions reinforce the need for inclusive systems that support the mental health needs of culturally diverse groups in society. They are also a starting point to discuss the needs of culturally diverse students in higher education institutions. As far back as 2011, 33% (up from 30% in 2001) of all higher education students in Australia had been born overseas, with the over 60 percent of these born in Asian countries (ABS, 2013). Further, the numbers of students of Aboriginal and Torres Strait Islander background have also been dramatically increasing over the last few decades. The 2016 Census identified 24,861 Aboriginal and Torres Strait Islander people who had completed a graduate or postgraduate degree, up from 7196 in 2001 (ABS, 2016). This increase in the numbers of Aboriginal and Torres Strait Islander peoples going through the higher education system also points to the need for systems and processes that respond to the particular mental health needs of these students.

Cultural diversity in the higher education sector is also a product of the proportion of international students at universities, proportions that have been increasing in the HICs over the last few decades. Bygrave et al. (2014) draw on a range of resources to demonstrate that international student enrollments in Canadian higher education institutions more than doubled in the last two decades and that both the UK and the United States continue to experience dramatically increased numbers of international student enrolments. In Australia, university enrollments of international students went up from around 125,000 in 2002 to just over 177,000 in 2019 (Austrade, 2021). The COVID-19 pandemic has, however, impacted quite negatively on the international student numbers in HICs over 2020–2021, and in the context of Australia, Hurley (2020) points out that current modeling suggests a reduction of 50% in international students in 2021 and further reductions depending on the nature of travel restrictions in subsequent years. Nevertheless, Australia continues to have a highly internationalized higher education sector, with at least every one in five students being an international student (Fozdar & Volet, 2016).

This diversity of the student body has to be considered very carefully with the understanding that cultural differences change the way that people view and experience mental health issues or mental illness, how they seek help, how they perceive the mental health systems and the practitioners and the therapies. Hernandez et al. (2009) describe culture as defining the problem and how it is understood as well as influencing what solutions are viewed as acceptable. In the words of the US Surgeon-General's report on culture, race, and ethnicity in mental health:

> The meaning of an illness refers to deep-seated attitudes and beliefs a culture holds about whether an illness is "real" or "imagined", whether it is of the body or the mind (or both), whether it warrants sympathy, how much stigma surrounds it, what might cause it, and what type of person might succumb to it. Cultural meanings of health and illness have real consequences in terms of whether people are motivated to seek treatment, how they cope with their symptoms, how supportive their families and communities are, where they seek help (mental health specialist, primary care provider, clergy, and/or traditional healer), the pathways they take to get services, and how well they fare in treatment. (USDHHS, 2001a, p. 26)

The cultural meanings of health and illness and their attendant consequences that are highlighted in this excerpt are explored in more detail in the next section, with the focus remaining on the implications for the mental health of culturally diverse students in higher education.

Cultural Diversity and Mental Health

One of the first areas in which culture plays a role in mental health is in terms of the perception of the *etiology* of disease. For example, two of the well-known alternative systems of medicine, Traditional Chinese Medicine and Ayurveda, ascribe ill-health to a lack of balance between elements such as Yin and Yang or Vata/Pitta/Kapha (Haque, 2010; Kirmayer, 2004). Further, these systems focus on treatment of the patient as a whole and do not emphasize the separation of body and mind (Libster, 2001; Trotter, 2000). These systems of medicine and the cultural understandings embedded in them assume considerable significance given that a high proportion, over 40%, of international students in HICs are from India and China (Bygrave et al., 2014). As with India and China, many countries have their own indigenous forms of medicine, and many people from these countries are used to accessing different forms of medicine for different illnesses or stages of disease. It must be pointed out here that the processes of globalization have dramatically reduced the influence of the medicine systems in their home countries while establishing Western medicine at the center. However, these medicine systems continue to play a part in the perceptions of health and health-seeking behavior of culturally diverse students from these countries. The plurality of these views of illness causality is presented by Helman (2007) as ranging from individual to the natural world to the social world, suggesting that every illness can emerge from multiple causes and that every culture would perceive these differently. Both indigenous students as well as other culturally diverse students could possibly be viewing illnesses and their causes quite differently, with attendant implications for managing these illnesses.

Culture also has strong influences on the health-seeking behavior of students from culturally diverse backgrounds. Research studies in HICs suggest that people from culturally diverse backgrounds tend to seek help much later than people from the majority communities in these countries and that they tend to present at much later stages of mental distress (FECCA, 2011; Nguyen & Bornheimer, 2014). There are several hypotheses presented to explain this phenomenon, and they have relevance in terms of working with culturally diverse students in higher education. *Stigma,* for example, plays a very important role in terms of the nature of health-seeking behavior. Unlike most physical illness, mental illness can often be perceived in a negative manner among particular cultural groups and can lead to people being rejected, discriminated against and excluded from social participation (Biswas et al., 2016; FECCA, 2011; WHO, 2001). The fear of stigma can be a very real one and can lead to people hiding their symptoms and not seeking professional help for as long as possible, perhaps until the symptoms are so acute that they become visible (USDHHS, 2001a). In the case of students in higher education, this could involve non-disclosure of mental illness for fear of what the immediate family would think or what other students of their culture would think of them.

In close association with stigma, the notion of *shame* can be an important factor in the health-related decision-making of culturally diverse individuals and groups. Hechanova and Waelde (2017) describe shame as one of the key elements that cause culturally diverse individuals and Asians in particular to access professional therapists late. They suggest that the significant role of the extended families in these contexts may exacerbate the impacts of shame because of the desire to protect the family reputation. The authors also refer to the nature of shame in relation to the person's fear of being seen as crazy by the mental health professional. And finally, they also reflect on the fear of speaking up to strangers, as a product of factors such as lack of trust or the fear of revisiting traumatic experiences. Hampton and Sharp (2013) have also described shame as involving external, internal and reflective shame and have argued that addressing these effects of shame on culturally diverse people is central to effective management of their mental health issues. The broad-based use of talk therapies needs reconsideration in this context as research indicates that they might not be appropriate in the context of working with every culturally diverse individual (Conrad & Barker, 2010; Gopalkrishnan, 2012). This has been described by the National Child Traumatic Stress Network in the United States as "talking about painful events may not be experienced as valuable or therapeutic by refugees from societies where psychological models are not hegemonic" (NCTSN, 2005, p. 32). Multi-modal approaches that incorporate a range of movement-based therapies, expressive therapies and culturally based healing practices could be considered in this context (Gopalkrishnan, 2020).

Racism and discrimination are also important elements that impact on the mental health status of culturally diverse individuals and groups. Older forms of racism that built on notions of biological "race superiority" have increasingly been debunked by scientific research and are increasingly being replaced by notions of "cultural superiority", notions which continue to impact adversely on the mental health of culturally diverse groups (Babacan & Gopalkrishnan, 2007; FECCA, 2011). The experience of racism and discrimination has a number of impacts on people, including social alienation, a fear of public spaces, loss of access to health and other services, depression, anxiety and the experience of panic attacks, just to name a few (FECCA, 2011;

Fernando, 2015). As mentioned earlier, First Nations peoples in HICs like Australia, Canada and the United States continue to be adversely impacted by these issues and the attendant mental health issues (Boksa et al., 2015). In their metareview of the literature relating to the issue of discrimination, Williams and Mohammed (2009, p. 39) focus particularly on the fact that discrimination has a very significant impact on a range of health outcomes across a number of population groups and that "lends credibility to the plausibility of perceived discrimination as an important emerging risk factor for disease". *Mainstream bias* and *stereotyping* are related factors that have implications on the mental health of diverse communities. Many researchers have reflected on the fact that the stereotyping of cultural groups can lead to inappropriate mental health interventions, misdiagnosis and overdiagnosis of particular groups and mishandling of the therapeutic encounter (Ahmad & Bradby, 2007; Fernando, 2015; NCTSN, 2005; USDHHS, 2001b). Concepts of normality and abnormality that are central to Western mental health systems are not generalizable across cultures and can lead to situations where "health practitioners overlook, misinterpret, stereotype or otherwise mishandle their encounters with those who might be viewed as different from them in their assessment, intervention and evaluation-planning processes" (Kline & Huff, 2007, p. 7). This raises the need for appropriate training to be provided to healthcare practitioners to enable them critically examine their assumptions and develop the appropriate attitudes, knowledge and skills to work effectively across cultures.

Two of the protective factors of mental health relevant to culturally diverse students are *coping* and *resilience*. Coping styles are the ways in which people cope with everyday stressors as well as extreme stressors, and these can vary across different cultures. Different cultures experience stressors differently and allocate social resources differently leading to distinctly different experiences of these stressors (Aldwin, 2004). Hechanova and Waelde (2017) posit that healing is a product of interdependence in collective cultures and that group health is as important as individual health in these cultures. This is quite in contrast to coping in Western cultures that can be quite embedded in notions of individual freedom and individual health. Similarly, resilience, the ability to do well in the face of adversity, can be a product of collective systems rather than individual traits. Kirmayer et al. (2011) discuss this in the context of the First Nations People of Canada, arguing that resilience emerges from shared cultural identity, collective history, language and spirituality and collective action. The incorporation of these ideas of diversity in coping and resilience also provides some direction in terms of appropriate approaches to supporting the mental health of culturally diverse students in higher education institutions, suggesting that community, family and cultural groups support could have as much of a role as more traditional mental health therapies.

The therapeutic relationship also needs to be considered in the context of cultural diversity. Power differentials in the context of indigenous peoples and the impacts of colonization have been mentioned earlier. Similar issues may arise with migrants and refugees in HICs, who may have a lived experience of racism and discrimination either in their home country or in the new host country (Williams & Mohammed, 2009). Additionally, many of the tools used by therapists, such as assessment tools, may not have linguistic, normative and cultural equivalence and could lead to inaccurate and inappropriate decision-making (Marsella, 2011). This lack of equivalence could be one possible reason for the over-representation of some cultural groups in the mental health systems of HICs (Fernando, 2015). Similarly, lack of a common language and inadequate use of trained interpreters can lead to issues in the therapeutic relationship and poor decision-making on the part of the clinician (FECCA, 2011). This aspect is also raised by Alpern et al. (2016) who draw on several research studies to emphasize that many medical professionals still do not use trained interpreters despite the evidence that using professional interpreters leads to improved patient satisfaction and outcomes. In the context of culturally diverse students in HICs, this issue may not have the same importance as with the general migrant and indigenous populations, given that students are expected to have particular levels of English language proficiency. However, it is an issue that merits consideration for interactions with parents and other community members in the context of dealing with mental health issues.

Much of the mental health support that culturally diverse students receive in HICs draws from Western notions of mind–body separation and the scientific method (Fernando, 2015; Sarafino, 2008). These approaches largely depend on the utilization of talk therapies and medication and derive from relatively monocultural understandings of mental health and mental illness. In particular, Tribe (2005, p. 8) points to the differences of such models that "focus on individual intrapsychic experience or individual pathology" as against the needs of other traditions that "may be based more on community or familial processes". In the context of supporting the mental health needs of students of diverse backgrounds, both university staff and mental health professionals would do well to have a deep understanding of the intersection of mental health and culture and to adopt frameworks that would allow them to work effectively across cultures. The range of factors discussed in this section is only some of ways in which culture impacts on mental health especially in the context of higher education. Nevertheless, they do provide direction in terms of possible approaches that could and do support the mental health of culturally diverse students.

Ways Forward

Accessing health care should be a matter of guaranteeing the individual's human rights and as such should not be compromised by cultural factors (Lood et al., 2015). Mainstream mental health systems are increasingly recognizing the importance of culture, and the incorporation of the *cultural formulation interview* into the DSM-5 is a good example of this recognition. However, this does not address some of the key issues of historical trauma, racism and discrimination, as well as cultural differences in perception of illness, health-seeking behavior, shame, stigma, coping styles and other factors that have been previously discussed. The acknowledgement of culture as an asset provides numerous opportunities to build more effective healthcare systems (Rubincam et al., 2016).

The development of *Integrative Health Services*, within and external to the higher education sector, would be a strong first step toward the effective support of the mental health of culturally diverse populations. At the moment, this term is used to focus on integrating mental health with primary health care as a way to address stigma and discrimination (Chen & Mak, 2008), and this is already in practice in Australia, for example, where the general practitioner is the first port of call for mental health issues. This form of integration is particularly useful in providing health care to people in regional and remote areas in low- and medium-income countries (LMICs) where resources are quite limited (Shidhaye et al., 2016). However, integrated health services could also provide avenues to integrate the *positive resources* in the community toward supporting the mental health needs of culturally diverse people. Some of these resources are people in the community, such as elders, community leaders, priests and other religious leaders and traditional healers (USDHHS, 2001a). The inclusion of such people into the mental health systems can work to address some of the issues of power, mistrust and discrimination that have been mentioned earlier. Further, particularly in the context of indigenous peoples, traditional healing practices could also be integrated into the health system. These have already been demonstrated to be efficacious in the context of Native Americans through the incorporation of sweat lodges, pipe ceremonies and talking circles by the Indian Health Service (Gone, 2013). Similarly O'Mahony and Donnelly (2007) argue that immigrants could benefit from the utilization of spiritual and traditional healing practices.

Many culturally diverse groups and individuals are used to the notion of medical plurality, where they may access different health systems based on the nature and severity of the disease (WHO, 2005). Many *Complementary and Alternative Medicine* systems have widespread acceptance across the world, and their efficacy is also being established through scientific research. The use of Yoga and Tai Chi for pain relief is a case in point where the U.S. Pain Management Inter-Agency Task Force states that both of these appear to be safe and beneficial for pain management while also being cost effective in group settings (PMTF, 2019). CAMs have widespread utilization in the HICs with as much as 63% of all adults in Australia and 36% in the United States utilizing some form of CAM to support health (NCCAM, 2010; Steel et al., 2018). Integrative health systems that utilize Western biomedical approaches in tandem with CAMs would be useful to support the mental health needs of culturally diverse students. Many of these CAM approaches can be easily incorporated into the higher education sector and are relatively cost-effective, especially where movement therapies are taught in group settings. However, this needs to be further supported with research, as much of the health needs of indigenous and other culturally diverse students remains under-researched (Lood et al., 2015).

Developing a *cultural partnerships* framework to work across cultures would form a very important part of supporting culturally diverse population mental health needs. Over the last few decades, *cultural competence* has been the framework of choice for working across cultures in the HICs (Gopalkrishnan, 2019b). However, this framework is either silent about or actively perpetuates issues of power differences, racism and discrimination and the voicelessness of marginalized groups (Pon, 2009; Sakamoto, 2007). A central element of any cultural partnership between academics/other professional staff and students would have to involve an acknowledgement of the historical placement of this relationship as well as the power differentials implicit within that. This is particularly true of working with First Nations students, who have to deal with these issues in many aspects of their educational experience. This is very well described by Day et al. (2015) as:

> …Indigenous students' engagements with Indigenous course content (or its omission) often amplify the affective aspects of learning. Students' responses to representations of Indigenous people, histories, knowledge, to lecturers' treatment of material and other students' responses, Students' perceptions of racism and exclusion, the anxiety/stress of academic demands associated with assessment, the anxiety/stress associated with the expectation that Indigenous students are Indigenous knowledge "experts", all provide additional emotional burdens and layers of challenge that can complicate the academic aspects of learning… (Day et al., 2015, p. 504).

Some of the issues highlighted in this excerpt, such as the lack of engagement, impacts of racism and discrimination and unrealistic expectations, are addressed by the focus on mutual learning in the cultural partnerships framework. Most intercultural frameworks emphasize the practitioner learning about the culture of the other and where the expert is trained in the competencies of working with diverse cultures (Bean, 2006). However, effective cultural partnerships would involve both individuals/groups learning from each other and where every interaction is a learning interaction (Gopalkrishnan, 2019b). In the process, both individuals/groups would develop better knowledge of each other, refine skills that would support these interactions and also nurture attitudes that would enable them to work effectively in the partnership. In the case of the experience of indigenous students described earlier, this partnership would involve academics, other staff and other students learning interactively with the indigenous students. This would also lead to a change in the power dynamics of the relationships and more equitable relationships.

Figure 1, as developed by the authors, delineates the nature of a cultural partnerships approach, where the interaction based on mutual learning leads to changes in both cultures and the creation of an area of mutual understanding.

Cultural partnerships need to be developed at different levels of practice including the micro, the mezzo and the macro. At the micro-level, the process would involve the education, training and skill development of both staff and students so that they can work with each other's culture in an equitable and nurturing manner. Both staff and students need to be able to explore their historical context and power relationships in a culturally safe way and develop mutual understandings that would enable them to work with these issues. Rather than adopting inappropriate attitudes of tolerance and adoption of the exotic, this approach would work with notions of mutuality, empowerment and inclusion (Gopalkrishnan, 2019a). This kind of approach would fit with the notion of the student as a purposive and agentive individual who has the capacity to engage with these issues (Day et al., 2015).

The mezzo level would involve the family and the community and their relationships with the higher education organization and its staff. Collaborative processes and some of the elements of integrative health systems mentioned earlier could be included in these relationships. Elders, religious leadership and traditional healers

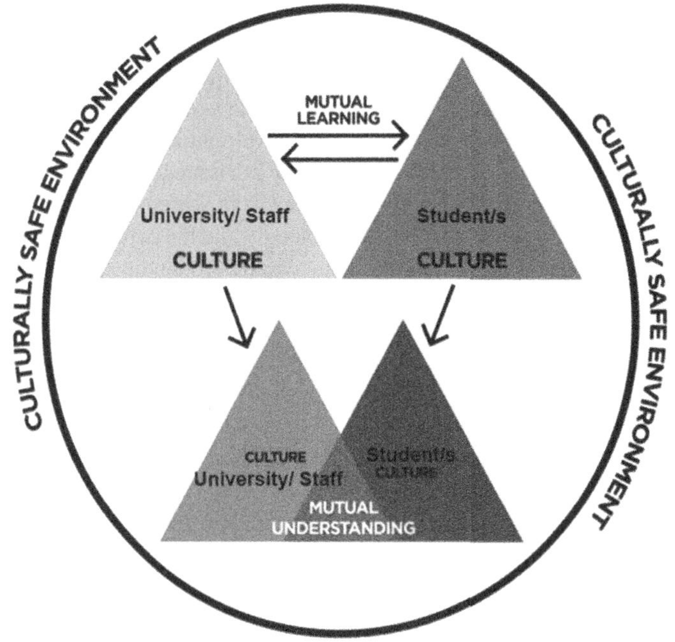

Fig. 1 Cultural partnerships

could all form part of the cultural partnerships developed at this level. Further, some of the exploration of issues of colonization, settlement, racism and discrimination could be engaged at this level too so as to change traditional patterns of domination–submission to more enlightened relationships (Bhugra, 2004; Chen, 2015). And finally, the development of appropriate policies and processes that support this work at the macro-level is an essential part of building effective cultural partnerships. They would involve more resource allocation and allocation of time than top-down approaches, but would ensure the long-term sustainability of such initiatives (Cox, 2009).

Conclusion

The mental health of culturally diverse students in higher education institutions is an important aspect of ensuring student success. In HICs, the cultural diversity of students includes First Nations students, students of migrant backgrounds as well as international students. Besides the numerous factors that impact the mental health of the general student population, there are several factors related to cultural diversity and mental health that need to be considered in addressing the needs of culturally diverse students. These include historical issues of trauma and dispossession, racism and discrimination, notions of cultural mistrust, settlement processes, stigma and shame and differing cultural views of mental health, just to name a few. In this context, the importance of a deep understanding of the impacts of these factors, as well as the need for adoption of new and creative ways of managing them, cannot be overstated. Integration, collaboration, and the development of cultural partnerships would be some of the ways that student mental health issues could be addressed. This could include the inclusion of positive resources from within the community, development of strategic alliances between the university and the community and building the attitudes, skills and knowledge of all stakeholders including the students themselves, staff (both academics and professional), as well as concerned people in the community. This process would enable more equitable and sustainable relationships to be built and would ensure better student outcomes.

References

ABS. (2013). *Hitting the books: Characteristics of higher education students.* Australian Bureau of Statistics.

ABS. (2016). *Education statistics for Aboriginal and Torres Strait Islander peoples.* Australian Bureau of Statistics. https://www.abs.gov.au/statistics/people/aboriginal-and-torres-strait-islander-peoples/education-statistics-aboriginal-and-torres-strait-islander-peoples/latest-release#key-statistics

ABS. (2017). *Cultural diversity in Australia.* Australian Bureau of Statistics. https://www.abs.gov.au/ausstats/abs@.nsf/Lookup/by%20Subject/2071.0~2016~Main%20Features~Cultural%20Diversity%20Data%20Summary~30

Ahmad, W. I. U., & Bradby, H. (2007). Locating ethnicity and health: Exploring concepts and contexts. *Sociology of Health & Illness, 29*(6), 795–801.

Aldwin, C. M. (2004). Culture, coping and resilience to stress. In *First International Conference on Operationalization of Gross National Happiness*, Thimphu.

Alpern, J. D., Davey, C. S., & Song, J. (2016). Perceived barriers to success for resident physicians interested in immigrant and refugee health. *BMC Medical Education, 16.* https://doi.org/10.1186/s12909-016-0696-z

Austrade. (2021). *Pivot tables: Enrolments and commencements 2002 onwards.* Australian Trade and Investment Commision. Retrieved April 15, 2021 from https://www.austrade.gov.au/australian/education/education-data/current-data/pivot-tables

Babacan, H., & Gopalkrishnan, N. (2005). Post traumatic experiences of refugee women. In C. Rabin (Ed.), *Understanding gender and culture in the helping process* (pp. 149–166). Wadsworth Group Thomson Learning.

Babacan, H., & Gopalkrishnan, N. (2007). *Racisms in the new world order: Realities of culture.* Cambridge Scholars Publishing.

Bean, R. (2006). *The effectiveness of cross-cultural training in the Australian context.* Department of Immigration and Multicultural Affairs.

Bélanger, A., Sabourin, P., Marois, G., Hook, J. V., & Vézina, S. (2019). A framework for the prospective analysis of ethno-cultural super-diversity. *Demographic Research, 41*, 293–330, 293A–293B. https://doi.org/10.4054/DemRes.2019.41.11

Bessarab, D., & Crawford, F. (2013). Trauma, grief and loss: The vulnerability of Aboriginal families in the child protection system. In B. Bennett, S. Green, S. Gilbert, & D. Bessarab (Eds.), *Our voices* (pp. 93–113). Palgrave Macmillan.

Bhugra, D. (2004). Migration, distress and cultural identity. *British Medical Bulletin, 69*, 129–141.

Bhugra, D., & Becker, M. A. (2005). Migration, cultural bereavement and cultural identity. *World Psychiatry: Official Journal of the World Psychiatric Association (WPA), 4*(1), 18–24. https://pubmed.ncbi.nlm.nih.gov/16633496. https://www.ncbi.nlm.nih.gov/pmc/articles/PMC1414713/

Biswas, J., Gangadhar, B. N., & Keshavan, M. (2016). Cross cultural variations in psychiatrists' perception of mental illness: A tool for teaching culture in psychiatry. *Asian Journal of Psychiatry, 23*, 1–7. https://doi.org/10.1016/j.ajp.2016.05.011

Boksa, P., Joober, R., & Kirmayer, L. J. (2015). Mental wellness in Canada's aboriginal communities: Striving toward reconciliation. *Journal of Psychiatry & Neuroscience, 40*(6), 363–365.

Bygrave, C., Asik-Dizdar, O., & Kaur Saini, G. (2014). From homogeneity to heterogeneity: the multicultural future of higher education. *On the Horizon, 22*(3), 199–209. https://doi.org/10.1108/OTH-05-2014-0016

Chen, G. M. (2015). Theorizing global community as cultural home in the new century. *International Journal of Intercultural Relations* (46), 73–81.

Chen, S. X., & Mak, W. W. S. (2008). Seeking professional help: Etiology beliefs about mental illness across cultures. *Journal of Counseling Psychology, 55*(4), 442–450.

Conrad, P., & Barker, K. K. (2010). The social construction of illness: Key insights and policy implications. *Journal of Health and Social Behavior, 51*, S67–S79. http://www.jstor.org.elibrary.jcu.edu.au/stable/20798317

Cox, P. (2009). "Connectivity": Seeking conditions and connections for radical discourses and praxes in health, mental health and social work. *Social Theory & Health, 7*(2), 170–186. https://doi.org/10.1057/sth.2009.9

Day, A., Nakata, V., Nakata, M., & Martin, G. (2015). Indigenous students' persistence in higher education in Australia: Contextualising models of change from psychology to understand and aid students' practices at a cultural interface. *Higher Education Research & Development, 34*(3), 501–512. https://doi.org/10.1080/07294360.2014.973379

FECCA. (2011). *Mental health and Australia's culturally and linguistically diverse communities: A submission to the Senate Standing Committee on Community Affairs.*

Fernando, S. (2015). *Race and culture in psychiatry*. Routledge.

Fozdar, F., & Volet, S. (2016). Cultural self-identification and orientations to cross-cultural mixing on an Australian University Campus. *Journal of Intercultural Studies, 37*(1), 51–68. https://doi.org/10.1080/07256868.2015.1119674

Gone, J. P. (2013). Redressing First Nations historical trauma: Theorizing mechanisms for indigenous culture as mental health treatment. *Transcultural Psychiatry, 50*(5), 683–706. https://doi.org/10.1177/1363461513487669

Gopalkrishnan, N. (2001). *Cultural diversity and civic participation in Queensland*. University of the Sunshine Coast.

Gopalkrishnan, N. (2012). *Yoga therapy and the health of refugees*. Curtin University. http://espace.library.curtin.edu.au:80/R?func=dbin-jump-full&local_base=gen01-era02&object_id=186711

Gopalkrishnan, N. (2019a). Cultural competence and beyond: Working across cultures in culturally dynamic partnerships. *The International Journal of Community and Social Development*,. https://doi.org/10.1177/2516602619826712

Gopalkrishnan, N. (2019b). Working with community groups. In S. Nipperess & W. Williams (Eds.), *Critical multicultural practice in social work*. Allen & Unwin.

Gopalkrishnan, N. (2020). Culture, diversity, and global health: Challenges and opportunities. In R. Haring, I. Kickbusch, D. Ganten, & M. Moeti (Eds.), *Handbook of global health* (pp. 1–33). Springer. https://doi.org/10.1007/978-3-030-05325-3_5-1.

Hampton, N. Z., & Sharp, S. E. (2013). Shame-focused attitudes toward mental health problems. *Rehabilitation Counseling Bulletin, 57*(3), 170–181. https://doi.org/10.1177/0034355213501722

Haque, A. (2010). Mental health concepts in Southeast Asia: Diagnostic considerations and treatment implications. *Psychology, Health & Medicine, 15*(2), 127–134. https://doi.org/10.1080/13548501003615266

Hechanova, R., & Waelde, L. (2017). The influence of culture on disaster mental health and psychosocial support interventions in Southeast Asia. *Mental Health, Religion & Culture, 20*(1), 31–44. https://doi.org/10.1080/13674676.2017.1322048

Helman, C. G. (2007). *Culture, health and illness* (5th ed.). Hodder Arnold.

Hernandez, M., Nesman, T., Mowery, D., Acevedo-Polakovich, I. D., & Callejas, L. M. (2009). Cultural competence: A literature review and conceptual model for mental health services. *Psychiatric Services, 60*(8), 1046–1050.

Hurley, P. (2020). *Coronavirus and international students.* Mitchell Institute, Victoria University.

IOM. (2020). *World migration report 2020.* International Organization for Migration.

Kirmayer, L. J. (2004). The cultural diversity of healing: meaning, metaphor and mechanism. *British Medical Bulletin* (69), 33–48.

Kirmayer, L. J., Dandeneau, S., Marshall, E., Phillips, M. K., & Williamson, K. J. (2011). Rethinking resilience from indigenous perspectives. *Canadian Journal of Psychiatry, 56*(2), 84–91.

Kline, M. V., & Huff, R. M. (2007). Health promotion in the context of culture. In M. V. Kline & R. M. Huff (Eds.), *Health promotion in multicultural populations* (pp. 3–22). Sage.

Libster, M. (2001). *Demonstrating care: The art of integrative nursing.* Delmar.

Lood, Q., Häggblom-Kronlöf, G., & Dahlin-Ivanoff, S. (2015). Health promotion programme design and efficacy in relation to ageing persons with culturally and linguistically diverse backgrounds: A systematic literature review and meta-analysis. *BMC Health Services Research, 15*, 560. https://doi.org/10.1186/s12913-015-1222-4

Luiking, M., Heckemann, B., Ali, P., Doorn, C. D., Ghosh, S., Kydd, A., Watson, R., & Patel, H. (2019). Migrants' healthcare experience: A meta-ethnography review of the literature. *Journal of Nursing Scholarship, 51*(1), 58–67. https://doi.org/10.1111/jnu.12442.

Marsella, A. J. (2011). Twelve critical issues for mental health professionals working with ethnoculturally diverse populations. *Psychology International, 22*(3), 7–10.

NCCAM. (2010). *What is complementary and alternative medicine.* National Center for Complementary and Alternative Medicine. Retrieved December 10, 2010 from http://nccam.nih.gov/health/whatiscam/

NCTSN. (2005). *Review of Child and Adolescent Refugee Mental Health White Paper.* National Child Traumatic Stress Network Refugee Trauma Task Force. Retrieved April 14, from www.NCTSNet.org

Nelson, S. E., & Wilson, K. (2017). The mental health of Indigenous peoples in Canada: A critical review of research. *Social Science & Medicine, 176*, 93–112. https://doi.org/10.1016/j.socscimed.2017.01.021.

Nguyen, D., & Bornheimer, L. A. (2014). Mental health service use types among Asian Americans with a psychiatric disorder: Considerations of culture and need. *The Journal of Behavioral Health Services & Research, 41*(4), 520–528. https://doi.org/10.1007/s11414-013-9383-6

O'Mahony, J. M., & Donnelly, T. T. (2007). The influence of culture on immigrant women's mental health experiences from the perspectives of health care providers. *Issues in Mental Health Nursing* (28), 453–471.

PMTF. (2019). *Pain management best practices iner-agency task force report.* U.S. Department of Helath and Human Services. https://www.hhs.gov/sites/default/files/pmtf-final-report-2019-05-23.pdf

Pon, G. (2009). Cultural competency as new racism: An ontology of forgetting. *Journal of Progressive Human Services, 20*(1), 59–71. https://doi.org/10.1080/10428230902871173

Rubincam, C., Lacombe-Duncan, A., & Newman, P. A. (2016). Taking culture seriously in biomedical HIV prevention trials: A meta-synthesis of qualitative studies. *Expert Review of Vaccines, 15*(3), 331–347. https://doi.org/10.1586/14760584.2016.1118349

Sakamoto, I. (2007). An anti-oppressive approach to cultural competence. *Canadian Social Work Review/revue Canadienne De Service Social, 24*(1), 105–114. https://doi.org/10.2307/41669865

Sarafino, E. P. (2008). *Health psychology: Biopsychosocial interactions* (6th ed.). Wiley.
Shidhaye, R., Shrivastava, S., Murhar, V., Samue, S., Ahuja, S., Ramaswamy, R., & Patel, V. (2016). Development and piloting of a plan for integrating mental health in primary care in Sehore district, Madhya Pradesh, India. *British Journal of Psychiatry, 208*(s56), S13–S20. https://doi.org/10.1192/bjp.bp.114.153700
Spencer-Oatey, H. (2008). *Culturally speaking: Culture, communication and politeness theory* (2nd ed.). Continuum.
Steel, A., McIntyre, E., Harnett, J., Foley, H., Adams, J., Sibbritt, D., Wardle, J., & Frawley, J. (2018). Complementary medicine use in the Australian population: Results of a nationally-representative cross-sectional survey. *Scientific Reports, 8*(1), 17325–17327. https://doi.org/10.1038/s41598-018-35508-y
Tribe, R. (2005). The mental health needs of refugees and asylum seekers. *The Mental Health Review, 10*(4), 8–15.
Trotter, G. (2000). Culture, ritual, and errors of repudiation. *Alternative Therapies in Health and Medicine, 6*(4), 62–68.
UN. (2019). *State of the world's indigenous peoples 4th volume*. United Nations.
UNHCR. (2017). *Statistical handbook 2016*.
USDHHS. (2001a). *Mental health: culture, race, and ethnicity: A supplement to mental health: A report of the Surgeon General*.
USDHHS. (2001b). *National standards for culturally & linguistically appropriate services in health care: Final report*. http://minorityhealth.hhs.gov/assets/pdf/checked/finalreport.pdf
Vertovec, S. (2007). Super-diversity and its implications. *Ethnic and Racial Studies, 30*(6), 1024–1054. https://doi.org/10.1080/01419870701599465
WB. (2021). *Indigenous peoples*. World Bank. Retrieved March 12, 2021 from https://www.worldbank.org/en/topic/indigenouspeoples
WHO. (2001). *The world health report 2001. Mental health: New understanding, new hope*. World Health Organization.
WHO. (2005). *National Policy on traditional medicine and regulation of herbal medicines—Report of a WHO global survey*. World Health Organization.
WHO. (2007). *Health of indigenous peoples*. World Health Organization. https://www.who.int/gender-equity-rights/knowledge/factsheet-indigenous-healthn-nov2007-eng.pdf?ua=1
Williams, D., & Mohammed, S. (2009). Discrimination and racial disparities in health: Evidence and needed research. *Journal of Behavioural Medicine, 32*(1), 20–47.

Narayan Gopalkrishnan is an internationally recognized academic with extensive experience in Australia and overseas, working in universities, NGOs and the private sector over the last 25 years. He lectures at James Cook University in the areas of community work, working with diverse communities, and mental health. Narayan was formerly the Founding Director of the Centre for Multicultural and Community Development, an academic research center of the University of the Sunshine Coast, Australia, which focused on research and development relating to multiculturalism and community development. Narayan's teaching and research interests relate to Community Development, Community and Ecological Sustainability, Cultural Diversity and Multiculturalism, Social Determinants of Health and Well Being, and Social Enterprise, and he has published widely in these areas.

Hurriyet Babacan is Research Director at Rural Economies Centre of Excellence, James Cook University. She has a distinguished career over the last 30 years in senior roles in higher education, public administration, and research and training. Hurriyet has published widely in national and international publications on a range of issues including multiculturalism, immigration, cultural diversity, racism, community and international development, social policy, and gender. She has co-authored 3 books on racism. She has published numerous books and articles including two publications for UNESCO. She has served on numerous ministerial and expert advisory committees.

She has been a member of two working parties for the Council of Europe/OECD on measuring wellbeing and social progress. Professor Babacan has led numerous national and international leadership, research and development projects, particularly in the Asia Pacific. Hurriyet has been recognised for her work through a number of awards including the Order of Australia, Bi-Centennial Medal awarded by the Prime Minister, 2002 and the Multicultural Services Award by the Premier of Queensland. Hurriyet was the Queensland State Finalist in the Telstra Business-women's Award in the for Government and Public Service category in 2003.

Investigating Whether Law Schools in the UK and Australia Are Workplaces that Support the Wellbeing of Law Teachers

Rachael Field, Caroline Strevens, and Colin James

Abstract There is now an extensive evidence-base across numerous countries demonstrating that approximately one-third of law students experience a decline in their wellbeing during their first year of legal education. As a result, law schools are seeking to enact strategies to prevent this decline and to positively support law student wellbeing—both through extra-curricula and curricula approaches. The success of these strategies depends largely on the capacity of law teachers and other faculty staff, and yet there is currently insufficient research on whether law teachers are well and able to support the wellbeing of their students. This chapter presents the results to-date of a longitudinal study conducted in the UK and Australia, both pre-COVID and post-COVID, considering the quality of the working life of law teachers in terms of the context of its impact on their capacity to promote law student wellbeing. We examine some of the prominent challenges that law teachers identify and recount some of their constructive suggestions which may assist law school managers and leaders in enacting structural and cultural change in support of the wellbeing of legal academics.

Introduction

Consistent with concerns about the wellbeing of academics in higher education more broadly (Carter & Goldie, 2018; Kinman, 2014), a recent development in the scholarship of law student and lawyer wellbeing has extended the focus of the field to include the wellbeing of law teachers (James et al., 2019, 2020; Wilson & Strevens, 2018).

R. Field (✉)
Faculty of Law, Bond University, Gold Coast, Australia
e-mail: rfield@bond.edu.au

C. Strevens
University of Portsmouth, Portsmouth, England, UK
e-mail: caroline.strevens@port.ac.uk

C. James
Australian National University, Canberra, Australia
e-mail: colin.james@anu.edu.au

A. P. Francis and M. A. Carter (eds.), *Mental Health and Higher Education in Australia*,
https://doi.org/10.1007/978-981-16-8040-3_5

The hypothesis of this research is that, if law student wellbeing is to be attended to in the hope of a positive flow-on effect for the practising legal profession, then the wellbeing of law teachers must be sound, and they must be supported by healthy workplace structures, practices and cultures. Indeed, law teachers are in a unique position of influence in terms of supporting law students not only to survive but also to thrive and flourish in what we know to be a stressful learning environment. For this reason, the wellbeing of law teachers in law schools is an important starting place for sustaining the wellbeing of law students—who in turn will make up the ranks of the future practising profession of law.

This chapter presents the qualitative results of national surveys of UK and Australian legal academics conducted in 2017 and 2020 exploring law teachers' perceptions of the quality of working life in their law school. First, the research methodology is discussed. Second, the results are explained with a focus on a thematic analysis of responses to the key qualitative open question of the survey: *Please explain what you think your university could do to improve staff quality of working life?* The chapter considers law teacher suggestions for the creation of law schools with healthy workplace structures, practices and cultures that are supportive of the wellbeing of law teachers and conducive to enabling law teachers to support the wellbeing of their students at law school and beyond.

It is important to emphasise that the suggestions and approaches discussed in this chapter are focussed on the structural and cultural changes law schools and universities can make to improve the quality of working life for law teachers. Our focus is not on approaches that hold individual law teachers responsible for building their own resilience and self-management skills, although we note that many law teachers are intentional about their own self-care.

Methodology

This project began in the UK in 2015 with a single study, following a 2014 pilot project. It was funded in part by the Legal Education Research Network (LERN) and led by Dr Clare Wilson and Caroline Strevens at the University of Portsmouth. The 2015 study has been documented and analysed by Wilson and Strevens (2018).

Through a collaboration of members of the UK Advancing Wellness in Law Network and the Australian Wellness Network for Law, the project has since developed into a longitudinal research project designed to understand how the academic workplace is experienced by legal educators in both countries, with a view to knowing more about the structural and cultural workplace stressors in law schools and giving voice to law teachers in terms of how these stressors might be addressed. Ethics approval for the conduct of the surveys was received from the Ethics Committees of Portsmouth University and the Australian National University for the 2017 survey, and Portsmouth University and Bond University for the 2020 survey.

In 2017, the second UK survey was issued contemporaneously with the first Australian survey using well-validated survey instruments such as the Quality of

Working Life (QoWL) (Easton & Van Laar, 2013, 2018), Stress Mindset (Crum et al., 2013), and the Work Engagement Scale (WEL) (Mills et al., 2012). Minor changes to the UK survey were necessary to adapt it to the Australian legal education context (Strevens et al., 2019a, b).

The 2017 UK survey was distributed by email with the assistance of the Law Learned Societies. The Australian survey was distributed with the help of Law Deans and Heads of Schools by email to teaching academics in all 40 Australian law schools and the College of Law. The 2020 survey was a shortened version issued after the emergence of the COVID-19 pandemic in July in the UK and in October in Australia. Again, the Law Learned Societies assisted with the distribution of the survey to law teachers in the UK. The Australasian Law Academics Association and the Wellness Network for Law assisted with the distribution of the Australian survey via their email lists.

This chapter reports on the qualitative responses to the question asked in 2017: *Please explain what you think your university could do to improve staff quality of working life?* And to the same question asked in 2020 along with two additional questions: *Is there anything arising out of the COVID-19 pandemic and responses to it that your University should implement or change to improve staff quality of working life in the short term?* and *Is there anything arising out of the COVID-19 pandemic and responses to it that your University should implement or change to improve staff quality of working life in the long term?*

The methodology applied in this project for gathering and analysing the qualitative data adopted a phenomenographical conceptual framework. Phenomenography is an interpretivist research methodology which enables the exploration of different ways in which people understand the same concept or phenomenon (Marton, 1981, 1986; Svensson, 1997). It is a methodology that can build a deep and rich understanding of a particular phenomenon; it is not a methodology that results in claims of proof-of-concept, or the identification of a single essence. Phenomenography originated in the late 1970s in education research (Prosser & Trigwell, 1997); but is now used extensively across a range of diverse disciplines (Kettunen & Tynjälä, 2018; Barnard et al., 1999; Walsh et al., 1993).

Phenomenography was chosen as the most appropriate methodology for achieving the research aims of this project in terms of exploring the phenomena of how law teachers experience law schools as workplaces, and how the quality of working life for law teachers might be improved. We make no claim that our data proves any one or more aspects of these phenomena.

In analysing the data, the survey responses were coded by the research team through a triangulated process, and levels of saturation in the emergence of dominant themes were reached quite quickly. The data analysis has also drawn on the principles of self-determination theory (SDT) which include the importance of intrinsic over extrinsic motivation and the 'psychological needs triad' of autonomy, competence and relatedness (Niemic & Ryan, 2009; Ryan & Deci, 2000).

Methodological limitations

The narratives found in the data are a snapshot of a small sample of self-selecting law teachers, and while they constitute a rich and indicative data set, the number of responses compared to the overall number of law teachers invited to participate in both countries is low. For this reason, statistically significant conclusions cannot be made. Further, we acknowledge that phenomenographical methods often involve the use of in-depth interviews, to inform and add to understandings of data gathered by a survey instrument (Feldon & Tofel-Grehl, 2018). Our intention is that future surveys in this ongoing study will include in-depth interviews with participants.

A Summary of the Results of the 2017 UK and Australian Law Teacher Studies

The UK survey in 2017 attracted 132 participants and the Australian survey, 160 participants. The UK respondents included 83 women, 48 men, and one person who preferred not to identify a gender. Most did not have a second job (78%), and there were equal numbers of participants who had worked in legal practice prior to becoming an academic compared with those who had not. Over 90% of the UK participants worked in a publicly-funded university. Respondents to the Australian study included 105 women, 50 men, two people identifying as transgender and three people who preferred not to identify a gender. Most were employed full-time (75%), and most currently worked at a law school in a publicly funded university (83%). Unlike the UK participants, most had worked in legal practice before becoming an academic (73%).

In 2017, well-prior to the impact of the COVID-19 pandemic, law teachers in both the UK and Australian studies gave wide-ranging responses to the question: 'Please explain what you think your university could do to improve staff quality of working life'? The key themes identified from the coding of responses in 2017 related to issues concerning: administrative burden, teacher support, workload, management styles, transparency, strategic priorities, autonomy, communication and respect.

These themes, when considered through the lens of SDT, generated two critical understandings of the experience of the participants in terms of the quality of their working life in law schools in the UK and Australia in 2017. First, many responding law teachers appeared to be unsettled and confused as a result of poor management styles, and a lack of clarity about institutional strategic direction and priorities; some also felt a need for stronger support from their institution and that workload and administrative burdens needed to be addressed. Second, most seemed to experience law school as a workplace where levels of transparency and respect were in need of improvement, and higher levels of communication and autonomy were needed.

Many responding law teachers in both the UK and Australia were concerned about sustaining and/or improving the quality of their work environment. While participants were very critical of university management and systems, their responses reflected a professional focus on offering ideas aimed at improving their institution and the sector, as well as the student learning experience. Although some comments related to the need for improved security of employment, relatively few referred to improved experiences or benefits for law teachers themselves.

The Overarching Theme of the Negative Impact of Neoliberalism on the Tertiary Sector

An overarching theme of the 2017 survey responses in both countries concerned criticism of neoliberal changes (market-driven, profit/revenue maximising, commodifying approaches) to the structures and functions of universities (Giroux, 2018; Thornton, 2001, 2007, 2011, 2014a, 2014b). For example, reference was made to an 'obsession' with rankings and metrics, and top-down, micro-management styles. Most participants observed these changes as impacting negatively on their experience of working as law teachers, as well as on the functioning of their institution and the quality of the student experience. One participant commented: '*Stop treating students like consumers, which is raising their expectations of staff to unattainable levels of "customer service"*'. A UK participant identified a 'gulf' between the values of the university, focussed on extrinsic values 'such as the size of an atrium' and the values of law teachers, focussed on the quality of the student experience. An Australian participant said: '*Universities should not be (operating) as marketing devices for some product*'. Another commented: *'university education is not merely and should never be merely transactional. It should be transformative for students (and staff)'*.

As a result, many law teachers indicated they felt professionally compromised, and that they had become workers subjected to evaluation and critique by consumer students with increasing influence. *'Anything a student wants, the student gets – people are scared to take the hard line because this will be undermined at faculty and university level' (Aus); 'the university is driven by the money they make from bums on seats' (Aus); 'I feel like an academic slave serving the university and its students' (UK).*

Many respondents observed that significant resources and management hours are spent justifying the latest 'restructure' that is driven more by university priorities and rankings instead of teachers' experiences of what policies and practices succeed in enhancing student learning. Many responses indicated change fatigue. *'Tedious and unnecessary administrative changes' (UK)* were noted, and there was concern that *'changes to systems, etc., are increasingly made without any reference to those of us on the coal-face who actually do the work' (Aus).* A UK law teacher commented: *'Arbitrary imposed change is productive of bad stress that can become disabling'.*

Significantly, the thematic analysis of the data below reveals a high level of consistency in the experiences of law school as a workplace for both UK and Australian law teachers in the 2017 study.

The Impact of Poor Management Styles, and Workload and Administrative Burdens in Combination with a Lack of Teacher Support

Poor Management Styles

Many teachers in both countries called for enhanced approaches to line management within law schools, with university management systems seen as *'ever more unwieldy' (UK)* and poor management styles recognised as creating *'significant stress for all staff' (UK)*. Many agreed that those in management roles need to develop and improve their management skills, and better understand, for example, the importance of *'nurturing and mentoring staff' (Aus)*. Another Australian law teacher observed that 'mediocre academics' often transfer into management as a way forward.

It was suggested in response to this issue, that Deans should be trained to *'make the difficult and sometimes unpopular decisions that ultimately are for everyone's benefit instead of pandering to those who are the loudest objectors' (Aus); 'line managers should be capable and willing to engage in collaborative management' (UK);* and staff should be included in *'important conversations' (Aus)*. Several participants mentioned a need to ensure appropriate responses to bullying allegations.

Workload Issues

Workloads were one aspect of a law teacher's working life that participants in both countries identified as not being managed well, with many responses noting increased and unmanageable workloads, a lack of clarity regarding expectations, unrealistic performance goals, along with inequities in workload allocation. Some indicative comments include: *'productive and efficient members of academic staff are rewarded with excessive workloads while less productive/less efficient academics have work taken from them' (UK); 'it is the struggle of trying to balance research and teaching that causes me the most stress' (Aus); 'pulled in many different directions: teaching, research and service' (Aus); 'clarity over the goals - is it research or is it the student experience? It can't be both' (UK).*

Administrative Burdens

In 2017, administrative burdens were identified as a significantly negative aspect of a law teacher's workload, with responses noting that administrative tasks are increasingly being devolved to academics simultaneously with requirements to deliver increasingly higher research and teaching outputs. Many respondents in both countries emphasised a need to reduce the bureaucratic demands on law teachers, predominantly because increased administrative work misdirects their time, energy and focus away from the core business of teaching students and engaging in scholarship and service.

For example, respondents commented: *'Get administrators to do administration and academics to do academic work' (UK)*; *'the university could improve staff quality of working life if it genuinely took into account the work (and the time needed) to deal with all the administration now ancillary to teaching' (Aus)*; *'it would be useful to slimline some of the admin we have to do' (UK); 'admin is much too burdensome and I spend way too much time trying to learn new admin systems - that then change the next semester. It's a waste of time' (Aus); 'resource administration better' (UK).*

A Lack of Teacher Support

Overall, law teachers in both countries expressed disappointment at the low levels of teacher support provided by their universities. This theme is consistent with poor management styles and concerns about workload issues and administrative burdens. Comments called for 'more', 'better', 'additional', 'back-up', 'more effective', 'proper', 'improved', 'greater', 'better resourced' and 'financial' support. A UK law teacher noted: *'Very little support is provided by my university to overcome any or all of these very demanding challenges'.*

The Impact of a Lack of Trust, Transparency and Respect, and the Need for Higher Levels of Communication and Autonomy

Trust, Transparency and Respect

In 2017, many academics indicated a lack of trust and confidence in university management. Indicative comments included: *'[the university] could try acting with integrity rather than making statements about integrity and values while turning this place into somewhere I am no longer proud to work' (Aus); 'I have no trust whatsoever in their ability' (UK).*

Relatedly, law teachers felt that levels of trust and confidence in them were low: *'interfere less and trust academics' judgement' (Aus); 'treat us as valued and trusted colleagues, rather than treating us as recalcitrant proletarians to be constantly flogged' (UK); 'it feels like the central university do not trust academics' (Aus).*

There were consistent calls in the UK and Australia for greater levels of respect for law teachers: *'notice our efforts and respect our professionalism instead of seeing us as a resource from which maximum value must be extracted' (UK); 'greater recognition and respect from management that the academics are professionals and form the backbone of the university' (Aus); 'show respect to all staff and not have Deans select favourites (whose lack of performance is widely recognised and demoralises other hard-working staff who contribute)' (UK); 'treat staff properly and with greater respect' (UK).*

Communication and Autonomy

Many academics reported inadequate communication and consultation, and that they felt alienated as a result of not being properly included in decisions, changes or improvements. Indicative comments included: *'better communication between management and staff' is needed (UK); 'it all comes down to communication. If communication and understanding are lacking, then everything else falls around you' (UK); 'stress and uncertainty could be avoided with proper communication' (Aus); 'good communication and a willingness, not just to listen, but to act upon the concerns raised consistently by staff, would go a long way in alleviating the stress and anxiety that is experienced by so many' (UK).*

Calls were also made for increased levels of autonomy: *'increase academic staff autonomy' (Aus); 'stop the erosion of academic autonomy' (Aus); 'there is too much autonomy in matters where support would assist and little or no autonomy in important pedagogical matters' (Aus).*

Summary of Results of the 2020 UK and Australian Law Teacher Studies

The UK survey in 2020 attracted 117 participants and the Australian survey, 43 participants. The substantial majority of respondents to the UK survey worked in public universities and worked full time. Of those who disclosed a gender 70% were female ($n = 72$) and 30% were male ($n = 32$). 59 (82%) female respondents disclosed having a caring responsibility as opposed to 21 (66%) male respondents.

There were 43 respondents to the Australian study in 2020 including 26 women and 17 men. Most were employed full-time (81%). Similar to the 2017 cohort, most had worked in legal practice before becoming an academic (88%); and most currently worked at a law school in a publicly funded university (81%).

The UK survey took place throughout July 2020. This was a time when COVID case numbers fell and non-essential businesses were permitted to open as restrictions were lifted.[1] It was also a time when it was clear that international students would not be travelling to the UK and applications from them were expected to decrease significantly. Domestic students were expected to defer starting their studies until

[1] The Devolved governments of England Scotland Wales and Northern Ireland have the power to make law to protect public health and thus each of these governments made differing choices about restrictions in response to the pandemic. For a summary of how the four nations manage differently see https://www.instituteforgovernment.org.uk/explainers/coronavirus-lockdown-rules-four-nations-uk.

2021, and increased numbers of requests for suspension of studies of continuing students were anticipated. There was increasing uncertainty about the EU student applications due to the looming Brexit deadline at the end of 2020.

As a result, competition between universities for students increased dramatically. League tables of universities who relied upon international student recruitment were published, and tales of financial embarrassment were discussed (Kernohan, 2020). Student number controls were imposed in 2020 and then promptly removed because of the chaos caused by the proposal to calculate grades for A level students unable to sit examinations. Universities were working under a cap on their undergraduate student numbers for the 2020–21 academic year, which was put in place to stop heightened competition between universities for students because of the COVID-19 pandemic. Universities had come under increasing pressure to honour all offers made to prospective students regardless of their A level results, putting them in danger of breaching their number caps and then being fined.

Furthermore, schools in England closed in March 2020. They reopened to some year groups in the summer term and to all pupils in September. Research into the impact upon parents working from home confirms the uneven manner in which this affected employees (Bevan, 2020) generally, and mothers in particular. Parents reported having to work in the evenings and on the weekend to meet the demands of their roles, and there was an increased sense of conflict between parent and professional.[2]

In person examinations were swept away as part of the impact of the pandemic. Urgent requests for 'no detriment policies' were experienced by most universities as student unions sought assurance that students would achieve pre-COVID grades despite the impact of the sudden move to fully online learning at the end of March 2020. This move was also unevenly felt, and universities rushed to lend computers and other IT equipment to those students needing support. Those experiencing disadvantage were impacted the most as they struggled with internet access and sharing devices and workspace with their wider family groups.

Overall, there was a sense of an enormous increase in teaching- and learning-related work that fell disproportionately on the teachers in universities who already had the most teaching responsibilities. This burden continued over the summer as third attempts at assessment were created to give students the maximum opportunity to progress to the next stage of their degree. In July, at the time the survey was completed, some of this was already apparent but perhaps not all. There had been warnings by government scientific advisers of a second wave in the autumn, but few imagined in July 2020, as trips to Europe returned briefly, what this would mean.

In Australia, the COVID-context to working life as an academic is also important to note. As for their UK counterparts, Australian law teachers also faced an unusually uncertain time when they were completing the survey. Law teachers in Australia were also being challenged by school closures and working from home, requests to design and develop quickly new online methods of teaching delivery and to master new online platforms, having to manage increased student concerns about the impact on

[2] https://eprints.soton.ac.uk/446405/1/Work_After_Lockdown_Insight_report_Jan_2021_1_.pdf.

their learning success of changes to the tertiary learning environment and financial pressures on law schools and faculties.

The following sections present the data obtained from UK and Australian law teachers to the question: 'Please explain what you think your university could do to improve staff quality of working life'?; along with responses to the question as to what their institutions could do to improve the quality of working life in the context of short- and long-term reactions to the challenges created by the COVID-19 pandemic. The key themes identified from the coding of responses in 2020 were very similar to, although slightly different in focus, from those identified in 2017. The dominant 2020 themes included: teacher support, flexible work practices, workload issues, transparency, strategic priorities, communication and recognition. The issues of administrative burden, management styles, autonomy and respect featured less frequently across the 2020 results.

Interestingly, more than a quarter of respondents to the Australian study indicated across the three questions that there was nothing more they considered their university could do. Indeed, the general tenor of the Australian 2020 survey results was that many law teachers appreciate the stress university administrators are under, and understand that very difficult decisions, such as those relating to increased teaching and administrative workloads, and redundancies, are unavoidable. Indicative comments included: *'My employer has been excellent in its response' (Aus); 'They are responding wisely and well' (Aus); 'Feeling very lucky to have a job …' (Aus).*

There were fewer examples of this within the UK data but there was an element of positivity and a recognition of the wider context: *'Overall my university promotes a good work–life balance and has given us a rest day (Friday) each week during lockdown. It could improve our working life more by minimising needless bureaucracy which is rampant but I think some of this bureaucracy is out of the university's control, e.g. coming from government' (UK).* In general, many—although not all—law teachers indicated an appreciation for teaching remotely, feeling more trusted to work from home, and yet they still called for more transparency around law school decisions. Responses also called for administrators to *'plan slower so that they don't have to keep changing' (Aus)* and to allow for Faculty-based (as opposed to central university) strategies to address workplace needs. The importance of prioritising job security was noted.

Summary of Responses to the Question About What Universities Should Implement or Change to Improve Staff Quality of Working Life in the Short Term and Long Term as a Result of the COVID-19 Pandemic

Although the survey asked separate questions in relation to short and long-term responses to the COVID-19 pandemic, the responses in both countries did not engage with this distinction in a meaningful way. The same themes emerged in both sets of answers, and some participants simply repeated their response for both questions. Therefore, our analysis of those questions has been combined. The key themes emerging in responses focussed on issues of: more teacher support, flexible work practices, better management of workload, clarity about strategic priorities, greater transparency, improved communication, and greater awareness and recognition.

In terms of *teacher support*, in Australia issues of COVID-safety were raised such as enhanced COVID-safe cleaning measures, *'help with social distancing' (Aus)* and *'better availability of PPE for FtoF teaching' (Aus)*. Comments also referred to *'more support for Internet and technology problems' (Aus)* and *'actual proper wellbeing supports of any kind would be helpful' (Aus)*. In contrast, the UK responses hardly mentioned COVID safety measures. However, there were some comments requesting more concern for staff wellbeing when contrasted with institutional concern for student wellbeing, for example, *'give consideration to staff wellbeing rather than making it all about students' (UK)*. There was also a request for support in the move to online learning in terms of the provision of improved software and training.

Greater *flexibility in work practices* was a strong theme in the 2020 responses particularly in relation to ensuring meetings are managed efficiently, online teaching is supported and working from home arrangements are clear. Also, flexibility was seen as necessary in terms of accommodating caring responsibilities—such as allowing extended marking periods, more support for women researchers and ensuring staff are adequately supported to work from home. Indicative comments included: *'continue with flexible working arrangements and allow staff (both academic and professional) to work from home as the need arises' (Aus)*, *'continue offering remote online participation in seminars and meetings' (Aus)*. *'Many things can be done from home! There is no need to have lots of face-to-face meetings (although online meetings need to be reduced too!). Perhaps a realisation that staff can be trusted to do our jobs and do not need constant interference from management' (UK)*. The UK responses had several very positive comments in relation to institutions that had supported increased flexibility and the number of positive items contrasts with the 2017 survey which was substantially negative: *'my experience is that the University has given me a good quality of working life, including flexible working arrangements when my children were of school age and also with caring for elderly parents'*.

In relation to the theme of *workload*, law teachers in 2020 noted a need for *'recognition of increased workloads' (Aus)* as a result of COVID, *'clearer workload responsibilities particularly in relation to teaching' (Aus)*, *'improved workload balance' (Aus)* and increased allowance for administrative workload *'to recognise the extra support given to students' (Aus)*. The UK responses mirrored these and requested clear recognition of the time taken to develop blended learning materials: *'more realistic workloads that reflect the true cost of time involved in work'*. Some participants noted that current workloads are 'unsustainable' and identified a need for *'individualised admin assistance' (Aus)*, *'reduce the absolutely crushing work overload' (UK)* and a need to fund casual staff (and treat them well) as a way of addressing issues of increased workload for full-time staff. One Australian participant commented that more should be expected from students *'in terms of their expectations and engagement in learning'*. Another asked for *'respect for research time during COVID'*.

In terms of clarity about *strategic priorities*, participants highlighted the need to *'prioritise staff job security, emphasise access to permanent/long-term employment and embrace greater accommodations/flexibility in work practices' (Aus)*. Some responses focussed on the need to *'rebalance the importance of teaching against research. Research has for too long been the only way to progress - the pandemic has shown how important teaching actually is and the skills required to be a good teacher are not simply innate' (UK)*. Suggestions were made to *'reduce the number of executive staff, cut back on administrative red tape and delegate more decision-making authority to Heads of School and middle management' (Aus)*. It was also suggested that universities should develop *'business plans that are contemporary and recognise the realities of 2020 and beyond' (Aus)*. One UK participant commented: *'Employ more staff instead of terminating contracts due to COVID-19. The work is very intense and results in mental and other health issues. We are asked to do more and more to cover for absent and dismissed colleagues, without any change in our contracts'*.

The need for greater *transparency* in relation to *'what is happening' (Aus)* was highlighted and linked to staff being in a position to make informed decisions. Comments called for transparency in terms of *'the university's survival plan' (Aus)*, *'decision-making surrounding workforce decisions' (Aus)* and the *'finances of the faculty and university' (Aus)*. *'Better communication, real inclusion and involvement of a range of people in discussions, sharing information and decision-making processes, recognising and admitting uncertainties' (UK)*.

Communication was a key theme of responses with law teachers asking for *'improvements in communication' (Aus)*, particularly in the context of working remotely and the appropriate use of email: *'Recognise that we are in fact working from our homes; emails talking about "return to work" imply that we are on some sort of extended holiday, when in fact we are busier than ever and having to use home resources to do university work' (UK)*. Suggestions were made for managers and leaders *'to check in with staff more regularly' (Aus)*, *'survey the staff' (Aus)*, provide reassurance *'regarding job security' (Aus)* and provide *'clearer communication about plans' (Aus)* and *'the reality of the institution's situation' (Aus)*. The UK responses included some positive comments of successful communication: *'The senior managers at my university have been fantastic throughout the COVID crisis, lots of helpful communication and regular updates' (UK)*; *'generally, good communication with a line manager helps create a good quality of working life' (UK)*.

One of the strongest themes in relation to short-term responses to COVID-19 was the need for greater *awareness and recognition*, particularly in relation to *'how hard people are working to maintain the student experience and teach well and the toll this can take on academics' (Aus)* and the reality that *'in the long term, many university positions are possibly going to be lost' (Aus)*. Comments called for increased awareness of: *'the additional demands (time, resources, professionalism, innovation, generosity) being imposed upon teaching academics' (Aus)*, *'the serious issues of increasing workloads over recent years. The pandemic has made this even more important with staff working longer hours and having the home as an office' (UK)*. Responses also called for greater recognition *'that research productivity has been much lower because of the additional workload required in teaching and administration' (Aus)*, and for acknowledgement that *'mental health issues in the current time (and more generally) are largely the product of structural/environmental factors, rather than individual deficiencies/practices' (Aus)*. An Australian participant sought recognition *'that doing online stuff well is expensive and time-consuming and constantly needs resources for review and revision' (Aus)*. Others noted a need for recognition of *'the stress and other practical impacts of COVID on research productivity' (Aus)*, *'the extra support given to students' (Aus)* and the efforts put into doing *'new flexible approaches well' (Aus)*.

Summary of Responses to the Question 'Please Explain What You Think Your University Could Do More Generally to Improve Staff Quality of Working Life'?

In response to this question, the same themes as for the questions about short- and long-term responses to the COVID-19 pandemic arose. There was an emphasis on supporting teachers, managing workloads, ensuring flexibility in work practice, improving communication and transparency in decision-making, and improving recognition of the new realities of working life as law teachers. An additional theme not evident in the earlier questions arose, however, regarding management styles and practices.

Participants called for *'more competent management'*, *'decreasing managerialism'*, *'decentralisation of decision-making and less central admin'*, and greater *'employment certainty' (Aus)*. Specific comments included: *'university management is undertaken by academics who, having moved up through the ranks, have little management/administration training and do not understand good decision-making or organisational requirements such as strong policies in areas such as harassment/bullying, family responsibilities, appropriate leadership. However, decisions made have profound effects upon individuals and organisations. In a publicly-funded university, this becomes an issue of public concern' (Aus)*; *'restrict the "thought bubble" ideas, rather have considered responses mindful of the commitments of staff - those in decision making roles inevitably are administrators who either do not know or who no longer recall the pressure of front-line delivery of education' (Aus)*; *'stop organisational change that is not warranted on the financial position of the university and stop simultaneously ramping up performance requirements' (Aus)*; *'stop expecting to get bigger, brighter, better all the time. We are good. Can't we just be "enough" for a while?' (Aus)*.

One Australian participant commented: *'think through how the various disparate imperatives work together and pull apart in light of current funding constraints: teaching, research, service. Presently we are being told to aim for excellence, but we do not have the time or resources to do so. We are told to research, but we are loaded up with teaching. We are told to design great units with innovative assessments, and then (directly, by the Dean) we are told that we need to "just do enough" because there's no sessional budget. We are told to get grants, but no-one has the time to write the applications which, for law, stand little chance of success anyway. And even if we were successful, we wouldn't have the time to devote to discharging them effectively either. Dark days indeed'.*

Similar comments are to be found in the UK data as indicated by this response: *'Reduce the culture of metrics and managerialism. Model workloads fully and properly. Spend money on staff not fancy buildings. Work to reduce overwork and glorification of business. Reduce micro-management and increase autonomy and freedom. Reduce competitiveness and foster collegiality. Recognise not everyone is good at everything and allow colleagues to allocate/share work between ourselves'.*

Discussion

The themes identified in this study about the stressful nature of the working life of law academics as expressed by respondents in the UK and Australia in 2017 and 2020 echo the international research about the stressors academics face at work more generally (Carter & Goldie, 2018; Catano et al., 2010; Kinman & Jones, 2008; Mudrak et al., 2018; Pignata et al., 2018; Pujol-Cols & Lazzaro-Salazar, 2018; Reevy & Deason, 2014; Winefield et al., 2008). Indeed, Wray and Kinman have said that the extant research 'indicates that academic staff may be at high risk of a range of psychosocial hazards related to their work and there is some evidence that the risk may be increasing' (2020, 3). Wray and Kinman also note, however, that there are challenges in systematically reviewing and drawing conclusions from this research because of the different methodologies adopted across the studies, particularly in relation to measurement and sampling (2020, 3).

Nevertheless, the existing body of research does provide a useful affirmation of the themes identified in our project. In addition, Wray and Kinman's identification of seven psychosocial hazards experienced by UK academics (2020) also affirms our themes. These hazards include: demands, control, support from managers and colleagues, relationships, role and change management.

In both our 2017 and 2020 studies, issues in relation to the impact of the neoliberal university on the quality of the working life of law teachers were apparent. This is consistent with the research examining the structure and function of higher education which highlights how the nature of academic work has changed in recent years as a result of, for example, 'increased student numbers with a more "consumer-driven" approach to their studies, increased pressure to undertake and publish research with "significance" and "reach", more rigorous teaching and learning policies and processes, and greater demand for entrepreneurial activity' (Wary & Kinman, 2020, 1 citing Kinman, 2001; Biron et al., 2008; Lynch, 2017; Nixon et al., 2018). The neoliberal university has been identified as a workplace in which there has been a shift away from collegiality and cooperation towards greater competition and marketisation fuelled by a target-centric, output-focussed culture (Deem et al., 2007; Nixon et al., 2018). It is also a place where management relationships are characterised by a lack of trust, transparency and respect. For example, low levels of satisfaction with communication and management practices have been reported by Kinman et al. (2006) and Teichler and Höhle (2013).

Our data indicate that law teachers associate the rise of the neoliberal university with a decline in their autonomy. Work autonomy has been found to be a stress-protective factor and is associated with positive work performance (Häusser et al., 2010; Zábrodská et al., 2016), a reduction in burnout and health problems, stronger job-commitment and better life-satisfaction levels (Boyd et al., 2011; Kinman & Jones, 2008; McClenahan et al., 2007; Taris et al., 2001). Traditionally, academic staff have had the benefit of high levels of autonomy, particularly in terms of their teaching and research (Musselin, 2007). Three decades ago in 1986, for example, Gmelch, Wilke and Lovrich found that work–stress is ameliorated by high job control and collegial cultures of support (Gmelch et al., 1986). However, the work of Henkel (2005), Kolsaker (2008) and Lee et al (2017) evidences that universities have become more manager-centric and focussed on performativity, monitoring, auditing academic performance and top-down management practices (Deem et al., 2007; Watts & Robertson, 2011) with associated reductions in worker autonomy.

One of the major concerns for law teachers identified in our project relates to unmanageable workloads, something attributable to an aspect of the neoliberal university which derives from pressures associated with external quality metrics and a focus on league tables (Carter & Goldie, 2018; Smith et al., 2011). Kinman (2001) and Long et al. (2019) have found that work overload is a key stressor for academics. Studies by Tytherleigh et al. (2005), Bentley and Kyvik (2012), Kinman (2014), Barkhuizen and Rothmann (2008), Biron et al. (2008), and Johnson et al. (2019) have also shown across a number of countries that academics cannot complete their work tasks in the time they have at work, and many have to work long hours to keep up with their workload. Further, studies by Kinman (2014), Winefield et al. (2008), and Fontinha et al. (2018) found high academic workloads to be associated with work–life imbalance. Unsurprisingly, work overload has also been associated with mental health problems (Barkhuizen & Rothmann, 2008; Kinman, 2019; Viljoen & Rothmann, 2009).

Our data indicates that a particular challenge with workload is the management of administrative burdens, alongside teaching and research responsibilities. This sits well with the findings of Kinman (2001), Teichler and Höhle (2013), Long et al. (2019), Bennett et al. (2018) and Chory and Offstein (2017) that role conflict is a key stressor for academics and with the work of Collins and Parry-Jones (2000) that found administrative burdens to be a significant source of stress for academic staff. Research in the UK by Bentley and Kyvik (2012) indicates that academics in that country report higher levels of administrative load than academics in other countries.

It is clear from both the results of our research and broader research internationally that the 'stressors associated with core aspects of academic work, … and the growing demands of the role' (Wray & Kinman, 2020, 2) are associated with low levels of quality in the working life of academics. Overall, our data calls for stronger support for academic staff from university managers, better communication and a return to autonomous and collegial approaches to academic life.

Conclusion

Across the 2017 and 2020 studies, law teachers in the UK and Australia have taken the opportunity to express both frustration about their working conditions and awareness about the impact of COVID-19 in terms of creating a new reality for life in the legal academy.

The 2020 research evidences somewhat of a change in the attitudes of law teachers from the 2017 research. The COVID-19 pandemic seems to have shifted the mindset of respondents, at least to some extent, away from the impact of neoliberalism and a focus on the mal-alignment of values between academics and institution towards a greater sense of shared goals and priorities. Nevertheless, there appears to be the potential for simple but effective changes to law schools as workplaces in terms of improving approaches to support, workloads, management styles, communication and transparency and acknowledgement and recognition.

The responses to the two surveys provide university managers and leaders, particularly in law schools, with some clear suggestions and feedback as to possible adjustments that will improve the quality of working life for law teachers. It is important that institutions hear these messages from staff because the wellbeing of law teachers is connected to the wellbeing of law students, and this in turn is connected to the wellbeing of the future practising legal profession.

References

Barnard, A., McCosker, H., & Gerber, R. (1999). Phenomenography: A qualitative research approach for exploring understanding in health care. *Qualitative Health Research, 9*(2), 212–226.

Barkhuizen, N., & Rothmann, S. (2008). Occupational stress of academic staff in South African Higher Education institutions. *South African Journal of Psychology, 38*(2), 321–336. https://doi.org/10.1177/008124630803800205

Bennett, D., Roberts, L., Ananthram, S., & Broughton, M. (2018). What is required to develop career pathways for teaching academics? *Higher Education, 75*(2), 271–286. https://doi.org/10.1007/s10734-017-0138-9

Bentley, P. J., & Kyvik, S. (2012). Academic work from a comparative perspective: A survey of faculty working time across 13 countries. *Higher Education, 63*(4), 529–547. https://doi.org/10.1007/s10734-011-9457-4

Bevan, S. (2020). Work without boundaries: Wellbeing in Covid-19 lockdown. *The Work-Life Balance Bulletin, British Psychological Society, 4*(1), 5–9.

Biron, C., Brun, J. P., & Ivers, H. (2008). Extent and sources of occupational stress in university staff. *Work, 30*(4), 511–522.

Boyd, C. M., Bakker, A. B., Pignata, A., Winefield, A., Gillespie, N., & Stough, C. (2011). A longitudinal test of the job demands-resources model among Australian university academics. *Applied Psychology, 60*(1), 112–140. https://doi.org/10.1111/j.1464-0597.2010.00429.x

Carter, M. A., & Goldie, D. (2018). Potential enablers of mental health and wellness for those teaching in tertiary education. *International Journal of Innovation, Creativity and Change, 4*(2), 3–20.

Catano, V., Francis, L., Haines, T., Kirpalani, H., Shannon, H., Stringer, B., & Lozanzki, L. (2010). Occupational stress in Canadian universities: A national survey. *International Journal of Stress Management, 17*(3), 232.

Chory, R. M., & Offstein, E. H. (2017). 'Your professor will know you as a person': Evaluating and rethinking the relational boundaries between faculty and students. *Journal of Management Education, 41*(1), 9–38. https://doi.org/10.1177/1052562916647986

Collins, S., & Parry-Jones, B. (2000). Stress: The perceptions of social work lectures in Britain. *British Journal of Social Work, 30*(6), 769–794. https://doi.org/10.1093/bjsw/30.6.769

Crum, A. J., Salovey, P., & Achor, S. (2013). Rethinking stress: The role of mindsets in determining the stress response. *Journal of Personality and Social Psychology, 104*(4), 716–733. https://doi.org/10.1037/a0031201

Deem, R., Hillyard, S., & Reed, M. (2007). *Knowledge, Higher Education, and the new managerialism: The changing management of UK universities.* Oxford University Press.

Easton, S., & Van Laar, D. (2013). QoWL (Quality of Working Life): What, how, and why? *Psychology Research, 3*(10), 596–605.

Easton, S., & Van Laar, D. (2018). *User manual for the Work-Related Quality of Life (WRQoL) Scale: A measure of quality of working life.* University of Portsmouth.

Feldon, D. F., & Tofel-Grehl, C. (2018). Phenomenography as a foundation for mixed models research. *American Behavioral Scientist, 62*(7), 887–899.

Fontinha, R., Van Laar, D., & Easton, S. (2018). Quality of working life of academics and researchers in the UK: The roles of contract type, tenure and university ranking. *Studies in Higher Education, 43*(4), 786–806. https://doi.org/10.1080/03075079.2016.1203890

Giroux, H. A. (2018). *Terror of neoliberalism: Authoritarianism and the eclipse of democracy.* Routledge.

Gmelch, W. H., Wilke, P., & Lovrich, N. (1986). Dimensions of stress among university faculty: Factor-analytic results from a national study. *Research in Higher Education, 24*(3), 266–286. https://doi.org/10.1007/BF00992075

Häusser, J. A., Mojzisch, A., Niesel, M., & Schulz-Hardt, S. (2010). Ten years on: A review of recent research on the job demand–control (-support) model and psychological wellbeing. *Work and Stress, 24*(1), 1–35.

Henkel, M. (2005). Academic identity and autonomy in a changing policy environment. *Higher Education, 49*(1–2), 155–176. https://doi.org/10.1007/s10734-004-2919-1

James, C., Strevens, C., Field, R., & Wilson, C. (2019). Fit your own oxygen mask first: The contemporary neoliberal university and the wellbeing of legal academics. In J. M. Marychurch & A. Sifris (Eds.), *Wellness for law: Making wellness core business.* LexisNexis.

James, C., Strevens, C., Field, R., & Wilson, C. (2020). The changing world of legal education: A comparison of law teachers' wellbeing and perceptions of stress at work in Australia and the UK. In J. Chan, P. Vines, & M. Legg (Eds.), *The impact of technology and innovation on the wellbeing of the legal profession.* Intersentia.

Johnson, S. J., Willis, S., & Evans, J. (2019). An examination of stressors, strain, and resilience in academic and non-academic UK university job roles. *International Journal of Stress Management, 26*(2), 162–172. https://doi.org/10.1037/str0000096

Kernohan, D. (2020). Which providers are exposed to a downturn in international recruitment? Wonkhe.com Blog, April 2, 2020. https://wonkhe.com/blogs/which-providers-are-exposed-to-a-downturn-in-international-recruitment/.

Kettunen, J., & Tynjälä, P. (2018). Applying phenomenography in guidance and counselling research. *British Journal of Guidance & Counselling, 46*(1), 1–11.

Kinman, G. (2001). Pressure points: A review of research on stressors and strains in UK academics. *Educational Psychology, 21*(4), 473–492. https://doi.org/10.1080/01443410120090849

Kinman, G. (2014). Doing more with less? Work and well-being in academics. *Somatechnics, 4*(2), 219–235. https://doi.org/10.3366/soma.2014.0129

Kinman, G. (2019). Effort-reward imbalance in academic employees: Examining different reward systems. *International Journal of Stress Management, 26*(2), 184–192. https://doi.org/10.1037/str0000128

Kinman, G., & Jones, F. (2008). Effort-reward imbalance and overcommitment: Predicting strain in academic employees in the United Kingdom. *International Journal of Stress Management, 15*(4), 381–395. https://doi.org/10.1037/a0013213

Kinman, G., Jones, F., & Kinman, R. (2006). The well-being of the UK academy, 1998–2004. *Quality in Higher Education, 12*(1), 15–27. https://doi.org/10.1080/13538320600685081

Kolsaker, A. (2008). Academic professionalism in the managerialist era: A study of English universities. *Studies in Higher Education, 33*(5), 513–525. https://doi.org/10.1080/03075070802372885

Lee, P., Miller, M., Kippenbrock, T., Rosen, C., & Emory, J. (2017). College nursing faculty job satisfaction and retention: A national perspective. *Journal of Professional Nursing, 33*(4), 261–266. https://doi.org/10.1016/j.profnurs.2017.01.001

LERN (Legal Education Research Network). *Findings of UK 2015 study*: https://ials.sas.ac.uk/sites/default/files/files/About%20us/Leadership%20%26%20Collaboration/LERN/LERN_Final_Report(C)_Perceptions_of_wellbeing_in_Law_Teachers.pdf.

Long, W., Northcote, M., Barnes, L., & Williams, A. (2019). Role conflict in the work of accounting academics in Australia. Paper presented at the Higher Education Research and Development Society of Australasia Conference, Auckland New Zealand, July 2–5.

Lynch, K. (2017). New managerialism in education: The organisational form of neoliberalism. In A. Abraham-Hamanoiel, D. Freedman, G. Khiabany, & K. Nash (Eds.), *Liberalism in neoliberal times: Dimensions, contradictions, limits* (pp. 159–163). Goldsmith's Press.

Marton, F. (1981). Phenomenography: Describing conceptions of the world around us. *Instructional Science, 10*, 177–200.

Marton, F. (1986). Phenomenography: A research approach investigating different understandings of reality. *Journal of Thought, 21*(2), 28–49.

McClenahan, C. A., Giles, M., & Mallett, J. (2007). The importance of context specificity in work stress research: A test of the demand-control-support model in academics. *Work and Stress, 21*(1), 85–95. https://doi.org/10.1080/02678370701264552

Mills, M. J., Culbertson, S. S., & Fullagar, C. J. (2012). Conceptualizing and measuring engagement: An analysis of the Utrecht Work Engagement Scale. *Journal of Happiness Studies, 13*(3), 519–545.

Mudrak, J., Zabrodska, K., Kveton, P., Jelinek, M., Blatny, M., Solcova, I., & Machovcova, K. (2018). Occupational well-being among university faculty: A job demands-resources model. *Research in Higher Education, 59*(3), 325–348. https://doi.org/10.1007/s11162-017-9467-x

Musselin, C. (2007). The transformation of academic work: Facts and analysis. In M. Kogan & U. Teichler (Eds.), *Key challenges to the academic profession* (pp. 175–190). Centre for Studies in Higher Education. https://files.eric.ed.gov/fulltext/ED502859.pdf.

Niemic, C. B., & Ryan, R. M. (2009). Autonomy, competence and relatedness in the classroom: Applying Self-Determination Theory to educational practice. *Theory and Research in Education, 7*(2), 133–144.

Nixon, E., Scullion, R., & Hearn, R. (2018). Her majesty the student: Marketised Higher Education and the narcissistic (dis)satisfactions of the student-consumer. *Studies in Higher Education, 43*(6), 927–943. https://doi.org/10.1080/03075079.2016.1196353

Pignata, S., Winefield, A. H., Boyd, C. M., & Provis, C. (2018). A qualitative study of HR/OHS stress interventions in Australian universities. *International Journal of Environmental Research and Public Health, 15*(1), 103.

Pujol-Cols, L., & Lazzaro-Salazar, M. (2018). Psychosocial risks and job satisfaction in Argentinian scholars: Exploring the moderating role of work engagement. *Journal of Work and Organizational Psychology, 34*(3), 145–156. https://doi.org/10.5093/jwop2018a17

Prosser, M., & Trigwell, K. (1997). Using phenomenography in the design of programs for teachers in higher education. *Higher Education Research & Development, 16*(1), 41–54.

Reevy, G. M., & Deason, G. (2014). Predictors of depression, stress, and anxiety among non-tenure track faculty. *Frontiers in Psychology*. https://doi.org/10.3389/fpsyg.2014.00701

Ryan, R. M., & Deci, E. L. (2000). Self-Determination Theory and the facilitation of intrinsic motivation, social development, and wellbeing. *American Psychologist, 55*(1), 68–78.

Smith, S., Ward, V., & House, A. (2011). 'Impact' in the proposals for the UK's research excellence framework: Shifting the boundaries of academic autonomy. *Research Policy, 40*(10), 1369–1379. https://doi.org/10.1016/j.respol.2011.05.026

Strevens, C., James, C., Field, R., & Wilson, C. (2019a). Fit your own oxygen mask first: The contemporary neoliberal university and the wellbeing of legal academics. Invited Keynote Presentation to the Wellness for Law Forum, Melbourne. https://law.unimelb.edu.au/wellness-for-law-forum.

Strevens, C., James, C., Field, R., & Wilson, C. (2019b). Student wellbeing through teacher wellbeing: A study with law teachers in the UK and Australia. *Student Success, 10*(3), 76–83. https://doi.org/10.5204/ssj.v10i3.1338.

Svensson, L. (1997). Theoretical foundations of phenomenography. *Higher Education Research & Development, 16*(2), 159–171.

Taris, T. W., Schreurs, P., & Van Iersel-Van Silfhout, I. (2001). Job stress, job strain, and psychological withdrawal among Dutch university staff: Towards a dual process model for the effects of occupational stress. *Work and Stress, 15*(4), 283–296. https://doi.org/10.1080/02678370110084049

Teichler, U., & Höhle, E. (Eds.). (2013). *The work situation of the academic profession in Europe: Findings of a survey in twelve countries*. Springer.

Thornton, M. (2001). Among the ruins: Law in the neo-liberal academy. *Windsor Year Book of Access to Justice, 20*, 3–23.

Thornton, M. (2007). The law school, the market and the new knowledge economy. *Legal Education Review, 17*, 1–26.

Thornton, M. (2011). *Privatising the public university: The case of law*. Routledge.

Thornton, M. (2014a). Legal education in the corporate university. *Annual Review of Law & Social Sciences, 10*, 19–35.

Thornton, M. (Ed.). (2014b). *Through a glass darkly: The social sciences look at the neoliberal university*. ANU Press.

Tytherleigh, M. Y., Webb, C., Cooper, C. L., & Ricketts, C. (2005). Occupational stress in UK Higher Education institutions: A comparative study of all staff categories. *Higher Education Research & Development, 24*(1), 41–61.

Viljoen, J. P., & Rothmann, S. (2009). Occupational stress, ill health and organisational commitment of employees at a university of technology. *SA Journal of Industrial Psychology, 35*(1), 67–77. https://doi.org/10.4102/sajip.v35i1.730

Walsh, E., et al. (1993). Physics students' understanding of relative speed: A phenomenographic study. *Journal of Research in Science Teaching, 30*(9), 1133–1148.

Watts, J., & Robertson, N. (2011). Burnout in university teaching staff: A systematic literature review. *Educational Research, 53*, 33–50. https://doi.org/10.1080/00131881.2011.552235

Winefield, T., Boyd, C., Saebel, J., & Pignata, S. (2008). Update on national university stress study. *Australian Universities' Review, 50*(1), 20–29. https://search.informit.com.au/documentSummary;dn=266240247331451;res=IELAPA. ISSN: 0818-8068.

Williams, G., Thomas, K., & Smith, A. P. (2017). Stress and well-being of university staff: An investigation using the demands-resources-individual effects (drive) model and well-being process questionnaire (WPQ). *Psychology, 8*, 1919–1940. https://doi.org/10.4236/psych.2017.812124

Wilson, C., & Strevens, C. (2018). Perceptions of psychological wellbeing in UK law academics. *The Law Teacher, 52*(3), 335–349.

Wray, S., & Kinman, G. (2020). The psychosocial hazards of academic work: an analysis of trends. *Studies in Higher Education*, 1–12.

Zábrodská, K., Mudrák, J., Květon, P., Machovcová, K., & Šolcová, I. (2016). Keeping marketisation at bay: The quality of academic worklife in Czech universities. *Sociologický Časopis/czech Sociological Review, 52*(3), 347–373. https://doi.org/10.13060/00380288.2016.52.3.262

Rachael Filed is a Professor of Law in the Bond University Faculty of Law, and Co-Director of the Bond Dispute Resolution Centre and Bond's Centre for Professional Legal Education. Her areas of teaching and research expertise include dispute resolution, family law and domestic violence, lawyer and law student well-being and legal education (particularly foundations of law and transition in, through and out of law school). Rachael is an Australian Learning and Teaching Fellow (2010), the winner of a National Teaching Citation (2008) and an Australian Teaching Excellence Award (2014), and she is a Senior Fellow of the Higher Education Academy. She founded the Australian Wellness Network for Law and co-founded the ADR Research Network. Rachael has been involved with Women's Legal Service, Brisbane since 1993 and is now an Ambassador for the Service. In 2013 Rachael was named Queensland Woman Lawyer of the Year and in 2020 she was elected to be an Academic Bencher of the Inner Temple in London.

Caroline Strevens is a professor in Legal Education, Head of the Law Department at the University of Portsmouth and immediate past Chair of the Association of Law Teachers. Caroline's academic career was preceded by a career in legal practice as a Solicitor. Caroline's primary research area is legal education including investigating how principles of positive psychology may influence well-being of staff and students in Higher Education. She is one of a team of UK academics who are supporting LawCare in the development of a research study that will look at the impact of work culture and working practices on the wellbeing of legal professionals.

Dr. Colin James is a solicitor and a senior lecturer with the Australian National University. He has PhD in history and other qualifications in law, coaching psychology and tertiary education. He teaches family law and practice, supervises in clinical legal education programs and serves on the management committees of law societies and community legal centres. His areas of practice include family law and domestic violence and his research areas include legal history, domestic violence, academic integrity, emotional intelligence, coaching psychology, professional development and wellbeing. Colin presents at many national and international conferences and has supervised PhDs and DBAs on diverse topic areas. He has published extensively and edited texts and his current research focus is vicarious trauma in professionals.

Employing Humanistic Teaching Approaches to Promote Student Wellbeing in Higher Education

Mark David Chong, Abraham P. Francis, Margaret Anne Carter, and Frank Darkwa Baffour

Abstract Given the increasing levels of stress, strain and anxiety brought about by "ongoing challenges of living independently, autonomous learning and peer competition [initially for better grades, and thereafter, for better jobs/careers] [as well as the] … financial challenges established by high tuition and living fees", tertiary-level students from across the world have sadly been experiencing significant wellbeing issues, including mental health complications. There is therefore an urgent need for educators to employ innovative means of engaging students to neutralise stressful situations that may arise from these global tertiary educational trends, as well as the increasingly demanding pressures generated as a result of needing to adjust to new academic environments and teacher–student relationships in a current COVID-19, as well as a future post-pandemic, world. To that end, this chapter will attempt to put forward the suggestion that humanistic teaching approaches would be ideally suited to address this serious malady inflicting the higher education sector.

Keywords Higher education challenges · Humanistic pedagogy/teaching philosophy · Mental health · Student wellbeing · Psychosocial problems/demands · COVID-19

M. D. Chong (✉) · A. P. Francis
James Cook University, Townsville, Australia
e-mail: markdavid.chong@jcu.edu.au

A. P. Francis
e-mail: Abraham.framcis@jcu.edu.au

M. A. Carter
Australian College of Applied Professions, Brisbane, Australia
e-mail: Margaret.Carter@acap.edu.au

F. D. Baffour
Lecturer in Social Work, Faculty of Art, Design, & Architecture, School of Social Sciences, University of New South Wales, Sydney, Australia
e-mail: f.baffour@unsw.edu.au

A. P. Francis and M. A. Carter (eds.), *Mental Health and Higher Education in Australia*,
https://doi.org/10.1007/978-981-16-8040-3_6

Introduction

Finding an innovative pedagogy that promotes sustainable wellbeing levels for higher education students has been a key aim for many universities, governments, educators and researchers. This is arguably due to the exponential increase in students experiencing mental health complications in higher education institutions globally (Averill & Major, 2020; Garbett & Thomas, 2020; Nandy et al., 2021). Further, the COVID-19 pandemic has exacerbated the challenges faced by higher education institutions to maintain the wellbeing of their students, and sadly, these difficulties that are confronted by such universities are expected to increase post-pandemic as well (Nandy et al., 2021).

In this chapter, the authors define "student wellbeing" as "…a sustainable positive mood and attitude, health, resilience, and satisfaction with self, relationships and experiences at …" an educational institution (Victorian Auditor-General, 2010, p. vii; see also Hill et al., 2021, pp. 171–172). Jones et al. (2021) speak of a more expansive definition of wellbeing that includes not only a student's mental health (cognitive and emotional) but also that of their physical and social wellbeing (p. 439). As these definitions would indicate, student wellbeing and the state of mental health are concepts that are often closely linked together. In fact, the World Health Organization (2001) defined mental health as being "a state of *well-being* [emphasis included] in which the individual realizes his or her own abilities, can cope with the normal stresses of life, can work productively and fruitfully, and is able to make a contribution to his or her community" (p. 1).

Maintaining high levels of student wellbeing has, however, been increasingly difficult to sustain, and as Hill et al. (2021) explained, there has been a

> … shift in the student population in universities across the globe, whereby the student body has significantly diversified and expanded … while experiencing ongoing challenges of living independently, autonomous learning and peer competition …. Alongside this, students face significant pressures including competition for graduate jobs and financial challenges established by high tuition and living fees …. These factors have meant that student mental health problems in higher education continue to rise internationally …. (p. 169).

There is therefore a need for educators to employ innovative means of engaging students to neutralise stressful situations that may arise from these global tertiary educational trends. There is, in fact, an urgent need for action given the increasingly demanding pressures generated in this current COVID-19, as well as future post-pandemic, world. This chapter will attempt to put forward the suggestion that humanistic teaching approaches would be ideally suited to address this serious malady inflicting the higher education sector.

Employing a suitable teaching pedagogy to achieve this is arguably a reasonable course of action to take. Garbett and Thomas (2020) contended that university staff play a significant role in higher education mental health promotion. More particularly, Baik et al. (2019) suggested that lecturers and administrators are stakeholders in students' wellbeing and that their effective engagement with learners is an antecedent to achieving wellbeing in higher education environments. The problem however is this—even though the extant literature has shown how enhanced levels of teacher-student engagement can lead to improved academic performance and student well-being (Hill et al., 2021; Jones et al., 2021; Pomerantz, 2006; Sandeen & Barr, 2006; Vibert & Shields, 2003), what is yet unclear, are the specific teaching philosophies that are needed in order to achieve this. To contribute to this discourse, the authors will focus on proposing a paradigm shift to a humanistic approach to teacher–student engagement that is built on the foundation of care, love, compassion, empathy and respectful relationships.

The Concept of Humanism

Humanism entails happiness, satisfaction and egalitarianism for all. It refers to the quintessential way of how a human being should engage with people in all spectrums of life (Rockwell, 2012). Cohen (2007) noted that "humanism is a way of being. It comprises a set of deep-seated personal convictions about one's obligations to others, especially others in need" (p. 1031). Humanism is, as Rüsen (2021), more fundamentally explained, a reflection of our intrinsic human dignity. Humanistic practice, therefore, endeavours to achieve the greater good for humanity and as such advocates for a world free from harm and quandaries (Cheruvalath, 2017).

The principles that underpin humanism—such as love, equal opportunity, respect, care, compassion, empathy and accommodation—look enticing and as such have attracted the interest of educators, researchers and practitioners in medicine, mental health and other psychosocial professions. For example, humanistic engagement with clients has been embraced by the fields of medicine, psychology, social work, business and mental health service providers (Bennegadi & Cyrulnik, 2020; Blatt et al., 2018; Cheruvalath, 2017; Rockwell, 2012; Shafiq et al., 2019). Given that these said professions (i.e. doctors, psychologists, social workers and so on) have adopted such an approach in their own fields of practice and continue to do so, it is reasonable for university administrators and academics to likewise explore the prospect that a humanistic pedagogy will have the same potential to promote academic excellence and wellbeing among students enrolled in higher education institutions.

A Humanistic Approach to Teaching

In a book entitled "*The Dispute between Philanthropinism and Humanism in the Educational Theory of our Time*" (1808; as cited in Fincham, 2011, pp. 95–96), Friedrich Immanuel Niethammer first coined the term "humanism" to describe a new liberal educational curriculum that was designed to facilitate a full expression of our humanity. Thus, to Niethammer, "education should not simply be concerned with the transmission of facts and figures, or even of reading, writing and arithmetic. It must also strive to bring to the surface our nobler selves, the best of what it means to be human" (Chong, 2018, p. 13). That said, Pring (2010) noted that the introduction of principles of humanism into educational settings can actually be traced back to the days of Aristotle in Ancient Greece. Aloni (2011, 2014) explained that there were five forms of humanistic education (as set out in Table 1).

Table 1 Humanistic teaching philosophies

S/No	Humanist pedagogical typology	Description
1	Classical-cultural framework	This is a rational and Enlightenment approach that "inherently implies the existence of an ideal of human perfection—comprising notions such as Paideia, virtue, nobility, justice, goodness, and beauty—that should serve as a universal and objective model for regulating the education of all human beings qua human beings" (Aloni, 2014, p. 2)
2	Romantic-naturalistic approach	This is "characterized by its fundamental premise that there exists in every one of us an "inner nature" or a "fixed self" that is fundamentally good and unique, and that pushes to unfold and actualize itself — in accordance with… [its] built-in code — toward healthy existence and full humanity. True education, therefore, consists of careful "drawing out" and attentive actualization of the individual's inner nature" (Aloni, 2014, p. 3)
3	Existential paradigm	This is a framework that rejects both the classical-cultural framework and the romantic-naturalist approach, in favour of seeking to "humanize their students by urging them to pursue neither ultimate truths nor self-realization, but [rather] to constantly choose, form, and create their identities and life-projects—enlarging their sense of freedom and responsibility for the meanings, values, and events that constitute the public as well as the private realms of their lives" (Aloni, 2014, pp. 3–4)
4	Radical-critical form	This approach contextualises educational issues within the broader themes of key cultural, social and economic inequalities as well as injustices and to that end strives to ensure that "pedagogy should become more political and the political more pedagogical" (Aloni, 2014, p.4)
5	Ecocentric participatory model	This framework eschews being exclusively anthropocentric and instead develops policies and practices that pursue "environmental and social sustainability, cosmopolitan-multicultural education, and education for a culture of peace and shared life" with nature as a whole (Aloni, 2014, pp. 4–5)

Although each approach accentuates particular imperatives, all of them still focus on developing the complete human being (mind, body and spirit), while at the same time ensuring that the core purpose of education (which is to impart socially-useful knowledge and skills) is achieved (Aloni, 2014). To this end, Rogers (1969), who has been credited as the modern father of humanistic education, noted how a holistic educational system that prioritises the needs of the learner (i.e. being student-centred) tends to succeed in producing individuals who are better prepared to address real-world challenges. The Association for Humanistic Education and Development in their 1982 report indicated that a humanistic education should aim to develop students to (i) function well in a complex situation; (ii) acquire skills that they will need in order to promote a self-belief that will bring out their potential and to function effectively in conflict situations and (iii) improve their understanding of their existence through the promotion of self-awareness and love for self and others. Furthermore, a humanistic educational system primes its teachers to be able to identify the uniqueness of each of their individual students, while helping them to address their specific needs as the latter strive to achieve their cherished goals and ambitions. As Moustakas (1966) suggested, for such a humanistic approach to be implemented, a deeper interpersonal relationship has to be developed and sustained between the teacher and his/her student. This is, of course, reminiscent of Jean-Jacques Rousseau's work "Emile or On Education' (1762). Some studies on humanistic education have also noted that such an interpersonal relationship works in favour of the students (Brumfit, 1984; Chong, 2018; Hanley et al., 2020; Sarem & Hamidi, 2013). Why? Because they feel loved and cared for; they feel a sense of belonging to the academic environment; and they perceive teachers as people whom they can safely confide in (Brumfit, 1984; Hanley et al., 2020). Similarly, Chong (2018) noted that a humanistic pedagogy is epitomised by caring and empathetic teacher–student engagements and relationships. As such, a humanistic teaching philosophy will help university staff to more empathetically understand their students' needs, which in turn will facilitate trust between them and hopefully encourage these students to more confidently confide in them when they are faced with pressing psychosocial demands or problems that impact upon their wellbeing at university.

Thus, it is arguable that a student-centred form of engagement that is built on respect, trust, compassion and care could act as a catalyst for the building of a much more healthy system of higher education. Javadi and Tahamsbi (2020) argued that a learning process that prioritises the "individual" and places them at the centre of learning "helps us get better education while allowing us to tackle more social issues" (p. 42). This is important because as Hanley et al. (2020) suggested, it contributes towards addressing students' needs and promoting their wellbeing. In particular, a humanistic pedagogy tends to create a more democratic learning environment where students' psychosocial (in addition to academic) needs are attended to (Aloni, 2011; Cicciarelli, 2007; Popovych et al., 2021; Tamrat, 2020).

Translating a Humanistic Teaching Philosophy into Implementable Principles

One practical way of imbuing our teaching methods with a humanistic philosophy was proposed by Chong (2018), who distilled from the relevant literature, seven core principles that, in his opinion, underpinned the implementation of a humanistic pedagogy. These principles are set out in Table 2.

To that end, Chong's (2018) humanistic teaching approach focused on preparing students to become the best that they can be. As Maslow (1954) so pithily put it: "what a man [or woman] can be, must be" (p. 46). Chong's (2018) humanistic pedagogical approach was premised on an adaptation of two humanistic pedagogical approaches that Aloni (2014) had previously described, i.e. the classical cultural and the romantic-naturalistic, paradigms. It should be noted that Chong (2018) was attempting to educate and nurture future criminal justice practitioners, who would invariably face extremely challenging circumstances in the course of their professional work. Consequently, it was critical to that not only would his teaching philosophy help to accentuate and celebrate "the individuality of each student as a most worthy end in itself" (via classical cultural humanism), it was equally important that his pedagogy would also encourage his students to strive "to harness that self-actualisation of individual goodness within each of ...[them], for the common good" (via romantic-naturalistic humanism) (Chong, 2018, p. 14).

This humanistic pedagogy goes beyond the mere acquisition of knowledge and extends itself to the wellbeing and holistic development of the student—mind, body and spirit. Among other benefits, this will also build resilience in them so that they will be better equipped to handle not only the normal but also abnormal stresses of life at university and in the real-world problems which we have already identified as being deleterious factors that negatively impact upon student wellbeing and mental health (Hill et al., 2021).

The Challenges of Implementing a Humanistic Pedagogy

The obstacles to operationalising such an approach potentially arise at two different levels: personal and institutional. In the case of the former, Chong (2018) explained how employing a humanistic pedagogical framework at his university was far from "smooth-sailing and full of success stories" (p. 23). The operationalising of those seven implementable principles outlined earlier in this chapter was an arduous task, requiring both copious amounts of time and effort to regularly and frequently mentor students as well as organise for them extra-curricular: (i) Criminology Lunch Events; (ii) Criminology Workshops and Mini-Conferences; (iii) University Open Day Criminology Stalls; (iv) Criminal Justice Movie and Lunch Events; (v) Special Criminology Lectures; (vi) Criminological Quiz Competitions; (vii) Criminal Justice

Table 2 Humanistic teaching principles

S/No	Humanistic pedagogical principles	Description
1	Caring for the individual student	Here, "[i]deally, a teacher has to go that "extra mile" for their students because that will really help to build trust and respect between them. Students need to know that you care for them - not just in abstract terms but rather in some concrete and personal way" (Chong, 2018, p. 15). This is because "[t]angible expressions of concern, both great and small, build trust; and with trust, effective mentoring at a later stage will be facilitated" (Chong, 2018, p. 15)
2	Aiding the student in self-discovery	This is a key part of the humanistic enterprise because the "… process of discovering who they really "are" is a critical stage in any student's journey towards self-actualisation" (Chong, 2018, p. 15)
3	Facilitating self-actualisation or the fulfilling of their potential	This is by no means an easy task to accomplish but it begins by finding out "…what the individual student wants out of life through discussions either individually or in small groups", and thereafter, personalising their undergraduate degree "programme and other scaffolding structures around those hopes and aspirations - taking specific account of the student's actual strengths and weaknesses" (Chong, 2018, p. 16)
4	Intensive mentoring	From a humanistic perspective, Chong (2018) asserted that intensive mentoring was "an ideal vehicle to facilitate the process of self-actualisation" (p. 16) although for it to be successful, it has to be tailored to meet the specific needs of the individual student. Furthermore, given the demanding nature of such an approach, Chong (2018) cautioned that "… getting the right balance between being a good teacher-mentor and being overly manipulative and domineering - ala-Svengali - is very fine indeed, particularly when such intensive mentoring may be considered by some to be overly invasive and dictatorial" (p. 17). One way of being sensitive towards this overbearing tendency is to constantly seek feedback from the students about how they are coping with such intensive supervision, monitoring and guidance

(continued)

Table 2 (continued)

S/No	Humanistic pedagogical principles	Description
5	Cultivating sound judgment and a sense of nobility or honour	As Carl Rogers once asserted, a good education should not only be from "the neck up" (1969, pp. 3–4). It must be more than simply developing our students' academic or cognitive prowess. Consequently, every lesson should also be an opportunity for a humanist teacher "to impart some deeper [life] lesson than that which is obvious" (Chong, 2018, p. 17)
6	Empowering the student	According to Chong (2018, pp. 17–18), there are two dimensions to empowerment, internal and external. Internal empowerment entails: "… having confidence in your students, and showing them that despite their need to be mentored, that by itself does not take away their agency and self-worth. If your students can see that you believe in them in a tangible way through the expenditure of your time, effort and concern, you will ultimately also give them an equally persuasive reason to believe in themselves; to engender a self-belief of worthiness and capability" (Chong, 2018, p. 17). External empowerment then builds upon the former by: "… ensuring that your students will be in the 'right place', at the 'right time', and with the 'right attributes'. This … will require the implementation of a holistic educational programme that encompasses scaffolding across a range of dimensions: mind, body and spirit; as well as opportunities to exercise those right attributes, for example by providing: (1) work integrated-learning internships; (2) in-house … conferences and workshops; (3) paid or unpaid research assistantships; (4) paid sessional tutorship; and (5) … training classes, etc." (Chong, 2018, p.18)
7	Leading by example	It should be noted here that this principle does not require our teachers to be morally or cognitively faultless. Rather, as Chong (2018) explained: "[o]ne of the most effective ways of mentoring is through one's own personal conduct; both good and bad. Everything a teacher-mentor does can be a teaching moment, and … [Chong reinforces] this by accentuating the fact that while "no one is perfect", particularly … [himself], we are all nevertheless called to do the right and noble thing. Even if we fail – and … [Chong reminds his students constantly that he is just as prone to error and poor judgement as the next person] – our obligation nonetheless is to keep trying; and when students see you do that, it inspires them to do the same" (p. 18)

Agency Recruitment Talks; (viii) Criminal Justice Agency Internships; (ix) Facebook Criminology Network; (x) Criminology Karate Club Classes and so on (Chong, 2018, pp. 19–23). It was also personally expensive to run these activities given the fact that university budgets have become increasingly tight due in part to governmental budget-tightening measures. The financial situation for certain disciplines in Australia is even more precarious now given governmental reluctance to invest more in the social sciences and humanities (Barnes, 2020; Sawczak, 2020). It was likewise an emotionally draining experience particularly when the affective chasms between teacher and students were not effectively bridged despite the numerous extra-curricular activities that were organised for them: student apathy being the main culprit in this regard (Chong, 2018, p. 24; see also Sage et al., 2012, in relation to the risk of teacher burnout). Additionally, there may also be a significant opportunity cost factor that had to be taken into account here, given that employing a rigorous humanistic pedagogical regime would probably result in less time for such academics to conduct research, publish scholarly works, as well as to apply for grants, consultancies and so on (Chong, 2018, p. 24).

At an institutional level, the impediments to employing a humanistic teaching philosophy are much more subtle. For example, teachers are often themselves taught to either directly or indirectly rely upon observable and/or mechanistic ways of teaching where the focus of learning is directed at skills development, usually at the expense of ensuring the overall or complete development of their students (Javadi & Tahamsbi, 2020). The relevant literature suggests that this mode of educating has continued to ignore the emotional aspects of learning, and it is arguable that this has contributed to the maintenance and/or escalation of the psychosocial challenges that students of higher education are confronted with (DeCarvalho, 1991; Hanley et al., 2020; Javadi & Tahamsbi, 2020; Sage et al., 2012). Other institutional challenges include

(i) the often-reactive as opposed to proactive approach that higher education institutions tend to take when addressing the wellbeing and mental health issues of their students. As previously highlighted, such problems in higher education are increasing at a significant rate. It has also been anticipated by recent studies that the COVID-19 pandemic will result in higher education students suffering from substantial socio-psychological damage (Nandy et al., 2021), thereby making a remedial (reactive) strategy less viable than a preventative (proactive) one.

(ii) the use by higher education institutions of traditional standardised learning regimes that are often narrow and teacher-centred (see Combs, 1961, 1966, 1988; DeCarvalho, 1991; Rogers, 1969). Scholars have argued that such an approach to teaching tends to ignore the learners' psychosocial needs and wellbeing (Hanley et al., 2020; Javadi & Tahamsbi, 2020; Tangney, 2014). It is thus arguable that this "mechanised" framework of teaching does not seek to develop the whole being of the student (to self-actualise) but merely to ingrain in them the skills needed to perform specific technical activities

(Javadi & Tahamsbi, 2020)—activities that are deemed to be valuable by commercial market forces and/or industry.

(iii) curriculums that are primarily developed and driven by higher education academic staff. This tends to create a static one-way channel where tertiary-level students become passive learners in their own educational journeys. There is, therefore, no pedagogical partnership between teacher and students in which the latter are given opportunities to meaningfully participate in developing what they will ultimately learn (Cook-Sather et al., 2019). That said, Bovill et al. (2016) noted how difficult it was to establish such partnerships due to there being "resistance to co-creating; navigating institutional structures, practice and norms; and establishing an inclusive co-creating approach" (p. 195). According to Bovill et al. (2016), resistance may actually arise from both staff and student alike. For example, more often than not, educators and students are quite comfortable in their traditional roles, and as a result, resistance may arise from the uncertainties concerning the effectiveness and suitability of their proposed new roles in these pedagogical partnerships. Other issues that could raise further opposition include the educators' lack of trust in the competence of their students to contribute to their learning as well as the students' own lack of belief that they can bring anything of real substance to the table (Bovill et al., 2016). Furthermore, such pedagogical partnerships would likely contravene existing systemic structures and cultural status quos (Cook-Sather et al., 2019). Finally, it is unclear what form will the eligibility criteria take in order to determine which student or groups of students would be involved in the co-creation of the curriculum. Depending on the specific nature of the inclusionary parameters, this could potentially result in accusations of biased representation and may well undermine the purpose of such student engagement/partnership in the first place (Bovill et al., 2016).

Conclusion

Given the challenges and disappointments involved in adopting a humanistic pedagogical approach to his teaching, Chong (2018) wistfully asked whether it was all worthwhile. The answer to that question would be a tentative "yes"—if the seven principles articulated earlier in this chapter are applied compassionately, comprehensively and consistently—positive results are possible (though not guaranteed). For example, enrolment figures, commencement statistics, course retention numbers and student feedback were—over a period of five years (from 2011 to 2015)—very positive indeed (Chong, 2018, pp. 24–25). More importantly, students expressed how cared for, and valued, they felt while studying at university, and that this had led to their decisions to study harder as well as to remain at university despite their personal problems that involved financial difficulties, familial conflicts, mental health issues, intimate partner relationship problems, medical ailments, employment/unemployment challenges and so on (Chong, 2018, pp. 15–18, 25).

The challenges, however, of implementing a humanistic pedagogy at tertiary-level institutions are manifold. As Aloni (2011) lamented:

> [i]t is a pity, ..., that the popularity of the values and tenets of humanistic education has failed to be translated and put to work in the real life of educational practice and schools' characteristics. (p. 45)

That, however, should not discourage academics and educators from seeking meaningful ways of infusing humanist values into their teaching, given how subsequent/resulting levels of student wellbeing and mental health have improved. Although this may well be a daunting endeavour to undertake, Aloni (2011) has provided us with a range of prescriptions to guide us in this regard, including, for example, the need to

(i) challenge our current perceptions and/or expectations of teachers to be merely "passive conduits" of educational messages to that of being "active shapers" of such knowledge (p. 36);
(ii) encourage our teachers to develop and strengthen their pedagogical presence (in line, of course, with their "new" professional image or identity of being "active shapers"), that is based on interpersonal trust, cultural idealism and a "practise what you preach" type of personality (p. 36);
(iii) promote a humanistic and democratic culture through educational policies that are premised on a/an: intellectual open-mindedness that is reasonable, logical, critical and empirically based; moral platform that is egalitarian, socially just/fair, respectful and considerate of others; active form of democratic citizenship that prioritises social responsibility and political involvement that is pluralistic, tolerant of differences and self-restrained; cultural richness; as well as being a "world citizen" (pp. 39–41) and
(iv) develop a humanistic school culture through a multifaceted cultivation of student personality; engendering a social climate of security and fairness; enriching instruction through the use of empowering dialogues (Socratic, Nietzschean, and so forth); adopting a communitarian approach and encouraging social involvement; providing students with a strong foundation in general education and cultural context; ensuring that students understand that education is supposed to be employed as a tool that can help them to self-actualise and their communities to flourish and finally
(v) to build and design educational/school infrastructure that not only facilitates safety but is also beautiful and welcoming (pp. 41–45).

Although there appears to be much work to be done, Aloni (2011) hoped that his detailed recommendations would provide us with sufficient signposts to translate humanistic pedagogies "from [simply being] a worthy and promising theory to a desirable and rewarding practice" (p. 45). For the sake of our students' wellbeing, it is likewise the hope of the authors that this chapter will provide educators, academics and university administrators with ideas, frameworks, principles and inspiration, to do the same.

References

Aloni, N. (2011). Humanistic education: From theory to practice. In W. Veugelers (Ed.), *Education and humanism: Linking autonomy and humanity* (pp. 35–46). Sense Publishers.

Aloni, N. (2014). Humanistic education. *Encyclopaedia of educational philosophy and theory*. Retrieved from http://www.mofet.macam.ac.il/prof/dialog/Documents/aloni%20ency%20humanism.pdf

Association for Humanistic Education and Development. (1982). *A position paper on humanistic education*. AHED.

Averill, R. M., & Major, J. (2020). What motivates higher education educators to innovate? Exploring competence, autonomy, and relatedness—and connections with wellbeing. *Educational Research, 62*(2), 146–161.

Baik, C., Larcombe, W., & Brooker, A. (2019). How universities can enhance student mental wellbeing: The student perspective. *Higher Education Research & Development, 38*(4), 674–687.

Barnes, J. (2020, 3 July). Defunding arts degrees is the latest battle in a 40-year culture war. *The Conversation*. Retrieved from https://theconversation.com/defunding-arts-degrees-is-the-latest-battle-in-a-40-year-culture-war-141689

Bennegadi, R., & Cyrulnik, B. (2020). Impact COVID-19 and mental health. *World Social Psychiatry, 2*(2), 115–119.

Blatt, B., Plack, M. M., & Simmens, S. J. (2018). Preparing interprofessional faculty to be humanistic mentors for medical students: The GW-Gold mentor development program. *Journal of Continuing Education in the Health Professions, 38*(2), 117–125.

Bovill, C., Cook-Sather, A., Felten, P., Millard, L., & Moore-Cherry, N. (2016). Addressing potential challenges in co-creating learning and teaching: Overcoming resistance, navigating institutional norms and ensuring inclusivity in student–staff partnerships. *Higher Education, 71*, 195–208.

Brumfit, C. J. (1984). *Communicative methodology in language teaching: The roles of fluency and accuracy*. Cambridge University Press.

Cheruvalath, R. (2017). Need for a shift from a philanthropic to humanistic approach to corporate social responsibility. *Annals of Public and Cooperative Economics, 88*(1), 121–136.

Chong, M. D. (2018). Humanistic education for the future 'crime fighters.' *International Journal of Criminal Justice Sciences, 13*(1), 10–28.

Cicciarelli, M. S. (2007). Behavioral, cognitive, and humanistic theories: Which theories do online instructors utilize. *International Journal of Information and Communication Technology Education, 3*(4), 1–12.

Cohen, J. J. (2007). Viewpoint. Linking professionalism to humanism: What it means, why it matters. *Academic Medicine, 82*(11), 1029–1032.

Combs, A. W. (1988). New assumptions for educational reform. *Educational Leadership, 45*(5), 38–40.

Combs, A. W. (1966). Teacher education - A problem in becoming. In E. B. Smith, H. C. Olsen, P. J. Johnson, & C. Barbour (Eds.), *Partnership in teacher education* (pp. 211–227). American Association of Colleges for Teacher Education, The Association for Student Teaching.

Combs, A. W. (1961). What can we become? *California Journal of Instructional Improvement, 4*(4), 15–23.

Cook-Sather, A., Bahti, M., & Ntem, A. (2019). *Pedagogical partnership: A how-to guide for faculty, students, and academic developers*. Elon University Center for Engaged Learning.

DeCarvalho, R. J. (1991). The humanistic paradigm in education. *The Humanistic Psychologist, 19*(1), 88–104.

Fincham, R. (2011). Humanistic values in German idealism. In C. Dierksmeier, W. Amann, E. von Kimakowitz, H. Spitzeck, & M. Pirson (Eds.), *Humanistic ethics in the age of globality*. Palgrave MacMillan.

Garbett, D., & Thomas, L. (2020). Developing inter-collegial friendships to sustain professional wellbeing in the academy. *Teachers and Teaching, 26*(3–4), 295–306.

Hanley, T., Winter, L. A., & Burrell, K. (2020). Supporting emotional well-being in schools in the context of austerity: An ecologically informed humanistic perspective. *British Journal of Educational Psychology, 90*, 1–18.

Hill, J., Healey, R. L., West, H., & Déry, C. (2021). Pedagogic partnership in higher education: Encountering emotion in learning and enhancing student wellbeing. *Journal of Geography in Higher Education, 45*(2), 167–185.

Javadi, Y., & Tahamsbi, M. (2020). Application of humanism teaching theory and humanistic approach to education in course-books. *Theory and Practice in Language Studies, 10*(1), 40–48.

Jones, E., Priestley, M., Brewster, L., Wilbraham, S. J., Hughes, G., & Spanner, L. (2021). Student wellbeing and assessment in higher education: The balancing act. *Assessment & Evaluation in Higher Education, 46*(3), 438–450.

Maslow, A. H. (1954). The instinctoid nature of basic needs. *Journal of Personality, 22*(326), 347.

Moustakas, C. (1966). *The authentic teacher: Sensitivity and awareness in the classroom*. Howard A. Doyle Publication.

Nandy, M., Lodh, S., & Tang, A. (2021). Lessons from Covid-19 and resilience model for higher education. *Industry & Higher Education, 35*(1), 3–9.

Pomerantz, N. K. (2006). Student engagement: A new paradigm for student affairs. *College Student Affairs Journal, 25*(2), 176–185.

Popovych, M., Levkulych, V., Khodanych, Y., & Popovych, T. (2021). Introducing the concepts and methods of humanism into education for ensuring quality sustainable development. *E3S Web of Conferences, 277*, 1–10.

Pring, R. (2010). The philosophy of education and educational practice. In R. Bailey, R. Barrow, D. Carr, & C. McCarthy (Eds.), *The SAGE handbook of philosophy of education* (pp. 55–66). Sage.

Rockwell, D. (2012). Humanizing mental health: Existentialism and the DSM-5: Can humanistic psychology light the way? *The Humanistic Psychologist, 40*(2), 207–211.

Rogers, C. R. (1969). *Freedom to learn*. Charles E. Merrill Publishing.

Rousseau, J.-J. (1762/1921). *Emile, or education* (Translated by Barbara Foxley, M. A.). J. M. Dent and Sons. Retrieved from: http://oll.libertyfund.org/titles/2256

Rüsen, J. (2021). *Humanism: Foundations, diversities, developments*. Routledge.

Sage, S. M., Adcock, S. S., & Dixon, A. L. (2012). Why humanistic teacher education still matters. *Action in Teacher Education, 34*(3), 204–220.

Sandeen, A., & Barr, M. (2006). *Critical issues for student affairs: Challenges and opportunities*. Jossey-Bass.

Sarem, S. N., & Hamidi, H. (2013). Humanistic education: Concerns, implications and applications. *Journal of Language Teaching & Research, 4*(1), 45–51.

Sawczak, K. (2020, 31 July). Funding changes endanger humanities and the social sciences. *The Weekend Australian* (online). Retrieved from: https://www.theaustralian.com.au/higher-education/funding-changes-endanger-humanities-and-the-social-sciences/news-story/45ee117d7e2c3549c3d857767d4477b3

Shafiq, H. M., Rafiq, M., & Mahmood, Z. (2019). Humanism and mental health of married female patients with systemic lupus erythematosus. *Pakistan Journal of Neurological Sciences, 14*(2), 34–39.

Tamrat, S. (2020). Re-thinking humanism as a guiding philosophy for education: A critical reflection on Ethiopian higher education institutions. *International Journal of Ethics Education, 5*, 187–195.

Tangney, S. (2014). Student-centred learning: A humanist perspective. *Teaching in Higher Education, 19*(3), 266–275.

Vibert, A. B., & Shields, C. (2003). Approaches to student engagement: Does ideology matter? *McGill Journal of Education, 38*(2), 221–240.

Victorian Auditor-General. (2010). *The effectiveness of student wellbeing programs and services*. Retrieved from: https://www.parliament.vic.gov.au/papers/govpub/VPARL2006-10No270.pdf

World Health Organization. (2001). *Strengthening mental health promotion* (Fact Sheet No.220). World Health Organization.

Mark David Chong is currently a Senior Lecturer in Criminology and Criminal Justice Studies. He was formerly the Director of Research Education at the School of Arts and Social Sciences, James Cook University, from 2012 to January 2015, and Acting Associate Dean of Research at the College of Arts, Society and Education, James Cook University, from July 2019 to September 2019 (3 months). He is also an External Assessor (grant applications) for the Social Sciences and Humanities Research Council of Canada. He graduated with a PhD in Law from the University of Sydney, where he received his Law School's Longworth Scholarship (2003), the Cooke, Cooke, Coghlan, Godfrey and Littlejohn Scholarship (2004), the Longworth Scholarship for Academic Merit (2006) and the Longworth Scholarship once again in 2007. He was initially trained as a criminal defence lawyer and later secured an LLM (Merit) in Criminology and Criminal Justice from Queen Mary, University of London.

Abraham P. Francis is an Associate Professor and currently the Head of Academic Group in Social Work and Human Services at James Cook University, Australia. He has worked with government, non-government and corporate sector and has developed many international partnerships. He taught social work at the Delhi University in India and worked as a senior mental health social worker with Country Health South Australia before moving to Townsville to join James Cook University. Dr. Francis has established many international partnerships and research collaborations with universities and non-government organisations.

He has extensively contributed to the literature on social work practice in mental health through his publications, convening conferences, establishing research networks and by developing consortiums. His other research interests are in the field of communities, criminal justice, international social work and gerontological social work. His excellence in teaching has been recognised on a number of occasions. For example, in 2010, he was a recipient of James Cook University's Inclusive Practice Award for his 'exceptional support for students with a disability'. In 2016, he received the university's '***Citation for Outstanding Contributions to Student Learning***' for his 'leadership and expertise in social work education in mental health that inspires and nurtures students to be competent, confident and compassionate practitioners'.

Dr. Francis was one of the finalists at the 2018 India ***Australia Business and Community Awards*** in the category of Community Services Excellence Award and Business Leader/Professional of the Year. In 2018, Dr. Francis received the NAPSWI (National Association of Professional Association Social Workers in India) Life Time Achievement Award for his outstanding contribution to social work education.

For more details—https://research.jcu.edu.au/portfolio/abraham.francis/.

Margaret Anne Carter's career in higher education, both in Singapore and in Australia, includes teaching, academic leadership, community service and research. In 2017, Margaret Anne was awarded the National Citation for Outstanding Contribution to Student Learning. Her strong research interests provide a solid foundation for the integration of expert theory and quality practice to promote academic excellence and high levels of student engagement, productivity and wellbeing. Contributing to a sense of social consciousness, Margaret Anne's research continues to generate new knowledge and insight to enhance student learning and experiences. Margaret Anne publishes in areas including teaching and learning in higher education, resilience, mental health and wellbeing, preventing cyber bullying, young children's social behaviour and character education in early childhood.

Frank Darkwa Baffour holds a Bachelor of Arts degree in Social Work, a Master of Philosophy degree in Social Work and a Ph.D. in Criminal Justice and Social Work. He is currently working as a casual academic in the Department of Social Work, James Cook University. As a Researcher, he employs critical theory, anti-oppressive practice and behavioural theories to understand crime, recidivism, intimate partner violence, offender treatment and rehabilitation, and higher education mental wellbeing. He received prestigious awards such as the James Cook University Excellence Doctoral Research Thesis Medal and passed his Ph.D. thesis with cum laude (rated within the top 5% of Ph.D. candidates worldwide). His work has been published in high-profile peer-reviewed journals such as the Journal of Interpersonal Violence, Victims and Offenders, Marriage and Family Review, to name a few.

Student Support in Rural Medical Education: What Does Evidence-Based Practice Look Like?

Anna Kokavec, Jane Harte, and Simone Ross

Abstract Every year, a small number of medical students will 'fail to thrive' (for several reasons) and need to repeat the year. The high cost of failure is a very strong motivator for medical schools to do everything possible to identify and support at-risk students (both academically and mentally). However, the challenge rests with knowing the best approach to take and making sure it is affordable, easily accessible, and valued by students. Evidence contained in the medical education literature highlights the importance of being able to identify students at risk of failure as early as possible. Once supports are in place, it is also important to make sure that the student is monitored for several months to ensure the intervention is working. Most medical schools, when questioned, claim to provide student support in one form or another. However, what this support looks like and whether the approach is even effective are often difficult to determine and even harder to evaluate. The aim of this chapter is to provide an overview of how student support can be provided to medical students by using the James Cook University medicine student risk management model as an example.

Keywords Rural medical education · Medical students · Evidence · Risk management

Introduction

Being accepted into a medical course in Australia and elsewhere is a highly competitive process (Groves et al., 2007; Parry et al., 2006; Wilkinson et al., 2008). Most medical schools receive more applications that can be accommodated in the medical

A. Kokavec (✉) · J. Harte · S. Ross
James Cook University, Townsville, Australia
e-mail: anna.kokavec@jcu.edu.au

J. Harte
e-mail: jane.harte@jcu.edu.au

S. Ross
e-mail: simone.ross@jcu.edu.au

A. P. Francis and M. A. Carter (eds.), *Mental Health and Higher Education in Australia*,
https://doi.org/10.1007/978-981-16-8040-3_7

program, which also means that medical schools can pick and choose who they let into their course (Laurence et al., 2010). There is general agreement that a high-tertiary entry score or grade point average is a valid predictor of success (Harris & Owen, 2007). However, it has been argued that competence as a medical practitioner and academic achievement in a medical school is dependent on more than just academic ability (Glick, 2000).

A structured interview almost always forms part of a medical program's selection process, the goal being to only select strong applicants who are most likely to successfully complete the course (Powis et al., 1988). Panel members are also on the lookout for students who may have been pressured into applying for medicine by parents or some other well-meaning relative (Yates, 2011). However, some claim that 'guesswork' is a large part of the selection process. After all, trying to predict future professional performance by using data collected up to a decade earlier is virtually impossible (Glick, 2000).

Risk of Academic Failure

Every year, a small number of students will 'fail to thrive' and need to repeat the year. Previous research has found that between 10 and 15% of medical students will struggle during their medical training (Yates & James, 2006). The risk of academic failure is higher during the first year of medical training when compared to subsequent years. However, the potential for failure exists at all stages of the medical training program (Yates, 2011).

Study success is often dependent on what else is going on in the student's life (Yates & James, 2006). Many medical students have sporadic difficulties, and when things become too hard to manage, the risk of academic failure is higher, particularly if they do not seek support (Malau-Aduli et al., 2020). Successful completion at any year level can be impacted when students experience: family difficulties, grief and loss, conflict with others; have a history of physical illness, mental illness, or disability; have poor social skills or low emotional intelligence; and lack life experience (Yates, 2011).

The High Cost of Failure

Failure is often accompanied by a very high personal cost that is borne (often in silence) by the student (Yates, 2011). The high academic entry requirements make getting into medical school a dream that only a few will ever experience (Laurence et al., 2010). A large proportion of medical students may have no prior experience of academic failure. Indeed, for many, their experience prior to getting into medical school would have been entirely the opposite, with most being top of their class and used to praise for achieving study excellence (Yates, 2011). Failing on its own can create a high degree of personal distress. However, when failing is coupled with financial hardship due to needing to repeat a year, shame of family finding out about the failure, and the stigma of being labeled a failure, the distress felt can be grossly amplified (Yates & James, 2009).

At the organizational level, every failure has some impact on university resources. Students who are struggling can place an increased load on resources that may already be under-staffed. For example, students who are struggling require a disproportionate amount of time to be spent on arranging meetings, organizing remediation, rescheduling examinations and practical assessments, and providing other forms of support. In some cases, time may also need to be spent arranging suitability to practice panels or assessing appeals against exclusion (Yates & James, 2009). The increased risk of litigation and antidiscrimination law makes it very difficult to exclude a student, and usually, course exclusion only occurs after repeated course failures, breaches in student agreements and other fit for practice criteria, all of which require several years of monitoring and support (Papadakis et al., 2004, 2005; Yates & James, 2009).

Whenever a student drops out of any course there is also a community cost. Most university places in Australia are subsidized by the Australian Government, while other medicine places only exist due to funding provided by private or public scholarships. Patient safety can also be impacted. For example, research has revealed an association between academic achievement and professional skills with academically at-risk students often failing later in their professional life (Papadakis et al., 2005; Yates & James, 2009).

What Does Support for Medical Students Look Like?

The high cost of failure is a very strong motivator for universities to do everything possible to ensure students can achieve to potential. However, academic success, even in very high achieving students, is never guaranteed. Most medical schools, when questioned, claim to provide academic support to their medical students (in one form or another). However, what this looks like is often difficult to determine and even harder to evaluate (Saks & Karl, 2004).

Data collected in the US in the early 2000's revealed that most medical schools (at the time) offered voluntary intervention programs with senior students often working alongside student support faculty members to provide interventions tailored to meet a student's needs (Saks & Karl, 2004). Other forms of support identified involve the provision of study skills workshops, so new students can develop appropriate note taking and examination preparation skills (Flavell, 1979; Mevarech & Amrany, 2008).

A key problem with voluntary programs, especially when there are already high demands being placed on students, is that the at-risk students often do not view them as a priority. Regardless of how many student messages are sent by faculty members, it is not unusual for the academically at-risk students to ignore offers of help (Cleland et al., 2005).

Medical students are not used to failing or asking for help; they are used to achieving and being the top of their class. Even the academically at-risk students think that if they work hard enough, they are going to get there, often overestimating their ability, the amount of effort, and depth of knowledge required (Cleland et al., 2008).

More recently, an integrated, school-wide model that comprises both behavioral and academic support has been proposed. The four-tier continuum of academic and behavioral support model focuses on early intervention and aims to maximize student engagement and performance by providing adequate instruction, small-group interventions, individualized support, and exit support (Stegers-Jager et al., 2017).

Mental Health

When a student first applies to enter a medical course, the rate of emotional disturbance is similar to what would be expected in the general population (Smith et al., 2007). However, when medical students are questioned about their mental health during medical training, the level of distress, depression, and anxiety is reportedly higher than the general population (Compton et al., 2008; Dyrbye et al., 2006; Firth, 1986). An early longitudinal study that investigated psychological distress in first year medical students ($N = 312$) found that the level of anxiety was approximately one SD above the mean when compared with nonpatient levels. Moreover, the percentage of students who reported symptoms of depression doubled as the study period progressed (Vitaliano et al., 1989).

Studies conducted in the U.S. in the early 2000's revealed that almost 49% of medical students experienced depressive symptoms (Dyrbye et al., 2007). Similarly, the level of distress experienced by Australian medical students was estimated to be four times higher than what would be expected in the general population (Leahy et al., 2010). The mental health of medical students continues to be a concern with recent data suggesting the rate of depression and anxiety and burnout in medical students could be as high as 27% and 50%, respectively (Dyrbye & Shanafelt, 2016; Rotenstein et al., 2016).

Upward of 24% of medical students may meet the criteria for depressive illness (Rotenstein et al., 2016). As a result, considerable effort has been put into developing educational interventions that bolster resilience and mindfulness (Daya & Hearn, 2018; Dobkin & Hutchinson, 2013; Farquhar et al., 2018; McAllister & McKinnon, 2009; Tempski et al., 2012). However, while these factors are known to be associated with well-being (Dyrbye et al., 2006; Ishak et al., 2013), a recent systematic review found there is little evidence to support the conclusion that these wellness interventions are helping medical students stay mentally well (Wasson et al., 2016).

Many medical schools have implemented wellness programs and stress reduction activities. However, these current efforts may overlook underlying cognitive distortions that students have about academic performance which can contribute to emotional distress. Medical students often achieve high scores on perfectionism dimensions (Enns et al., 2001), and a significant positive correlation has been noted between perfectionism and the level of distress in medical students (Henning et al., 1998). Additionally, a large proportion of medical students also doubt their abilities, feel like a fraud, and find it difficult to accept their accomplishment, a condition known as 'imposter phenomenon' or 'imposter syndrome' (Gottlieb et al., 2020).

A significant association has been noted between dysfunctional thought patterns linked to perfectionism and impostor phenomenon, and feelings of shame, embarrassment, and inadequacy. The standards medical students set for themselves are often unrealistic, and there is a tendency to compare themselves to others, which leads to even greater feelings of inadequacy. This creates a negative cycle whereby negative thoughts create negative feelings, which in turn result in medical students experiencing a higher rate of depression and anxiety (Hu et al., 2019).

The challenge for any medical school is to be able to support its students in a way that is affordable, easily accessible, valued by students, and effective in meeting its goal of supporting students who (for a range of factors) are at risk of failure. The aim of this chapter is to discuss how this can be achieved by using the James Cook University medicine student risk management model as an example.

James Cook University Medicine Student Risk Management Model

James Cook University (JCU), located in regional Queensland, Australia, offers a six-year undergraduate Bachelor of Medicine and Bachelor of Surgery course (MBBS). The unique nature of the JCU medicine course is that it is focused on rural, remote, indigenous, and tropical health with the view to produce medical practitioners who are trained and prepared for working in these areas of need (Malau-Aduli et al., 2017; Woolley et al., 2021).

The MBBS is divided into two distinct parts, MBBS1-3 is referred to as the 'foundation' years and MBBS4-6 as being the 'clinical' years. MBBS1-3 is very similar to many university science degrees, except with numerous health system science subjects, extensive clinical skills training, and the requirement that students are to undertake some placement during each year.

Due to the age at which students leave high school in Queensland, new recruits into the JCU MBBS can be as young as 17 years old. All students commence their training at the main Townsville campus (MBBS1-3) and then are asked to choose whether they want to stay in Townsville or move to the Cairns campus (MBBS4-6). At the end of MBBS-4, students can opt to move to the Mackay campus (MBBS5-6). Many students take up the offer of moving campuses largely because of the learning and placement opportunities this presents.

Regional, Rural, and Remote Students

According to Harding and Wilson (2008), medical students are more likely to succeed in their first year if they are encouraged to invest time on task, regularly attend class lectures and tutorials, balance their commitments, develop a social network, have a clear reason or goal for attending university, engage with the online environment, and have some measure of academic self-confidence. Conversely, medical students may be at higher risk of dropping out if they do not meet the above criteria, in addition to being the first in their family to attend university and/or are a member of a minority or disadvantaged group.

The rate of access, participation, retention, and success for regional and remote students (RRR) when compared to their urban counterparts is lower, and this trend has been evident for several years. An independent review into regional, rural, and remote education was commissioned by the Australian Government in 2017 as a way of trying to identify what could be done to ensure students who do not reside in large cities can achieve to their full potential. Accommodation was identified as a key factor, which makes sense given that many RRR are forced to move away from home to study (Hasley, 2018).

The selection process for incoming students focuses on identifying students who prefer working in rural and remote areas (Sen Gupta et al., 2012; Woolley & Ray, 2019). Because of this, more than 80% of our incoming MBBS students move away from home to attend JCU. For RRR students, the prospect of relocating, living in a high-cost locality, and moving away from family can be a daunting experience. A RRR student is more likely to be the first in family to attend university, and the pressure to succeed is often quite high. Many have moved from a small community where everyone knows everyone else and losing that sense of belonging and the feelings this creates can be difficult to manage. Many RRR students experience homesickness and feelings of loneliness severe enough to need to access counseling services (Matthews et al., 2018).

Managing At-Risk Students

The evidence suggests that medical students can fail at any stage of their medical training (Yates, 2011), and students who come from RRR areas may be at even greater risk of course failure (Matthews et al., 2018). This highlights the importance of making sure that student achievement across all years of the medical program is monitored, at-risk students can be easily identified, and vulnerable students who need support are referred to the appropriate services. Figure 1 provides an overview of the JCU MBBS Student Management Risk Model.

From Fig. 1, we can see that the student support, course support, and learning support areas are all well placed to provide advice on how to access a range of support

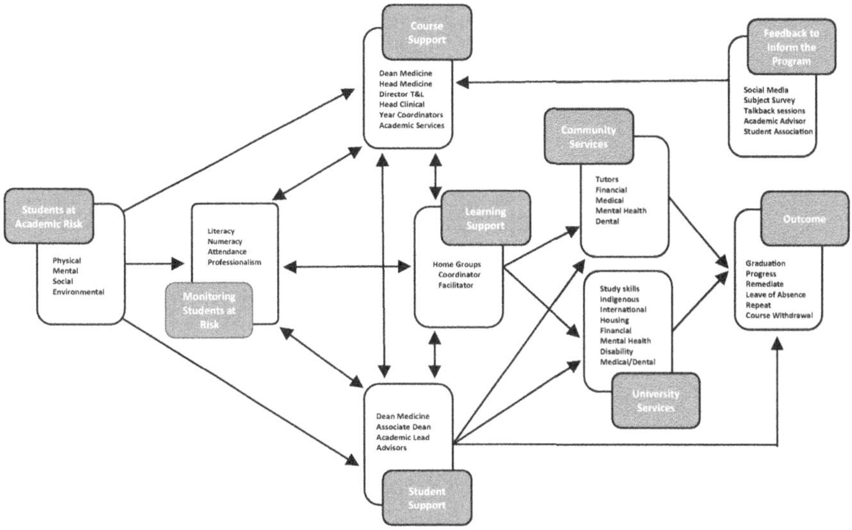

Fig. 1 James Cook University medicine student risk management model. Arrows indicate communication pathways for provision of student support

services. It is not unusual for students who need support to be referred to university-wide services (e.g., JCU Counseling, JCU Health, JCU Dental, JCU Access*ibility*, JCU Student Association (JCUSA), JCU Medical Student Association (JCUMSA), JCU Learning center, and JCU Indigenous Education and Research Center). Moreover, students can also be directed to community-based services, especially if university services are overwhelmed and experiencing unusually long wait-times, which often occurs during the examination period.

However, promoting academic success is not just about referring students to external support services. After all, how do we know that a student even needs a referral? Embedded into the JCU MBBS course are mechanisms that help to identify students who may be struggling both academically and psychologically at all year levels. However, due to space restrictions only an outline of support mechanisms currently in place for JCU medical students enrolled in the foundation years will be provided in the next few sections.

MBBS Home Group Program

One way that we assist our students to build early connections, friendships and achieve academic success is participation in the Home Group Program. The JCU Home Group Program (HGP) focuses on near-peer teaching from senior students to junior, in small groups of eight to ten students (Cate & Durning, 2007; Bene & Bergus, 2014). In 2015, the HGP was awarded a JCU Citation for Outstanding Contribution

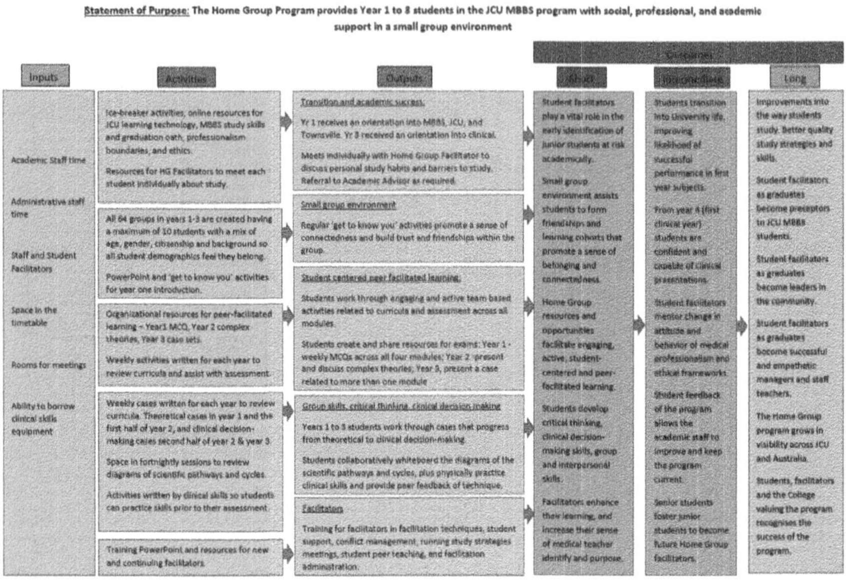

Fig. 2 Program logic model of the Bachelor of Medicine Bachelor of Surgery Home Group Program

to Student Learning, for being a unique program to foster student connectedness, academic engagement, and success in a regional medicine undergraduate program.

The HGP is a compulsory program for MBBS1-3 students providing social, professional, and academic support in small groups (see Fig. 2 for the Home Group Program Logic Model). Each group is facilitated by an academic staff member and/or a senior student who is required to be two MBBS years in advance of the students they are working with.

Home Group Program Design

The HGP has three values and five goals. The values are simply educational, supportive, and fun, whereas the goals are:

Goal 1: Facilitate transition to university life, improving likelihood of successful performance in first-year subjects.

Goal 2: Provide students with a small-group environment to assist them to form friendships and learning cohorts that promote a sense of belonging and connectedness.

Goal 3: Provide resources and opportunities to facilitate engaging, active, student-centered, and peer-facilitated learning.

Goal 4: Provide students to develop critical thinking, clinical decision-making skills, group, and interpersonal skills.

Goal 5: Provide opportunities for facilitators to enhance their learning and increase their sense of medical teacher identity and purpose.

The first half of the program in the first year, 13-week study period, is a social and regional orientation to their fellow students, MBBS, JCU, and Townsville. Content in the program closely follows the MBBS program, so the small-group environment allows the students to talk through their learning, while aiding them in developing friendships and learning cohorts.

Early in each study period, every first- and second-year student meets with their facilitator in an individual meeting to review their first assignment. This assignment focuses on their study skills and the development of a learning and life plan. During this meeting, if required, students are also offered referral to the Academic Advisor. This means that the near-peer facilitators play a vital role in the early identification of students at risk academically.

Two types of peer teaching are provided. First is the near-peer teaching from senior student facilitator to junior students. The second is the peer teaching from student-to-student within the educational design of the program. The first-year students write one multiple choice question (MCQ) each week for a mini-quiz which assists them to engage in collaborative learning and problem solving, with the question writer required to explain the answer, which encourages higher-order thinking skills (Grainger et al., 2018). In the evaluation of the program, more than 80% of first-year students advice that they use their peer created and facilitated MCQ questions as a study resource in preparation for exams.

Second-year students present concepts they are struggling with, and third year students present a short patient case study, all of which encourage self-reflection, verbal presentation skills, and problem-solving skills. Third year students, who will be in the clinical years in the following year, are practicing to present cases to clinicians.

The development of critical thinking and clinical decision-making skills, group and interpersonal skills is essential. In all years, cases are linked directly to topics taught in the subject modules. In first year, they receive theoretical cases. In second year, these progress over time to clinical decision-making cases. In third year, all cases involve clinical decision-making. Regarding the cases, two versions are provided: a student version and a facilitator version with answers and relevant Web sites. Further, all groups are provided the opportunity to borrow clinical skills equipment to practice these skills after they have been learned in class with the clinical skills lecturer.

For facilitators, there is clear and specific training in how to present and facilitate the cases and peer-learning for quality group work. Using a four-point Likert scale (1 = not satisfactory, 2 = satisfactory, 3 = good, 4 = very good), the first-year students across both study periods of 2019 ($n = 342$, 85%) ranked facilitators *group management skills*, and *enabling the group to share knowledge and teach each other* at a mean of 3.71 and 3.73, respectively. Regarding transition to university, students recognize their near-peer facilitators as key to easing their transition (Malau-Aduli et al., 2021).

Both values of 'educational' and 'supportive,' are easily identified in the discussion above regarding the program. The value of 'fun,' however, is viewed easily as part of the informal format of the weekly group meetings. Each group is encouraged to bring food for social enjoyment, short weekly icebreakers are recommended, plus celebration of students' lives is encouraged (e.g., birthdays, driver's license) *with* cake!

Building Resilience

The evidence suggests that medical students who experience depressive symptoms often do not seek support. For example, it has previously been reported that the usual way for a medical student to deal with mood disturbance is to brush it aside, pretend it is not happening, and try to push through the problem (Chew-Graham et al., 2003). Unfortunately, this type of approach often leads to mood symptoms worsening, which has an impact on grades, class attendance, and self-esteem (Storrie et al., 2010).

Studies have shown that mental health and resilience can be improved by providing medical students with learning that focuses on building resilience and self-care. Moreover, early intervention that allows first-year medical students to develop positive coping strategies is claimed to be key to promoting well-being (Shapiro, 2000).

Health Professional Self-care Program

The Health Professional Self-care Program (HPSC) is an 8-week mindfulness and self-care program specifically designed to support first-year students. The HPSC was introduced as a way of helping new students transition from high school to studying medicine at university. The program's aim is to decrease distress of first-year students throughout their transition, while teaching them positive coping mechanisms and stress-relieving techniques.

The HPSC program started in 2016 and balances the exploration of the research underpinning well-being frameworks, such as neuroscience and psychology, while also delivering practical exercises. Practical techniques include stress management, single pointed focus, open awareness, and body scanning. Since its inception, the HPSC has been evaluated. Successes of the program for first-year medical students include reduced study-related stress, reduced exam-related stress, and development of effective coping skills (Ross et al., 2020).

MBBS Student Support

The Associate Dean of Students (ADS) is responsible for overseeing the MBBS student support area. The MBBS program is delivered at several locations within North Queensland, so out of necessity, the college has a team of academic advisors who work collaboratively to ensure MBBS students are supported.

The ADS role, which reports directly to the Medical Dean, is largely responsible for all matters relating to student suitability and well-being. The ADS role is supported by the Academic Lead Student Support (ALSS), who works closely with the ADS, providing administration support and acting as a proxy for the ADS within the college, as required. However, most of the pastoral care and student support assessment is the responsibility of the Academic Advisor.

Members of the Academic Advisor team, headed by the ADS, work collaboratively to ensure students across the entire six-year program are supported. It is not unusual for the ALSS to discuss student needs with the ADS and in very complex cases with other academic advisors. However, personal information relating to a student's family, physical, or mental health is never shared with educators responsible for teaching and assessment in the MBBS program.

What is an Academic Advisor?

The main role of Academic Advisors (AA) in the medical program is to assist students with course planning, electives, remediation, and progression. Students are allocated an AA for each year of their course. The AAs are primarily academic staff who may or may not have academic duties. However, academic duties undertaken by an AA is not related to the year or years for which they act as an advisor.

The role of the AA has expanded over the years in relation to variation in the needs of MBBS students. As a result, the role of the AA in the MBBS largely depends on the years for which the AA is responsible. However, in broad terms, the AA role may include:

- Working within a community of advisers.
- Working with students who may have academic and/or personal support requirements.
- Working with students to address absenteeism and other aspects of professionalism.
- Supporting academic coordinators and professional staff with respect to any student concerns.
- Advising the MBBS Course Coordinator on assessment decisions.

Pastoral Care

When a student reports experiencing personal difficulties, they are usually referred to the AA for assessment and support. Meeting with students who have personal issues (including health and welfare) forms a large part of the AA role. However, while the AA provides pastoral care, the MBBS student support area does not provide a counseling or medical service. If students require the services of a health professional, the AA will usually direct students to the appropriate health service that best meets their needs.

Student Contracts

All students who are returning from a leave of absence (LOA) or are repeating a year are required to meet with the AA several times during the year. The purpose of the meeting is to discuss any academic or personal issues that could potentially impact progress and put in place strategies to ensure success in the current year. As part of the remediation plan, all students are required to sign a student contract, which clearly outlines the expectations of the medical college.

Student Attendance

Student attendance is monitored closely in both study periods across all year levels. Attendance is known to be an indicator of unprofessional behavior and lack of coping (Papadakis et al., 2005; Rogers & Ballantyne, 2010). Electronic sign-in is required for mandatory on-campus sessions. Any student with an excessive number of unexplained absences is referred to the AA who will aim to identify the cause and develop a remediation plan. A weekly attendance report is sent to the Year-level Coordinator, AA, and members of the academic services team, which allows students at risk of failing to be easily identified and interventions put in place to support vulnerable students.

Identifying Students at Risk of Failing

The MBBS has several mandatory activities that have been specifically designed to identify students at risk of failing. All students who are identified as needing support are directed toward appropriate self-help resources. Support can range from provision of academic support strategies (literacy, numeracy, and study technique support) through to more specific support for individual assessment activities and/or subject materials. For example,

- Mandatory in-course quizzes are scheduled in weeks 5 and 10 of each study period in order to provide MBBS1-3 students with some indication of how they are tracking. Any student who scores below 70% is contacted by the Year-level Coordinator and given another opportunity to submit.
- All MBBS-1 students are required to complete the post-entry English language assessment task (PELA) in study period 1. The PELA is completed as part of a joint collaboration between the JCU Learning Center and Medical School and involves students completing a hurdle writing assessment task, which is designed to identify students who may require support with academic writing. All students identified as needing literacy support are automatically referred to the JCU Learning Center for assistance.
- MBBS-1 students must also complete a numeracy assessment. However, this is scheduled in the second half of the year. Attendance at a numeracy workshop that (again) is delivered as part of a joint collaboration between the JCU Learning Center and Medical School is a mandatory requirement of the course. During the workshop, MBBS-1 students are advised of the expected numeracy standards for medical students in the first year of their program. All students who do not meet the hurdle requirement (70% grade on the exam) are automatically referred to LTSE for additional support.

There are also several optional academic support activities that are available to support medical students. These activities are designed to promote effective study and coping habits. For example,

- Optional laboratory sessions for general learning session (GLS) activities that require laboratory exposure. This is useful for students who feel rushed during the regular session and may need extra time to integrate the learning. For example, optional laboratory sessions are available for histology and anatomy.
- Optional clinical skills sessions to assist with the development of practical skills.
- Integrative sessions introduce understanding research, peer-review processes, and publication data; library services (including accessing and assessing peer-reviewed publications); generic study skills and exam preparation.
- A journal club is run to allow students to engage in the process of critical review and analysis.

Professionalism and Leadership

The professionalism education and leadership (PEAL) e-portfolio aims to link student's self-reflection of experiences and learning to the MBBS Professionalism and Leadership learning outcomes. The PEAL focuses on the reflective practice of students professional and leadership journey in medicine and provides an avenue for assessors to identify potential students at risk both psychologically and academically. Assessors are encouraged to recommend students to seek advice from the AA when they identify 'at risk' behavior as part of a student's writing.

Individual Learning and Life Plan

In each study period of MBBS1-3, all students are required to create an individual learning and life plan (ILP). The aim of the ILP is to assist students to develop, review, reflect, and adjust study habits. The ILP is an assessment that sits within the PEAL program and is supervised by home group facilitators.

When constructing an ILP, students have an opportunity to request a referral to an AA. Home group facilitators can also recommend a student makes an appointment to see the AA. In this instance, communication between the home group and student support areas is important, and it is not unusual for a home group facilitator or home group coordinator to contact the AA if they are concerned about the well being of a student. The home group facilitator is well positioned to be able to identify students who are struggling, and a referral for extra support can be made to the AA or LTSE directly, as appropriate.

Professionalism Indicator Report

Research data suggests that academic performance and professional conduct are closely related. Moreover, the two unprofessional behaviors in medical students that are highly predictive of disciplinary action following graduation are: (1) severe irresponsibility (e.g., unreliable attendance and/or not following up on assigned tasks); and (2) severely diminished capacity for self-improvement (e.g., failure to accept constructive criticism, argumentativeness, and/or display of poor attitude) (Papadakis et al., 2005; Rogers & Ballantyne, 2010).

In the MBBS, professionalism is partly assessed via the Professionalism Indicator Report (PIR). The introduction of the PIR assessment for MBBS1-4 students is a recent innovation aimed at more easily identifying students who may be at risk of failure (and otherwise). The introduction of the PIR has provided the medical school with a framework for the provision of academic support to ensure there is a plan for students to learn and improve.

The PIR is issued individually to each student in each study period and provides an itemized summary of a suite of professionalism indicators, including attendance, timely submission of assessments, completion of pre-placement requirements (such as a police check, obtaining a blue card, organizing requisite vaccinations, etc.), and interpersonal communication. Data for the PIR is collected by college staff across the study period and provided to students by email at the same time as feedback on exam performance.

The AA is often the first point of contact for course-specific academic staffs who have concerns about a student's professionalism. For example, it is not unusual for an AA to be contacted by the Year-level Coordinator, Home Group Coordinator, or Academic Services team when there are concerns about attendance, interpersonal communication, or assessment submission. Students who (according to the PIR) are deemed to be 'borderline' or 'below expected standard' are referred for remediation to the Year-level Coordinator and AA, respectively.

Student Feedback to Inform the Outcomes

The medical school welcomes student feedback and is motivated to effect positive change by working with students in an open and constructive manner. Several student feedback pathways exist. For example, communication between the JCU Medical Student Association and college staff is promoted by allowing student membership at college committee meetings. Other feedback options include all year student-focused feedback sessions, subject evaluation surveys, lecturer evaluation surveys, and one-on-one communication between students and student support staff.

On-Campus Versus Online?

In 2020, the COVID-19 pandemic resulted in Australian universities shifting to online learning. The MBBS1-3 program in early 2020 was quickly adapted so that medical students enrolled in the foundation years could continue their training. While some students reported finding online learning difficult, there were many students who preferred the flexibility that online learning provided, so much so that when on-campus learning returned in the second half of 2020, many students wanted the online learning to continue.

Moving away from home is known to be a significant risk factor for failure in RRR students, especially in their first year of study (Matthews et al., 2018). The introduction of online learning meant many of our students could return home. After all, if everything was being delivered online, there was no need for students to be away from the support provided by family and friends, living alone or with strangers, and paying rent in Townsville.

Students being allowed to complete their learning online were reflected in the 2019/2020 student success data. A lower number of failures were noted, especially in the first year, compared to the previous year despite the interruption to the first-year university experience and stress of studying during a pandemic. In 2020, only 16 MBBS1-3 students failed the year (MBBS1 = 9, MBBS2 = 3, MBBS3 = 4) compared to the 29 students who failed in 2019 (MBBS1 = 18, MBBS2 = 9, MBBS3 = 2). A slightly lower number of leave of absence applications was also noted in 2020 with a total of 16 students applying to take a leave of absence due to special consideration factors compared to 19 students in the previous year. At JCU, there are approximately 200 students enrolled at each year level and the number of failures recorded represents less than 3% and 5% of the enrolments in 2020 and 2019, respectively.

Conclusions

At JCU, much thought and effort has gone into ensuring our medical students have every opportunity to achieve academic success. There are several student support mechanisms (that do not rely on voluntary participation) embedded into the MBBS program. This allows at-risk medical students to be easily identified, monitored, and managed throughout the year, at all year levels.

The student support model employed by the JCU medical school relies on effective communication between university services staff, academics, and student support staff. Communication between all areas is key to the success of this model because it ensures at-risk students can be identified and directed to appropriate support services as soon as they are needed.

Student support is not just about teaching students how to take good notes, recommending students hire a tutor, or make an appointment to see a counselor. Student support needs to be proactive and able to identify when there is a problem before the problem gets so big, it becomes overwhelming, and results in failure.

It is important that at-risk students can be identified quickly, interventions put in place immediately, and students monitored throughout the year to ensure a student does not fall through the cracks. Lastly, building resilience and promoting self-care are important to ensure students have the tools to be able to deal with the many stressors that are just part and parcel of medical training and, eventually, medical practice.

References

Benè, K. L., & Bergus, G. (2014). When learners become teachers: A review of peer teaching in medical student education. *Family Medicine, 46*, 783–787.

Cate, O. T., & Durning, S. (2007). Peer teaching in medical education: Twelve reasons to move from theory to practice. *Medical Teacher, 29*, 591–599.

Chew-Graham, C. A., Rogers, A., & Yassin, N. (2003). 'I wouldn't want it on my CV or their records': Medical students' experiences of help-seeking for mental health problems. *Medical Education, 37*, 873–880.

Cleland, J., Arnold, R., & Chesser, A. (2005). Failing finals is often a surprise for the student but not the teacher: Identifying difficulties and supporting students with academic difficulties. *Medical Teacher, 27*, 504–508.

Cleland, J., Milne, A., Sinclair, H., & Lee, A. J. (2008). Cohort study on predicting grades: Is performance on early MBChB assessments predictive of later undergraduate grades? *Medical Education, 42*, 676–683.

Compton, M. T., Carrera, J., & Frank, E. (2008). Stress and depressive symptoms/dysphoria among US medical students results from a large, nationally representative survey. *Journal of Nervous and Mental Disease, 196*, 891–897.

Daya, Z., & Hearn, J. H. (2018). Mindfulness interventions in medical education: A systematic review of their impact on medical student stress, depression, fatigue and burnout. *Medical Teacher, 40*, 146–153.

Dobkin, P. L., & Hutchinson, T. A. (2013). Teaching mindfulness in medical school: Where are we now and where are we going? *Medical Education, 47*, 768–779.

Dyrbye, L., & Shanafelt, T. (2016). A narrative review on burnout experienced by medical students and residents. *Medical Education, 50*, 132–149.

Dyrbye, L. N., Thomas, M. R., Eacker, A., Harper, W., Massie, F. S., Jr., Power, D. V., et al. (2007). Race, ethnicity, and medical student well-being in the United States. *Archives of Internal Medicine, 167*, 2103–2109.

Dyrbye, L. N., Thomas, M. R., & Shanafelt, T. D. (2006). Systematic review of depression, anxiety, and other indicators of psychological distress among U.S. and Canadian medical students. *Academic Medicine, 81*, 354–373.

Enns, M. W., Cox, B. J., Sareen, F., & Freeman, P. (2001). Adaptive and maladaptive perfectionism in medical students: A longitudinal investigation. *Medical Education, 35*, 1034–1042.

Farquhar, J. M., Kamei, R. K., & Vidyarthi, A. R. (2018). Strategies for enhancing medical student resilience: Student and faculty member perspectives. *International Journal of Medical Education, 9*, 1–6.

Firth, J. (1986). Levels and sources of stress in medical students. *British Medical Journal Clinical Research Education, 292*, 1177–1180.

Flavell, J. H. (1979). Metacognition and cognitive monitoring: A new area of cognitive—Developmental inquiry. *American Psychologist, 34*, 906–911.

Glick, S. M. (2000). Selection for entry to medicine and specialist training. *Medical Teacher, 22*, 443–447.

Gottlieb, M., Chungm, A., Battaglioli, N., Sebok-Syer, S. S., & Kalantari, A. (2020). Impostor syndrome among physicians and physicians in training: A scoping review. *Medical Education, 54*, 116–124.

Grainger, R., Dai, W., Osborne, E., et al. (2018). Medical students create multiple-choice questions for learning in pathology education: A pilot study. *BMC Medical Education, 18*, 201.

Groves, M. A., Gordon, J., & Ryan, G. (2007). Entry tests for graduate medical programs: Is it time to re-think? *Medical Journal of Australia, 186*, 120–123.

Harding, D. W., & Wilson, I. G. (2008). Medical school selection criteria and the prediction of academic performance. *The Medical Journal of Australia, 189*, 234–235.

Harris, S., & Owen, C. (2007). Discerning quality: Using the multiple mini-interview in student selection for the Australian National University Medical School. *Medical Education, 41*, 234–241.

Hasley, J. (2018). *Independent review into regional, rural and remote education*. Commonwealth of Australia.

Henning, K., Ey, S., & Shaw, D. (1998). Perfectionism, the imposter phenomenon and psychological adjustment in medical, dental, nursing and pharmacy students. *Medical Education, 32*, 456–464.

Hu, K. S., Chibnall, J. T., & Slavin, S. J. (2019). Maladaptive perfectionism, impostorism, and cognitive distortions: Threats to the mental health of pre-clinical medical students. *Academic Psychiatry, 43*, 381–385.

Ishak, W., Nikravesh, R., Lederer, S., Perry, R., Ogunyemi, D., & Bernstein, C. (2013). Burnout in medical students: A systematic review. *The Clinical Teacher, 10*, 242–245.

Laurence, C. O., Turnbull, D. A., Briggs, N. E., & Robinson, J. S. (2010). Applicant characteristics and their influence on success: Results from an analysis of applicants to the University of Adelaide Medical School, 2004–2007. *Medical Jouranal of Australia, 192*, 212–216.

Leahy, C. M., Peterson, R. F., Wilson, I. G., Newbury, J. W., Tonkin, A. L., & Turnbull, D. (2010). Distress levels and self-reported treatment rates for medicine, law, psychology and mechanical engineering tertiary students: Cross-sectional study. *Australian and New Zealand Journal of Psychiatry, 44*, 608–615.

Malau-Aduli, B. S., Adu, M. D., Alele, F., Jones, K., Drovandi, A., Mylrea, M., Sfera, K., Ross, S., & Jennings, E. (2021). Adjusting to university: Perceptions of first-year health professions students. *Public Library of Science ONE, 16*, e0251634.

Malau-Aduli, B. S., O'Connor, T., Ray, R. A., van der Kruk, Y., Bellingan, M., & Teague, P. (2017). Risk factors associated with academic difficulty in an Australian regionally located medical school. *BMC Medical Education, 17*, 266.

Malau-Aduli, B. S., Ray, R. A., O'Connor, T., van der Kruk, Y., Alele, F. O., & Bellingan, M. (2020). Dealing with academic difficulty in medical school: A pilot study. *Education Sciences, 10*, 83.
Matthews, D., Milgate, G., & Clarke, L. (2018). *Assessment of university support services for regional and remote students on transition to university*. Commonwealth Department of Education and Training.
McAllister, M., & McKinnon, J. (2009). The importance of teaching and learning resilience in the health disciplines: A critical review of the literature. *Nurse Education Today, 29*, 371–379.
Mevarech, Z. R., & Amrany, C. (2008). Immediate and delayed effects of meta-cognitive instruction on regulation of cognition and mathematics achievement. *Metacognition and Learning, 3*, 147–157.
Papadakis, M., Hodgson, C., Teherani, A., & Kohatsu, N. (2004). Unprofessional behavior in medical school is associated with subsequent disciplinary action by a State Medical Board. *Academic Medicine, 79*, 244–249.
Papadakis, M., Teherani, A., Banach, M., Knettler, T., Rattner, S., Stern, D., Veloski, J., & Hodgson, C. (2005). Disciplinary action by Medical Boards and prior behaviour in medical school. *New England Journal of Medicine, 353*, 2673–2682.
Parry, J., Mathers, J., Stevens, A., Parsons, A., Lilford, R., Spurgeon, P., & Thomas, H. (2006). Admissions processes for five year medical courses at English schools: Review. *British Medical Journal, 332*, 1005–1009.
Powis, D. A., Neame, R. L. B., Bristow, T., & Murphy, L. B. (1988). The objective structured interview for medical student selection. *British Medical Journal (clinical Research Education), 296*, 765.
Rogers, W., & Ballantyne, A. (2010). Towards a practical definition of professional behaviour. *Journal of Medical Ethics, 36*, 250–254.
Ross, S. J., Owens, K., Roberts, A., Jennings, E., & Mylrea, M. (2020). Mindfulness training: Success in reducing first year health professional students' study and exam related stress. *Health Professions Education, 6*, 162–169.
Rotenstein, L. S., Ramos, M. A., Torre, M., Segal, J. B., Peluso, M. J., Guille, C., et al. (2016). Prevalence of depression, depressive symptoms, and suicidal ideation among medical students: A systematic review and meta-analysis. *JAMA, 316*, 2214–2236.
Saks, N. S., & Karl, S. (2004). Academic support services in U.S. and Canadian medical schools. *Medical Education Online, 9*, 4348.
Sen Gupta, T., Murray, R. B., & Ray, R. A. (2012). Only the best: Medical student selection in Australia. *Medical Journal Australia, 196*, 357.
Shapiro, S. L. (2000). Stress management in medical education: A review of the literature. *Academic Medicine, 75*, 748–759.
Smith, C .K., Peterson, D. F., Degenhardt, B. F., & Johnson, J. C. (2007). Depression, anxiety, and perceived hassles among entering medical students. *Psychology Health & Medicine, 12*, 31–39.
Stegers-Jager, K. M., Cohen-Schotanus, J., & Themmen, A. P. N. (2017). The four-tier continuum of academic and behavioral support (4T-CABS) model: An integrated model for medical student success. *Academic Medicine, 92*, 1525–1530.
Storrie, K., Ahern, K., & Tuckett, A. (2010). A systematic review: Students with mental health problems—A growing problem. *International Journal of Nursing Practice, 16*, 1–6.
Tempski, P., Martins, M. A., & Paro, H. B. M. S. (2012). Teaching and learning resilience: A new agenda in medical education. *Medical Education, 46*, 343–348.
Vitaliano, P. P., Maiuro, R. D., Russo, J., & Mitchell, E. S. (1989). Medical student distress. A longitudinal study. *Journal of Nervous & Mental Disease, 177*, 70–76.
Wasson, L. T., Cusmano, A., Meli, L., Louh, I., Falzon, L., Hampsey, M., Young, G., Shaffer, J., & Davidson, K. W. (2016). Association between learning environment interventions and medical student well-being: A systematic review. *JAMA, 316*, 2237–2252.
Wilkinson, D., Zhang, J., Byrne, G. J., Luke, H., Ozolins, I. Z., Parker, M. H., & Peterson, R. F. (2008). Medical school selection criteria and the prediction of academic performance: Evidence

leading to change in policy and practice at the University of Queensland. *Medical Journal of Australia, 188*, 349–354.
Woolley, T., & Ray, R. A. (2019). Effectiveness of regional medical schools in attracting and retaining students for early-career practice in the local area: The James Cook University experience. *Australian Journal of Rural Health, 27*, 125–131.
Woolley, T., Ross, S., Larkins, S., Sen Gupta, T., & Whaleboat, D. (2021). "We learnt it, then we lived it": Influencing medical students' intentions towards rural practice and generalist careers via a socially-accountable curriculum. *Medical Teacher, 43*, 93–100.
Yates, J. (2011). Development of a 'toolkit' to identify medical students at risk of failure to thrive on the course: An exploratory retrospective case study. *BMC Medical Education, 11*, 95.
Yates, J., & James, D. (2006). Predicting the "strugglers": A case-control study of students at Nottingham University Medical School. *British Medical Journal, 332*, 1009.
Yates, J., & James, D. (2009). Risk factors at medical school for subsequent professional misconduct: Multicenter retrospective case-control study. *British Medical Journal, 340,* c2040.

Anna Kokavec (Ph.D.) is a registered psychologist, mental health educator and addiction researcher. Anna has more than 20 years experience working with young adults in academic, organisational, and clinical settings. She is currently the Academic Lead Student Support for the College of Medicine and Dentistry and has an academic appointment as Senior Lecturer Medical Education, Student Support, and Professional Practice at James Cook University. Anna is internationally known for her work with young adults in the alcohol area.

Jane Harte (Ph.D.) is a registered corporate psychologist and academic. Jane has more than 25 years experience working in medical education in Australia at the fellowship, graduate and undergraduate levels and is currently the Associate Dean Students in the College of Medicine and Dentistry at James Cook University. She has published in a variety of areas, including neuropsychology, medical education, and incentives for rural medical practice.

Simone Ross (MDR) is a Senior Lecturer in Medical Education in the College of Medicine and Dentistry at James Cook University. Simone teaches, mentors, and supervises students in several domestic and international student support programs. Simone was a consultant in the role of Program Manager with the Training for Health Equity Network (2011–2019) and has published in a variety of health professional education areas, including mindfulness, medical leadership, health equity, and social accountability.

Interdisciplinary Research Initiatives

Exploring Visual Art Students' Wellbeing: A Multi-level Research Approach

Eileen Siddins

Abstract Australian mental health literature acknowledges the complexity of students' university experiences by providing increasingly sophisticated knowledge and evidence-based strategies to promote student mental health. In doing so, some researchers have directed their attention to the unique contexts, learning preferences, and wellbeing needs that students might have according to their chosen area of study. Such research is promising and can guide the development of interventions that are tailored to students' disciplines and learning objectives. However, this is an emerging area of research, and the wellbeing of students from different study areas, like the visual arts, has not yet been comprehensively explored. To cultivate further scholarly discussion about mental health in Australian universities, this chapter presents mixed methods research called Visual Arts Wellbeing (VAW). VAW was designed as a multi-level needs assessment to collect empirical data during 2018 and 2019, to better describe the breadth and complexity of Australian visual art students' experiences and perspectives relevant to student wellbeing. Consequently, the VAW research findings contribute original knowledge by presenting the voices of an underrepresented student group and propose wellbeing interventions that improve students' creative learning experiences while supporting and protecting their mental health.

Keywords Visual art undergraduates · Student wellbeing · Mixed methods research

Recently, Australian research has identified whole-of-university and student-centred approaches to support students' mental health (Orygen, 2020; Productivity Commission, 2020). These approaches often address the need for early and proactive action, to enhance the students' university experience and assist students' management of their wellbeing before mental health difficulties reduce their quality of life. Although few institution and sector-wide interventions have been designed to create supportive learning environments (Larcombe et al., 2021), an emerging body of literature has begun to recognise the unique experiences and wellbeing needs of students

E. Siddins (✉)
James Cook University, Townsville, Australia
e-mail: eileen.siddins@my.jcu.edu.au

A. P. Francis and M. A. Carter (eds.), *Mental Health and Higher Education in Australia*,
https://doi.org/10.1007/978-981-16-8040-3_8

from different study areas (Baik et al., 2019). These study areas include law (Field et al., 2013; Tang & Ferguson, 2014), medicine (Saravanan & Wilks, 2014; Slavin et al., 2014), nursing (McAllister & McKinnon, 2009), social work (Adamson et al., 2012), education (Knight et al., 2013), veterinary science (Fritschi et al., 2009), and performing arts (Huddy, 2016; Moyle, 2019).

Australian literature has provided examples of curricula that have been designed to support visual art students' wellbeing. The Interior Visualisation II subject (McAuliffe et al., 2015) and Design Thinking for Social Innovation (Bhuva, 2018) are notable examples. However, further research can increase understanding of visual art students' learning contexts, disciplinary differences, and perspectives on improving their mental health, to inform future interventions (Baik et al., 2019). This chapter discusses how the Visual Arts Wellbeing (VAW) research was designed to increase this understanding. Although VAW represents the voices and complex experiences of visual art students, there is potential for this research approach to be adapted for research in other study areas, to explore different students' disciplinary experiences and wellbeing needs. Hence, the purpose of this chapter is to draw from the author's doctorate thesis (Siddins, 2021) and outline the VAW research design, to benefit future designs of discipline-specific research. This is achieved by identifying a rationale for the research, outlining the methodology, and overviewing the research findings from 247 survey respondents and 29 interview participants.

A Rationale for the VAW Research Project

Like other university students, art students experience unique challenges that can influence their wellbeing (Baik et al., 2019). Some of these challenges relate to students' creative training, at times consisting of long hours (Lee, 2019), management of ambiguous and self-regulated learning (Greene et al., 2019; Sawyer, 2019; Shreeve et al., 2010), pressure to produce original artwork (Lipson et al., 2016), and critiques of artwork that are heavily linked to students' personal ideas and identity (Lindström, 2015; Logan, 2013). Despite research indicating art educators' support of their students' wellbeing needs (Brooker et al., 2017), Australian literature also recognises dysfunctional power relationships between art students and their educators (Seton & Trouton, 2014) and influences on the students' university experience due to discipline-based reform packages recently approved by the Australian government (Daly & Lewis, 2020; Tjia et al., 2020). As Patston et al. (2018) note, devaluing social perceptions are challenging for artists and art students, who may need to consistently defend their decisions to pursue creative art careers (Bennett & Hennekam, 2018). Difficult career prospects and financial hardship offer additional insights into Australian art students' wellbeing and their high risk of attrition (Cherastidtham et al., 2018; QILT, 2019). These students potentially experience anticipatory distress about life after graduation (Cloonan, 2008; Oakley, 2009), and financial hardship is linked with students' mental health difficulties (Universities Australia, 2018).

Cross-disciplinary research on undergraduate students' wellbeing necessitates furthered understanding of art students' wellbeing needs (Baik et al., 2019). For example, one Australian study ($N = 4{,}711$) that compared law students' distress with other students found that undergraduate art students reported higher rates of anxiety and depression than the participants studying in other fields (Larcombe et al., 2015). Another study from the United States ($N = 64{,}519$) found that art and design undergraduate, masters, and doctorate students had an increased likelihood of mental health difficulties (Lipson et al., 2016). Empirical research (Elias & Berg-Cross, 2009) focussing on the wellbeing of fine art students ($N = 75$) similarly indicated that participants experienced sub-optimal wellbeing. Although these studies are often founded on the self-reports of voluntary respondents and confirmatory research is necessary, the findings suggest that Australian art students also have wellbeing needs that can be identified and supported during their education.

Methodology

Australian music, dance, and acting students are increasingly given access to supportive performance psychology content in their curricula (Moyle, 2019). However, there are limited evidence-based interventions that support the wellbeing of Australian visual art undergraduates studying disciplines such as painting, ceramics, animation, and design (Siddins, 2018). To present evidence to facilitate future interventions, the VAW research project was established. This research provides a descriptive needs assessment that explored the visual art undergraduates' resilience, mental health, and wellbeing, to answer the overarching research question: how can visual art students' current wellbeing be improved and sustained during their higher education? Given literature indicates that dysfunctional power relationships at university diminish art students' agency (Seton & Trouton, 2014), this research was designed to empower students and represent their opinions on how to foster student wellbeing. Visual art students were, thus, considered providers of valuable insights (Busher, 2012) and co-producers of research recommendations (Dollinger & Mercer-Mapstone, 2019) to improve student wellbeing.

Theoretical Framework

Representing the voices of university students through a descriptive wellbeing needs assessment requires a theoretical framework that accommodates multiple complexities. Students' wellbeing and university experiences are complex (Orygen, 2020), and interventions that foster student mental health and resilience require sensitivity to social and cultural variables (Liebenberg & Ungar, 2009). Furthermore, student wellbeing researchers need to build trusting relationships with students to ensure they are comfortable and confident with sharing their unique opinions about

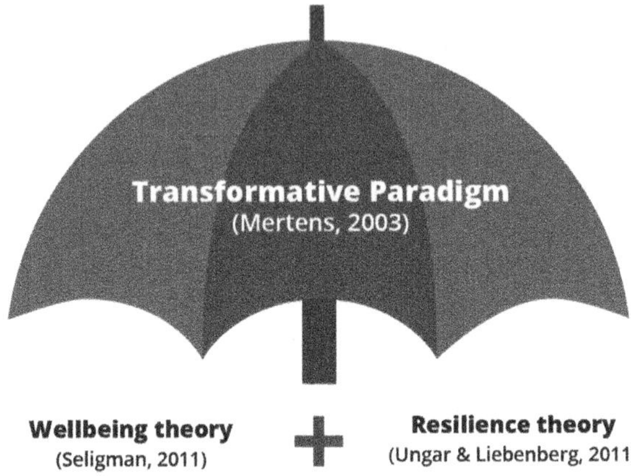

Fig. 1 Transformative paradigm as an 'umbrella' theoretical framework

wellbeing. To accommodate these requirements, the theoretical framework adopted for this research included the transformative paradigm (Mertens, 2009), wellbeing (Seligman, 2011), and resilience theories (Ungar & Liebenberg, 2011). The transformative paradigm, visualised as an umbrella in Fig. 1, supports multiple theories to empower the researched, facilitate multi-level mixed methods, and offer crystallised interpretations of participant views (Mertens, 2009, 2015).

This research was designed with an overarching ethical objective: do no harm to all involved in the research. Transformative researchers extend upon this objective by seeking to empower and respect the moral agency of the researched (Hugman et al., 2011; Mertens, 2009). The author carefully designed the research methodology by seeking advice to protect and empower participants. This process involved speaking to members of Australian art communities (Siddins, 2018) and university communities including counselling and psychology academics. Professional development like the Mental Health First Aid Course (Kitchener et al., 2010) was also completed and ethics approval provided by a Higher Research Ethics Committee before data collection. Subsequent steps that were taken to respect, empower, and protect the participants are detailed in the author's thesis (Siddins, 2021).

Research Methods

A parallel mixed methods approach was used to describe visual art students' wellbeing needs within higher education contexts. To direct this mixed research and answer the research question stated earlier, two research objectives were designed:

1. describe the current mental health, resilience, and wellbeing of Australian visual art students in higher education; and
2. explore ways to improve and sustain Australian visual art students' wellbeing through their higher education.

Parallel mixed methods offer flexibility by enabling separate strands of data collection, analysis, and interpretation (Creswell & Plano Clark, 2011). Given the descriptive nature of the research question and objectives, this research did not diagnose students with compromised mental health. Instead, the research prioritised qualitative data to sensitively explore the deeper meaning and contexts that marginalised communities can experience (Sweetman et al., 2010).

The VAW methods design converged two research strands to provide a multi-level needs assessment. These strands gathered data from the same sample through one online mixed methods survey and semi-structured interviews. The self-administered and cross-sectional online survey first established an understanding of participants' wellbeing, resilience, and psychological distress. In 15–20 min, participants responded to three short response questions and three scales: the PERMA Profiler (Butler & Kern, 2016), the Brief Resilience Scale (Smith et al., 2008), and the Self-administered K6 scale (Kessler et al., 2002). After completing the survey, participants were invited to share richer and more contextualised qualitative data through 30–60-min intensive interviews (Charmaz, 2006).

These data collection methods were designed to emphasise participants' strengths as well as their responses to challenges (Liebenberg & Ungar, 2009; Seligman, 2011). The survey scales were chosen for their compatibility with the theoretical framework, their ability to provide a descriptive profile of a smaller sample, and to ensure a shorter survey length to maintain participant engagement. The PERMA Profiler (Butler & Kern, 2016) was used to seek a contextualised understanding of human flourishing. This scale draws from wellbeing theory and integrates a range of indicators, including the five wellbeing domains: positive emotion, engagement, positive relationships, meaning, and accomplishment (Seligman, 2011). The PERMA Profiler applies a 23-item scale and asks positively worded questions using an 11-point Likert scale, anchored by 0 = never or not at all and 10 = always or completely.

Following the PERMA Profiler, participants were asked questions about their resilience and psychological distress. The Brief Resilience Scale (Smith et al., 2008) measured participants' ability to bounce back from stress through six items using a five-point Likert scale (1 = strongly disagree and 5 = strongly agree). The Australian version of K6, a six-item non-specific distress scale, was used to measure participants' psychological distress (Australian Bureau of Statistics, 2012; Kessler et al., 2002). Participants responded to this scale by considering how frequently they experienced symptoms including hopelessness, restlessness, and depression by using a five-point Likert scale (1 = none of the time and 5 = all of the time). The reliability and internal consistency of all survey scales are detailed in the author's thesis (Siddins, 2021).

Qualitative data collection was prioritised in this research, to provide detailed comparative insights into the unambiguous quantitative data (Este et al., 2009). Both the short responses in the online survey and the interview questions were designed to gather rich, meaningful, and contextual data regarding visual art students' wellbeing needs and ways to enhance students' wellbeing at university. The short response questions explored participants' social anxiety and their tendency to compare themselves with others (Larcombe & Fethers, 2013), how they coped with university challenges, and how their university could support their mental health and wellbeing. Similarly, the interview questions asked participants to describe what resilience and wellbeing meant to them, their coping strategies, and ways to improve students' university experiences to foster resilience and support students' mental health.

Participant Recruitment and Demographics

A criterion was developed to purposefully select participants who were Australian undergraduate students enroled in visual art degrees. These students were recruited if they studied disciplines including:

1. fine arts (including painting, drawing, print, sculpture, ceramics, and/or textiles),
2. illustration and design (including graphic and interactive, UX or UI design), and
3. digital arts (including digital illustration and animation).

As previously mentioned, the survey respondents were invited to participate in interviews once they had finished the survey. Although this recruitment strategy staggered the pacing of parallel strands, it supported the comparison of mixed data given the data from both strands were gathered from the same sample (Creswell et al., 2008). The survey remained active between August 2018 and February 2019. After data cleansing, 247 survey participant responses were retained for analysis. A total of 78 survey participants expressed interest in the interviews, and by December 2018, 29 participants were interviewed.[1] The participant demographics are displayed in Table 1.

The survey ($S = 247$) and interview participants ($I = 29$) practised similar visual art disciplines. Many survey ($s = 103$) and interview participants ($i = 12$) identified primarily with design disciplines (including graphic, game, and interactive design), whereas other participants identified with different new media disciplines, including animation and film ($s = 35$, $i = 7$), or disciplines including ceramics, drawing, painting, printmaking, textiles, and fashion ($s = 100$, $i = 10$). The remaining survey participants described their visual art practice as multi-disciplinary or involving other disciplines such as studio practice, conceptual art, art history, and installation.

[1] These participants' privacy is protected through survey anonymity and maintaining interview data confidentiality. For the remainder of this chapter, the survey participants will be referred to by their ID name followed by their described primary discipline (e.g. SP1, painting), or they will be counted with a value represented by 's' (e.g. $s = 24$). The interview participants will be referred to by their ID name and discipline (e.g. IP1, painting) and counted with a value represented by 'i' (e.g. $i = 3$). When both survey and interview participants are counted together, a lowercase '$s + i$' is used (e.g. $s + i = 12$).

Table 1 Participant demographics

Survey participant demographics				Interview participant demographics			
		s[a]	%			i[b]	%
Gender	Female	201	81.38	Gender	Female	20	68.97
	Male	36	14.57		Male	8	27.59
	Prefer not to say	3	1.21		Non-binary	1	3.45
	Prefer to self-describe[2]	7	2.83				
	Gender total	247	100.00		Gender total	29	100.00
Age groups	15–17 years old	3	1.21	Age groups	15–17 years old	0	0.00
	18–24 years old	170	68.83		18–24 years old	13	44.83
	25–34 years old	43	17.41		25–34 years old	10	34.48
	35–44 years old	12	4.86		35–44 years old	1	3.45
	45–54 years old	10	4.05		45–54 years old	4	13.79
	55–64 years old	8	3.24		55–64 years old	1	3.45
	65–74 years old	1	0.40		65–74 years old	0	0.00
	Age total	247	100.00		Age total	29	100.00
Location	Australian Capital Territory	15	6.07	Location	Australian Capital Territory	0	0.00
	New South Wales	47	19.03		New South Wales	4	13.79
	Queensland	68	27.53		Queensland	16	55.17
	South Australia	30	12.15		South Australia	1	3.45
	Tasmania	26	10.53		Tasmania	1	3.45
	Victoria	44	17.81		Victoria	5	17.24
	Western Australia	17	6.88		Western Australia	2	6.90
	Location total	247	100.00		Location total	29	100.00
Mode	Full-time attendance	213	86.23	Mode	Full-time attendance	23	79.31
	Part-time attendance	34	13.77		Part-time attendance	6	20.69

(continued)

Table 1 (continued)

Survey participant demographics				Interview participant demographics			
		s^{a}	%			i^{b}	%
	Attendance total	247	100.00		Attendance total	29	100.00

[a] Please refer to the first footnote above

[b] Self-descriptions of gender included a gender ($s = 1$), androgynous/queer ($s = 1$), ftm male ($s = 1$), gender fluid ($s = 1$), and non-binary ($s = 3$)

Analysis

The theoretical framework and applied thematic analysis (Guest et al., 2012) were used to conduct a reflexive and reflective analysis of participants' diverse responses. One key reflexive practice involved the use of interpretive forms during the analysis of interview data. For each interview, one interpretive form was completed to assess aspects of the data quality including silences and contradictions in the recorded dialogue between interviewer and participant (Arvay, 2003; Guest et al., 2012). These forms were used to develop interview summaries consisting of three to five keywords and a narrative description of the interview. In June 2019, the summaries were sent to interview participants to verify how their opinions were represented. Many participants responded to the summaries (response rate = 80.77%) by describing the interpretation as acceptable. Five interview participants also used this member checking process to update the author on their student life, highlighting changes in the way that they now understood and overcame their own challenges and recent successes in their student life.

Given the VAW project prioritised qualitative research, analysis began by first coding the qualitative interview and survey data separately, then mixing this data for comparison. The interview data were inductively approached using applied thematic analysis (Guest et al., 2012) with a limited reading of research literature in the first stage of analysis (Bazeley, 2013) to ensure scientific discourse did not undermine inclusive and empowering research practice (Liebenberg & Ungar, 2009). The same approach was applied to the following analysis of survey qualitative data and mixing of qualitative data from both strands. When comparing interview and survey codes, only slight alterations to themes were required. A key alteration was comparison, a theme that initially referred to interview participants' discussion of critiques but later accommodated survey participants' frequent discussion of comparison or self-comparison of their artwork. This theme is presented in Table 5.

Descriptive statistical analysis was used to find the mean and internal reliability (Cronbach's alpha) of the PERMA Profiler, Self-administered K6 scale, and Brief Resilience Scale. The K6 and Brief Resilience Scale findings were sorted into score categories, as detailed in Tables 3 and 4. However, the PERMA Profiler is designed to be descriptive rather than prescriptive (Butler & Kern, 2016) and does not specify 'high' or 'low' categories, to accommodate wellbeing as a multileveled and fluid state. The PERMA Profiler scores were thus compared with a validation sample (Butler & Kern, 2016), to offer insights into the descriptive wellbeing profile of participants.

The survey and interview participants provided a breadth and complexity of evidence relevant to visual art students' university experiences and wellbeing. To ensure a multileveled representation of these student voices, a full descriptive narrative structured by qualitative themes was reported in the author's thesis, alongside tabular displays outlining patterns and silences in the quantitative and mixed data (Siddins, 2021). In this chapter, a summary of these mixed findings is discussed. The findings are split into two sections defined by the research objectives. A description of participants' mental health, resilience, and wellbeing in the context of their university experiences is first presented by reporting quantitative results and summarising qualitative findings. This qualitative summary is followed by an overview of participants' expressed ways to improve and sustain student wellbeing during their university education.

Describing the Participants' University Experiences and Wellbeing

Quantitative Findings

In this section, the quantitative PERMA Profiler, Self-administered K6, and Brief Resilience Scale findings are presented. The PERMA Profiler scores were calculated by finding the mean of item scores that are sorted into wellbeing domains, as outlined in Table 2. The mean scores (ranging from 0–10) and the internal consistency scores are displayed for comparison. Despite the scales' weaker engagement domain alpha (Butler & Kern, 2016), the internal consistency of all wellbeing domains was satisfactory ($a = 0.86$). While comparing the survey and validation sample scores, the survey participants could be described as having sub-optimal functioning in all domains, except engagement (Siddins, 2021).

The K6 scores were first calculated by finding the sum of all items and categorising the total using dichotomous score groupings (Kessler et al., 2010). These dichotomous score categories included No Probable Mental Ill-health (scores between 6 and 18) and Probable Mental Ill-health (scores between 19 and 30). A total of 143 survey participants were sorted into the No Probable Mental Ill-health category, whereas 101 survey participants were sorted into the Probable Mental Ill-health category. In addition to these findings, the internal reliability and mean score (ranging from 1 to 5) of each scale item are presented in Table 3. The findings show that a larger portion (57.89%) of the survey participants were not at risk of mental ill-health. The percentage (40.89%) of participants who were identified as having Probable Mental Ill-health, however, is still concerning.

Table 2 Mean and coefficient of PERMA profiler responses compared with the validation sample

Domains	Survey sample		Validation sample (Butler & Kern, 2016)			
	S	Mean	*a*	*N*	Mean	*a*
Positive emotion[a]	247	5.60	0.84	31,965	6.69	0.88
Engagement[b]	247	7.18	0.50	31,962	7.25	0.72
Relationships[c]	247	6.24	0.80	31,940	6.90	0.82
Meaning[d]	247	5.64	0.87	31,931	7.06	0.90
Accomplishment[e]	247	6.40	0.70	31,963	7.21	0.79
Overall wellbeing[f]	247	6.13	0.92	31,966	7.02	0.94
Negative emotion[g]	247	5.73	0.63	31,386	4.46	0.71
Physical health[h]	247	5.26	0.82	30,601	6.94	0.92
Lonely[i]	247	5.75	–	–	–	–
Total	247	5.99	0.86	31,966	–	–

[a] Domain includes three positive emotion items
[b] Domain includes three engagement items
[c] Domain includes three relationship items
[d] Domain includes three meaning items
[e] Domain includes three accomplishment items
[f] Domain includes all of the positive emotion, engagement, relationship, meaning, and accomplishment items as well as the one happiness item
[g] Domain includes three negative emotion items
[h] Domain includes three health items
[i] Domain includes a single loneliness item and is not comprehensively listed in validation sample findings

Table 3 Mean and internal reliability of Self-administered K6

K6 items	*s*	Missing	Mean	*a*
Nervous[a]	245	2	3.27	0.82
Hopless[b]	244	3	2.60	0.79
Restless or fidgety[c]	245	2	3.08	0.85
Depressed[d]	245	2	2.33	0.79
Everything is an effort[e]	245	2	3.22	0.80
Worthless[f]	245	2	2.50	0.81
Total items (6 items)			2.83	0.84

[a] How often did you feel nervous?
[b] How often did you feel hopeless?
[c] How often did you feel restless or fidgety?
[d] How often did you feel so depressed that nothing could cheer you up?
[e] How often did you feel that everything was an effort?
[f] How often did you feel worthless?

Table 4 Mean, internal reliability, and score categories of Brief Resilience Scale

Item	*s*	Missing	Mean	*a*	Score categories
Bounce back[a]	244	3	3.16	0.84	Average resilience
Recover[b]	244	3	2.88	0.84	Low resilience
Come through difficult times[c]	244	3	2.78	0.86	Low resilience
(Rev) making it through stressful times[d]	243	4	2.70	0.84	Low resilience
(Rev) snap back[e]	243	4	2.83	0.82	Low resilience
(Rev) get over setbacks[g]	243	4	2.87	0.84	Low resilience
Total of all items (6 items)			2.87	0.86	Low resilience

[a] I tend to bounce back quickly after hard times
[b] It does not take me long to recover from a stressful event
[c] I usually come through difficult times with little trouble
[d] (R) I have a hard time making it through stressful events
[e] (R) It is hard for me to snap back when something bad happens
[f] (R) I tend to take a long time to get over setbacks in my life

The Brief Resilience Scale scores were calculated by finding the mean of individual items after reverse coding three negatively worded items. These scores were sorted into three categories: low resilience (scores below 3.00), average resilience (scores between 3.00 and 4.30), and high resilience (scores above 4.30). The score means and score categories are displayed alongside the internal reliability scores in Table 4. On average, the findings presented in Table 4 show that this survey sample had low to average levels of resilience. Comparison with the published mean scores for validation samples ($M = 3.53$–3.98, Smith et al., 2008) also indicates that the total mean of all items for this survey sample ($M = 2.87$) is low.

Qualitative Findings

The qualitative findings presented in Table 5 below explore participants' university experiences and offer insights into how their experiences influence their wellbeing. Table 5 summarises the qualitative findings by listing notable findings and exemplar participant quotes categorised by key themes. This table includes multiple participant opinions, and the frequency that these opinions were expressed is included in parenthesis. Although serving as a summary of the student voices, Table 5 provides insights into visual art students' learning preferences and their perspectives on the unique contexts of their creative learning, as some participants explained when comparing their experience with other degrees:

> I find it can be quite easy to do well [in my dual business degree] because of the obvious structure. Whereas in the creative industries, there is no right or wrong. When you are creating something, there are literally infinite ways you could create it. I think that can be quite overwhelming at times... (IP 14, design)

Table 5 Key themes relevant to participants' university experience and wellbeing

Key themes	Notable findings expressed by participants (frequency)	Exemplar quotes
Views on art student wellbeing	Optimal wellbeing linked with creative productivity ($i = 3$) Previously struggled with or could improve resilience ($i = 8$) Mental health difficulties stigmatised ($s + i = 15$)	Currently, it [discussing wellbeing] feels much more taboo, especially because of the stereotypes that visual art students face (SP 110, painting) … you do not want to appear weak to other people (IP 21, interactive design)
Views on broader university experience	University experience positively influences student wellbeing ($s + i = 45$) Unforeseen aspects of university are challenging ($s + i = 30$) Decline of art courses, lack of funding, staff redundancy ($s + i = 24$) External pressures including: • work and financial hardship ($s + i = 27$) • excessive travel times ($s + i = 5$) • relationship challenges ($s + i = 29$)	My university is currently ending my degree programme and cancelling a lot of the classes I need to graduate—these changes are stressful … (SP 149, graphic design) Just having enough money to sustain a study, to have secure accommodation, the real basics I think are really challenging for students (IP 17, printmaking)
Staff–student relationships	Staffs are inclusive, respectful, and understanding ($s + i = 26$) Staffs do not understand or care about student wellbeing ($s + i = 12$) Participants contemplated staff workload restrictions and duty of care ($s + i = 12$) Supportive staff encounters ($s + i = 74$) Unsupportive staff encounters ($s + i = 44$) Less formal student–staff relationships are ideal ($s + i = 12$)	We can just talk and have natural conversations. You do not have to be worried about what you say or what they might think. They are really open. And, that really helps (IP 18, interactive design) The current teaching and coordinating staff are too busy to talk, so it is difficult to cope sometimes (SP 197, ceramics)
Professional on-campus support services	Range of healthcare, financial, and legal aid services available ($s + i = 58$) Accessible and effective ($s + i = 28$) Inaccessible and require improvement ($s + i = 19$) Participants or their peers did not use services ($s + i = 32$)	There is counselling, there is student services, and there are all sorts of support (IP 5, painting) The mental health support team at uni has not been that helpful in the past (SP 158, graphic design)

(continued)

Table 5 (continued)

Key themes	Notable findings expressed by participants (frequency)	Exemplar quotes
Peer and friend relationships	Participants felt more supported in creative community ($s + i = 19$) Friends are ill-equipped to help ($s + i = 15$) Lonely or isolated from peers ($s + i = 38$) Peers have sub-optimal wellbeing ($s + i = 10$) Peers are focussed and successful in creative endeavours ($s + i = 10$) Positive group assessment experience ($s + i = 6$) Negative group assessment experience ($s + i = 13$) Peers have unrealistic or indifferent views on their learning and degree outcomes ($s + i = 8$)	It [brainstorming solutions to creative problems with peers] creates all kinds of connections. You become closer as friends as well (IP 22, interactive design) I do not have many close friends within my degree because art tends to get lonely (SP 213, drawing)
Relationship with time	Did not feel pressured by time restraints ($s + i = 4$) University is busy, intense, and fast-paced ($s + i = 82$) Time pressures prevent self-management and creative learning processes ($s + i = 44$) Challenge of assessment deadlines not being interspersed ($s + i = 14$) Competent with time management ($s + i = 37$) Expressed need to improve time management ($s + i = 21$)	I make detailed plans on what I need to achieve each day. (SP 20, graphic design) … it is just, uni, uni, uni, uni, uni, uni, uni all the time. It takes up—not, more my brain space (IP 1, new media art) Assignment's due … if I am too immersed in my work, I often forgot to eat (IP 20, interactive design)
Expressed characteristics of creative learning	Learning not clearly defined nor focussed on reciting a fixed cannon of knowledge ($s + i = 37$) Self-regulated learning and reliance on feedback ($s + i = 21$) Creative skills take a long time to learn and apply to projects ($s + i = 12$) Pressured to think creatively and produce original work ($s + i = 13$) Incorporated aspects of identity and life into artwork ($s + i = 23$) Frequently immersed in emotion ($s + i = 3$)	Art is not marked or judged by its capacity to be right or wrong, like maths. Art is judged by opinion and skill (SP 66, graphic design) … I have a good GPA, but when people are looking at hiring me for a job, they will be looking for a portfolio (IP 24, interactive design) I put all of my self-worth into my degree because it is one of my passions (IP 4, interior design)

(continued)

Table 5 (continued)

Key themes	Notable findings expressed by participants (frequency)	Exemplar quotes
Views on comparison	Concerned about being graded with minimal bias ($s + i = 18$) Invested a lot of effort and time into creative work but unsure if efforts were recognised ($s + i = 48$) Viewed creative abilities as an extension of their self-worth ($s + i = 11$) Compared art with peers or artists online ($s + i = 62$) Felt inferior, intimidated, or worried that work was at a lesser quality ($s + i = 110$) Worried others criticised them for: • lacking acceptable creative style ($s + i = 12$) • lacking talent or innovative thinking ($s + i = 21$) • age differences ($s + i = 11$) • limited understanding or intellectual capacity ($s + i = 17$) • inability to convey ideas ($s + i = 30$) • limited technical or manual skills ($s + i = 28$) • inability to reach standards of audience ($s + i = 122$) Not worried about others' views on art ($s + i = 65$) Prioritised constructive feedback over positive feedback ($s + i = 9$) Prioritised their own opinions over others ($s + i = 28$)	I always worry that my design work will be viewed as amateur and that it may seem like I have no idea what I am doing (SP 43, graphic design) I occasionally worry that my art is not good enough, but this thought pushes me to try harder and strive to achieve the goals I set myself (SP 232, drawing) I particularly like our lecturers because most of the people I talk to or get feedback from for my art are generally quite blunt and outspoken (IP 11, drawing) It is hard to imagine that your art will be displayed one day seeing all the other amazing art displayed. There is great subconscious competition in the arts (SP 186, painting) Since a lot of your heart and soul and often aspects of yourself and life end up in the work, a criticism of it can feel like a criticism of yourself (SP 12, sculpture)
Views on the future	Had not yet considered future work but confident they would learn more on the topic later in their degree ($i = 10$) Discussed clear goals for future ($s + i = 19$) Actively sought or already engaged in tasks that exposed them to the industry ($s + i = 19$) Aware of limited creative work positions ($s + i = 19$) Found degree suitable and prepared students for the future ($s + i = 12$) Wondered about degree's capacity to prepare students ($s + i = 15$) Lacked support or skills to meet industry standards ($s + i = 78$)	I spoke to two people, and they really solidified what I want to do with my career (IP 7, new media art) I am technically a designer because I am studying a design degree. But, I do not feel like I necessarily have the knowledge or skills to say that (IP 14, design) … we are constantly inundated with 'reality checks' from faculty and organisations like Artsource, about how tough/impossible/miserable/financially crippling it is to be a practising artist. As if we are not all already painfully aware of the fact! (SP 215, painting)

(continued)

Table 5 (continued)

Key themes	Notable findings expressed by participants (frequency)	Exemplar quotes
Creative identity	Cherished ability to self-express and enjoyed therapeutic benefits of creating ($s + i = 43$) Felt compelled to create ($s + i = 16$) University restricted creative self-expression ($s + i = 19$) Social perspectives devalued artists and art students ($s + i = 22$)	We are at our happiest when we have the conditions to create (SP 171, sculpture) If the university could recognise us as hard-working students and not just lost souls doing a fine art degree … I think it would help us not feel left out compared to other university degrees (SP 84, printmaking) I do not think there is a lot of people working office jobs that have to go to work every day and have a bunch of people commenting that what they do is not valuable and what they do has no purpose in society (IP 23, painting)
Insights about self-management	Each student is responsible for their self-management ($s + i = 34$) Avoided or preferred not to seek help ($s + i = 43$) Mentioned help-seeking and self-management barriers: • stigma ($s + i = 21$) • lack of professional support ($s + i = 34$) • lack of motivation ($s + i = 9$) • time pressures($s + i = 13$) Found help-seeking unnecessary ($s + i = 7$) Managed better alone ($s + i = 2$)	My biggest issue is realising when I need help, and that it is okay to ask for help. I never really want to bombard anyone with my issues (SP 89, graphic design) That afternoon happened to be a day where I had [a] full day of classes all day. There was no way to [get] some time where I could drop in and see them (IP 28, ceramics) I think there are quite a few support systems at university, and you just need to reach out and actually use them (SP 176, drawing)
Cognitive coping strategies	Forgave or reminded selves that high standards are not always necessary ($s + i = 16$) Refocused on positive aspects of task and university objectives ($s + i = 58$) Took things less seriously ($s + i = 22$) Reflected on improvement ($s + i = 10$) Pushed through university challenges and unpleasant emotions until university break ($s + i = 41$)	… you sort of have to move on or keep going. Keep going (IP 16, painting) I try to just remember that I love to create, and my work makes me happy, so it must be worth it! (SP 106, drawing)

(continued)

Table 5 (continued)

Key themes	Notable findings expressed by participants (frequency)	Exemplar quotes
Behavioural coping strategies	Set aside time to rest ($s + i = 37$) Participated in recreational activities ($s + i = 123$) Exercised ($s + i = 43$) Used meditation, self-help resources, and mindfulness activities ($s + i = 33$) Used time management ($s + i = 37$) Listened to music ($s + i = 18$) Created art ($s + i = 27$) Healthy diet and avoidance of alcohol or drugs ($s + i = 10$) Unhealthy diet or reliance on alcohol or drugs ($s + i = 33$) Procrastinated or avoided tasks ($s + i = 32$) Self-harmed ($s + i = 2$) Cried ($s + i = 8$)	… you can express yourself through your art and that is definitely something that I do if I am feeling stressed … (IP 15, animation) Just walking around and stuff …. it is just really peaceful, so you can just empty your mind I guess (IP 6, new media) I enjoy sport and my casual job to help forget about uni stresses for a brief period (SP 60, graphic design) Often, I procrastinate a lot until I find the motivation to get it done (SP 195, animation)
Social coping strategies	Friendships were support during university ($s + i = 121$) Spoke with friends about challenges ($s + i = 63$) Socialised with friends to relax ($s + i = 25$) Socialised with family and partner to relax ($s + i = 13$) Spoke with family and partner about challenges ($s + i = 53$) Unavailable support networks with family or partner ($s + i = 18$) Academic support and wellbeing assistance from teaching and professional staff ($s + i = 85$) Assistance from on-campus support services ($s + i = 58$) Off-campus professional support: • therapists ($s + i = 5$) • psychologists ($s + i = 20$) • psychiatrists ($s + i = 10$) • hospital ($s + i = 2$) • general practitioners and other healthcare providers ($s + i = 10$)	Talking to friends, breaking things down, and understanding what it is exactly I am feeling and why (SP 167, animation) The university helps a lot through their services for special consideration and close contact to lecturers (SP 253, painting) I usually seek help from friends or family. It is always good to talk about it with people you trust who are doing the same course, so they relate and you do not feel as alone (SP 250, painting)

Furthermore, the findings highlighted potential areas for interventions to foster student resilience and wellbeing. These areas include time management, preparation for future careers, the ability to embrace uncertainty, and managing comparison or self-comparison of art. Different comments displayed in Table 5 highlight how participants expressed being engaged with their creative work, using words including 'passion', 'happiest', and 'goals'. Such engagement indicates a potential to apply students' creative strengths to support their wellbeing. Subsequently, visual art students might benefit from further opportunities to engage in creative activity:

> [Art can be used] to build up mental resilience first… I think they need to talk about that early on in the game, what the benefits are of actually being creative and doing creative things… (IP 11, painting)

When discussing ways that visual art students coped with university challenges, participants expressed varied opinions about self-management. These opinions sometimes reflected the ways that participants acquired self-management skills as they progressed with their visual art degrees ($s + i = 30$):

> Now is a good time to do it because I have all of the support available to me. That is just something I can carry with me through the rest of my life. (IP 12, animation)

This quote highlights how universities are ideally placed to foster students' resilience and their development of adaptive coping strategies that benefit students well after they leave university. Similar sentiment was expressed by participants when they identified ways to improve university experiences and enhance student wellbeing.

Exploring Ways to Improve and Sustain Student Wellbeing

When responding to questions about improving their education, participants expanded upon their description of their wellbeing needs. In some cases, survey and interview participants who had not detailed their own university challenges during the earlier stages of data collection provided new information when they began recommending changes to improve university experiences. This rich information was used to further understand the participants' wellbeing needs and areas for positive change. Such findings are sorted into key themes and summarised in Table 6.

One notable finding summarised in Table 6 necessitated the alignment of future interventions with students' learning motivations and creative goals. To develop effective and sustainable intervention, participants ($s + i = 11$) affirmed the need for settings-based interventions that are engaging and accommodating of each student's subjective views on their disciplinary learning (Kern et al., 2019; Orygen, 2020). As stated by one participant, students may not enjoy the benefits of creating if it is not relevant to their study goals:

> … let us say you are doing some course and they are like 'Alright, let us paint for half an hour', they are obviously going to [think] 'well this has nothing to do with the course, so why are we doing this?' (IP 21, interactive design).

Table 6 Key themes relevant to participants' recommendations for change

Key themes	Notable findings expressed by participants (frequency)	Exemplar quotes
Views on change	Did not provide detailed recommendations for change ($s + i = 25$) Change needs to be relevant, engaging, and accommodating of students' subjective views and learning goals ($s + i = 11$) Wellbeing learning needs to be normalised or compulsory ($i = 3$)	Weaving these constructs into the fabric of the degree rather than as an option …. promotes normalisation … (IP 3, graphic design) I think if there was something that was compulsory … (IP 27, interactive design)
Broad change to university	Requested change related to: degree structure or current campus isolation ($s + i = 18$) culture and social perceptions on mental health and art education ($s + i = 14$) issues surrounding government and university funding and discontinuation of courses ($s + i = 12$)	I think there is too much work crammed into a period of time that is far too short (SP 105, multi-disciplinary) I think there needs to be a bigger support for the arts in general, particularly in more regional areas, as courses are getting cut, and it is becoming harder and harder to study the arts at universities (SP 241, new media art)
Change to on-campus support services	Increased promotion and accessibility of professional healthcare services ($s + i = 32$) Increased online and on-campus support services ($s + i = 35$) Free gym facilities ($s + i = 2$) Online industry and university support platforms ($s + i = 5$)	Needs more specialised mental health support in regards to students specifically studying in the faculty of arts … (SP 207, graphic design) I would probably ask for more health specialists around the smaller satellite campuses (IP 10, new media art)
Social support changes	Increased student art groups or social clubs ($s + i = 15$) Space for university staff and students to socialise ($s + i = 22$) Relaxing and fun activities including swings, puzzles, painting, weaving, movies, or camps ($s + i = 23$)	More social groups relevant to my degree. The classroom oft is dead quiet because no one knows each other. Some way to break that ice and create some new genuine friends (SP 37, graphic design) … like a drop-in structured art-making opportunity for any student of any discipline (IP 17, printmaking)
Change across art departments	More equipment and art supplies ($s + i = 2$) Improved enrolment and course advice ($s + i = 25$) Curricula, extracurricular, or co-curricular: • creative training ($s + i = 54$) • time management or self-motivation training ($s + i = 10$) • self-management and resilience training ($s + i = 27$) Staff training to increase mental health literacy ($s + i = 40$) Staff training to prevent uncomfortable or distressing staff–student relations ($s + i = 23$)	… uni could have more opportunities to do practise and have more machines to improve my skills (IP 13, ceramics) Better training for staff to recognise distress (as opposed to stress) … Let students know that some things will be hard and that anxiety and stress are part of life, but there is a limit (SP 240, glassmaking)

(continued)

Table 6 (continued)

Key themes	Notable findings expressed by participants (frequency)	Exemplar quotes
Curricula change	Reassess weight and pacing of assessment and content delivery ($s + i = 19$) Focus assessment on topics about resilience and wellbeing ($s + i = 20$) Improve balance of theory and practise taught ($s + i = 25$) Teach more creative skills ($s + i = 31$) Reassess if subjects are irrelevant or restrict student progress compared to subjects that are essential ($s + i = 26$) External learning options or class recordings ($s + i = 7$) Contact hours with teachers for mentoring support ($s + i = 24$)	Evaluating the amount of time expected to be in the studio making and the pressure of a workload (SP 244, printmaking) In general, the courses would benefit from being more organised and clearly expressed … to ease the burden on students with unnecessary confusion and uncertainty (SP 189, animation)
Industry-related change	Increased relevant career preparation and advice ($s + i = 46$) Compulsory internships or subjects that incorporate work experience into assessment ($s + i = 12$) Guest speakers discuss challenges and coping strategies ($s + i = 17$) Networking events like industry nights ($s + i = 20$) Field trips ($s + i = 2$) Classroom discussions about creative industries and securing work ($s + i = 14$)	If I was taught how to be an effective freelancer and how to contact potential employers, I think I would feel a lot more secure in my future (SP 114, graphic design) I think there could be talks from practising artists about how they manage their art practice and their day to day life. Also, how they manage stress, rejections, setbacks, etc. (SP 208, printmaking)

During their interview, this interactive design student continued to discuss alternative strategies, such as an assessment that requires students to analyse how professionals in their field managed industry-related challenges.

The findings support the need for collaboration between university, creative art, and mental health communities to develop effective and sustainable intervention. For example participants ($s + i = 46$) requested further exposure to the industry and advice to help mitigate anticipatory stress about the future. This requires the active involvement of university staff, creative industry members—and potential support from mental health experts—to nurture students' realistic expectations and self-management strategies in preparation for the creative workforce. Similar collaborations currently exist between Australian creative industries and mental health communities. The Mentally Healthy Change Group and the Never Not Creative community[2] provide notable examples of collaborative events like Asking for a Friend (Never Not Creative, 2020) to address the wellbeing needs of artists.

Discussion and Further Recommendations

The VAW research was designed to describe participants' wellbeing needs rather than diagnose compromised mental health. However, the mixed findings drawn from participant responses did describe visual art students' lower levels of resilience and sub-optimal wellbeing. These findings are consistent with other research on Australian university students' mental health (Rickwood et al., 2017; Stallman, 2010) and international cross-disciplinary research that identifies art students as experiencing wellbeing challenges (Lipson et al., 2016). The rich qualitative findings supported other research literature by highlighting participants' challenges such as managing ambiguous and self-regulated learning (Greene et al., 2019), devaluing social perceptions of artists (Patston et al., 2018), and value judgments or comparisons of artwork that are heavily linked to art students' identities (Lindström, 2015; Logan, 2013). These challenges, and other findings presented in Tables 5 and 6, provide further understanding of visual art students' university experiences to inform future intervention.

These VAW research findings necessitate transformation to establish more supportive learning environments that protect student wellbeing (Larcombe et al., 2021). Visual art students are primarily responsible for their wellbeing and provide valuable insights about ways to enhance university experiences to protect student wellbeing in university settings (Baik et al., 2019; Busher, 2012). However, art students' efforts to improve their university experiences can be disempowered by the educational systems in which they operate (Seton & Trouton, 2014). To support and empower students as agents of change and address the overarching research question, the findings identified positive areas of change for Australian visual art education.

[2] For more information, visit www.mentally-healthy.org and www.nevernotcreative.org.

This research argues that positive change will be more effective if university interventions align with students' discipline of study and their learning goals. Hence, the research recommendations require the involvement of those who are able to reposition their power and cultivate active transformation within higher education and art communities. Key university stakeholders, academic and professional staff, wellbeing support services, artists, art graduates, and art students may all partake in the recommended changes summarised below:

- reassess how current curricula supports student wellbeing by including content that is coherently organised, distributes power, and prevents uncomfortably evocative, discriminatory, or disengaging content;
- improve the quality and accessibility of online and on-campus support services;
- improve training and support for university staff to respond to mental health difficulties, practise respect for students' wellbeing, and empower student agency;
- implement preventative wellbeing interventions into curricula by ensuring that these interventions are relevant to the student's creative learning goals;
- cultivate supportive creative communities on campus, including student support groups;
- increase industry engagement to prepare students for challenges they will experience in the creative workforce.

The mixed findings that are summarised in this chapter reaffirm the importance for multi-level needs assessments of students' wellbeing. For example the students' heterogeneous coping strategies summarised in Table 5 provide a clear reminder that there is no 'one size fits all' approach to helping artists cope with challenges (Mentally Healthy, 2020). Interventions, thus, need to be multileveled and grounded in evidence to accommodate students' multifaceted wellbeing needs. One strength of the VAW research was the mixed methods design. The qualitative findings extended understanding of the quantitative findings by adding rich and contextualised detail regarding the breadth of visual art students' diverse university experiences. These findings revealed students' strengths, the challenges they experienced, and ways to support their wellbeing, while they manage these challenges.

However, the findings are not exhaustive, and some limitations merit further research attention. Transformative research is conducted to allow the voices of the researched to be heard and the VAW research included participatory action methods such as member checking of interview summaries. Despite this, the participants were not given the opportunity to offer feedback on the final research recommendations. Voluntary self-reports are also limited given findings can be influenced by recall and social desirability. Without further research to evaluate, refine, and implement strategies for change, nuanced conclusions cannot be drawn from the research recommendations. Instead, the methods design outlined in this chapter could be foundational for further research on the wellbeing needs of discipline-specific cohorts or research guiding the development of wellbeing-focussed interventions for visual art students.

The VAW research contributes original knowledge pertaining to Australian visual art undergraduates' wellbeing. By representing the students' voices and exploring their views, this transformative research has provided an original evidence base that can be used to develop discipline-specific solutions to promote Australian visual art students' wellbeing. Given the COVID-19 pandemic has altered the creative workforce and creative art education (Coates et al., 2020; Daly & Lewis, 2020), students will arguably need to manage additional financial, educational, and social challenges (Siddins, 2021). It is, thus, imperative that these students are taught how to protect their wellbeing and prepare for future challenges. Now is the time for Australian university stakeholders to heed the call for wellbeing intervention, particularly for those enroled in creative art degrees.

Acknowledgements The research outlined in this paper was supported by the Australian Government Research Training Program Scholarship.

References

Adamson, C., Beddoe, L., & Davys, A. (2012). Building resilient practitioners: Definitions and practitioner understandings. *British Journal of Social Work, 2014*(44), 522–541.

Arvay, M. (2003). Doing reflexivity: A collaborative narrative approach. In L. Finlay & B. Gough (Eds.), *Reflexivity: A practical guide for researchers in health and social sciences* (pp. 163–175). Wiley, Incorporated. http://ebookcentral.proquest.com/lib/jcu/detail.action?docID=351401

Australian Bureau of Statistics. (2012). *Information Paper: Use of the Kessler Psychological Distress Scale in ABS Health Surveys, Australia, 2007–08.* www.abs.gov.au/ausstats/abs@.nsf/Lookup/1BF12FE00641EA89CA2579D50015D70F?opendocument

Baik, C., Larcombe, W., & Brooker, A. (2019). How universities can enhance student mental wellbeing: The student perspective. *Higher Education Research & Development, 38*(4), 674–687. https://doi.org/10.1080/07294360.2019.1576596

Bazeley, P. (2013). *Qualitative data analysis: Practical Strategies* (S. Jai, Ed.). SAGE Publications.

Bennett, D., & Hennekam, S. (2018). Self-authorship and creative industries workers' career decision-making. *Human Relations, 71*(11), 1454–1477.

Bhuva, N. (2018). Using a co-experience approach to improve international students' classroom experience: a practice report from within an Australian higher education setting. *International Journal of Innovation, Creativity and Change, 4*(3, Special Edition), 81–97.

Brooker, A., Baik, C., & Larcombe, W. (2017). Understanding academic educator's work in supporting student wellbeing. *Research and Development in Higher Education: Curriculum Transformation, 40*, 50–60.

Busher, H. (2012). Students as expert witnesses of teaching and learning. *Management in Education, 26*(3), 113–119. https://doi.org/10.1177/0892020612445679

Butler, J., & Kern, M. L. (2016). The PERMA Profiler: A brief multidimensional measure of flourishing. *International Journal of Wellbeing, 6*(3), 1–48.

Charmaz, K. (2006). *Constructing grounded theory: a practical guide through qualitative analysis.* Sage.

Cherastidtham, I., Norton, A., & Mackey, W. (2018). *University attrition: what helps and what hinders university completion?*

Cloonan, D. (2008). Observations when counselling trainee artists. *Journal of the Australian and New Zealand Student Services Association* (31), 42–55.

Coates, B., Cowgill, M., Chen, T., & Mackey, W. (2020). *Shutdown: Estimating the COVID-19 employment shock.* Grattan Institute.

Creswell, J. W., & Plano Clark, V. L. (2011). *Designing and conducting mixed methods research* (2nd ed.). Sage.

Creswell, J. W., Plano Clark, V. L., & Garrett, A. L. (2008). Methodological issues in conducting mixed methods research designs. In M. M. Bergman (Ed.), *Advances in mixed methods research* (pp. 66–83). Sage.

Daly, A., & Lewis, P. (2020). The proposed job-ready graduate package: A misguided arrow missing its target. *Australian Journal of Labour Economics, 23*(2), 231–251.

Dollinger, M., & Mercer-Mapstone, L. (2019). What's in a name? Unpacking students' roles in higher education through neoliberal and social justice lenses. *Teaching & Learning Inquiry, 7*(2), 73–89.

Elias, D. M. G., & Berg-Cross, L. (2009). An Exploration of motivations of fine art students in relation to mental and physical well-being. *Journal of College Student Psychotherapy, 23*(4), 228–238. https://doi.org/10.1080/87568220903163850

Este, D., Sitter, K., & Maclaurin, B. (2009). Using mixed methods to understand youth resilience. In L. Liebenberg & M. Ungar (Eds.), *Researching resilience* (pp. 201–224). University of Toronto Press.

Field, R., Duffy, J., & Huggins, A. (2013). Supporting transition to law school and student well-being: The role of professional legal identity. *The International Journal of the First Year in Higher Education, 4*(2), 15–25. https://doi.org/10.5204/intjfyhe.v4i2.167

Fritschi, L., Morrison, D., Shirangi, A., & Day, L. (2009). Psychological well-being of Australian veterinarians. *Australian Veterinary Journal, 87*(3), 76–81. https://doi.org/10.1111/j.1751-0813.2009.00391.x

Greene, J. A., Freed, R., & Sawyer, R. K. (2019). Fostering creative performance in art and design education via self-regulated learning. *Instructional Science, 47*(2), 127–149. https://doi.org/10.1007/s11251-018-9479-8

Guest, G., MacQueen, K., & Namey, E. (2012). *Applied thematic analysis*. Sage. https://methods.sagepub.com/book/applied-thematic-analysis

Huddy, A. (2016). Performance enhancement: A whole of person approach to first year Dance students' transition into tertiary training. *Performance Enhancement & Health, 4*(1–2), 27–34. https://doi.org/10.1016/j.peh.2015.09.005

Hugman, R., Pittaway, E., & Bartolomei, L. (2011). When 'do no harm' is not enough: The ethics of research with refugees and Other vulnerable groups. *The British Journal of Social Work, 41*(7), 1271–1287. https://doi.org/10.1093/bjsw/bcr013

Kern, M. L., Williams, P., Spong, C., Colla, R., Sharma, K., Downie, A., Taylor, J. A., Sharp, S., Siokou, C., & Oades, L. G. (2019). Systems informed positive psychology. *The Journal of Positive Psychology*, 1–11. https://doi.org/10.1080/17439760.2019.1639799

Kessler, R. C., Andrews, G., Colpe, L. J., Hiripi, E., Mroczek, D. K., Normand, S. L. T., Walters, E. E., & Zaslavsky, A. M. (2002). Short screening scales to monitor population prevalences and trends in non-specific psychological distress. *Psychological Medicine, 32*(6), 959–976. https://doi.org/10.1017/S0033291702006074

Kessler, R. C., Green, J. G., Gruber, M. J., Sampson, N. A., Bromet, E., Cuitan, M., ... & Zaslavsky, A. M. (2010). Screening for serious mental illness in the general population with the K6 screening scale: Results from the WHO World Mental Health (WMH) survey initiative. *International Journal of Methods in Psychiatric Research, 19*(S1), 4–22. https://doi.org/10.1002/mpr.310

Kitchener, B. A., Jorm, A. F., Kelly, C. D., & Orygen Research, C. (2010). *Mental health first aid manual* (2nd ed.). Orygen Youth Health Research Centre. www.orygen.org.au/Policy/University-Mental-Health-Framework

Knight, C., Hardy, S., & Knight, B. (2013). Social innovation, resilience and the higher degree research experience. *International Journal of Innovation, Creativity and Change, 1*(1), 37–50.

Larcombe, W., Baik, C., & Finch, S. (2021). Exploring course experiences that predict psychological distress and mental wellbeing in Australian undergraduate and graduate coursework students. *Higher Education Research & Development*, 1–16. https://doi.org/10.1080/07294360.2020.1865284

Larcombe, W., & Fethers, K. (2013). Schooling the blues? An investigation of factors associated with psychological distress among law students. *UNSW Law Journal, 36*(2), 390–436.

Larcombe, W., Finch, S., & Sore, R. (2015). Who's distressed? Not only law students: Psychological distress levels in university students across diverse fields of study. *The Sydney Law Review, 37*(2), 243–273.
Lee, F. M. (2019). *Comparing students who do and do not study the fine arts: Mental health, stress and time spent on academic work*. Oklahoma State University.
Liebenberg, L., & Ungar, M. (2009). *Researching resilience*. University of Toronto Press. http://ebookcentral.proquest.com/lib/jcu/detail.action?docID=4672933
Lindström, S. (2015). Constructions of professional subjectivity at the fine arts college. *Professions and Professionalism, 5*(2). https://doi.org/10.7577/pp.869
Lipson, S. K., Zhou, S., Wagner, B., Beck, K., & Eisenberg, D. (2016). Major differences: Variations in undergraduate and graduate student mental health and treatment utilization across academic disciplines. *Journal of College Student Psychotherapy, 30*(1), 23–41. https://doi.org/10.1080/87568225.2016.1105657
Logan, C. (2013). Living artists: Identity, independence and engagement in fine art learning. *Art, Design & Communication in Higher Education, 12*(1), 33–48. https://doi.org/10.1386/adch.12.1.33_1
McAllister, M., & McKinnon, T. (2009). The importance of teaching and learning resilience in the health disciplines: A critical review of the literature. *Nurse Education Today, 29*(4), 371–379.
McAuliffe, M., Martin, P., Cameron, L., & Hankinson, J. (2015). Embedding metacognitive skills in spatial design education. *International Journal of Innovation, Creativity and Change, 2*(2).
Mentally Healthy. (2020). *Mentally Healthy 2020 Research*. Mentally Healthy. www.mentally-healthy.org/resources-collection/mentally-healthy-2020; www.youtube.com/watch?v=KzQ_914hCg0&feature=youtu.be
Mertens, D. M. (2009). *Transformative research and evaluation*. The Guilford Press.
Mertens, D. M. (2015). *Research and evaluation in education and psychology: Integrating diversity with quantitative, qualitative, and mixed methods*. Sage.
Moyle, G. M. (2019). Coaching performing artists. *Consulting Psychology Journal: Practice and Research, 71*(2), 97–106. https://doi.org/10.1037/cpb0000127
Never Not Creative. (2020). *Asking for a friend*. www.nevernotcreative.org/asking-for-a-friend
Oakley, K. (2009). From Bohemia to Britart—Art students over 50 years. *Cultural Trends, 18*(4), 281–294. https://doi.org/10.1080/09548960903268105
Orygen. (2020). *Australian University Mental Health Framework* (pp. 1–29). Orygen.
Patston, T. J., Cropley, D. H., Marrone, R. L., & Kaufman, J. C. (2018). Teacher implicit beliefs of creativity: Is there an arts bias? *Teaching and Teacher Education, 75*, 366–374. https://doi.org/10.1016/j.tate.2018.08.001
Productivity Commission. (2020). *Mental health* (Report no. 95, Issue. www.pc.gov.au/inquiries/completed/mental-health#report
QILT. (2019). *2019 graduate outcomes survey—Longitudinal National report* (Graduate Outcomes Survey—Longitudinal (GOS-L), Issue. www.qilt.edu.au/qilt-surveys/graduate-employment
Rickwood, D., Telford, N., O'Sullivan, S., Crisp, D., & Magyar, R. (2017). *National tertiary student wellbeing survey 2016*. www.headspace.org.au/assets/Uploads/headspace-NUS-Publication-Digital.pdf
Saravanan, C., & Wilks, R. (2014). Medical students' experience of and reaction to stress: The role of depression and anxiety. *The Scientific World Journal, 2014*, 1–8.
Sawyer, R. K. (2019). The role of failure in learning how to create in art and design. *Thinking Skills and Creativity, 33*, 1–10. https://doi.org/10.1016/j.tsc.2018.08.002
Seligman, M. E. P. (2011). *Flourish*. Free Press.
Seton, M., & Trouton, L. (2014). Deconstructing the taken-for-grantedness of institutional knowledge and power in arts education: restoring the voice of the creative student. In W. Midgley, A. Davies, & M. E. Oliver (Eds.), *Echoes ethics and issues of voice in education research* (pp. 95–109). Sense Publishers.

Siddins, E. (2018). Paving the way for unique wellbeing intervention in visual art curricula. *International Journal of Innovation, Creativity and Change, 4*(3 Special Edition November), 33–48. http://www.ijicc.net/images/Vol4_iss3_spec_ed_nov_2018/Eileen_Siddins.pdf

Siddins, E. (2021). *The visual arts wellbeing project: A wellbeing needs assessment of visual arts students in Australian universities* [Doctoral thesis, James Cook University]. Townsville, Australia.

Shreeve, A., Sims, E., & Trowler, P. (2010). 'A kind of exchange': Learning from art and design teaching. *Higher Education Research & Development, 29*(2), 125–138. https://doi.org/10.1080/07294360903384269

Slavin, S. J., Schindler, D. L., & Chibnall, J. T. (2014). Medical Student Mental Health 3.0: Improving student wellness through curricular changes. *Academic Medicine, 89*(4), 573–577. https://doi.org/10.1097/acm.0000000000000166

Smith, B. W., Dalen, J., Wiggins, K., Tooley, E., Christopher, P., & Bernard, J. (2008). The brief resilience scale: Assessing the ability to bounce back. *International Journal of Behavioral Medicine, 15*(3), 194–200. https://doi.org/10.1080/10705500802222972

Stallman, H. (2010). Psychological distress in university students: A comparison with general population data. *Australian Psychologist, 45*(4), 249–257.

Sweetman, D., Badiee, M., & Creswell, J. W. (2010). Use of the transformative framework in mixed methods studies. *Qualitative Inquiry, 16*(6), 441–454. https://doi.org/10.1177/1077800410364610

Tang, S., & Ferguson, A. (2014). The possibility of wellbeing: Preliminary results from surveys of Australian professional legal education students. *QUT Law Review, 14*(1), 27–51. https://doi.org/10.5204/qutlr.v14i1.521

Tjia, T., Marshman, I., Beard, J., & Baré, E. (2020). Australian university workforce responses to COVID-19 pandemic: reacting to a short-term crisis or planning for longer term challenges? https://melbourne-cshe.unimelb.edu.au/lh-martin-institute/fellow-voices/australian-university-workforce-responses-to-covid-19-pandemic

Ungar, M., & Liebenberg, L. (2011). Assessing resilience across cultures using mixed methods: Construction of the child and youth resilience measure. *Journal of Mixed Methods Research, 5*(2), 126–149. https://doi.org/10.1177/1558689811400607

Universities Australia. (2018). *2017 Universities Australia student finances survey* (Student Finances Survey, Issue). www.universitiesaustralia.edu.au/policy-submissions/teaching-learning-funding/student-finances-survey

Eileen Siddins has interest in transforming university art curriculum to benefit art students' wellbeing and resilience. Her research is published by the International Journal of Innovation, Creativity and Change, Journal of Arts & Humanities and the Australian Council of Arts & Design Schools. You can find more information about her research at www.wellartist.org.

Reimagining Higher Education Curricula for Creative and Performing Artists: Creating More Resilient and Industry-Ready Graduates

Ryan Daniel

Abstract Creative and performing artists often experience heightened levels of mental health distress, experiences increasingly recognised in the discourse and the academic literature. Some students studying the arts at the higher education level may even bring with them pre-existing mental health issues, which can affect their capacities for learning and career preparation. On completing their studies, graduates enter a sector that offers particular challenges in terms of significant competition for employment, non-linear work patterns, precarious resource bases and physical and mental stressors associated with the nature of artistic work. An artist therefore requires resilience and mental strength to cope with the realities of their practice. This chapter surveys recent research literature relevant to artists and mental health, it identifies several implications for higher education programs in the arts, and suggests ways curricula might be reimagined to respond to a post-pandemic world which is likely to offer significant challenges for artists.

Keywords Artists · Mental health · Higher education · Curriculum · Covid-19

Introduction

Students around the world sign up to higher education creative and performing arts programs hoping to secure a career in creative industries. Governments also invest in creative industries in both developed and developing countries, recognising the value that arts, creativity and culture bring to the economy. In an increasingly consumer focussed global society, where creative experiences and entertainment are sought after in a range of informal and formal settings, the demand for and production of creative content has accelerated in recent decades. Whilst the global Covid-19 pandemic that emerged in early 2020 has had a major impact and slowed global economies (including the creative industries sector), there is evidence that in lock-down individuals and societies have turned to the arts as a form of refuge and respite.

R. Daniel (✉)
James Cook University, Townsville, Australia
e-mail: ryan.daniel@jcu.edu.au

A. P. Francis and M. A. Carter (eds.), *Mental Health and Higher Education in Australia*,
https://doi.org/10.1007/978-981-16-8040-3_9

Hence, there is ongoing demand for creative work and for new forms of content. Like all members of society, artists will face new challenges adjusting to a changed world, increased unpredictability and the "new normal". Those involved in the education and training of artists will also have a very important role to play, particularly those in higher education who are required to prepare graduates for the world of work and very challenging careers.

This chapter focusses on three key topics relevant to artists. The first is the standard discourse that continues to link artists and mental health conditions (Hays, 2017). This includes such perceptions and stereotypes of the "mad artist" with predilections for and higher rates of psychopathological conditions, the "starving artist" who suffers in order to produce "great art", and the "frivolous artist" who is perceived by some segments of society as engaging in time-wasting activity that has little to no public impact and value. The second topic is the impact of the current global pandemic on creative industries. Covid-19 is taking a toll on the mental health of artists, and will have a long-term effect. At the same time, it is affecting art-making and may result in significant change in modes of production and consumption. The third topic is the future for higher education creative and performing arts programs, which this chapter argues will need to change dramatically in order to recognise and address the mental stressors associated with a career in creative industries. These stressors are likely to be significantly exacerbated as a result of the current global pandemic. In the current crisis the world needs artists more than ever, as they can provide the means by which millions find refuge in the beauty that the arts provide. Therefore, it becomes even more important that higher education providers revisit their curricula in order that they prepare graduate artists for the new normal, and that graduates are better equipped to deal with the various and ongoing mental stressors they will face.

Artists: History, Perceptions and Mental Health

For centuries, philosophers and authors have explored the relationship between artists and mental health (Kaufman, 2016). As far back as the Greek philosophers including Plato, prominent thinkers have considered the extent to which the creative gene or "genius" is caused by external factors such as the "muse" or divine intervention, and if it requires the influence of psychopathological conditions or mind-altering substances. These various stigmas are largely perceptions that have become ingrained in society where clear understandings of creativity and the creative process remain elusive (Barron, 1963; Ceci & Kumar, 2016; Kaufman, 2016; Lubart, 2018; Runco, 2014; Steptoe, 1998; Wiggins et al., 2015). An increasing number of authors have considered and interrogated these complex issues, with significant growth in the literature in the last two decades. Consensus is yet to be achieved in relation to the personality traits or experience required for high-level creativity, the external forces or conditions that need to be in place, and the processes associated with moving from creative intent through to creative realisation (Botella et al., 2018; Sternberg, 2018; Wilson, 2018).

Artists who aim to make a living from their creativity are exposed to intense scrutiny and judgement by live and online audiences, as well as the broader artistic community. The explosion in online activity through the internet has meant that artists are exposed to an extra element of scrutiny, much of which can be anonymous and potentially lead to heightened stress. Artists also have to determine the extent to which they want to establish an online presence and to engage with social media. They are subject to the views, preferences and policies of a number of stakeholders with significant power in the relevant cultural field (Bourdieu, 1984), such as directors, producers, funding agents, critics, commentators and government agencies. At times, these stakeholders apply subjective judgements in assessing the quality or suitability of particular artists, which can have a major effect on self-esteem and self-confidence for the performing artist (for example musician, actor, dancer) who undertakes countless auditions for roles and for paid work (Moyle, 2019). Online audiences are also increasingly active in evaluating and commenting on artists and their creativity, thereby adding an additional layer of scrutiny and potential stress (Adipa, 2019). Key agents in the field have the capacity to foster and accelerate careers, or to stymie and curtail them. This constant pressure has an impact on the mental health of artists who are striving for artistic, personal and career success.

An additional and well-documented layer of stress for artists results from the widely acknowledged oversupply of creative labour (Menger, 1999; Towse & Hernández, 2020), with many facing significant job insecurity, lower earnings and the need to undertake non-artistic or bread-and-butter work in order to survive and sustain their art practice. The stereotype of the actor, painter, film maker or musician having to wait tables, make coffees, or stack supermarket shelves is a reality for many aspiring creatives (Higdon & Chapman, 2020; Ivcevic et al., 2020). World famous actors such as Julianne Moore, Sandra Bullock, Chris Pratt and Jon Hamm all spent several years waiting tables before achieving Hollywood success and fame. Whilst this experience of undertaking the type of work that enables but does not enhance a career is not limited to aspiring artists, it is relatively common amongst them, and it remains an entrenched stereotype in western society.

Like many important figures in history, many high-profile artists have achieved an almost celebrity-like status, often due as much to their personal challenges and mental health conditions as to their creative work. The list of artists is extensive and ranges from writers such as Virginia Woolf and Ernest Hemingway, to painters Vincent Van Gogh and Edward Munch, composers Wolfgang Amadeus Mozart and Ludwig van Beethoven to contemporary popular musicians such as Jimmy Hendrix, Amy Winehouse and Kurt Cobain. In recent decades, numerous artists—musicians in particular—have succumbed to suicide at a young age, largely as a result of their battles with mental health whilst dealing with their celebrity status. One of the recent tragic deaths involved the Swedish electronic-music artist Avicii, who "reached almost absurd levels of fame, success, wealth and adoration. Sadly, his success came [with the] heavy cost of anxiety, depression, heavy alcoholism, and ultimately suicide" (Mayoras & Mayoras, 2019). Avicii was only 28 years old when he ended his life in 2018.

Full-time artists face similar physical and mental stressors as do sporting professionals. Those in performing arts fields such as dance, music and acrobatics can be prone to serious and long-term physical injuries. Dancers are at risk from feet, knee, and hip injuries; instrumental musicians risk injuries to hands, neck and back; and singers risk damage to their vocal organ (Kwok & Eslick, 2019; Moyle, 2019; Stanek et al., 2017). In a recent study involving college-level musicians in the United States, Stanek et al. (2017) found that of 1007 survey participants, 67% experienced pain, however few of these actively reported seeking medical help and support. Like those involved in professional sport, artists who face short- or longer-term injuries and the need to manage their body are exposed to the mental stressors associated with regular bouts of pain and enforced inactivity, loss of earnings, the risk of permanent damage and at worse, a curtailed career. Whilst those in professional sport often have the ongoing support of physiotherapists, masseurs, personal trainers, sports psychologists and dieticians, this is far less common for professional artists given the lack of funding available across the sector for these services (Moyle, 2019).

High-profile celebrity artists and sporting professionals have in recent years had a positive impact in relation to mental health awareness, with more and more individuals prepared to reveal to the public their personal battles with mental illness. In the entertainment world, current celebrities including Lady Gaga, Demi Lovato, Ben Affleck and Leonardo DiCaprio have revealed their struggles, as have sporting greats such as Michael Phelps, Amanda Beard, Serena Williams, Frank Bruno and Jerry West. Whilst celebrities and sporting greats have an important role to play in raising awareness of the seriousness of mental illness, as well as the potential ways to seek support in dealing with challenges, they also suffer very easily at the power of the masses. For example, Franssen (2020) refers to the breakdown and recovery of performer Demi Lovato in recent years, describing how the Lovato story "demonstrates the paradoxical cultural status of celebrities: they embody success, glamour and beauty; yet at the same time, society fosters a fetishistic fascination for their downfall" (p. 103).

Recent authors continue to refer to the need for non-artistic skills and support for those working in creative industries. Patkovic (2020), for example, contends there is minimal literature on the concept of resilience in relation to musicians, proceeding to argue that the three most important factors for them are "optimism, self-esteem and personal support provided by trusted persons" (p. 74). He then compares the careers of three famous musicians (Beethoven, Vladimir Horowitz, Glenn Gould) with three contemporary artists currently working professionally (two accordion players, one ballet dancer). Whilst a very small sample, Patkovic (2020) identified that what all six had in common was a "trustworthy person or mentor in their own life who stood by them and gave them the support they needed in difficult times" (p. 76). He proceeds to argue for three key dimensions in music education: the encouragement of networking amongst musicians, the implementation of resilience as a formal subject of study and a system where every musician has a personal mentor whose primary role is to provide positive support. Whilst arguing that the mentoring element is the most important aspect of the three, Patkovic (2020) does not provide any detail of how this might work in practice.

Bacon (2016) also argues for the importance of finding an appropriate mentor for those engaging in the solitary practice of creative writing. Citing numerous examples of mentors and mentees in history, such as Aristotle and Plato, Picasso and his father, Van Gogh and Jean-François Millet, Bacon (2016) proposes that a "good mentor will nurture the creative practitioner through vital interrogations that add value to their practice" (p. 181). For prospective artists, this arguably works particularly well in the area of higher degree research supervision, where the expert supervisor mentors the student in a one-on-one capacity, although if this relationship is fraught with tensions it can be highly problematic for both parties (Bacon, 2016; Batty et al., 2020). Bacon (2016) therefore argues that an artist needs to "discern unhealthy mentor relationships and act swiftly to substitute or reconfigure them, and equally have the cognisance to leverage from worthy mentor partnerships" (p. 190).

The 2020 Pandemic, Art and the Future of Creative Industries

The arts sector has been one of the biggest casualties of the Covid-19 pandemic (Eikhof, 2020). At the time of writing this chapter, the global situation was dire. In the United Kingdom (UK), Brown's (2020) description of the impact on the performing arts sector notes the "thousands of jobs already lost [with] politicians and unions warning of a 'tsunami' to come". Turnover in the UK cultural economy was expected to drop 30% during 2020, with 400,000 people or 20% of the cultural workforce to lose their employment. In the United States, it is likely that 2.7 million jobs and more than $150 billion in sales will be lost, with a Brookings institute research report claiming that the consequent "lasting damage to the creative sector will drastically undercut [American] culture, well-being, and quality of life" (Florida & Seman, 2020). In Europe the situation is also dire, and a report from the McKinsey company proposes that 50% of jobs in the arts and entertainment sector are at risk, potentially resulting in 1.7 million unemployed workers (Chinn et al., 2020). In Australia, a research report by the Grattan institute proposes that up to 75% of workers in the creative and performing arts are likely to lose their jobs, this more than three times the average for the total Australian workforce (Caust, 2020).

Government rescue or recovery packages for artists have been problematic, in that they have typically focussed on institutions and businesses whilst the majority of artists work as freelancers or by contract to contract. As a result, most artists are unable to access these programs. In countries such as the UK and Australia, rescue packages for the arts have been late to emerge, with ongoing uncertainty about how these packages work and who is eligible. It has also been suggested that these support and recovery programs may only delay inevitable disaster (Guardian Writers, 2020). In addition to calls for urgent and ongoing government support, there are emerging views that business models in the arts will need to drastically change. For example, Eikhof (2020) proposes that less use of permanent contracts, cuts to salaries and rates, recruitment via contacts rather than expensive advertising processes will all need to considered. Debates exist about the rapid move to online delivery of cultural products, with Midgette (2020) suggesting that if this stopgap measure continues to gather momentum in the longer term, it will result in an extremely competitive market for capturing audiences. Ultimately, there is an emerging consensus that whilst most workers in all industries will be prone to increased stress and mental health conditions (Pfefferbaum & North, 2020), artists are arguably one of the more at-risk groups given their already precarious work conditions and struggle to survive financially.

Implications for Higher Education Programs in Creative and Performing Arts in the "New Normal"

Recent decades have seen significant growth in the numbers of students enrolling in higher education programs in the creative and performing arts (Daniel & Johnstone, 2017). As argued by Higdon and Chapman (2020), the comfort of higher education is a great attraction for many artists and it may be the case that in the post-pandemic recession, even more prospective artists will enrol in study. Whilst the full economic and social impact of the global pandemic on the higher education sector is yet to be fully realised, it is likely the case that institutions and educators will need to continue to look for new models of delivery. If travel restrictions, social distancing and lockdowns remain in place for some time, perhaps even years, the education and training of artists through traditional face to face methods and small cohorts—where they are often in close proximity to each other—will need to be revisited. In addition, graduates are likely to face a very different arts industry in the future. The view by Higdon and Chapman (2020) that student artists "perceive the university world as safe and the graduate world as precarious and unsafe" (p. 272) may be exacerbated in future years, as the arts sector struggles to rebuild, to restore income streams, and where government and philanthropic funding is likely to be less available and far more competitive.

The calls for higher education programs in the arts to consider change continue, given the mismatch between the supply of labour and the volume of work available in the sector (Higdon & Chapman, 2020). These calls for change are strongly related to ongoing views in the discourse that students in arts programs are prone to and often suffer mental health stressors that other students may not (Higdon & Chapman, 2020). Therefore, Higdon and Chapman (2020) highlight the need for specific curricula that address "anxiety and mental health as well as financial and relational stress … [but also] ensure that students do not become over-supported and thus afraid of making the transition" (p. 280) to the world of work. Moyle (2019) argues that one of the greatest challenges relates to funding the inclusion of performance psychology into higher education arts programs, where students would be provided with fundamental skills in performance psychology and knowledge of the range of support strategies and services available to them that they may require in the future.

In terms of specific strategies that higher education providers might consider, one theme relates to mentoring involving industry professionals and through mentored projects. For example, Botstein (2020) contends that professional musicians "need to work more closely with higher education" (p. 359). Another theme is that proposed by Bell and Bell (2016), who argue that entrepreneurship education should not be the sole domain of business schools but that they should be university wide, given they "may be missing potential entrepreneurs enrolled in more technical and creative courses of study" (p. 335). In their study, 32 participants from a range of fields including creative arts took part in a business plan creation process—in groups—where three winners were eventually chosen and provided with start-up funds and ongoing mentoring support. Bell and Bell (2016) stated that the "most successful team had a robust combination of interdisciplinary members from the schools of business, psychology and *fine arts*" [author's italics] (p. 340).

Traditionally, creative and performing arts schools have tended to be focussed on developing an individual's technical and expressive skills. The notion of the painter, musician, writer and designer spending days and nights in the studio has been a tradition and thus stereotype. Whilst to some extent this remains a requirement, it comes with a cost, namely isolation, stress, exposure to what can be subjective and harsh criticism at times, all of which have significant potential to contribute to or exacerbate mental health issues. Taking the leap into a new paradigm where students are encouraged to diversify their practice and focus beyond individual training to include a range of additional activities and learning experiences is not necessarily straightforward, but the world of work post the pandemic would suggest that there is no longer the option to rest on traditions and old styles of working. Botstein (2020), in relation to music performances in concert halls specifically, reflects on the question of "whether something akin to the past would ever resume. And if it would not, what would the future hold" (p. 352). Similarly, Tregear (2020) questions the future for extremely costly and urban-centric Opera companies and their business models, arguing that "a return to anything like our pre-COVID operatic culture is unlikely". This would suggest that higher education programs at least formally introduce students to new methods and locations for presenting creative work, that do not necessarily involve the traditional performance venue, gallery or museum amongst others. How to effectively use alternative physical spaces, online platforms, virtual collaboration and social media is likely to be key to the future for artists, hence an area to be considered as part of higher education.

In summary, this chapter proposes that higher education academics consider a new curriculum that, in addition to individual skill development in an area or areas of artistic practice, allows students to develop specialised skills and knowledge in the following areas:

- Industry practices via mentoring and through mentored projects in live or virtual environments;

- Online technologies and communication systems including social media platforms;
- Entrepreneurship and alternative business models that are applicable to artists; and
- Psychology principles, mental health, resilience and wellbeing.

The challenge for educators is to consider how these various areas might be embedded, sequenced and delivered, given it would rely on teams of staff and multiple areas of expertise. It would require significant rethinking and revision to traditional models. The various areas of skill and knowledge development cited above would also potentially suit as part of the ongoing development of a "career preparation" portfolio that students work on and update during the course of their studies.

Conclusions

The new normal for the arts in higher education is likely to be very challenging for students, academics and institutional leaders. Students are likely to face an uncertain future, including novel ways of working and sustaining a career. Academics are under pressure to perform at a high level in teaching, research, engagement and all of the accompanying administrative and operational tasks associated with an increasing focus on return on investment and accountability. Given the enormous financial shocks being experienced around the world, including a significant and to some extent still unknown stress on higher education budgets, the future will rely on academics who are prepared to be courageous, to take risks and to acknowledge that graduates are likely to face a very different future. How institutions might move to courses that enable artists to develop their passion but also important complementary skills and knowledge is not easy to determine and resolve quickly. Whilst this challenge is not insurmountable, if the sector is to have artists equipped to deal with the new normal and its associated pressures and potential impact on their mental health, higher education providers will need to be supported and encouraged to rethink the ways in which they prepare graduates for a future with its many unknowns, but also a future with many opportunities yet to be determined.

Acknowledgements The author wishes to thank Dr. Claire Brennan, the peer reviewers and the Editors for their valuable suggestions and feedback.

References

Adipa, P. (2019). Talking events: How social interaction and discourse shape cultural participation, aesthetic evaluation, and meaning-making. *Poetics, 77*, 101381.

Bacon, E. (2016). Creative practice–finding the right mentor. *New Writing, 13*(2), 180–193.

Barron, F. (1963). *Creativity and psychological health: Origins of personal vitality and creative freedom*. Van Nostrand.
Batty, C., Ellison, E., Owens, A., & Brien, D. (2020). Mapping the emotional journey of the doctoral 'hero': Challenges faced and breakthroughs made by creative arts and humanities candidates. *Arts and Humanities in Higher Education, 19*(4), 354–376.
Bell, R., & Bell, H. (2016). Replicating the networking, mentoring and venture creation benefits of entrepreneurship centres on a shoestring: A student-centred approach to entrepreneurship education and venture creation. *Industry and Higher Education, 30*(5), 334–343.
Botella, M., Zenasni, F., & Lubart, T. (2018). What are the stages of the creative process? What visual art students are saying. *Frontiers in Psychology, 9*(2266), 1–13.
Botstein, L. (2020). The future of music in America: The challenge of the COVID-19 pandemic. *The Musical Quarterly, 102*(4), 351–360. https://doi.org/10.1093/musqtl/gdaa007
Bourdieu, P. (1984) *Distinction: A social critique of the judgment of taste*. Harvard University Press.
Brown, M. (2020, 4 September). Theatres must reopen to curb job losses, says West End star Paul Whitehouse. *The Guardian*. https://www.theguardian.com/stage/2020/sep/03/coronavirus-theatres-must-reopen-says-west-end-star-paul-whitehouse
Caust, J. (2020, April 29). Cornavirus: 3 in 4 Australians employed in the creative and performing arts could lose their jobs. *The Conversation*. https://tinyurl.com/hxasxp5h
Ceci, M. W., & Kumar, V. (2016). A correlational study of creativity, happiness, motivation, and stress from creative pursuits. *Journal of Happiness Studies, 17*(2), 609–626.
Chinn, D., Klier, J., Stern, S., & Tesfu, S. (2020, April 19). *Safeguarding Europe's livelihoods: Mitigating the employment impact of COVID-19*. McKinsey & Company. https://www.mckinsey.com/industries/public-and-social-sector/our-insights/safeguarding-europes-livelihoods-mitigating-the-employment-impact-of-covid-19
Daniel, R., & Johnstone, R. (2017). Becoming an artist: Exploring the motivations of undergraduate students at a regional Australian University. *Studies in Higher Education, 42*(6), 1015–1032.
Eikhof, D. (2020). COVID-19, inclusion and workforce diversity in the cultural economy: What now, what next? *Cultural Trends*, 1–17. https://doi.org/10.1080/09548963.2020.1802202
Florida, R., & Seman, M. (2020, August 11). *Lost art: Measuring COVID-19's devastating impact on America's creative economy*. Brookings Institute. https://www.brookings.edu/research/lost-art-measuring-covid-19s-devastating-impact-on-americas-creative-economy/
Franssen, G. (2020). The celebritization of self-care: The celebrity health narrative of Demi Lovato and the sickscape of mental illness. *European Journal of Cultural Studies, 23*(1), 89–111.
Guardian Writers. (2020, June 18). *World spends to protect culture from economic ruin*. https://www.theguardian.com/culture/2020/jun/18/world-spends-to-protect-culture-from-economic-ruin
Hays, K. (2017). Performance psychology with performing artists. Oxford *Research Encyclopedia of Psychology*. https://oxfordre.com/psychology/view/10.1093/acrefore/9780190236557.001.0001/acrefore-9780190236557-e-191
Higdon, R., & Chapman, K. (2020). *A dramatic existence: Undergraduate preparations for a creative life in the performance industries*. Industry and Higher Education. https://journals.sagepub.com/doi/10.1177/0950422220912979
Ivcevic, Z., Grossman, E., & Ranjan, A. (2020). Patterns of psychological vulnerabilities and resources in artists and nonartists. *Psychology of Aesthetics, Creativity, and the Arts*. https://doi.org/10.1037/aca0000309
Kaufman, J. (2016). *Creativity 101*. Springer.
Kwok, M., & Eslick, G. (2019). The impact of vocal and laryngeal pathologies among professional singers: A meta-analysis. *Journal of Voice, 33*(1), 58–65.
Lubart, T. (2018). *Creative process*. Springer.
Mayoras, D., & Mayoras, A. (2019, January 8). Avicii died without a will but illustrated an important lesson. *Forbes*. https://www.forbes.com/sites/trialandheirs/2019/01/08/avicii-died-without-a-will-but-illustrated-an-important-lesson/#3a0a154377dc
Menger, P.-M. (1999). Artistic labour markets and careers. *Annual Review of Sociology, 25*, 541–574.

Midgette, A. (2020, April 27). Furloughed musicians and a new digital frontier: Performing arts in the COVID-19 shutdown. *Vanity Fair*. https://www.vanityfair.com/style/2020/04/performing-arts-in-the-covid-19-shutdown
Moyle, G. (2019). Coaching performing artists. *Consulting Psychology Journal: Practice and Research, 71*(2), 97–106. https://doi.org/10.1037/cpb0000127
Patkovic, D. (2020). Resilience in music–viewpoints of artists' abilities to deal with crises in life. *Trio, 9*(1), 70–77.
Pfefferbaum, B., & North, C. (2020). Mental health and the Covid-19 pandemic. *New England Journal of Medicine*. https://www.nejm.org/doi/full/10.1056/NEJMp2008017
Runco, M. (2014). *Creativity: Theories and themes: Research, development, and practice*. Elsevier.
Stanek, J., Komes, K., & Murdock, F. (2017). A cross-sectional study of pain among US college music students and faculty. *Medical Problems of Performing Artists, 32*(1), 20–26.
Steptoe, A. (1998). *Genius and the mind: Studies of creativity and temperament*. Oxford University Press.
Sternberg, R. (2018). A triangular theory of creativity. *Psychology of Aesthetics, Creativity, and the Arts, 12*(1), 50–67.
Towse, R., & Hernández, T. (Eds.). (2020). *Handbook of cultural economics*. Edward Elgar.
Tregear, P. (2020, September 8). As COVID wreaks havoc in the performing arts, do we still need a national opera company? *The Conversation*. https://tinyurl.com/d3xep7n8
Wiggins, G., Tyack, P., Scharff, C., & Rohrmeier, M. (2015). The evolutionary roots of creativity: mechanisms and motivations. *Philosophical Transactions of the Royal Society B: Biological Sciences, 370* (1664). https://royalsocietypublishing.org/doi/full/10.1098/rstb.2014.0099
Wilson, J. (2018). *Artists in the university: Positioning artistic research in higher education*. Springer.

Ryan Daniel holds a Bachelor of Music Honours degree (Class I and University Medal), a Master of Music degree in chamber music performance and research, and a Ph.D. in piano pedagogy. He also holds the FTCL (Trinity) and L.Mus.A (AMEB) performance diplomas. He is currently a senior researcher in creative arts and creative industries at James Cook University, Australia, with over 50 peer-reviewed publications to date. His research is published in *Creative Industries, International Journal of Cultural Policy, Creativity Studies, Asia-Pacific Journal for Art Education, Local Economy, Australian Journal of Career Development, Arts and Humanities in Higher Education, CoDesign, Music Education Research* and the *British Journal of Music Education*. Professor Daniel has achieved significant awards for his teaching, including the JCU Vice Chancellor's citation for teaching excellence (2004, 2006) as well as a national teaching excellence citation (2010). He has also been twice winner of the Supervisory Panel of the Year award for his contributions to team-based Ph.D. supervision (2019, 2020).

Embedding an Aboriginal Well-Being Intervention in Australian Social Work Curriculum

Fiona Gardner, Mary Whiteside, and Rachael Sanders

Abstract The Australian higher education sector is increasingly concerned about the mental health and well-being of students. Within this context, the unique stressors that can impact the well-being for students enrolled in social work degrees need to be studied. Students come to social work from a range of backgrounds and embark on a journey of learning to work with diverse groups in a complex and changing social service sector. For some students, this can be somewhat daunting and overwhelming, particularly when coupled with personal challenges they may be facing themselves. This chapter introduces a curriculum-based response to student well-being in social work studies. In a foundational first-year subject, students are introduced to an Aboriginal Family Well-being Empowerment program and an embedded process of critical reflection. The subject promotes ethics, self-awareness, confidence, critical thinking, relationship management and interpersonal skills. Pilot research of the impact of the subject highlights its relevance for enhancing student well-being, foundational social work skill development and students' capacity to manage an increasingly complex and changing world.

Introduction

Ensuring the mental health and well-being of students is an increasing concern in Australian higher education (Rickwood et al., 2016). This is particularly the case for academics supporting social work students who come from a wide range of backgrounds and embark on what can be a personally challenging journey of learning to work with diverse groups in a complex and changing social service sector. Given

---

F. Gardner (✉) · M. Whiteside · R. Sanders
La Trobe University, Bundoora, Australia
e-mail: F.Gardner@latrobe.edu.au

M. Whiteside
e-mail: M.Whiteside@latrobe.edu.au

R. Sanders
e-mail: R.Sanders@latrobe.edu.au

A. P. Francis and M. A. Carter (eds.), *Mental Health and Higher Education in Australia*,
https://doi.org/10.1007/978-981-16-8040-3_10

that many students have personal issues, including mental health concerns, social work studies can feel somewhat daunting and overwhelming.

This chapter introduces a curriculum-based response to student well-being for first-year students, providing them with a foundation for their studies and a pre-emptive response to these concerns. In their *Reflective Communication* subject, students are introduced to an Aboriginal Family Well-being Empowerment program. Pilot research on the impact of this subject highlights its relevance for enhancing student well-being, foundational social work skill development and student's capacity to manage an increasingly complex and changing world (Whiteside et al, 2017).

Background

The Australian higher education sector is increasingly concerned about the mental health and well-being of students; however, formal evidence is limited. Orygen, the National Centre of Excellence in Youth Mental Health, aptly named their 2017 research project *Under the Radar: The mental health of Australian university students* as a way of highlighting the lack of evidence. However, a study conducted in 2016, by the National Union of Students in partnership with Headspace, a mental health agency focused on young people, reported that of the 3300 survey respondents, 65% of the 2636 respondents aged between 17 and 25 reported high or very high psychological distress, with 53% of students over 25 reporting the same levels (Rickwood et al., 2016). While the authors of this report point out that this may be due, in part, to self-selection, given the concept of well-being is defined by one's own perception and is therefore highly subjective, students' own judgement of psychological distress is important.

Browne et al. (2017) suggest a number of risk factors related to poor mental health among university students, including academic pressure and performance expectations, financial pressures and low SES, coming from rural and regional areas and/or being an Aboriginal or Torres Strait Islander. Both anecdotal information and more formal data from counselling services (Andrews, 2016) indicate that the number of higher education students with mental health issues continues to increase. However, a recent Australian study by Burns and Crisp (2019) did not find an increased level of mental illness among people in tertiary education, inferring the rise in support service engagement is due to students' increased willingness to seek help. Whether there is a rise in the prevalence of mental illness or the number of students seeking support, our experience as social work educators is that more students need extra support related to mental health issues, particularly in relation to anxiety and depression.

As with other student cohorts, there remains a need for more research on the mental health of social work students, with international evidence indicating a significant level of depression (Ting, 2011). Some students fear their mental illness will mean they are seen as not fit for practice, so they are reluctant to divulge it. Furthermore, many social work students avoid seeking help due to stigma, distrust and concerns about confidentiality and cultural competence (Ting, 2011). There are unique stressors that can impact well-being for students enrolled in social work degrees. They are from a wide range of backgrounds but also need to work with many groups with experiences different from their own in an uncertain and constantly changing context. This is particularly confronting when these students experience personal challenges to their health and well-being.

There is an expectation that social work students develop self-awareness, with Trevithick (2012) suggesting the capacity to constructively reflect on our own experiences and understand their possible influence on our behaviour is an integral part of social work practice. Chenoweth and McAuliffe (2017) emphasise the importance of social workers and social work students knowing themselves, understanding their own motivations and the relevance of their own family and personal history. Related to this, these authors propose that each student needs to "(p)repare yourself to be challenged about your views of the world and your morals and values" (Chenoweth & McAuliffe, 2017, p. 3).

Given these expectations, their own anxieties and those of the people they will be working with, social work students need to manage their own mental health and learn greater resilience. Essentially, social workers need to be able to cope with the emotional demands of the job without these impacting their mental health and well-being (Cuartero & Campos-Vidal, 2019). Grant and Kinman (2012) observed that trainee social workers who were more resilient were also more psychologically healthy and that emotional intelligence, reflective ability, empathy and social confidence are predictors of resilience. However, while self-awareness can help build resilience, the focus on this in the social work course can be unsettling or challenging for students with past traumatic or distressing experiences.

Curriculum-Based Response to Foster Student Well-Being: Reflective Practice Subject

This chapter introduces a curriculum-based response to these issues of student well-being and to building self-awareness and related resilience, in an Australian social work higher education context. In a foundational first-year subject, students are introduced to an Aboriginal Family Well-being Empowerment program (Aboriginal Education Development Branch, 2002) in combination with an embedded process of critically reflecting on their feelings, thoughts, assumptions, values and reactions to the subject.

From a First Nations perspective "(m)ental health results from an adjustment to one's life circumstances. This adjustment allows ease instead of dis-ease and can be developed further into the idea of self-actualisation" (Grieves, 2009, p. 44). This is firmly connected to Spirituality: "a state of being that includes knowledge, calmness, acceptance and tolerance, balance and focus, inner strength, cleansing and inner peace, feeling whole, an understanding of cultural roots and 'deep well-being'"(Grieves, 2006, p.52). An understanding of the interconnections between a holistic approach to well-being is embedded in the Family Well-being Framework (Whiteside et al, 2014). As such, the subject fosters self-awareness, confidence, critical thinking, being ethical, relationship management and interpersonal skills.

Our pilot research of the impact of the subject highlights its relevance for enhancing student well-being, foundational social work skill development and student capacity to manage an increasingly complex and changing world (Whiteside et al., 2017). Developing the capacity to reflect on our own well-being, and how to influence it, is a significant aspect of the subject. It is hoped this will provide a foundation for effective social work practice by workers who are able to practice self-care for their own mental health and well-being as well as that of their clients and co-workers.

Reflective Practice Subject

Background to the FWB Empowerment Program

One of the authors (Mary Whiteside) is part of an Indigenous-led university and community research partnership seeking to strengthen the evidence for the Aboriginal Family Well-being Empowerment program (FWB). Developed in 1993, by The Aboriginal Employment Development Branch (AEDB) of the TAFE South Australia, the program adopts the premise that physical, emotional, mental and spiritual well-being enables people to take greater control for their lives at personal and community levels (Whiteside et al., 2014). The program involves a structured reflective process through which participants explore topics such as human qualities, basic human needs, managing emotions and relationships, life journey and conflict resolution. Participation in the program has been shown to bring about transformative life changes for participants. Participants report building resilience, improving problem-solving and relationship skills, engaging more fully in education and employment and participating in collective efforts for organisational and community change (Whiteside et al., 2014, 2017).

In some of the organisations where the program has been delivered, including Queensland child protection services, Aboriginal participants have called for non-Aboriginal workers to train in FWB as a means for enabling culturally sensitive practice (Whiteside et al., 2006). This aligns with the call within social work to integrate the understanding of Aboriginal and Torres Strait Islander knowledges in social work education and practice (Zubrzycki et al., 2014) and to practice in culturally responsive ways (Australian Association of Social Work, 2015). With permission from Aboriginal leaders and TAFE South Australia, social work academics at La Trobe university made the decision to trial FWB within the first year of their social work course as a strategy for student well-being, foundational skill development and, most importantly, to learn from Aboriginal Australians about a culturally respectful approach to practice, including the need to be critically reflective (Zubrzycki et al., 2014).

How the FWB Program Is Used in the Subject

In our adaption of the FWB program, students are taken through a variety of topics in weekly two-hour workshops. Given that students are asked to reflect on their experiences, assumptions and values, a key first step is to create a culturally safe space for learning through the negotiation of a class group agreement. This is a significant part of establishing an effective group process. Students are encouraged to develop group guidelines that would help them to feel comfortable in exploring their own experiences. Students are often surprised that this is an expectation of the subject, making such comments as: "*I never expected to have to be talking about myself*".

In each group, educators facilitate explorations of how differently students may feel about engaging in self-reflection and how to allow for and be respectful of such differences. The preferred group culture generally includes protective qualities such as valuing and respecting different opinions, being honest and trustworthy, respecting others and self, keeping what's shared in class confidential, being non-judgemental, open and not making assumptions, recognising each other's strengths and being brave about sharing but also respectful of people's right not to share on some occasions.

Students are introduced to the subject's reflective model, foundational skills in helping others and theory of group work to enable them to facilitate the subsequent FWB topics with their peers in small groups. In the following weeks students work through the FWB topics of Human Values and Qualities; Basic Human Needs; Understanding Relationships; Life Journey; Conflict Resolution; Understanding Emotions and Crisis; Beliefs and Attitudes; and Self Care. Students are provided with a modified version of the FWB facilitator guide and topic handouts, as well as online resources such as facilitation demonstration videos and academic literature addressing empowerment, well-being and other concepts related to the weekly topic. Subject tutors receive training in course facilitation prior to subject commencement.

The FWB topics have clear connections to the mental health and well-being of students. The topic Basic Human Needs, for example, encourages students to think about what their own needs are in terms of physical, mental, spiritual and social well-being. In small groups totalling 5 or 6 students, students identify how they recognise and aim to fulfil their needs in these particular areas. The topic Emotions and Crisis fosters sharing of how emotions can be helpful or unhelpful in engaging with a crisis, but also how students have previously managed crises and how this could be helpful for building resilience. The weekly concepts that are explored in the smaller groups are discussed further in the whole of class discussions to allow the class facilitator to model the ideas and to talk about how the students found the experience. Students use the reflective model and the key questions outlined in the next section to more deeply interrogate their reaction to each topic and the implications for social work practice.

Reflective Model

The model for reflection used in the subject is based on the critically reflective approach developed by Fook and Gardner (2007) with a specific set of questions outlined in Gardner (2014). Here, critical reflection is defined as a "way of understanding and engaging with interconnections between an experience; the emotions, thoughts and reactions and actions related to that experience; meaning: what matters about the experience, including related assumptions and values at a fundamental level; and the influence of social context and history both individually and collectively with the expectation of the critically reflective process leading to socially just change" (Gardner, 2014, p. 34).

The critically reflective process is underpinned by four theoretical aspects. First, reflective practice emphasises the exploration of reactions and related assumptions by articulating beliefs and values that are often unconscious (Schon, 1983). Secondly, reflexivity encourages the exploration of "how we present to others, how we are perceived and the context within which we engage as well as our role and specific mandate" (Walsh, 2012, p. 192). This partly means acknowledging that the way we perceive ourselves and how others perceive us are not necessarily the same—and by implication, how we see others and how they see themselves may also differ. Postmodern thinking affirms there are many ways of perceiving and understanding any given person and situation and encourages us to see the discourses that influence our assumptions, those "general expectations about how society should be ordered, who has power and influence and how people should act" (Gardner, 2016, p. 51). This is complemented by critical social theory which makes explicit the assumptions and expectations of the wider social culture and context and how these influence individual and community experiences. As Fook (2012, p. 65) points out, this means having an "understanding of how the ways we talk about our world, that is, our frameworks, for understanding our social worlds, actually also construct it". The aim of the critically reflective process is to use these theoretical ideas to more deeply understand reactions to particular experiences given the context in which they occur. The theories are implicit in the questions asked in the process. These questions are highlighted in the next paragraph.

There are four stages to this reflective process. In Stage 1a, a student or worker identifies an experience that has caused some degree of discomfort or is puzzling to them in some way. They then use reflective questions to identify their reactions (i.e. *How did I react?, What were my feelings and thoughts?*), the meaning they attribute to the experience and reactions (i.e. *What was important to me?, Why did this matter to me?, What underlying values, beliefs, assumptions were there for me?)* and the context that surrounded the experience and reactions (i.e. *What was the background and how was my experience influenced by my individual family history and social context and to society I live in?*). This process generally leads to a deeper beginning understanding about why the experience has been significant and an identification of the meaning attached to it, including the unconscious assumptions made. Given this is a foundational first-year subject educators ask students to use this part of the reflective process, to help them develop their skills in self-awareness, knowing that we build on the next phases of the reflective process in subsequent subjects.

In Stage 1b of the reflective process, the student/worker would use similar reflective questions to explore the experience from the perspective of another person who has been part of the experience, such as asking what might have mattered for the other person. In Stage 1c, the student/worker then re-examines their perception of the experience to see whether they now perceive it differently. Finally, in Stage Two the student/worker explores the implications for change, either in their assumptions or in possible changed actions.

What generally emerges from this process is that the person reflecting reaches a deeper understanding of where they were coming from: the particular assumptions and values that they were reacting from, which they may choose to affirm or change. An example follows.

Terry, had an experience where she reacted angrily to another student, Will, who was not as quick to complete their part of an assignment group task as Terry would have liked. When Terry was asked what values and assumptions were there for you? Terry realised that she had assumed that everyone would have the same expectations as she did: that a group assignment needed to be the first priority in her life and that being organised and efficient and finishing the task early was important. Terry remembered that Will had mentioned in the first class that their young daughter had significant health issues. This encouraged Terry to see that Will would have had very different priorities which she could well understand. Terry also remembered the class discussion about differences in personality which meant that some people like her had a high need for closure for getting things done and became anxious and stressed if this didn't happen. Terry could see that others were relaxed and less stressed about leaving things to the last minute. When Terry returned to thinking about her own reaction, Terry realised that another assumption she had was that not only should everyone be the same but be the same as her. When asked how might your reaction be influenced by your family and social context?, Terry thought about her family and to some extent the society in which she lived, and Terry could see that her organised, task-centred approach was often validated, but that it had limitations in raising her anxiety levels and in not recognising the importance of relationships. Having understood this, Terry was better able to raise the issue of how to work together effectively in the group without becoming unhelpfully angry with Will. Terry was able to recognise that sometimes she put a lot of unhelpful pressure on herself to finish tasks early and that she needed a new assumption related to her own self-care and well-being.

Because the weekly FWB topics draw on students' personal experiences, they are found to be contextually relevant for critical reflection and the two elements of the subject are highly compatible. The subject's assessment tasks provide an opportunity for students to test their learning and enhance their knowledge through real-life experience. Students are required to keep a weekly journal using the reflective model, facilitate a FWB program topic with a group beyond the classroom (e.g. with family, friends or other students) and then write an academic report based on this experience, and design an innovative group presentation of a FWB topic. All of these helps demonstrate the subject's core learning outcomes, but also aim to improve student well-being and mental health.

Findings and Discussion

This subject has been taught for 5 years with over 800 students from metropolitan and rural campuses. Each year the subject receives well above average scores on university student feedback surveys. A mixed methods study undertaken in 2016 by Whiteside et al. (2017) found significant changes on empowerment and well-being measures that were delivered pre and post the subject, suggesting that the subject is highly relevant for student mental health and well-being.

Building Self-awareness and Confidence

Qualitatively, students referred to building self-awareness and confidence, being able to better manage the stresses associated with day-to-day life and strengthening relationships that were important to them. Students could see they were gaining knowledge that was relevant to their future professional life, and this helped them to engage more fully with their university studies (Whiteside et al., 2017). The following quotations are illustrative of these findings:

> "The FWB program has helped me look at my life from a different perspective and has allowed me to reflect on life wants and choices in a way that has allowed me to grow as a person"
>
> "It has helped me to understand myself and my emotions more clearly as well as dealing with different stages of my life"
>
> "FWB made me realise how strong and resilient I am as an individual and how I have overcome hard times in my life. This made me feel empowered and satisfied with life"
>
> "Most of all the FWB has strengthened and helped me overcome the fear of not being successful and dealing with normal stresses in everyday life"
>
> "FWB enabled me to be aware of the way in which I conduct myself, the way I interact with others, the way it affects others and how I can inspire others to make positive changes in others' lives"
>
> "FWB has enabled me to see my inner strengths and values. I know I can achieve whatever I want to"

In addition to these findings, as facilitators of this subject the authors have systematically considered their experience of the student groups combined with material from student journals that provide powerful examples of positive change in students' attitudes, assumptions and values over the course of a semester. Students enter the course at different levels of social, emotional, mental and spiritual well-being. They come with a range of values, beliefs and assumptions; and they hold varying levels of skill in communication, group work and critical reflection. For some, these ideas are familiar and the FWB content serves to strengthen their skills by providing new and interesting topics to reflect upon in a group setting. For others, the chasm between who they espouse to be as budding social workers and the way they interact with the group is more expansive. Inevitably, some students are more vocal and others more reserved. Regardless of where students begin, the shift in values, attitudes and ways of interacting with others is evident in the weekly journals. We have outlined themes from these journals below:

Using Journaling to Explore Thoughts, Feelings and Assumptions

The journal is a useful platform for students to reflect on and share their thoughts, feelings and assumptions. We have been pleasantly surprised about how honest some students are at revealing inner thoughts that they may otherwise not readily admit to others. Facilitators help foster a safe non-judgemental environment, and this is evident in journal entries in which students have shared intimate views and experiences. Many journals proved to be an excellent record of change, revelation and positive development. Some students shifted from a place of judgement and even a dismissive attitude towards others' thoughts and feelings, to an empathetic acceptance of difference. Students turned what they first considered to be an annoyance into a valued source of learning.

Changing Beliefs and Attitudes

An example of new learnings came from a group where it became clear that some students placed greater value on shared storytelling as a form of learning/teaching compared with others, and this influenced their level of contribution. This appeared to be linked to stage of life, with noteworthy differences between younger and older students. There were young students who were quite critical of older students "over" sharing their life experiences, considering them indulgent and time-wasting. Similarly, some older students were quite judgemental of what they perceived to be younger students' lack of engagement and reluctance to share their stories, assuming that they were lazy or too selfish to create a communal learning experience. It became evident that as the students' levels of self-awareness and ability to empathise increased, their opinions changed, and they became more understanding and responsive to their peers' experiences. Students could appreciate having their values and attitudes challenged as Chenoweth and McAuliffe (2017) advocate. Younger students came to appreciate what they could learn from the older students who had a more diverse range of life experiences, and the older students were more forgiving of the younger students' stage of life development and held more realistic expectations of them. Students developed a deeper group bond based on trust, empathy, acceptance (of self and others) and authenticity. This demonstrates how the FWB program improved students' well-being and how the reflective process worked to bring about positive change.

Need for Self-empowerment

The reflective journals also provided evidence of why a program that fosters self-empowerment is important, as demonstrated in the following example. The second week of student-facilitated groups focusses on four basic human needs – physical, emotional, spiritual and mental. Several students mentioned their reluctance to share stories that would reveal their Christian beliefs because they thought that they may be judged harshly by their peers. These women, in their early 20 s, said that they draw strength, comfort and wisdom from their religion, but they did not feel they could be open about the ways in which it adds to their well-being in case it meant they were treated differently. This is the antithesis of what the program aims to nurture—empowerment—and highlights the importance of overcoming notions of "othering", both real and perceived. This is not to suggest that their peers would have judged them or treated them differently, but this is a poignant example about how assumptions can hold us back from revealing ourselves and being authentic to our beliefs, thereby degrading our authenticity, which is ultimately disempowering and may impact our mental health. In this example, the journals have had an unintended positive outcome, in that the class facilitator has learned about some students' trepidation about sharing these values, which can be addressed in future classes by highlighting the benefits that some people gain from being a member of an organised religion.

Learning from the Experiences of Others

A final anecdotal example of the benefits of the subject on student's mental health is the moments in which students said something along the lines of "I didn't think they had had such a difficult background … they seem so happy and together" in response to hearing one of their peer's difficult life experiences. There have been several instances in which students come to learn that they assumed people must have had an easier upbringing than they had because they did not appear to be damaged or "messed up". From this, students learned two important lessons. Firstly, that holding assumptions about others is unhelpful because it restricts relationship building. Secondly, as Grant and Kinman (2012) suggest they came to connect self-awareness with well-being, to learn the meaning of resilience and that they too could develop wisdom, kindness, inner peace and accomplish their goals and desires despite the adversities that they had faced. The FWB program offers a space to learn about other people's experiences and the ways they develop their sense of self and notions of well-being—sometimes in spite of great adversity. The reflective component of the subject helps students to uncover their assumptions and learn that empowerment is a choice, and they can choose to drive their approach to life regardless of their history.

Conclusions

Our experience demonstrates the value of this kind of experiential shared learning and the related benefits in terms of mental health, well-being and the development of greater resilience. The FWB program offers a space to learn about other people's experiences and the ways they develop their sense of self, well-being and self-empowerment. The reflective component of the subject helps students to uncover their assumptions and what they take for granted, thereby learning that their reactions, actions and sense of empowerment are a choice that they can control. The combination of the FWB program and the reflective journal help students develop self-awareness and foster self-empowerment, which together aid in positive well-being and mental health.

However, there are challenges that need to be made explicit and managed effectively. We are asking students to be vulnerable by revealing their own experiences, some of which are painful. It is essential that we ensure that the process is sufficiently safe so that students who have experienced past trauma are not further traumatised and that students see this as an enabling and supportive process leading to greater resilience. It is also important that we don't reinforce unhelpful power differences, asking students to be self-revealing while we as the educators remain unknown.

What helps here is being prepared to demonstrate our own vulnerability by using an example from our own experience: as Savaya (2013, p.185) indicates "My self-disclosure increased the students' confidence in me as someone who was intimately acquainted with the process I was asking them to undergo and also learned from her critical reflection". It is essential to set the class up with a clear and mutually supportive group culture, exploring with each class their particular hopes and fears related to this kind of reflective experience (Fook & Gardner, 2007). If the group doesn't themselves name these, we need to make explicit the importance of confidentiality, being non-judgemental and to self-monitor what they choose to reveal.

Due to the uncertainty of COVID-19, this year the subject's authors are trialling this as on online subject. This has its own challenges with less easy access to seeing how each smaller group in the class is engaging at the same time. However, early indications are that students continue to engage well with the process, possibly finding some security in being in their home or chosen environment. In the light of these changes, are repeating the 2016 study (Whiteside et al., 2017) of the subject to gain greater understanding of both the impact of COVID-19 on our social work students' mental health and well-being and the experience of undertaking this subject in an online format.

To conclude, embedding a curriculum-based approach to improving student well-being has not only brought benefits in students' ability to manage life stresses but it has also taught foundational skills for professional social work practice. The integration of a model of critical reflection with the opportunity to experience an Aboriginal Family Well-being Empowerment program has been very effective and highlights the opportunities for learning from Aboriginal Australia.

Acknowledgements With thanks to the Aboriginal leaders and TAFE South Australia who have allowed the Family Well-being Program material to be used in this subject and to the students who have participated so constructively in this subject and contributed to the research.

References

Aboriginal Education Development Branch. (2002). *Family wellbeing curriculum document*. TAFE South Australia

Andrews, A. (2016). ANZSSA Heads of Counselling Services Benchmarking Survey. (2013). Summary report. *Journal of the Australian and New Zealand Student Services Association, 47*.

Australian Association of Social Work (AASW). (2015). *Preparing for culturally responsive and inclusive social work practice in Australia: Working with Aboriginal and Torres Strait Islander peoples*. http://www.aasw.asn.au/document/item/7006

Browne, V., Munro, J., & Cass, J. (2017). The mental health of Australian university students. *Journal of the Australian and New Zealand Student Services Association, 50*, 51–62.

Burns, R. A., & Crisp, D. A. (2019). The long-term mental health of Australia's tertiary students. *Social Psychiatry and Psychiatric Epidemiology*. https://doi.org/10.1007/s00127-019-01806-7

Chenoweth, L., & McAuliffe, D. (2017). *The road to social work and human services practice*. Cengage Learning.

Cuartero, E. C., & Campos-Vidal, J. F. (2019). Self-care behaviours and their relationship with satisfaction and compassion fatigue levels among social workers. *Social Work in Health Care, 58*(3), 274–290. https://doi.org/10.1080/00981389.2018.1558164

Fook, J. (2012). *Social work: A critical approach to practice.* Sage Publications.

Fook, J., & Gardner, F. (2007). *Practising critical reflection: A resource handbook.* Open University Press.

Gardner, F. (2014). *Being critically reflective.* Palgrave Macmillan.

Gardner, F. (2016). *Working with human service organisations* (2nd ed.). Oxford.

Grant, L., & Kinman, G. (2012). Enhancing wellbeing in social work students: Building resilience in the next generation. *Social Work Education, 31*(5), 605–621.

Grieves, V. (2009). *Aboriginal spirituality: Aboriginal philosophy the basis of Aboriginal social and emotional wellbeing.* Darwin: Discussion Paper No 9, Cooperative Research Centre for Aboriginal Health.

Grieves, V. (2006). Indigenous wellbeing: a framework for governments' cultural heritage activities. NSW Department of Environment and Conservation, Sydney at https://www.google.com/search?client=firefox-bd&q=Grieves%2C+V.+2006+Indigenous+Wellbeing%3A+A+Framework+for+Governments%27+Cultural+Heritage+Activities

Orygen: The National Centre of Excellence in Youth Mental Health. (2017). Under the radar: The mental health of Australian university students. Retrieved from https://www.orygen.org.au/Policy/Policy-Reports/Under-the-radar/OrygenUnder_the_radar_report

Rickwood, D., Telfor, N., O'Sullivan, S., Crisp, D., & Magyar, R. (2016). National Tertiary Student Wellbeing Survey 2016. Retrieved from https://headspace.org.au/assets/Uploads/headspace-NUS-Publication-Digital.pdf

Savaya, R. (2013). Critical reflection: Training to social workers. In J. Fook & F. Gardner (Eds.), *Critical reflection in context.* Routledge.

Schon, D. (1983). *The reflective practitioner: How professionals think in action.* Basic Books.

Ting, L. (2011). Depressive symptoms in a sample of social work students and reasons preventing students from using mental health services: An exploratory study. *Journal of Social Work Education, 47*(2), 253–268.

Trevithick, P. (2012). *Social work skills and knowledge: A practice handbook* (3rd ed.). Oxford University Press.

Walsh, T. (2012). Shedding light on the expert witness role in child welfare work: The value of social constructionism. In S. Witkin (Ed.), *Social construction and social work practice* (pp. 240–322). Columbia University Press.

Whiteside, M., Bould, E., Tsey, K., Cadet-James, Y., Venville, A., & Morris, M. (2017). Promoting 21st century student competencies: Piloting a wellbeing intervention. *Australian Social Work.* https://doi.org/10.1080/0312407X.2016.1263351

Whiteside, M., Tsey, K., Cadet-James, Y., & McCalman, J. (2014). *Promoting aboriginal health: The family wellbeing empowerment approach.* Springer Briefs in Public Health. Springer.

Whiteside, M., Tsey, K., McCalman, J., Cadet-James, Y., & Wilson, A. (2006). Empowerment as a framework for indigenous workforce development and organisational change. *Australian Social Work, 59*(4), 422–434.

Zubrzycki, J., Green, S., Jones, V., Stratton, K., Young,S., & Bessarab, D. (2014). *Getting it right: Creating partnerships for change. Integrating aboriginal and torres strait islander knowledges in social work education and practice. Teaching and learning framework.* Australian Government Office for Learning and Teaching.

Fiona Gardner is Associate Professor and Discipline Lead for Social Work and Social Policy at the Rural Health School, La Trobe University, based in Victoria, Australia. She is particularly interested in the use of critical reflection as a theory and process for understanding and changing practice. She has developed a framework for critical spirituality which encourages practitioners to see the spiritual (what makes life meaningful) as a key aspect of practice. Her current research is focused on establishing the value of spiritual care in health settings and on the use of critical reflection in education to change the classroom experience.

Mary Whiteside an Adjunct Associate Professor in Social Work and Social Policy at La Trobe University, She has a long history of involvement in research and development in health, education and community settings, including Australian Aboriginal and international contexts. The focus of her research primarily involves empowerment and wellbeing at individual and community levels, and changes in professional practice using qualitative and participatory research approaches.

Rachael Sanders is a Lecturer in Social Work and Social Policy at La Trobe University. Rachael is passionate about the power of knowledge and education and its role in individual and social wellbeing through critical thinking and social support. She has been a social worker for ten years and worked in research and academia for over twenty years, during which time she has developed a keen interest in critical reflection and its role in both personal and professional health and wellbeing.

Promoting the Mental Wellbeing of Law Students Through the Curriculum and Communities of Practice

Ozlem Susler and Alperhan Babacan

Abstract Empirical studies in Australia demonstrate that a large number of law students experience disproportionately elevated levels of psychological distress when compared to students studying in other disciplines. Psychological distress throughout a student's tertiary journey can adversely impact on a student's ability to learn effectively and hamper their tertiary experience. This chapter commences with a discussion of the findings of empirical studies examining psychological distress amongst law students in Australia. These empirical studies were selected from major reviews con in Australian law schools as well as studies conducted in the United States. This discussion is followed by an identification of the factors which contribute to elevated levels of stress amongst law students. Factors that contribute to psychological distress amongst law students are primarily based on the analytical, didactic and adversarial manner in which the legal education curriculum is modelled and delivered, which in turn results in heavy workloads and intense student academic competition. Another key factor is the lack of social connectedness. The final part of the chapter offers curricular interventions to reform the legal education curriculum through the enhancement of mindfulness and resilience and the adoption of a transformative approach to learning coupled with provision of supports for online students through fostering a sense of community and belonging.

Keywords Legal education · Mental wellbeing · Law students · Legal education curriculum

O. Susler (✉)
LaTrobe University Law School, Melbourne, Australia
e-mail: o.susler@latrobe.edu.au

A. Babacan
Barrister and Solicitor of the Supreme Court of Victoria and High Court, Melbourne, Australia
e-mail: alperhanbabacan@gmail.com

A. P. Francis and M. A. Carter (eds.), *Mental Health and Higher Education in Australia*,
https://doi.org/10.1007/978-981-16-8040-3_11

Introduction

The student experience at university has received increased attention in recent decades. Previous research demonstrates that the transition to and studying at university can be stressful for students (Dyson & Renk, 2006; Friedlander et al., 2007; Munro & Pooley, 2009). Numerous studies in recent decades indicate high numbers of law students in Australian law schools are emotionally distressed about their learning and teaching experiences. (Beaton Consulting, 2011; Crowley-Cyr, 2014; Duffy et al., 2011; Field & Duffy, 2012; Field & Kift, 2010; Hall, 2009; Kelk et al., 2009; Larcombe et al., 2012, 2013; Lester et al., 2011; O'Brien et al., 2011; Parker, 2014; Skead & Rogers, 2014; Tani & Vines, 2009; Watson & Field, 2011).

When compared with students from other disciplines, law students are far more likely to suffer from anxiety and stress (Appleby & Bourke, 2014; Stallman, 2010). Overwhelmingly, the evidence in Australia which is similar to findings in the United States points to the fact that the nature of the legal education curriculum, namely the adversarial modelling of legal education within a didactic teaching framework—placing emphasis on legal doctrine—is an important contributor to student stress levels through the promotion of a competitive and individualistic learning environment that is marks and outcomes driven (Appleby & Bourke, 2014; Baron, 2013; Duffy et al., 2011; Field & Duffy, 2012; Larcombe et al., 2012, 2013; O'Brien, 2011; Sheldon & Krieger, 2014, 2007).

Studies on the mental wellbeing of law students provide abundant evidence that there is an urgent need for law schools to implement effective strategies by way of curricular redesign and the enhancement of the student experience. In response to the adverse findings relating to the emotional wellbeing of law students, some law schools have implemented strategies directed at addressing the high levels of student distress (Galloway & Jones, 2014; Huggins, 2012; O'Brien, 2011) which include provision of pastoral care (Galloway & Bradshaw, 2010), introducing reflective practice into the law curriculum as opposed to solely focusing on doctrinal teaching (Galloway & Jones, 2014) and emphasis by some law schools on alternative dispute resolution (Galloway & Jones, 2014). Notwithstanding positive initiatives being introduced by some law schools to address this issue, such measures are not widespread.

This chapter commences with an examination of the findings of research, which document the mental wellbeing of law students in Australia. The empirical studies considered in this chapter have been selected from major reviews conducted into the mental health of law students in Australian law schools. Additionally, consideration has been given to longitudinal studies on mental health and the impact of legal education in the United States. These studies were selected based on their specific focus on the impact of the law curriculum and the workload on the mental wellbeing of law students. The common finding in these studies is that the mental wellbeing of law students has been adversely affected by high workloads, a Socratic teaching method, coupled with the competitive nature of legal education and that these needed to be remedied. Therefore, a critical approach has been adopted by the authors to identify gaps in the literature with respect to the best manner in which mental health issues faced by law students can be effectively reduced, both in the short-term and long-term through transformative learning, resilience, mindfulness and communities of practice.

The authors then conduct an assessment of the legal education curriculum and practices as a contributory cause of the emotional distress suffered by law students and an overview of some positive initiatives undertaken by a number of law schools to address the mental health needs of their law students. In recognition of the rigidity of legal education curriculum as a cause of the high levels of emotional distress experienced by law students, the final part of the chapter provides suggestions in the areas of curricular reform and student supports. It is acknowledged and noted that the provision of non-academic supports also plays an important role in addressing the mental wellbeing of students. These matters have been addressed in past research (Appleby & Bourke, 2014; Crowley-Cyr et al., 2014; Field & Duffy, 2012; Field et al., 2015; Friedlander et al., 2007; Lester et al., 2011) with the focus of this chapter being devoted to the need for curricular change.

The Wellbeing of Law Students in Australia

Over the last decade, numerous studies have provided evidence of significant levels of psychological distress amongst law students in Australia (Beaton Consulting, 2011; Crowley-Cyr, 2014; Duffy et al., 2011; Field & Duffy, 2012; Field & Kift, 2010; Hall, 2009; Kelk et al., 2009; Larcombe et al., 2012, 2013; Lester et al., 2011; O'Brien et al., 2011; Parker, 2014; Skead & Rogers, 2014; Tani & Vines, 2009; Watson & Field, 2011). These reports express concern about the alarmingly high levels of emotional distress amongst law students which exceed their peers from other disciplines and their non-student peers in the wider community (Appleby & Bourke, 2014).

The Brain & Mind Research Institute Report (hereinafter referred to as the 'BMRI Report') (Kelk et al., 2009) surveyed 741 law students at 13 Australian law schools. Findings reported that 35.5% of law students experienced high levels of emotional distress, significantly higher than students studying in any other discipline and people aged between 18 and 34 in the general population (Kelk et al., 2009). Whilst the BMRI Report could not identify the exact causes of psychological distress amongst law students, the report points to the highly competitive nature of legal education as one factor for the high levels of distress amongst law students. The recommendations of the BMRI Report included increasing awareness of mental health issues within the student body and amongst law staff, offering supports to distressed students and the preparation of law students and legal professionals for normal forms of stress in the workplace (Kelk et al., 2009).

Tani and Vines (2009) who conducted a cross-sectional study of students at the University of New South Wales found that, in contrast to students studying in other disciplines including those studying medicine, law students demonstrated much higher levels of emotional distress. Tani and Vines (2009) advance that law students are highly competitive and lack social connectedness during their law degree. In 2010, Leahy et al. (2010) conducted a cross-sectional study of the distress levels amongst students studying in different faculties at the University of Adelaide. The report revealed that of the 955 students who were surveyed, 48% were psychologically distressed. Law students were by far the worst affected in the cohort, with 58% of law students stating that they were emotionally distressed. This figure was higher than engineering and medical science students.

A longitudinal study of the emotional distress experienced by law students was conducted at Monash University, Law Faculty in 2011. This research examined whether there were changes to stress, anxiety and depression levels throughout their first year of the law degree at Monash University (Lester et al., 2011). The findings showed that whereas 8.5% of first year students reported mild to high levels of depression in the early part of their first year of study, the percentage of students who felt distressed by the end of the first year rose to 15% (Lester et al., 2011).

In 2011, O'Brien, Tang and Hall published their research on the mental wellbeing of first year law students studying law at the Australian National University, examining whether stress levels changed throughout their first-year experience. During the beginning of their first year, the results indicated that 14.3% of law students suffered from moderate to severe symptoms of depression. This figure rose to 31.5% by the end of the first year (O'Brien et al., 2011).

A Melbourne University study conducted by Larcombe et al. (2013) examined students from both the Bachelor of Law and Juris Doctor programs and found that students from both degrees experienced high levels of anxiety, stress and depression (Larcombe et al., 2013). Similarly, a University of Western Australia study examined students from both the Bachelor of Law and Juris Doctor programs and found that students from both degrees experienced high levels of anxiety, stress and depression, replicating the findings of the Melbourne University study (Skead & Rogers, 2014).

Cross-sectional studies reveal that not only do law students experience higher levels of distress compared with students studying in other disciplines, the law school curriculum and practices are the likely source of the psychological distress (Field & Duffy, 2012). Longitudinal studies can also enable law schools to identify the precise points during the law degree where psychological distress is being faced by law students and at what point in the degree the wellbeing of students deteriorate (Field & Duffy, 2012). Furthermore, the research also suggests that stress levels are not confined to the first year and continue throughout the law degree and into their first years of legal practice, thereby revealing that law students are inadequately equipped with the requisite skills and resilience to cope with the rigours of legal practice (Appleby & Bourke, 2014).

Emotional distress is also high amongst the legal profession. The BMRI Report found that almost one in three solicitors demonstrated anxiety, stress and depression (Kelk et al., 2009). The Queensland Legal Services Commissioner's Report on stress levels of legal practitioners confirmed that 30% of practitioners who faced disciplinary processes had underlying issues with emotional distress (Britton, 2009). Other research (Beaton Consulting, 2011) demonstrates that 40% of legal practitioners across Australia displayed symptoms of anxiety and depression.

Collectively, the findings of the research in Australia are consistent with longitudinal studies conducted in the United States since the 1980s (Benjamin et al., 1986; Iijima, 1998, 2002; Krieger, 1999, 2002, 2008; Pritchard & McIntosh, 2003; Sheldon & Krieger, 2004, 2007). These findings clearly point to the fact that the legal education curriculum and law school practices contribute to the higher levels of emotional distress suffered by law students and are confirmed by Australian legal academics, who have specifically referred to the legal education curriculum as a strong contributory factor to high levels of emotional distress experienced by law students (Appleby & Bourke, 2014; Baron, 2013; Crowley Cyr, 2014; Field & Duffy, 2012; Field & Kift, 2010; Field et al., 2015; Galloway & Jones, 2014; Hall, 2009; Larcombe et al., 2012 & 2013; Lester et al., 2011; O'Brien, 2011; O'Brien et al., 2011; Skead & Rogers, 2014).

The State of the Legal Education Curriculum in Australia

Legal education is preoccupied with the instilling of legal and technical thinking within a doctrinal paradigm (Galloway, 2008). There is a general absence of the embedding of critique and alternative perspectives within the law degree (Thornton, 2001) and a lack of student-centred approaches to teaching and learning (Carruthers et al., 2012). Legal thinking processes are conservative and doctrinal in nature as well as logical, which reinforces a highly competitive advocate who is individualistic (James, 2000; Keyes & Johnstone, 2004). This in turn provides little scope for the enhancement of creative thinking and other soft skills (Sullivan et al., 2007). The law curriculum traditionally focuses on case law and legislation and the solving of legal problems through adversarial means (Keyes & Johnstone, 2004). From a pedagogic perspective, legal education is highly teacher-centric and Socratic in nature (Kelk et al., 2009). Hence over the decades, little attention is paid to alternative and critical pedagogies (Keyes & Johnstone, 2004). The 11 core units termed 'Priestly 11' across all Australian law degrees have been termed outmoded in content and inflexible in their approach (International Legal Services Advisory Council, 2004).

Through many articles in the last decade, Australian legal education academics have acknowledged that the legal education curriculum is a significant contributory factor to the psychological distress suffered by law students. This is primarily due to heavy workloads, inadequate feedback and a lack of social connectedness, the adversarial and competitive nature of legal education, the teacher-centric—Socratic methods adopted in teaching and a preoccupation with academic results and ranking (Appleby & Bourke, 2014; Baron, 2013; Crowley Cyr, 2014; Field & Duffy, 2012; Field & Kift, 2010; Field et al., 2015; Galloway & Jones, 2014; Huggins, 2012; Larcombe et al., 2012, 2013; Lester et al., 2011; Skead & Rogers, 2014). Thornton (2004) advances that economic drivers associated with the higher education sector and the law schools, have resulted in a conservative approach to the provision of legal education and placed it within a vocational and compartmentalised framework.

Similarly, studies conducted in the United States advance that the law school curriculum and its practices are an important causative factor to the emotional distress suffered by law students (Sheldon & Krieger, 2007, 2008). In particular, characteristics associated with the adversarial and didactic nature of the education and the competitive nature of the educational and employment outcomes sought, contributed to heightened stress, anxiety and depression amongst students in the United States (Iijima, 1998, 2002; Krieger, 1999, 2002, 2008; Sheldon & Krieger, 2007).

In 2000, the Australian Law Reform Commission was critical of the traditional manner in which legal education was taught and recommended for broader engagement with the law and skills enhancement (Australian Law Reform Commission, 2000). A Call was made to increase soft skills which are essential for graduates to not only enhance legal practice, but also to build professional relationships, develop resilience and to cope with changes impacting upon law and the legal practice (Appleby & Bourke, 2014; Field & Duffy, 2012; Larcombe et al., 2013; O'Brien et al., 2011). Notwithstanding these calls, innovative change in legal education has not been widespread across Australian law schools in recent decades.

Overwhelmingly, research conducted over the last decade has strongly recommended for the implementation of effective practices and strategies to address the high levels of distress through changes to law school culture and curriculum redesign. Given the strength of the empirical evidence, law schools have a positive obligation to enhance the psychological wellbeing of their students, through the provision of student support services and curriculum-based changes (Field & Duffy, 2012). It is critical for law schools to not only identify, but to modify both the curriculum and institutional factors which cause high levels of stress amongst law students.

Law School Strategies to Address the Mental Wellbeing of Students

Following the adverse findings of these various Australian reports, some law schools have implemented strategies and changes to the law curriculum to address the issue of emotional wellbeing of law students. In 2009, the Council of Australian Law Deans (CALD) developed the *Threshold Learning Outcomes for Legal Education* to specifically promote student wellbeing and self-management (Council of Australian Law Deans, 2009). Threshold Learning Outcome (TLO) 6 encourages law schools to implement strategies and practices, so that students will be able to (a) learn and work independently, (b) reflect on and assess their own capabilities and performance and (c) make use of feedback as appropriate, to support personal and professional development. TLO 6 draws on the United Kingdom's QAA Subject Benchmark Statement for law students which places emphasis on the ability of law students to act independently in planning and completing tasks, to reflect on their own learning, to seek and make use of feedback and to ensure that students are able to understand

and manage their emotions and self-awareness (Council of Australian Law Deans, 2009).

Additionally, in 2013, the CALD adopted the *Good Practice Guidelines for Promoting Law Student Well-Being* which encourage law schools to actively educate and disseminate information regarding mental illness and student distress to staff and students (Council of Australian Law Deans, 2013). The guidelines provide broad recommendations for law schools to enhance student wellbeing. Some of these guidelines include dissemination of information about mental health to staff and students, preparation of students for stresses in the study of law, the offering of mentoring programs and fostering relationships between students and those who have expertise in promoting student wellbeing (Council of Australian Law Deans, 2013). It should be noted that the CALD Guidelines and Threshold Learning Outcomes are recommendatory and are not mandated. A majority of law schools in Australia have not formally or holistically adopted the CALD Threshold Learning Outcomes or the CALD Guidelines.

Close to a decade ago, curricular strategies to enhance student wellbeing and resilience were adopted by one university through the embedding of appropriate pedagogies into the law curriculum. For example, the Queensland University of Technology (QUT) revised its law curriculum in the first year elective unit entitled *Lawyering and Dispute Resolution*. Key changes to the curriculum included variation of the learning outcomes and assessment tasks, the introduction of a focus on positive professional identity, the positive role of lawyers in society and non-adversarialism. Active and engaged learning and small group work was encouraged. The unit provided a learning environment that motivated and provided students with the will power to persevere with their studies and the fostering of a professional identity through reflective activities, problem-based tasks and interactive classes (Field & Duffy, 2012). A further example in 2014 by the University of Southern Queensland, is utilisation of a dialogue methodology in its first year law unit to provide a voice to students and to enable the sharing of experiences relating to psychological issues that are associated with the study of law. In addition to sharing of experiences, the class fostered an awareness of mental wellbeing and provided links to support services (Crowley-Cyr, 2014).

Since 2009, transition pedagogies were embedded into first year units at Monash University's LLB Program which also featured practical strategies to nurture resilience and coping behaviours including mindfulness. A comprehensive peer mentor program was introduced in 2008, with the aim of providing a structured support network and fostering a sense of support and community (Lester et al., 2011). Some 75 percent of the University of Southern Queensland's law students study online, (Crowley-Cyr) which can be isolating and lead to student attrition. The Law School at the University of Southern Queensland undertook measures to enhance the online student experience, as there was an absence of communities of practice and a lack of contact between on-campus and online students. A supportive online environment was created for students to share information about the barriers to studying, via online forums. Additionally, a meet and greet forum was organised for online students in 2012 (Crowley-Cyr, 2014).

Although there has been a shift away from the traditional focus of legal education by some law schools with a conscious effort to address the emotional wellbeing of their students, a teacher focused, doctrinal approach continues to dominate the legal education landscape (Appleby & Bourke, 2014; Galloway & Jones, 2014; Thornton, 2001), with students being required to address and resolve legal issues presented to them within the traditional discourses of doctrinal law. For example, a survey of almost half of property law teachers across Australia found that there was little emphasis on alternative pedagogies and student-centred approaches, but rather an emphasis on doctrinal analysis and exams across the property law units taught in Australian universities (Carruthers et al., 2012).

Whilst the measures implemented by the various Australian law schools are to be commended, there is a real need to address the pressing issue of emotional distress amongst law students. Given the strength of the research conducted over the last decade which strongly points to the legal education curriculum and practices as a contributing factor to the wellbeing of law students, there is an urgent need to implement radical changes to the legal education curriculum. Additionally, given the high levels of emotional distress amongst legal practitioners, it is also critical to not only provide strategies and practices to address emotional distress at university, but also to prepare graduates to cope effectively with pressures and change in the workforce through mindfulness, resilience-building activities and practices, as well as transformative pedagogies which are likely to be readily transferred to legal practice following graduation.

Addressing the Emotional Wellbeing of Law Students Through Curriculum Change

The introduction of mindfulness practices and resilience-building pedagogies embedded in a transformative education framework to teaching and learning, can equip students with the skills to cope with their studies and gain an increased awareness of the sources of their own anxiety. Transformative pedagogies which replace the traditional didactic approaches to teaching of law can provide students with broader critical and constructive thinking processes, which can encourage creative thinking and problem-solving capabilities to enable students to overcome barriers they may face during their studies and in the workforce. Additionally, communities of practice are advanced for students studying law via the online medium.

Mindfulness Practices and Building Resilience

The introduction of education on mindfulness into the law school curriculum to increase students' psychological literacy levels, would be most beneficial. Mindfulness is defined as bringing one's complete attention to the experiences occurring in the present moment in a non-judgemental or accepting way (Baer et al., 2006). Mindfulness involves acknowledging pleasant and unpleasant experiences which may arise in our daily lives and accepting that judging or resisting such experiences may heighten the impact of these experiences, particularly negative ones (Hassed et al., 2009).

Mindfulness research suggests that students who can reflect on their feelings and how they think are not only more likely to review the effectiveness of their own learning strategies, but to also cope with the demands, pressures and frustrations associated with their law school experience (Brockbank & McGill, 2007; Rogers, 2012; Schon, 1983; Sparrow, 2009). The practice of mindfulness involves the purposeful process of being attentive of moment-to-moment awareness, without passing judgment. Mindfulness-based interventions have proven to be beneficial in reducing stress, anxiety and depression, (Khoury et al., 2013) as mindfulness-based self-efficacy can encourage the regulation of emotion, distress tolerance, an ability to normalise difficulties and the taking of responsibility (Cayoun, 2012). Mindfulness can be practiced through meditation or through journaling and reflecting on one's learning experiences (James, 2011; Rogers, 2012).

Mindfulness meditation can be most beneficial for stress management, which is an essential tool for law students as it can support mental wellbeing. Keng et al. (2011) examined Mindfulness-Based Stress Reduction (MBSR) programs in American Colleges and found that the program had overall benefits in reducing stress, anxiety and psychological depression in American college students. In Australia, Monash University introduced MBSR in its Faculty of Medicine, Nursing and Health Sciences. First year students undertook a Health Enhancement Program as part of their core curriculum entitled Health Enhancement Program (HEP), which included components relating to mindfulness-based stress management. (Hassed et al., 2009). Students who participated were surveyed throughout the year. The results demonstrated HEP's significant contribution to student wellbeing, through a reduction in their stress and anxiety levels (Hassed et al., 2009).

Resilience-building activities can be highly beneficial to reducing student stress levels, thus, law schools can enhance resilience through such activities. Resilience is seen a set of attitudes and behaviours which are associated with an individual's ability to cope with and to adapt in the face of risk and stress (Holdsworth et al., 2018; Walker et al., 2006). Central to most definitions of resilience is the concept of 'enduring through difficult situations' and 'bouncing back' from a stressful situation (Holdsworth et al., 2018; Shimi & Manwaring, 2017).

The conceptualisation of 'resilience' is important as this will impact on the pedagogic strategies employed by law schools. The promotion of student resilience is based not merely on narrow constructs associated with coping at university, but one based on an awareness of self, wider environments, the ability to maintain a current system, to understand and cope with wider socio-economic–political impacts and change as well as the ability to influence change of existing systems, where transformation is preferred to maintaining the status quo (Krause, 2017). Such changes would go a long way to not only enable students to cope with the pressures and demands associated with their university studies, but can also be readily transferred to the workforce to enable students to understand and navigate workplace related pressures, change and uncertainty. Mindfulness and resilience-building activities are likely to strengthen coping and longer-term resilience, through the improvement of student awareness of the sources of their own anxiety and stress, thereby helping students to cope with the challenges they face and to develop best practices.

Student Transformation

Legal education creates and reinforces a particular mode of thinking (Thornton, 1994, 2001). Knowledge is acquired and presented in accordance with legal disciplinary methods and conventions, and hence, the status quo is maintained. Traditional technical definitions of legal skills are no longer in themselves suited to the practice of law in the twenty-first century, which now necessitates a critique and confrontation of legal technicalism and the inclusion of skills that encompass a broader understanding of self and society, including understanding its impacts upon the law and legal practice (Appleby & Bourke, 2014; Field & Duffy, 2012).

Transformative pedagogies are proposed as an alternative educational framework to the current didactic and teacher-centric approaches to legal education, to better prepare law students to cope within the university setting as well as for their careers following graduation (McAllister & McKinnon, 2009). Transformative pedagogies utilise critical and constructive thinking practices to encourage learners to analyse and understand practices, including the socio-economic–political impacts on the law and workforce and creative ways of thinking to solve problems, thereby overcoming barriers (Mezirow, 1991, 2000).

The transformative learning process involves transforming frames of reference through critical reflection, an evaluation of contested beliefs through dialogue, the taking of action about one's reflective insight and critically assessing the action taken. Central to transformative learning is that students' paradigms or views are subject to deep shifts, which may create new meanings through expanded consciousness. Such shifts may transform the manner in which students view themselves, society, the law, legal processes and wider impacts on the law and legal system (Mezirow, 2000). Perspective transformation involves the learner engaging in critical self-reflection of their own assumptions and the ways in which the learner's views of the world may be distorted or limited (Shore & Friere, 1986). Through the experience of a disorienting dilemma, learners may engender a change in the manner in which they view the law, the workforce and society, thus opening themselves up to alternatives and in turn changing their perceptions, thereby enabling the potential for enhanced resilience, effective coping and self-management (Mezirow, 1991).

The adoption of a critical and reflective approach to the teaching of law can encourage building resilience and mindfulness into the legal education curriculum, so that learning is likely to move from an adaptive perspective to one of personal understanding, self-management and personal transformation.

Fostering a Sense of Belonging for Online Students

Many students are now studying law (and other disciplines) via the online medium. Researchers are arguing that studying via the online medium can be isolating and may lead to pressure, stress and isolation (LaPadula, 2003). The advent of COVID-19 across the globe has meant that many universities have had to offer their classes solely via the online medium. It is therefore important to provide online law students with appropriate student supports in the form of online orientation and communities of practice. To successfully study in the online medium, students need to feel supported and not isolated from their institution, peers and instructors (LaPadula, 2003), and this carries equal weight to adequate instructional content (LaPadula, 2003; Tinto, 1975 and 1997). Research demonstrates that the quantity and quality of interactions offered to learners can result in increased levels of satisfaction with the course studied (Brindley, 2000; Lee, 2010).

The offering of tailored online orientation programs to online students, aids the transition into the university and the semester therefore, boosting the confidence of this cohort from the outset (Britto & Rush, 2013). A thorough online orientation program needs to cover a number of areas including: the course/unit and its structure and content, technology used to deliver the course, connecting online students with their peers and instructors, thereby providing a sense of belonging, as well as informing them about how to access learner support services (Britto & Rush, 2013; Williford et al., 2001).

Technology can play an integral role in the formation and operation of learning communities to foster collaboration and interaction with other learners. More than 20 years ago, Palloff and Pratt (1999, 21) suggested, '*Community is no longer a place-based concept*', though it may nonetheless be considered a '*conscious community*' with shared goals, communication styles and behavioural norms. For the purposes of distance education, in 1999, Palloff and Pratt (1999, 23) consider "geographically disconnected people becoming 'connected' in a community with several purposes, but with a shared interest" whereby all participants contribute to the exploration of subject matter, so as to enable a better understanding of the topic at hand and the perspectives of other members. Learning communities are essential in fostering meaningful sharing and reflection, provision of support, minimising isolation associated with studying online and thereby positively contributing to stress minimisation and student retention.

Conclusion

This chapter has examined the emotional distress suffered by law students in Australian law schools and the causes of such distress. The legal education curriculum and practices have been identified as a significant contributing factor to student stress levels, warranting the wellbeing of law students to be addressed through effective curricular reform which encourages mindfulness, self-awareness, resilience and a transformative approach to teaching and learning.

Students who are able to reflect on their values, attitudes and reactions are more likely to be aware of and to cope better with their own stressors and anxiety, as well as be more likely to seek assistance when they feel pressure or confusion, leading to anxiety. These skills are also highly relevant and transferable to their careers in the legal profession or non-legal workforce, following graduation.

In order to effectively design curricular and non-curricular interventions to improve law student wellbeing, it is essential to ensure that law schools gain a better understanding of the broad and specific factors which contribute to students' psychological distress. This includes impacts of the curriculum, assessment practices, the teaching and learning practices on student thinking styles and the impact of the competitive and adversarial nature of legal education on student social interactions and sense of connectedness.

More extensive and longitudinal research needs to be conducted on the mental wellbeing of law students including specific aspects of the law schools' experience, combined with a detailed analysis of the benefits of any pedagogic interventions undertaken to address the issues, so that further refinements can be made.

References

Appleby, M., & Bourke, J. (2014). Promoting law student mental health literacy and wellbeing: A case study from the College of Law Australia. *International Journal of Clinical Legal Education, 20*(1), 461–498.

Australian Law Reform Commission. (2000). *Managing justice: A review of the Federal civil justice system*, Report No. 89, Available at: https://www.alrc.gov.au/publication/managing-justice-a-review-of-the-federal-civil-justice-system-alrc-report-89/

Baer, R. A., Smith, G. T., Hopkins, J., Krietemeyer, J., & Toney, L. (2006). Using self-report assessment methods to explore facets of mindfulness. *Assessment, 13*(1), 27–45.

Baron, P. (2013). A dangerous cult: Response to the effect of the market. *Legal Education Review, 23*(2), 273–289.

Beaton Consulting and Beyond Blue. (2011). *Mental health in the workplace*. Available at: http://www.beatonglobal.com/pdfs/Anxiety_and_depression_in_the_workplace.pdf

Benjamin, G., Kaszniak, A., Sales, B., & Shanfield, S. B. (1986). The role of legal education in producing psychological distress among law students and lawyers. *Law and Social Inquiry, 11*(2), 225–252.

Brindley, J. E. (2000). *The effects of a social support intervention on distance learner behaviour*. Ph.D. dissertation, University of Ottawa.

Britto, M., & Rush, S. (2013). Developing and implementing comprehensive student support services for online students. *Journal of Asynchronous Learning Networks, 17*(1), 29–42.

Britton, J. (2009). *Lawyers, emotional distress and regulation.* Presented at Bar Association of Queensland Conference. Available at: http://www.lsc.qld.gov.au/__data/assets/pdf_file/0006/106197/lawyers-emotional-distress-and-regulation.pdf

Brockbank, A., & McGill, I. (2007). *Facilitating reflective learning in higher education.* (2nd ed) McGraw Hill.

Carruthers, J., Skead, N., & Galloway, K. (2012). Teaching property Law in Australia in the 21st Century: What we do now, what should we do in the future? *Australian Property Law Journal, 21*(1), 57–76.

Cayoun, B. (2012). The mindfulness-based self-efficacy scale—revised. MiCBT Institute. Available at: https://mindfulness.net.au

Council of Australian Law Deans. (2013). *Promoting law student wellbeing good practice guidelines for law school.* Available at: https://cald.asn.au/wp-content/uploads/2017/11/Promoting-Law-Student-Well-Being-Good-Practice-Guidelines-for-Law-Schools-March-2013-and-revised-September-2014.pdf

Council of Australian Law Deans. (2009). *Threshold learning outcomes for Bachelor of Laws.* Available at: (https://cald.asn.au/wp-content/uploads/2017/11/LLB-TLOsKiftetalLTASStandardsStatement2010-TLOs-LLB2.pdf)

Crowley-Cyr, L. (2014). Promoting mental wellbeing of law students: Breaking down stigma and building bridges with support services in the online learning environment. *Queensland University of Technology Law Review, 14*(1), 129–152. Wellness for Law (Special Edition).

Duffy, J., Field, R., & Shirley, M. (2011). Engaging law students to promote psychological health. *Alternative Law Journal, 36*(4), 250–254.

Dyson, R., & Renk, K. (2006). Freshmen adaptation to university life: Depressive symptoms, stress, and coping. *Journal of Clinical Psychology, 62*(10), 1231–1244.

Field, R., & Duffy, J. (2012). Better to light a single candle than to curse the darkness: promoting law student well-being through a first year law subject. *Queensland University of Technology Law and Justice Journal, 12*(1), 133–156.

Field, R., Duffy, J., & Huggins, A. (2015). Teaching independent learning skills in the first year: A positive psychology strategy for promoting law student well-being. *Journal of Learning Design, 8*(2), 1–10.

Field, R., & Kift, S. (2010). Addressing the high levels of psychological distress in law students through intentional assessment and feedback design in the first year law curriculum. *International Journal of the First Year in Higher Education, 1*(1), 65–756.

Friedlander, L. J., Reid, G. J., Shupak, N., & Cribbie, R. (2007). Social support, self-esteem, and stress as predictors of adjustment to university among first-year undergraduates. *Journal of College Student Development, 48*, 259–274.

Galloway, K. (2008). Statutory modification of contract law in Queensland: A new equilibrium or entrenching the old power order? *James Cook University Law Review, 15*, 67–96.

Galloway, K., & Bradshaw, R. (2010). Responding to changed parameters of the law student: A reflection on pastoral care in the law school. *Journal of the Australasian Law Teachers Association, 3*, 101–112.

Galloway, K., & Jones, P. (2014). Guarding our identities: The dilemma of transformation in the legal academy. *Queensland University of Technology Law Review, 14*(1), 15–26. Wellness for Law (Special Edition).

Hall, K. (2009). Do we really want to know? Recognising the importance of student psychological wellbeing in Australian law schools. *Queensland University of Technology Law and Justice Journal, 9*(1), 1–12

Hassed, C., de Lisle, S., Sullivan, G., & Pier, C. (2009). Enhancing the health of medical students: Outcomes of an integrated mindfulness and lifestyle program. *Advances in Health Science Education Theory and Practice, 14*(3), 387–398.

Holdsworth, S., Turner, M., & Scott-Young, C. M. (2018). Not drowning, waving resilience and university: A student perspective. *Studies in Higher Education, 43*(11), 1837–1853.
Huggins, A. (2012). Autonomy supportive curriculum design: A salient factor in promoting law students' wellbeing. *University of New South Wales Law Journal, 35*(3), 683–716.
Iijima, A. (1998). Lessons learned: Legal education and law student dysfunction. *Journal of Legal Education, 48*(4), 524–536.
Iijima, A. (2002). The collaborative legal studies program: A work in progress. *Kansas Journal of Law and Public Policy, 12*, 143–154.
International Legal Education and Training Committee. (2004). Internationalisation of the Australian Law Degree (p. 7). International Legal Services Advisory Council.
James, C. (2011). Law student wellbeing: Benefits of promoting psychological literacy and self. *Legal Education Review, 21*(2), 281–233.
James, N. (2000). A brief history of critique in Australian legal education. *Melbourne University Law Review, 24*(3), 965–981.
Kelk, N., Luscombe, G., Medlow, S., &Hickie, I. (2009). *Courting the blues: Attitudes towards depression in Australian law students and lawyers*. Brain & Mind Research Institute. Available at: https://cald.asn.au/wp-content/uploads/2017/11/BMRI-Report-Courting-the-BluesLaw-Report-Website-version-4-May-091.pdf
Keng, S. L., Smoski, M. J., & Robins, C. J. (2011). Effects of mindfulness on psychological health: A review of empirical studies. *Clinical Psychology Review, 31*(6), 1041–1056.
Keyes, M., & Johnstone, R. (2004). Changing legal education: Rhetoric, reality, and prospects for the future. *Sydney Law Review, 26*(4), 537. Available at: http://classic.austlii.edu.au/au/journals/SydLawRw/2004/26.html
Khoury, B., Lecomte, T., Fortin, G., Masse, M., Therien, P., Bouchard, V., Chapleau, M., Paquin, K., & Hofmann, S. G. (2013). Mindfulness-based therapy: A comprehensive meta-analysis. *Clinical Psychology Review, 33*, 763–771.
Krause, D. (2017). *Linking resilience thinking and transformative change*. Resilience Centre and the Resilience Alliance in Stockholm, Sweden, 17 August 2017. Available at: http://www.unrisd.org/resilience-krause
Krieger, L. S. (2008). Human nature as a new guiding philosophy for legal education and the profession. *Washburn Law Journal, 47*(2), 247–312.
Krieger, L. S. (2002). Institutional denial about the dark side of law school, and fresh empirical guidance for constructively breaking the silence. *Journal of Legal Education, 52*, 112–129.
Krieger, L. S. (1999). What we're not telling law students-and lawyers—that they really need to know: some thoughts-in-action toward revitalizing the profession from its roots. *Journal of Law and Health, 13*, 3–46.
LaPadula, M. (2003). A comprehensive look at online student support services for distance learners. *American Journal of Distance Education, 17*(2), 119–129.
Larcombe, W., Tubaga, L., Malkin, I., Nicholson, P., & Tokatlidis, O. (2013). Does an improved experience of law school protect students against depression, anxiety and stress? An empirical study of wellbeing and the law school experience of LLB and JD students. *Sydney Law Review, 35*(2), 406–432.
Larcombe, W., Malkin, I., & Nicholson, P. (2012). Law students' motivations, expectations and levels of psychological distress: Evidence and connections. *Legal Education Review, 22*(1), 85–95.
Leahy, C. M., Peterson, R. F., Wilson, I. G., Newbury, J. W., Tonkin, A. L., & Turnbull, D. (2010). Distress levels and self-reported treatment rates for medicine, law, psychology and mechanical engineering tertiary students: Cross-sectional study. *Australia and New Zealand Journal of Psychiatry, July, 44*(7), 608–615.
Lee, J. W. (2010). Online support service quality, online learning acceptance, and student satisfaction. *Internet and Higher Education, 13*(4), 277–283.
Lester, A., England, L., & Antolak-Saper, N. (2011). Health and wellbeing in the first year: The law school experience. *Alternative Law Journal, 36*(1), 47–49.

Mcallister, M., & McKinnon, J. (2009). The importance of teaching and learning resilience in the health disciplines: A critical review of the literature. *Nurse Education Today, 29*(4), 371–379.
Mezirow, J. (1991). *Transformative dimensions of adult learning*. Josse-Bass.
Mezirow, J. (2000). *Learning to think like and adult. Core concepts of transformation theory*. In J. Mezirow (Ed.), *Learning as transformation: Critical perspectives on a theory in progress*. Josse-Bass.
Munro, B., & Pooley, J. (2009). Differences in resilience and university adjustment between school leaver and mature entry university students. *The Australian Community Psychologist, 21*, 50–61.
O'Brien, M. O., Tang, S., & Hall, K. (2011). Changing our thinking: Empirical research on law student wellbeing, thinking styles and the law curriculum. *Legal Education Review, 21*(2), 149–182.
O'Brien, M. T. (2011). Facing down the gladiators: Addressing law school's hidden adversarial curriculum. *Monash Law Review, 37*(1), 43–56.
Palloff, R. M., & Pratt, K. (1999). *Building learning communities in cyberspace: Effective strategies for the online classroom*. Jossey-Bass.
Parker, C. (2014). The 'moral panic' over psychological wellbeing in the legal profession: A personal or political ethical response. *University of New South Wales Law Review, 37*(3), 1103–1141.
Pritchard, M., & McIntosh, D. (2003). What predicts adjustment among law students? A longitudinal panel study. *The Journal of Social Psychology, 143*(6), 727–745.
Rogers, S. L. (2012). The mindful law school: An integrative approach to transforming legal education. *Touro Law Review, 28*, 1189–1205.
Schon, D. A. (1983). *The reflective practitioner: How professionals think in action*. Basic Books.
Sheldon, K. M., & Krieger, L. (2004). Does legal education have undermining effects on law students? Evaluating changes in motivation, values, and well-being. *Behavioural Science and the Law, 22*, 261–286.
Sheldon, K. M., & Krieger, L. S. (2007). Understanding the negative effects of legal education on law students: A longitudinal test of self-determination theory. *Personality and Social Psychology, 33*(6), 883–897.
Shimi, J., & Manwaring, G. (2017). The resilient graduate. In C. Normand, L. Anderson (Eds.) (2017), *Graduate attributes in higher education: Attitudes on attributes from across the disciplines*. Routledge.
Sheldon, K. M., & Krieger L. S. (2014). Service job lawyers are happier than money job lawyers, despite their lower income. *The Journal of Positive Psychology, 9*(3), 219–226.
Shore, I., & Friere, P. (1986). *A pedagogy for liberation. Dialogues on transforming education*. Bergin & Garvey.
Skead, N., & Rogers, S. L. (2014). Stress, anxiety and depression in law students: How student behaviours affect student wellbeing. *Monash University Law Review, 40*(2), 564–587.
Sparrow, C. (2009). Reflective student practitioner—An example integrating clinical experience into the curriculum. *International Journal of Clinical Education, 14*, 70–76.
Stallman, H. M. (2010). Psychological distress in university students: A comparison with general population data. *Australian Psychologist, 45*(4), 249–257.
Sullivan, W. M., Colby, A., Wegner, J. W., Bond, L. & Shulman, L. S. (2007). *Educating lawyers: Preparation for the profession of law* ('Carnegie Report'). Jossey Bass.
Tani, M., & Vines, P. (2009). Law students' attitudes to education: Pointers to depression in the legal academy and the profession? *Legal Education Review 19*(1/2), 3–39.
Tinto, V. (1997). Classrooms as communities: Exploring the educational character of student persistence. *Journal of Higher Education, 68*, 599–623.
Thornton, M. (1994). Discord in the academy: The case of the feminist scholar. *The Australian Feminist Law Journal, 3*, 53–65.
Thornton, M. (2001). The demise of diversity in legal education: Globalisation and the new knowledge economy. *International Journal of the Legal Profession, 8*(1), 37–56.
Thornton, M. (2004). The idea of the university and the contemporary legal academy, *Sydney Law Review, 26*(4), 481–502.

Walker, C., Gleaves, A., & Grey, J. (2006). Can students within higher education learn to be resilient and, educationally speaking, does it matter? *Educational Studies, 32*(3), 251–264.
Watson, P., & Field, R. (2011). Promoting student wellbeing and resilience at law school. In S. Kift, M. Sanson, J. Cowley, & Watson, P. (Eds.), *Excellence and innovation in legal education* (pp. 389–419). LexisNexis.
Williford, M. A., Chapman, L. C., & Kahrig, T. (2001). The university experience course: A longitudinal study of student performance, retention, and graduation. *Journal of College Student Retention: Research, Theory & Practice.,* 2, 327–340.

Ozlem Susler is a graduate of the University of Melbourne and La Trobe University. She holds degrees in Arts, Education and Law and has been admitted as a Barrister and Solicitor of the Supreme Court of Victoria. She is a graduate member of the Chartered Institute of Arbitrators and is a Nationally Accredited mediator in Australia. Özlem is a senior lecturer at La Trobe University School of Law, where she is the Director of Postgraduate Programs. Her research focus is on international dispute resolution processes. She is also interested in the scholarship of learning and teaching in legal education.

Alperhan Babacan holds Honours degrees in Law and Political Science, a Ph.D. and a Graduate Certificate in Tertiary Teaching in Learning. Dr. Babacan is admitted as a Barrister and Solicitor of the Supreme Court of Victoria and High Court of Australia and has extensive experience in legal practice and legal education. In academia, Dr. Babacan has held various senior positions including as Chair of Criminology at Navitas, deputy head of School at Swinburne university and as Director of the Juris Doctor program at RMIT University. Dr. Babacan has extensive experience in unit and course development, accreditation and review. He has published very widely in the areas of law, criminology and teaching and learning in the higher education sector with a specific focus on the scholarship of learning in legal education.

How Perfectionism, Procrastination and Parenting Styles Impact Students Mental Health and How Mindfulness and Self-Compassion May be the Antidote

Kaz Mitchell

Abstract The mental health of students in higher education is of major concern, given the high levels of psychological distress that is known to exist amongst this cohort. In this literature review, evidence is presented based on research across three decades: it reveals a link between insecure attachment bonding in early childhood to maladaptive perfectionism as a means to feel worthy, oftentimes leading to procrastination as an unhelpful strategy to avoid the anxiety of possibly not meeting expectations. As a result, the student may experience conflicting "parts"—the part that wants to achieve high standards and the part that appears to self-sabotage—and this internal conflict appears to lead to high levels of shame, anxiety and depression. The mediator showing to effectively manage the cycle of shame that ensues when these "parts" are engaged is mindfulness and self-compassion. Suggestions for how to create a non-shaming, safe and encouraging environment include workshops that teach students *and* teachers about the autonomic nervous system and how to self-regulate emotions through the use of mindfulness and self-compassion techniques. As the research reveals, creating safety is the key to good outcomes both academically and from a mental health perspective.

Introduction

The following literature review covers three decades of well-documented research into the impact of maladaptive perfectionism on the mental health and wellbeing of students in higher education. This chapter will draw from three key areas of interconnected research linking maladaptive perfectionism, procrastination and early childhood attachment bonds to an increased susceptibility to depression and anxiety within student populations. Additionally, a review of literature will demonstrate the ways in which mindfulness and self-compassion (supported by neuroscience) can

K. Mitchell (✉)
Australian College of Applied Psychology, Sydney, Australia
e-mail: Kaz.Mitchell@acap.edu.au

A. P. Francis and M. A. Carter (eds.), *Mental Health and Higher Education in Australia*,
https://doi.org/10.1007/978-981-16-8040-3_12

help manage the intense feelings of shame associated with the need to appear perfect and a desire to hide imperfections.

A recent meta-analysis indicates a disturbing indication that perfectionism amongst young people is on the rise, with evidence to suggest that current generations are more demanding of themselves than ever before (Curran & Hill, 2019). Equally worrisome are details emerging from a meta-analysis showing a marked decrease of secure attachments among American college students, and an increase in insecure attachments (Konrath et al., 2014). A secure attachment style is necessary to form healthy, trusting relationships as well as fostering the development of skills and coping strategies for emotional self-regulation. Having an insecure attachment style is a predictor for maladaptive perfectionism (Konrath et al., 2014). For these reasons, it is timely to review the research to develop more effective and sustainable ways of supporting students to manage their study workloads in ways that do not sacrifice their mental health.

Common Causes of Student Stress

International studies show that over 50% of college students across a range of disciplines procrastinate, delay or fail to complete assessments, in many cases leading to poor outcomes and high levels of withdrawal from the course (Burnam et al., 2014; Steel, 2007; Veness, 2016). Novice university students report feeling overwhelmed by the sheer volume of new information they are expected to understand and critically evaluate (Barker et al., 2018; Ramsden, 2003; Sorout et al., 2020). According to a recent Australian report, "more than half of tertiary students aged 16–25 years reported high or very high psychological distress, while 35.4% had thoughts of self-harm or suicide" (Australian University Mental Health Framework, 2020, p. 8). Additionally, an increase in cortisol levels (the stress hormone) has been reported during assessment and exam periods (Concerto et al., 2017). For students with low self-esteem and low levels of self-efficacy, this stress can lead to feelings of panic, high levels of anxiety and depression (Manap et al., 2019; Tobin & Dunkley, 2020; Wood et al., 2015), all of which can lead to poor coping mechanisms in an attempt to manage distress, such as the compulsion towards maladaptive perfectionism and task avoidance.

Perfectionism

Over the past three decades studies highlight the difference between adaptive and maladaptive perfectionism (Flett et al., 2014; Mirzairad et al., 2017; Rice & Mirzadeh, 2000; Smith et al., 2021; Ulu & Tezer, 2010; Vanstone & Hicks, 2019). Adaptive perfectionists are predicted by traits such as conscientiousness, openness and extraversion, whereas maladaptive perfectionism is related to neuroticism, anxiety and avoidant behaviours. Maladaptive perfectionists also display a lack of self-efficacy and problem-solving skills and seem less able to regulate their emotions (Abdollahi et al., 2018).

Hewitt et al., (1991) observed and named three types of perfectionism: self-oriented, other-oriented and socially prescribed perfectionism; terms still used today. Self-oriented perfectionism is displayed through excessive striving towards exceptionally high standards and is generally adaptive in nature; other-oriented perfectionists place high standards and expectations on others, and finally, socially prescribed perfectionism stems from a perceived need (real or imagined) to meet the demands of others in order to maintain a sense of self-worth (Hewitt et al., 1991). Socially prescribed perfectionism is commonly linked with higher levels of procrastination, anxiety and higher rates of suicide (Smith et al., Smith, Speth, et al., 2017; Smith et al., Smith, Sherry, et al., 2017, Smith, Speth, et al., 2017, Smith, Vidovic, et al., 2017).

Procrastination

A plethora of studies indicate a relationship between procrastination and socially prescribed perfectionism (Burns et al., 2000; Champika & Weiss, 2014; Rice et al., 2012; Smith et al., Smith, Sherry, et al., 2017). Given there are several negative consequences attached to chronic procrastination amongst student populations, including poor grades, course withdrawal, time wasting and self-handicapping behaviour (Ozer et al., 2014), this is an area of concern that higher education institutions would be well advised to address.

In a seminal meta-analytic and theoretical review of procrastination as a self-regulatory failure, Steel (2007) defines procrastination as "to voluntarily delay an intended course of action despite expecting to be worse off for the delay" (p. 66). While Steel's definition is an accurate description for chronic procrastinators, Ferrari, who is another leading researcher in the study of procrastination (Ferrari, 2001; Ferrari & Diaz-Morales, 2014; Goroshit et al., 2020; Tibbett and Ferrari, 2019), explains that many people consider their procrastination as something that is helpful, believing they work best under pressure (Ferrari, 2001). Klingsieck (2013) names this "arousal procrastination" due to a perceived increase in motivation to act at the last minute. However, research reveals compelling evidence to suggest that chronic procrastinators were more likely to "choke under pressure" (Ferrari, 2001, p. 403). These are important points, as it can be difficult for students to hear that their procrastination is detrimental not only to their studies, but also for their mental health and wellbeing.

Academic procrastination often starts as a reaction to fear of failure, and students who procrastinate generally suffer from varying degrees of worry and anxiety (Burns et al., 2000); low self-esteem; decreased optimism and higher levels of depression than those who are either non-perfectionists or adaptive perfectionists (Klingsieck, 2013). While some students may lack in conscientiousness and genuinely not care how well they do, those students who have a strong need for approval and habitually procrastinate appear to be doing so to delay experiencing shame (Fee & Tangney, 2000; Hewitt, et al., 1991).

Students who habitually procrastinate do so due to negative self-evaluation and impossibly high standards they set for themselves (Burns et al., 2000; Martincekova & Enright, 2018). Ozer et al. (2014) draw attention to studies showing procrastinators maintain a strong focus on high personal standards matched with doubts about their ability to meet their own and others high expectations.

According to the seminal work of Flett et al. (1992), a common precursor to the development of socially prescribed perfectionism and its unhelpful ally, chronic procrastination is high parental expectations in combination with high parental criticism during early childhood. The long-term effects of this style of parenting lead to the internalization of shame and the development of an internal critic, which vociferously induces feelings of worthlessness, self-loathing and is the antithesis to healthy childhood development.

Parenting Styles

Rogers (1951), the founder of person centred counselling, based his practice on the theory that humans require positive regard from others and a sense of self-worth to reach their true potential. The greatest barrier to achieving maximum potential are "conditions of worth", defined as the types of expectations and demands that are laid down by parents as well as societal pressures and later internalized as an inner critic (Rogers, 1951). Mearns and Thorne (2007) describe conditions of worth as akin to wearing a straitjacket, as it leaves a person's sense of self-worth conditioned upon "winning approval and avoiding disapproval, and this means that their range of behaviour is severely restricted for they can only behave in ways which are sure to be acceptable to others" (p. 11). In a similar vein, Starley (2019) suggests that maladaptive perfectionists develop an unhelpful core schema early in life based on the belief that self-worth is synonymous with achieving high standards. Not surprisingly, this strategy of aiming to please others through performing to an exceptionally high standard often backfires resulting in poorer results or complete disengagement from the course. From here, the cycle of shame grows stronger, leading to problems with mental health that if not dealt with may become entrenched.

The term secure attachment bonds is associated with acclaimed psychoanalyst John Bowlby (1988) who observed that young children developed internal working models of themselves and others dependent on the parenting styles of their caretakers. Infants who received nurture, care, consistency and unconditional support from their parents developed a view of themselves as worthy and loveable (secure attachment); whereas infants who were frequently ignored, chastised and shamed for their efforts developed an unhelpful internal working model of themselves as unworthy (insecure attachment) (Speirs & Finch, 2006). Bartholomew and Horowitz (1991) took Bowlby's model a step further to describe four distinct adult attachment styles: secure, preoccupied, dismissing or fearful. Secure attachment in early childhood results in the person feeling comfortable with intimacy and equally at ease in solitude as an adult: These individuals are confident to seek out comfort from others, but can just as easily self-soothe. Preoccupied attachment styles require the comfort of others to regulate their emotions, despite the fact past experience tells them to be wary of rejection; fearful attachment styles lead to a fear of intimacy resulting in social avoidance, even although the individual desperately longs for connection, and finally, dismissing attachment styles disregard the need for intimacy altogether and are seemingly content to regulate their own emotions, but sacrificing close, intimate attachments in the process (Bartholomew & Horowitz, 1991; Mikulincer & Shaver, 2016).

Mikulincer and Shaver (2016) also report a suggested link between avoidant attachment styles and distancing coping strategies: Such a person is likely to deny they are stressed and divert their attention away from anxious feelings through disengagement strategies and procrastination. This has been confirmed in various studies reporting avoidant people showing physiological symptoms of high anxiety even although outwardly they seem calm and identify as feeling fine (Gillath et al., 2009; Goodall, 2015; Kidd et al., 2013; Maunder et al., 2006; Mikulincer & Shaver, 2016).

It has now been reasonably established, through several studies over the last two decades, that adult attachment styles play a part in the process of developing either adaptive or maladaptive perfectionism (Champika & Weiss, 2014; Gnilka et al., 2013; Kobac et al., 2016; Noble et al., 2011; Smith et al., 2021). Securely attached individuals are more likely to be satisfied with their efforts, while insecurely attached persons may never be pleased by their own attempts (Ulu & Tezer, 2010). Secure individuals are more able to confront challenges, because they view the world optimistically and have a sense of mastery over their lives, whereas insecure individuals are more likely to succumb to fear of criticism and avoid moving out of their comfort zone (Cassidy, 2016; Mikulincer, 1995). Students with secure attachment are likely to find it easier to strive towards perfectionism without the fear of failure or social disapproval, allowing them the freedom to pursue challenges that insecurely attached individuals may find too terrifying (Rice et al., 2005).

Authoritarian parenting, a style demonstrated by high levels of demands and high expectations in conjunction with a non-responsive attitude towards children's emotional needs, frequently leads to maladaptive perfectionism (Speirs & Finch, 2006). Additionally, Chen et al., (2012) note that neglectful parenting (often accompanied by withdrawal of love at sensitive moments) or overly intrusive parenting (particularly when shaming is present) may also be precursors to the development of both insecure attachment bonding and maladaptive perfectionism.

Speirs & Finch, (2006) describe the anxiety of trying to please others in an attempt to avoid rejection. Moreover, these individuals tend to blame themselves when they fail to gain acceptance and abnegate their own needs over the demands of others to win back favour. When parents emphasize performance over the emotional experience of their children, they are likely to foster the belief that being perfect is more important than satisfying emotional needs. Conversely, Rice and Mirzadeh (2000) point out that some children who are insecurely attached may begin to idealize themselves as perfect as a means to mask their feelings of unworthiness, which can lead to narcissism. This claim is supported by recent research suggesting that pathological narcissism is a result of insecurely attached adolescents and young people's efforts to maintain their ideal self in the face of unrealistic expectations (van Shie et al. (2021).

Gnilka et al. (2013), Noble et al., (2011) suggest that persons identified as maladaptive perfectionists with either an avoidant or anxious attachment style result in increased depression, hopelessness and dissatisfaction in life. In contrast, adaptive perfectionism was positively associated with life satisfaction and negatively associated with depression. Similarly, Rice and Mirzadeh (2000) demonstrate that children with secure attachments are more likely to experience either adaptive perfectionistic tendencies or to be non-perfectionists, as they can accept themselves as less than perfect.

Regulating the Autonomic Nervous System: Developing Tools to Mediate Perfectionism, Procrastination and Attachment Needs

Experiencing secure attachment bonds in early childhood is necessary for infants to regulate their autonomic nervous system (ANS) (Deits-Lebehn et al., 2020), which responds to cues of safety, danger and life-threatening situations (Dana, 2018). The ANS is divided into two parts, the sympathetic nervous system (SNS) and the parasympathetic nervous system (PNS). Together the SNS and PNS manage energy demands through a balancing act of either mobilization of energy (the domain of the SNS fight or flight response) or conservation of energy (the PNS rest and digest system/immobilization during moments of life-threatening danger). Through loving, attuned interactions between the infant and caregiver, a child gradually learns how to feel soothed and to eventually internalize that experience in order to self-soothe during times of stress (Lundin, 2020). Without these experiences, the child never truly develops the capacity to regulate their own emotions successfully: the definition of insecure attachment bonding.

According to Siegel (2007, 2019, 2020), resonance is the experience we feel when we are "felt" by another person who "sees" us and connects to us with compassion and empathy. Feeling safe in the company of another is the result of neuroception; a term to describe the ability of our ANS to respond to cues of safety, danger and life-threatening situations (Dana, 2018). By listening to vocal intonation and observing body language and facial expressions, we can tell if it is safe to approach or retreat.

Influential neuroscientist Panksepp (1998) spent decades in his pursuit to map and understand human and animal emotions, providing current researchers with information about the subcortical areas of the brain that may one day provide answers to the formation of human personality (Davis & Montag, 2018).

Panksepp's Seven Primal Emotional Systems.

Primary emotional system	Functions
The SEEKING system	Situation evaluation Facilitates learning Displayed as enthusiasm, curiosity and searching
The RAGE system	A response to frustration when basic needs are blocked by others or the environment
The FEAR system	Fight or flight response to protect against real or perceived threats
The LUST system	In service of procreation. Connected to the SEEKING system
The CARE system	In service of safety and stability. Displayed as love, affection and tenderness
The PANIC system	A call for help during times of separation distress when care is no longer accessible
The PLAY system	Associated with learning, creativity, social bonding and positive emotions

Panksepp et al. (2019) describe the ways in which early childhood experiences influence the wiring of these emotional systems, either negatively or positively. For example, children who are denied opportunities for play may find social engagement opportunities frightening. Insecure children are likely to become insecure adults, as such, the SEEKING, CARE and PLAY systems may be underdeveloped, and the FEAR and PANIC systems may be too sensitive (Panksepp et al., 2019). The SEEKING and CARE systems are essential to the development of a secure attachment style and also for the regulation of emotions (Gilbert & Procter, 2006). The SEEKING system has an arousing and activating effect, most likely driven by a surge of dopamine, whereas as the CARE system appears to generate the production of oxytocin, which is known to regulate the stress hormone cortisol (Gilbert & Procter, 2006). When caregivers provide their children with opportunities to feel safe, the child will explore (SEEKING) and use their imagination (PLAY), whereas children who experience unsafe feelings as the result of shame, criticism and negative evaluation are likely to experience high levels of cortisol and find themselves caught up in the PANIC and FEAR systems (Gilbert & Procter, 2006). Witness chronic procrastinators who fear failing, and you see an attempt to avoid the PANIC and FEAR systems: This works as a strategy in the short term, but only delays and heightens the inevitable consequences. This leads us back to the importance of self-soothing and self-regulating the nervous system and how understanding heart rate variability offers new insights into anxiety and cognitive function.

According to research conducted by Steffen and et al., (2020), persons with an insecure attachment style tend to have lower heart rate variability (HRV). HRV refers to the length of intervals between heartbeats (Shearer et al., 2016). According to Petrocchi and Cheli (2019), higher HRV (i.e. more variability between heart beats) is related to an increased capacity to regulate stress and arousal and is also associated with increased metacognitive awareness, focused attention and working memory (Petrocchi & Cheli, 2019). The benefits of a flexible ANS are that it enables swift emotional responses to various situations (Burg et al., 2012). It helps individuals to move between social engagement behaviours to a threat response and back into safety quickly and effectively rather than becoming "stuck" in a chronic threat response (Steffen et al., 2020). This is important because when the threat system is activated and the ANS triggers either a fight, flight or freeze response to perceived danger, the prefrontal cortex disengages to such a degree that a person's higher-order cognitive abilities are seriously hampered (Matos & Steindl, 2020).

Slade et al. (2009) discovered that in tests measuring attention and executive function, those who demonstrated signs of maladaptive perfectionism did less well than adaptive perfectionists, suggesting that attempts to avoid making errors in an effort to gain approval have a negative effect on working memory, attention and planning. Furthermore, Lo and Abbot (2013) found that students who identified as maladaptive perfectionists were not only more emotionally distressed than their counterparts, but also demonstrated significant dysfunctional cognitive processing (Lo & Abbott, 2013). However, while Robinson and Abramovitch (2020) found further proof that maladaptive perfectionism leads to significant psychological disturbances they found *no* evidence to suggest it hampers executive functioning at a neuropsychological level. Robinson and Abramovitch (2020) conclude that with such a limited and contradictory degree of research into this area of concern, further studies are critical to understanding the full impact of maladaptive perfectionism on executive function. Nevertheless, assuming that stress does have at least some negative effect on executive functioning in the short term, supporting students to cope with stress would appear self-evident.

Returning to the topic of HRV and the regulation of emotions, it is helpful to place it in the context of the PNS and in particular to the role of the vagus nerve (Fiskum, 2019). The vagus nerve is the longest nerve in the body, reaching from the brain and connected to major organs throughout the body. It is divided into two branches, namely ventral and dorsal. The ventral pathway leads to feelings of safety and connection, and the dorsal pathway leads to disconnection as part of a response to extreme threat. According to Dana (2018), "when we feel frozen, numb, or "not there", the dorsal vagus has taken control" (p. 9). The ventral "brake" assists in keeping our threat responses, including the sympathetic response of fight or flight as well as the dorsal collapse, at bay (Fiskum, 2019).

The most effective way to increase HRV through ventral vagal activity is through interpersonal relationships that feel safe as well as learning to develop the capacity for self-compassion (Petrocchi & Cheli, 2019). Mindfully present states that are paired with self-compassion have been observed to increase HRV and indicate a capacity for self-regulation (Beck et al., 2017; Burg et al., 2012; Shearer et al., 2016). In other words, higher education students who are self-aware and practice self-compassion will also foster a healthier perspective in regards to their studies, as well as develop a secure attachment style.

Mindfulness and Self-Compassion

Paying attention to the present moment without judgement (mindfulness) has been found to reduce stress and improve emotional regulation amongst college students (Cherry & Wilcox, 2020). Short and Mazmanian (2013) note the absence of worry and rumination in those who regularly practice mindfulness, and that mindfulness significantly lowers socially prescribed perfectionism. Similarly, Motie et al., (2019) found that mindfulness-based practice not only decreased anxiety and procrastination but also enhanced self-esteem and self-efficacy. In contrast, Shearer et al., (2016) report links to increased rumination, depression, anxiety, struggles with emotion regulation, avoidant behaviours, self-consciousness, social anxiety and absent-mindedness in those with low levels of mindfulness. Williams (2008) supports the view that when people are mindfully aware of the present moment they can also choose to disengage from states of rumination and negative thinking.

Tobin and Dunkley (2020) note that those students who set high standards for themselves are less at risk of developing anxiety or depression if they engage in mindfulness and self-compassion techniques; nor does it take a great deal of effort to be effective. This is supported by the research of Beck et al. (2017), who found that spending twenty minutes per day doing simple yoga stretches and paying attention to the breath reduced student stress across an entire academic semester, particularly in regards to managing maladaptive perfectionism without sacrificing high grades.

Internal conflict can be a very distressing component for perfectionists who procrastinate and can be the cause of deep shame (Matos & Steindl, 2020). Self-criticism is linked to an increased vulnerability to stress, social anxiety and depression, whereas increased self-compassion has been shown to improve symptoms of psychological distress (Shahar et al., 2014). The dynamic of self-criticism is displayed as an internal dialogue between a part of the self-judging and attacking another weaker and submissive part of the self. Shahar et al., (2014) describe the attacking part of "expressing contempt, whereas the attacked part is left with feelings of powerlessness, worthlessness, depression and anxiety" (p. 347). Whelton and Greenbert (2005) describe the self-critic as feeling "helplessly yoked to an interior taskmaster, against whom they never competitively win, and to whom they often submit, feeling overwhelmed, resentful, and secretly vanquished" (p. 1583). Additionally, Steel (2007) suggests that while choosing to procrastinate may be associated with the short-term alleviation of anxiety, in the long run, it proves an unhelpful strategy that perpetuates the cycle of shame.

Martincekova and Enright (2018) found that students who were able to forgive themselves for their avoidant behaviour were quicker to recover from setbacks to their study and in doing so were more able to avoid the cycle of shame. Students with high levels of self-compassion do not have the same need to enhance or defend their self-esteem through performance-based goals and yet tend to do well in their studies based on their motivation to be curious and to master tasks for their own growth (Neff, 2003). More importantly, self-compassionate students do not need to hide their limitations. Neff and Germer (2013) claim "because self-compassionate people do not berate themselves when they fail, they are less afraid of failure and more able to take on new challenges" (p. 31). In this regard, it is easy to make the link to Panksepp's (1998; 2019) emotional networks: students who are skilled in self-regulating through self-compassion are activated to SEEK and PLAY, whereas those in the throes of shame and self-criticism are driven by FEAR and PANIC.

Reviewing the literature in a meta-analysis of the association between self-compassion and psychopathology, MacBeth and Gumley (2012) found compelling evidence to suggest that self-compassion decreases mental health symptoms by reducing time ruminating. Likewise, Raes (2010) reports findings showing that self-compassion leads to less rumination, resulting in less depression and anxiety. Self-compassion has also been demonstrated to increase self-efficacy (Booker & Dunsmore, 2019; Pandey et al., 2020).

According to Petrocchi and Cheli (2019), compassion is an expression of Panksepp's (1998) CARE system, and it is through the act of self-care that a person can learn to self-soothe. During acts of kindness towards the self while stressed, the fight-flight-freeze response becomes inhibited (Petrocchi & Cheli, 2019; Steffen et al., 2020), and cortisol levels drop. The ability to self-soothe would clearly be an asset to students who are experiencing shame and self-loathing when they are in a fight/flight/or freeze reaction while tackling important assessment tasks.

Neuroscience provides another perspective regarding the formation of negative thinking and rumination. Any repetition of cognitive or behavioural patterns leads to the development and strengthening of neural networks (Cozolino, 2017). Self-criticism, once it has become firmly entrenched, will inevitably become the "go to" frame of mind when a person is under stress. Once a network has become strong enough it becomes the default mode of operating. We slip into old patterns with ease because of this neurological process, and it is by-and-large helpful as it means we can go about everyday tasks without much cognitive effort.

The voice of the internal critic, unfortunately, can easily become one of those default networks that are easily channelled and hard to ignore. Compassionate Mind Training (CMT) was developed to teach the practice of self-acceptance to people who experience high levels of self-criticism and related shame (Gilbert & Procter, 2006; Halamova et al., 2020). CMT aims to change unhelpful neural networks, such as automatic self-criticism, replacing it with a new, kinder and more supportive internal champion that has a chance of becoming the dominant mental pathway when the person is faced with a stressful situation. The first step is to recognize that attempts to avoid mistakes and/or self-harm behaviours are maladaptive coping strategies activated in an effort to regulate painful situations. The next step is to identify what the underlying fear is, such as the fear of being rejected. The third step is to acknowledge procrastination and general attempts to avoid stressful situations as "safety behaviours", which may be helpful in the short term as they alleviate anxiety but lead to increased shame over the long term when the person "fails" again (Gilbert & Procter, 2006). Instead of perpetuating the cycle of shame/avoid/shame/avoid, the person is encouraged to practice the act of self-compassion, which translates as recognizing the suffering they are experiencing and to want to help ease the suffering (Neff, 2003).

Neff (2003) makes the point that self-compassion is not the same as self-pity, which leads to disconnection as the person becomes engrossed with their own suffering and cannot see the pain others experience. Nor must people avoid or repress their emotions because it is only through witnessing pain that compassion comes alive. The benefit of this level of self-awareness is an increased capacity to self-regulate the nervous system resulting in a reduction in cortisol levels, enabling individuals to concentrate on the task at hand rather than getting into a panic and procrastinating as a maladaptive means to regulate unpleasant emotions.

Building Resilience: How Educational Institutions Can Support Students

Higher education administrators and leaders on campus need to raise awareness that academic stress is a real possibility and that anxiety is a common experience (Leblanc & Marques, 2019; Misra & McKean, 2000), while also reassuring students that minimizing stress is the key to successful completion of the course (Huckins et al., 2020). Planning to support students to manage their performance anxiety requires various different strategies, including teaching practical problem-solving skills regarding time management strategies and the like, but also teaching students how to self-soothe under stress and the benefits of mindfulness and self-compassion. Students can also benefit from gaining a better understanding of the difference between *wanting* to achieve excellent standards and *needing* to prove their self-worth through the grades they receive.

Wei et al., (2006) recommend helping students understand their attachment styles and how this relates to their maladaptive perfectionist tendencies and why they may use procrastination as a means to avoid feeling anxious (and how this increases their anxiety over the long haul). Creating a supportive higher education teaching and learning environment to alleviate the sense of loneliness that is often experienced by new students is also of high importance (Carr et al., 2013). Conversely, while encouraging social interactions may be of benefit for some students, educators need to be careful when encouraging students to work together in groups, as recent findings highlight the need to be sensitive to the needs of avoidant personalities (Lavy, 2017). In such cases, Lavy (2017) suggests making room to provide assistance in dealing with their difficulties working with others and to provide positive feedback to "help them overcome their negative view of themselves as group members" (p. 184).

Students in higher education who are experiencing high levels of stress and use procrastination as a strategy to cope can be helped by learning to successfully engage with the stressor rather than their customary approach of avoiding the problem. According to Steffen et al., (2020) "When people avoid a recurring stressor they never fully deal with that stressor and it is never resolved. When people engage with a recurring stressor they have the opportunity to work through the stress and increase their ability to cope, which improves HRV in the long term" (p. 61).

Perfectionists can be overly defensive, particularly if they are put in a position where they feel embarrassed, humiliated or shamed (Besser et al., 2010). For this reason, it is important that support is given in ways that minimize the risk of shaming. Students who are highly self-critical often have a need to withdraw in response to shame. For such hypersensitive students, feedback may result in further shame no matter how sensitively worded. Delivering assessment feedback using audio recordings, where tone of voice can convey support rather than perceived criticism, is a worthwhile option (McCarthy, 2015).

Curriculum design and delivery of content are other areas that can make a difference to student stress levels (Ramsden, 2003). Ambrose et al. (2010) explain the process of learning as a relatively slow process of building upon learned associations. Neural networks in the brain take time to be established, usually through repeated exposure to information, observation and practice. As the brain keeps learning, the more interlinked and complex the neural networks become, enabling the person to perform increasingly complex tasks (Cozolino, 2017). A teacher who has studied their topic of interest for many years has a highly organized set of networks that make it easy for them to explain and understand information quickly and efficiently. They may become frustrated with students who are struggling to grasp concepts and theories that to the teacher seem easy, and this frustration may lead to further stress for the struggling student: Remember, body language, tone of voice, and eye contact convey either threat or safety cues. Teachers and curriculum writers can organize material in ways that support the creation of neural networks, i.e. by not overloading the content and giving plenty of opportunities to instil information so that it becomes imbedded. Clear goals and feedback on progress are also recommended. As Biggs and Tang (2011) state, "driving in a thick fog is highly unpleasant. So is learning in one" (p. 45).

Conclusion

The literature examined throughout this chapter demonstrates a connection to early childhood bonds to securely attached caregivers and healthy adult self-esteem. Securely attached individuals strive towards goals that challenge them but do not threaten their self-worth when they do fail or miss the target of their attempts at perfection. People with insecure attachments are prone to worrying about the availability of support if they do not meet others expectations. Higher education students with an insecure attachment style are at a higher risk of developing maladaptive perfectionism and using procrastination as an unhelpful coping mechanism: this combination of factors leaves them prone to shame because they are unable to live the lives they want for themselves. In turn, this leaves the person vulnerable to mental health problems, including anxiety, depression and thoughts of suicide.

Suggestions for creating a healthy higher education teaching and learning environment are: making sure that all teachers create a safe environment that down-regulates the ANS threat response as far as possible; providing feedback in non-shaming terms and providing opportunities to encourage engagement; developing a curriculum that is designed to avoid overloading students' capacity to learn effectively; teaching students strategies such as time management skills; educating students about their nervous system and the negative effects of self-criticism and most important of all, delivering ongoing face-to-face and online workshops teaching the skills of mindfulness and self-compassion so that students can learn to self-soothe and learn to be kind to themselves when they are under pressure. Teachers and curriculum designers working in higher education can all contribute to creating opportunities to activate the SEEKING system by engaging with the materials with open curiosity, to activate the PLAY system to encourage creative thinking and to reduce FEAR and PANIC by creating safety through an environment that provides a great deal of CARE.

References

Abdollahi, A., Hosseinian, S., & Asmundson, G. J. G. (2018). Coping styles mediate perfectionism associations with depression among undergraduate students. *The Journal of General Psychology, 145*(1), 93–105. https://doi.org/10.1080/00221309.2017.1421137

Ambrose, S. A., Bridges, M. W., DiPietro, M., Lovett, M. C., & Norman, M. K. (2010). *How learning works: 7 research-based principles for smart teaching*. Jossey-Bass.

Barker, E. T., Howard, A. L., Villemaire-Krajden, & Galambos, N. L. (2018). The rise and fall of depressive symptoms and academic stress in two samples of university students. *Journal of Youth and Adolescence, 47*, 1252–1266. https://doi.org/10.1007/s10964-018-0822-9

Bartholomew, K., & Horowitz, L. M. (1991). Attachment styles among young adults: A test of a four-category model. *Journal of Personality and Social Psychology, 61*(2), 226–244.

Beck, A. R., Verticchio, H., Seeman, S., Milliken, E., & Schaab, H. (2017). A mindfulness practice for communication sciences and disorders undergraduate and speech-language pathology graduate students: Effects on stress, self-compassion, and perfectionism. *American Journal of Speech-Language Pathology, 26*, 893–907. https://doi.org/10.1044/2017_AJSLP-16-0172

Besser, A., Flett, G. L., & Hewitt, P. L. (2010). Perfectionistic self-presentation and trait perfectionism in social problem-solving ability and depressive symptoms. *Journal of Applied Social Psychology, 40*(8), 2121–2154.

Biggs, J., & Tang, C. (2011). *Teaching for quality learning at university* (4th ed.). McGraw Hill.

Booker, J. A., & Dunsmore, J. C. (2019). Testing direct and indirect ties of self-compassion with subjective well-being. *Journal of Happiness Studies: An Interdisciplinary Forum on Subjective Well-Being, 20*(5), 1563–1585. https://doi.org/10.1007/s10902-018-0011-2.

Bowlby, J. (1988). *A secure base: Parent-child attachment and healthy human development*. Basic Books.

Burg, J. M., Wolf, O. T., & Michalak, J. (2012). Mindfulness as self-regulated attention: Associations with heart rate variability. *Swiss Journal of Psychology, 71*(3), 135–139. https://doi.org/10.1024/1421-0185/a000080

Burnam, A., Komarraju, M., Hamel, R., & Nadler, D. R. (2014). Do adaptive perfectionism and self-determined motivation reduce academic procrastination? *Learning and Individual Differences, 36*, 165–172. https://doi.org/10.1016/j.lindif.2014.10.009

Burns, L. R., Dittman, K., Nguyen, N.-L., & Mitchelson, J. K. (2000). Academic procrastination, perfectionism, and control: Associations with vigilant and avoidant coping. In J. R. Ferrari & T. A. Pychyl (Eds.). Procrastination: current issues and new directions [Special Issue]. *Journal of Social Behaviour and Personality, 2000*(15), 35–46.

Carr, S., Colthurst, K., Coyle, M., & Elliot, D. (2013). Attachment dimensions as predictors of mental health and psychosocial well-being in transition to university. *European Journal of Psychology of Education, 28,* 157–172. https://doi.org/10.1007/s10212-012-0106-9

Cassidy, J. (2016). The nature of the child's ties. In J. Cassidy & P. R. Shaver (Eds.), *Handbook of attachment: Theory, research and clinical application* (3rd ed.). The Guildford Press.

Champika, K. S., & Weiss, A. (2014). Mediating perceived parenting styles—Test anxiety relationships: Academic procrastination and maladaptive perfectionism. *Learning and Individual Differences, 34,* 77–85.

Chen, C., Hewitt, P. L., Flett, G. L., Cassels, T. G., Birch, S., & Blasberg, J. S. (2012). Insecure attachment, perfectionistic self-presentation, and social disconnection in adolescents. *Personality and Individual Differences, 52,* 936–941. https://doi.org/10.1016/j.paid.2012.02.009

Cherry, M. L., & Wilcox, M. M. (2020). Decreasing perceived and academic stress through emotion regulation and nonjudging with trauma-exposed college students. *International Journal of Stress Management, 27*(2), 101–110. https://doi.org/10.1037/str0000138

Concerto, C., Patel, D., Infortuna, C., Chusid, E., Muscatello, M. R., Bruno, A., Zoccali, R., Aguglia, E., & Battaglia, F. (2017). Academic stress disrupts cortical plasticity in graduate students. *International Journal of the Biology of Stress, 20*(2), 212–216. https://doi.org/10.1080/10253890.2017.1301424

Cozolino, L. (2017). *The neuroscience of psychotherapy: Healing the social brain* (3rd ed.). W. W. Norton & Company.

Curran, T., & Hill, A. P. (2019). Perfectionism is increasing over time: A meta-analysis of birth cohort differences from 1989 to 2016. *Psychological Bulletin, 145*(4), 401–429. https://doi.org/10.1037/bul0000138

Dana, D. (2018). *The polyvagal theory in therapy: Engaging the rhythm of regulation.* W. W. Norton & Company.

Davis, K. L., & Montag, C. (2018). A tribute to Jaak Panksepp. *Personal Neuroscience.* https://doi.org/10.1017/pen.20185

Deits-Lebehn, C., Baucom, J. W., Crenshaw, A. O., Smith, T. W., & Baucom, B. R. W. (2020). Incorporating physiology into the study of psychotherapy process. *American Psychological Association, 67*(4), 488–499. https://doi.org/10.1037/cou0000391

Fee, R. L., & Tangney, J. P. (2000). Procrastination: A means of avoiding shame or guilt? In J. R. Ferrari & T. A. Pychyl (Eds.), Procrastination: current issues and new directions [Special Issue]. *Journal of Social Behaviour and Personality, 2000*(15), 167–184.

Ferrari, J. R. (2001). Procrastination as self-regulation failure of performance: Effects of cognitive load, self-awareness, and time limits on 'working best under pressure.' *European Journal of Personality, 15,* 391–406. https://doi.org/10.1002/per.413

Ferrari, J. F., & Diaz-Morales. (2014). Procrastination and mental health coping: A brief report related to students. *Individual Differences Research, 12*(1), 1–7.

Fiskum, C. (2019). Psychotherapy beyond all the words: Dyadic expansion, vagal regulation, and biofeedback in psychotherapy. *Journal of Psychotherapy Integration, 29*(4), 412–425. https://doi.org/10.1037/int0000174

Flett, G. L., Besser, A., & Hewitt, P. L. (2014). Perfectionism and interpersonal orientations in depression: An analysis of validation seeking and rejection sensitivity in a community sample of young adults. *Psychiatry, 77*(1), 67–85.

Flett, G. L., Blankstein, K. R., Hewitt, P. L., & Koledin, S. (1992). Components of perfectionism and procrastination in college students. *Social Behaviour and Personality, 20*(2), 85–94. https://doi.org/10.2444/sbp.1992.20.2.85

Gilbert, P., & Procter, S. (2006). Compassionate mind training for people with high shame and self-criticism: Overview and pilot study of a group therapy approach. *Clinical Psychology and Psychotherapy, 13,* 353–379. https://doi.org/10.1002/cpp.507

Gillath, O., Giesbrecht, B., & Shaver, P. R. (2009). Attachment, attention, and cognitive control: Attachment style and performance on general attention tasks. *Journal of Experimental Social Psychology, 45,* 647–654.

Gnilka, P. B., Ashby, J. S., & Noble, C. M. (2013). Adaptive and maladaptive perfectionism as mediators of adult attachment styles and depression, hopelessness, and life satisfaction. *Journal of Counseling & Development, 91*, 78–86.

Goodall, K. (2015). Individual differences in the regulation of positive emotion: The role of attachment and self-esteem. *Personality and Individual Differences, 74*, 208–213.

Goroshit, M., Meirav, H., & Ferrari, J. R. (2020). Life-domain regret regarding procrastination (LDR-P). Scale validation in the United States and Israel. *Current Psychology, 39*(3), 900–912. https://doi.org/10.1007/s12144-018-9801-2.

Halamova, J., Kanovsky, M., Pacutova, A., & Kupeli, N. (2020). Randomised controlled trial of an online version of compassion mind training in a nonclinical sample. *Europe's Journal of Psychology, 16*(2), 262–279. https://doi.org/10.5964/ejop.v16i2.1683

Hewitt, P. L., Flett, G. L., & Blankstein, K. R. (1991). Perfectionism and neuroticism in psychiatric patients and college students. *Personality and Individual Differences, 12*, 273–279.

Huckins, J. F., DaSilva, A. W., Hedlund, E. L., Murphy, E. I., & Rogers, C. (2020). Causal factors of anxiety and depression in college students: Longitudinal ecological momentary assessment and causal analysis using Peter and Clark momentary conditional independence. *JMIR Mental Health; Toronto, 7*(6), 1–9. https://doi.org/10.2196/16684

Klingsieck, K. B. (2013). Procrastination: When good things don't come to those who wait. *European Psychologist, 18*(1), 24–34. https://doi.org/10.1027/1016-9040/a000138

Kidd, T., Hamer, M., & Steptoe, A. (2013). Adult attachment style and cortisol responses across the day in older adults. *Psychophysiology, 50*, 841–847.

Kobac, R., Zajac, K., & Madsen, S.D. (2016). Attachment disruptions, reparative processes, and psychopathology: Theoretical and clinical implications. In J. Cassidy & P. R. Shaver (Eds.). *Handbook of attachment: Theory, research, and clinical implications*, (3rd ed.). The Guildford Press.

Konrath, S. H., Chopik, J., Hsing, C. K. & O'Brien, E. (2014). Changes in adult attachment styles in American college students over time: A meta-analysis. *Personal and Social Psychology Review, 18*(4), 326–348. https://doi.org/10.1177/1088868314530516

Lavy, S. (2017). Who benefits from group work in higher education? An attachment theory perspective. *Higher Education, 73*, 175–187. https://doi.org/10.1007/s10734-016-0006-z

Leblanc, N. J., & Marques, L. (2019). *Anxiety in college: What we know and how to cope*. Harvard Health Publishing. https://www.health.harvard.edu/blog/anxiety-in-college-what-we-know-and-how-to-cope-2019052816729

Lo, A., & Abbott, M. J. (2013). The impact of manipulating expected standards of performance for adaptive, maladaptive, and non-perfectionists. *Cognitive Theory Research, 37*, 762–778. https://doi.org/10.1007/s10608-013-9528-1

Lundin, L. (2020). Online narrative about panic attacks: Interpreted within a psychodynamic framework. *Social Work in Mental Health, 18*(3), 349–365. https://doi.org/10.1080/15332985.2020.1744500

McCarthy, J. (2015). Evaluating written, audio and video feedback in higher education summative assessment tasks. *Issues in Educational Research, 25*(2), 153–169. https://www.iier.org.au/iier25/mccarthy.html

MacBeth, A., & Gumley, A. (2012). Exploring compassion: A meta-analysis of the association between self-compassion and psychopathology. *Clinical Psychology Review, 32*(6), 545–552.

Manap, R., Hamid, S. A., & Ghani, M. A. (2019). Depression, anxiety and stress among undergraduate students. *Journal of Social Sciences and Humanities, 16*(2), 1–7.

Maunder, R. G., Lancee, W. J., Nolan, R. P., Hunter, J. J., & Tannenbaum, D. W. (2006). The relationship of attachment insecurity to subjective stress and autonomic function during standardized acute stress in healthy adults. *Journal of Psychosomatic Research, 60*, 283–290.

Martincekova, L., & Enright, R. D. (2018). The effects of self-forgiveness and shame-proneness on procrastination: Exploring the mediating role of affect. *Current Psychology, 39*, 428–437.

Matos, M., & Steindl, S. R. (2020). "You are already all you need to be": A case illustration of compassion-focused therapy for shame and perfectionism. *Journal of Clinical Psychology, 76*, 2079–2096. https://doi.org/10.1002/jclp.23055

Mearns, D., & Thorne, B. (2007). *Person-centred counselling in action* (3rd ed.). Sage.

Mikulincer, M. (1995). Attachment style and the mental representation of the self. *Journal of Personality and Social Psychology, 69*(6), 1203–1215.

Mikulincer, M., & Shaver, P. R. (2016). Adult attachment and emotion regulation. In J. Cassidy & P. R. Shaver (Eds.). *Handbook of attachment: Theory, research, and clinical applications* (3rd ed.). The Guildford Press.

Mirzairad, R., Haydari, A., Pasha, R., Ehteshamzadeh, P., & Makvandi. (2017). The relationship between perfectionism and psychological distress with mediation of coping styles and self-esteem. *International Journal of Mental Health and Addiction, 15*, 614–620. https://doi.org/10.1007/s11469-016-9689-8

Misra, R., & McKean, M. (2000). College students' academic stress and its relation to their anxiety, time management, and leisure satisfaction. *American Journal of Health Studies, 16*(1), 41–51.

Motie, H., Heidari, M., Bagherian, F., & Zarani (2019). Providing mindfulness-based educational package for evaluating academic procrastination. *Iranian Journal of Psychiatry and Clinical Psychology, 25*(1), 26–28. https://doi.org/10.32598/ijpcp.25.1.25

Neff, K. D. (2003). The development and validation of a scale to measure self-compassion. *Self and Identity, 2*, 223–250. https://doi.org/10.1080/15298860390209035

Neff, K. D., & Germer, C. (2013). A pilot study and randomized controlled trial of the mindful self-compassion program. *Journal of Clinical Psychology, 69*(1), 28–44. https://doi.org/10.1002/jclp.21923

Noble, C., Ashby, J. S., Ellis, M. B., Matheny, K. B., Gnilka, P. B., Clark, K. M., & Bell, C. M. (2011). Adult attachment style differences among adaptive, maladaptive, and nonperfectionists. *American Psychological Association*, 1–4.

Orygen, (2020). *Australian university mental health framework report*, Orygen.

Ozer, B. U., O'Callaghan, J., Bokszczanin, A., Ederer, E., & Essau, C. (2014). Dynamic interplay of depression, perfectionism and self-regulation on procrastination. *British Journal of Guidance and Counselling, 42*(3), 309–319. https://doi.org/10.1080/03069885.2014.896454

Pandey, R., Tiwar, G. K., Parihar, P., & Rai, P. K., (2020). The relationship between self-esteem and self-forgiveness: Understanding the mediating role of positive and negative self-compassion. *Research Gate*. https://doi.org/10.22541/au.158981530.01103201

Panksepp, J. (1998). *Affective neuroscience: The foundations of human and animal emotions*. Oxford University Press.

Panksepp, J., Clarici, A., Vandekerckhove, M., & Yovell, Y. (2019). Neuro-evolutionary foundations of infant minds: From psychoanalytic visions of how primal emotions guide constructions of human minds towards affective neuroscientific understanding of emotions and their disorders. *Psychoanalytic Inquiry, 39*(1), 36–51. https://doi.org/10.1080/07351690.2019.1549910

Petrocchi, N., & Cheli, S. (2019). The social brain and heart rate variability: Implications for psychotherapy. *Psychology and Psychotherapy: Theory, Research and Practice, 92*, 208–223. https://doi.org/10.1111/papt.12224

Raes, F. (2010). Rumination and worry as mediators of the relationship between self-compassion and depression and anxiety. *Personality and Individual Differences, 48*, 757–761. https://doi.org/10.1016/j.paid.2010.01.023

Ramsden, P. (2003). *Learning to teach in higher education* (2nd ed.). Routledge.

Rice, K. G., & Mirzadeh, S. A. (2000). Perfectionism, attachment, and adjustment. *Journal of Counseling Psychology, 47*(2), 238–250. https://doi.org/10.1037//0022-0167.47.2.238

Rice, K. G., Lopez, F. G., & Vergara, D. (2005). Parental/social influences on perfectionism and adult attachment orientation. *Journal of Social and Clinical Psychology, 24*(4), 580–605.

Rice, K. G., Richardson, C. M. E., & Clark, D. (2012). Perfectionism, procrastination, and psychological distress. *American Psychological Association, 59*(2), 288–302. https://doi.org/10.1037/a0026643

Robinson, A., & Abramovitch, A. (2020). A neuropsychological investigation of perfectionism. *Behaviour Therapy, 51*, 488–502.
Rogers, C. (1951). *Client-centered therapy*. Constable.
Shahar, B., Szsepsenwol, O., Zilcha-Mano, S., Haim, N., Zamir, O., Levi-Yeshuvi, S., & Levit-Binnun, N. (2014). A wait-list randomized controlled trial of loving-kindness meditation programme for self-criticism. *Clinical Psychology and Psychotherapy, 22*, 346–356. https://doi.org/10.1002/c00.1893
Shearer, A., Hunt, M., Chowdhury, M., & Nicol, L. (2016). Effects of a brief mindfulness meditation intervention on student stress and heart rate variability. *International Journal of Stress Management, 23*(2), 232–254. https://doi.org/10.1037/a0039814
Short, M. M., & Mazmanian, D. (2013). Perfectionism and negative repetitive thoughts: Examining a multiple mediator model in relation to mindfulness. *Personality and Individual Differences, 55*, 716–721. https://doi.org/10.1016/j.paid.2013.05.026
Siegel, D. J. (2007). *The mindful brain: Reflections and attunement in the cultivating of well-being*. W. W. Norton & Company.
Siegel, D. J. (2019). The mind in psychotherapy: An interpersonal neurobiology framework for understanding and cultivating mental health. *Psychology and Psychotherapy: Theory, Research and Practice* 92, 224–237. https://doi.org/10.1111/papt.12228
Siegel, D. J. (2020). Aware: The science and practice of presence. *American Medical WRiters Association, 35*(1), 13–19.
Slade, P. D., Coppel, D. B., & Townes, B. D. (2009). Neurocognitive correlates of positive and negative perfectionism. *International Journal of Neuroscience, 119*, 1741–1754. https://doi.org/10.1080/00207450902915212
Smith, M. M., Sherry, S. B., Saklofske, D. H., & Mushqaush, A. R. (2017). Clarifying the perfectionism-procrastination relationship using a 7-day, 14-occasion daily diary study. *Personality and Individual Differences, 112*, 117–123. https://doi.org/10.1016/j.paid.2017.02.059
Smith, M. M., Speth, T. A., Sherry, S. B., Saklofske, D. H., Stewart, S. H., & Glowacka, M. (2017). Is socially prescribed perfectionism veridical? A new take on the stressfulness of perfectionism. *Personality and Individual Differences, 110*, 115–118. https://doi.org/10.1016/j.paid.2017.01.031
Smith, M. M., Vidovic, V., Sherry, S. B., & Saklofske, D. H. (2017). Self-oriented perfectionism and socially prescribed perfectionism add incrementally to the prediction of suicide ideation beyond hopelessness: A meta-analysis of 15 studies. In U. Kumar (Ed.) *Handbook of suicidal behavior* (pp. 349–369). Springer. https://doi.org/10.1007/978-981-10-4816-6_19
Smith, M. M., Sherry, S. B., Ge, S. Y. J., Hewitt, P. L., Flett, G. L., & Baggley, D. L. (2021). Multidimensional perfectionism turns 30: A review of known knowns and unknown unknowns. *Canadian Psychology*. https://doi.org/10.1037/cap0000288
Sorout, J., Kodidala, S. R., Soni, H., Singh, P., & Sharma, N. (2020). Effects of academic stress on physical activity level and cognitive functions in first year medical students: An observational study. *Asian Journal of Medical Sciences, 11*(5), 8–11.
Speirs, K. L., & Finch, H. (2006). Perfectionism in high-ability students: Relational precursors and influences on achievement motivation. *The Gifted Child Quarterly, 50*(3), 238–273.
Starley, D. (2019). Perfectionism: A challenging but worthwhile research area for educational psychology. *Educational Psychology in Practice, 35*(2), 121–146. https://doi.org/10.1080/02667363.2018.1539949
Steel, P. (2007). The nature of procrastination: A meta-analytic and theoretical review of quintessential self-regulatory failure. *The American Psychological Association, 133*(1), 65–94. https://doi.org/10.1037/0033-2909.133.1.65
Steffen, P. R., Foxx, J., Cattani, K., Alldredge, C., Austin, T., & Burlingame, G. M. (2020). Impact of a 12-week group-based compassion focused therapy intervention on heart rate variability. *Applied Psychophysiology and Biofeedback, 46*, 61–68. https://doi.org/10.1007/s10484-020-09487-8
Tibbett, T. P., & Ferrari, J. F. (2019). Return to the origin: What creates procrastination identity? *Current Issues in Personality Psychology, 1*, 1–7. https://doi.org/10.5114/cipp.2018.75648

Tobin, R., & Dunkley, D. M. (2020). Self-critical perfectionism and lower mindfulness and self-compassion predict anxious and depressive symptoms over two years. *Behaviour Research and Therapy, 136*, 1–12. https://doi.org/10.1016/j.brat.2020.103780

Ulu, I. P., & Tezer, E. (2010). Adaptive and maladaptive perfectionism, adult attachment, and big five personality traits. *The Journal of Psychology, 144*(4), 327–340.

Van Shie, C. C., Jarman, H. L., Reis, S., & Grenyer, B. F. S. (2021). Narcissistic traits in young people and how experiencing shame relates to current attachment challenges. *BMC Psychiatry, 21*(246), 1–10. https://doi.org/10.1186/s12888-021-03249-4

Vanstone, D. M., & Hicks, R. E. (2019). Transitioning to university: Coping styles as mediators between adaptive-maladaptive perfectionism and test anxiety. *Personality and Individual Differences, 141,* 68–75. https://doi.org/10.1016/j.paid.2018.12.026

Veness, B. G. (2016). *The wicked problem of university student mental health.* Report to the Winston Churchill Memorial Trust.

Wei, M., Heppner, P. P., Russell, D. W., & Young, S. K. (2006). Maladaptive perfectionism and ineffective coping as mediators between attachment and future depression: A prospective analysis. *Journal of Counseling Psychology, 53*(1), 67–79. https://doi.org/10.1037/0022-0167.53.1.67

Whelton, W. J., & Greenbert, L. S. (2005). Emotion in self-criticism. *Personality and Individual Differences, 38,* 1583–1595. https://doi.org/10.1016/j.paid.2004.09.024

Williams, J. M. G. (2008). Mindfulness, depression and modes of mind. *Cognitive Therapy Research, 32,* 721–733. https://doi.org/10.1007/s10608-008-9204-z

Wood, C. M., Cano-Vindel, A., & Salguero, J. M. (2015). A multi-factor model of panic disorder: Results of a preliminary study integrating the role of perfectionism, stress, physiological anxiety and anxiety sensitivity. *Anales De Psicologia, 31,* 481–487. https://doi.org/10.6018/analesps.31.2.184241

Kaz Mitchell is a psychotherapist in private practice and a lecturer at the Australian College of Applied Psychology. Kaz Mitchell has over 30 years experience supporting people towards mental health and wellbeing. Prior to moving into private practice and education, Kaz worked for 25 years within mental health services both in Australia and in Scotland (her place of birth). She is fully qualified as an Art Therapist and has a Masters in Counselling and Psychotherapy. Kaz is currently researching her interest in neuroscience as it relates to psychotherapy, particularly the role mindfulness and self-compassion play in regulating emotions, with the intention of beginning a Ph.D.

The Higher Education Experience of Students During the COVID-19 Pandemic and the Impact on Mental Well-Being: A Review of the Literature

Saradamoyee Chatterjee

Abstract The COVID-19 pandemic substantially impacted higher education worldwide (Yang in High Educ Res Dev 39:1317–1321, 2020). The virus containment measures enforced the closure of the educational institutions and steered the transformation of most learning, teaching and assessment (LTA) to a virtual format (Watermeyer et al. in High Educ, 1–19, 2020). However, this transformation is not without unforeseen consequences (Burns et al. in Front Educ 5:1–10, 2020). This chapter first evaluates the impact of the virtual transformation of higher education on students reviewing research studies across five countries. The result shows that although the students benefited from the flexibility and autonomy of online learning, a few drawbacks of online learning, such as inaccessibility to appropriate digital technology and devices, an absence of face-to-face social interactions with teachers and peers, distance from campus facilities, and prolonged screen time, adversely affected the whole learning experience, with potential mental health consequences. In addition, the lifestyle changes and different pandemic-related stressors triggered negative mental health consequences on students. Subsequently, studies across ten countries are reviewed to understand the mental health challenges and coping strategies adopted by the students during the pandemic. The findings reveal that the students experienced low mental well-being during the pandemic. The prominent symptoms included anxiety, stress and depression with an associated adverse impact on concentration, eating and sleeping. COVID-19 lockdowns intensified mental health challenges and the two-week quarantine periods were an unpleasant experience for students. The students adopted a range of positive and negative coping mechanisms in response to their mental health difficulties. The chapter concludes with suggested measures to minimise the pandemic-related mental health challenges of the students.

Keywords COVID-19 · College students · Higher education · Lockdown · Quarantine · Mental health · Coping

S. Chatterjee (✉)
Centre of Development Studies, University of Cambridge, Cambridge, UK

A. P. Francis and M. A. Carter (eds.), *Mental Health and Higher Education in Australia*,
https://doi.org/10.1007/978-981-16-8040-3_13

Introduction

The extensive spread of COVID-19 pandemic generated the largest disruption of education systems in human history, affecting nearly 1.6 billion learners in more than 190 countries (UN, 2020). Wuhan in Hubei Province of China was the epicentre of the infection outbreak caused by a novel coronavirus, SARS-CoV-2 (Zhu, 2020) and from there the highly contagious and deadly virus spread rapidly across the globe. The World Health Organization declared the outbreak a pandemic in March 2020 and outlined public health measures for countries to stop the human-to-human transmission of the outbreak (WHO Timeline, 2020a). Following the guidelines of the WHO, countries primarily enforced a combination of three kinds of containment measures such as *social distancing, lockdown and quarantine* (WHO, 2020a, 2020b, 2020c; Bedford et al., 2020). The impacted countries imposed travel restrictions and enforced lockdown within their countries. In order to prevent the gathering of large crowds in a closed space, the governments directed the cessation of non-essential services including the closure of public places and other sites that were a threat to effective social distancing. In addition, people were advised to work from home and remain at home as much as possible (Bedford et al., 2020; GOV.UK, 2020; Sahu, 2020). The WHO indicated that these measures would profoundly affect individuals, communities and societies by bringing social and economic life to a near stop (WHO, 2020a, 2020b, 2020c). The adverse economic impact, the WHO estimates, is the risk of nearly half of the world's 3.3 billion global workforce losing their livelihoods (WHO, 2020a, 2020b, 2020c).

Among the urgent measures to contain the virus was the closedown of educational institutions, including the schools and universities worldwide, and transferring all modes of teaching online. Around 94% of the students across the globe were affected by this measure, with up to 99% in low and lower–middle-income countries (UN 2020). Not only education, a pandemic is also known to induce an adverse effect on mental health. The lessons from past epidemics have shown that the spread of infection, constraints on physical movement and social activities, and sudden and radical lifestyle changes accentuate or generate new stressors in the affected population including fear and worry for themselves and their loved ones (Mental Health Foundation, 2021; Shah et al., 2020; Son et al., 2020). Initially, the dominant mental health concerns focussed on health workers, key workers, patients, children, people with disabilities, and the general population (Santos et al., 2020; Son et al., 2020). The young minds with formidable challenges to adjust to an altered educational environment were not the primary focus.

It is known that mental health difficulties can beset anyone at any time and for some students, an unfamiliar higher education environment can be very stressful (Universities UK, 2015). Therefore, students' mental health in higher education has been an increasing concern that the COVID-19 challenges will affect students' academic performance (Son et al., 2020). With the onset of the pandemic, students had to adjust considerably to an altered learning space and an array of lifestyle changes, the repercussions of which were predicted to be profound (Burns et al., 2020).

This chapter analyses the impact of the COVID-19 pandemic on students in higher education and the mental health challenges experienced by them during the pandemic. The analysis is primarily based on review of the existing literature of the COVID-19-related impact on students in higher education and their mental health. The chapter first discusses the methodology of conducting this review and proceeds to discuss the pandemic impact on higher education and mental health of students.

Methodology

An electronic search was generated using a few keywords, i.e. COVID-19, higher education, students, mental health, lockdown and quarantine, using different blends. The studies conducted on the mental health of the general population are excluded from this review. Twenty-one empirical studies explicitly conducted on students in higher education during 2020–21 were selected for review. A separate search on coping strategies was not attempted as those were discussed by the studies examining the mental health challenges of students. In addition, literature related to coronavirus pandemic, online education, mental health challenges of college students in general, the psychological impact of lockdown and quarantine were consulted to build the conceptual background and understand the measures to minimise the mental health impact of the pandemic on students.

This chapter is divided into two sections. The first section discusses the higher education arrangements during the pandemic and evaluates the impact on students drawing upon research studies in five countries. The second section analyses the impact of COVID-19 on the mental health of students reviewing research studies from fourteen countries. The overall impact, lockdown, and the quarantine-specific impact of the pandemic on mental health and the students' coping strategies were analysed. The chapter concludes with suggested measures to minimise the mental health challenges of this group during the pandemic. The significance of this chapter is attributed to the fact that to the best of the author's knowledge, there is no other scholarly contribution attempting a comprehensive view of the impact of higher education arrangements during the pandemic on students and their mental health challenges. Understanding these challenges is pertinent to examining the effectiveness of higher education arrangements during a crisis like a pandemic and help devising ways to minimise the impact of the pandemic on the mental well-being of students.

Higher Education Arrangements in the COVID-19 Pandemic

As mentioned earlier, the COVID-19 lockdowns and social distancing measures led to the closures of schools and higher education institutions in the affected countries (Pokhrel & Chetri, 2021). However, Watermeyer et al. (2020) explained that this closure did not mean 'cessation of all learning, teaching, and assessment (LTA)'.

Instead, higher education courses were expected to be delivered via 'digital interface' without any change in the curriculum or compromise on the quality. Very rapidly, most LTA were transformed to a virtual format (Watermeyer et al., 2020). As the first country affected by the pandemic, China was the earliest to adopt the 'Suspending Classes without Stopping Learning' policy, and all of the higher education teachings moved online (Yang, 2020). Other affected countries followed a similar path. In the USA, the University of Washington became the first university to shift to online instruction in response to COVID-19. Other institutions in the USA soon followed (Weeden & Cornwell, 2020). The UK government expected most HE provisions in the UK to be online, with buildings open only for essential workers and students essentially requiring in-person teaching (Department of Education, UK, 2020). Universities Australia (2020) issued guidance to continue university activities with appropriate risk mitigation measures. The 130,000 staff working in universities in Australia moved to deliver whole courses online (Universities Australia, 2020). This mass migration of LTA online has not been witnessed before. A wide array of discussions is generated worldwide to examine the effectiveness of online learning, including the opportunities and challenges offered in this virtual model of education (Yang, 2020).

Online Higher Education During the Pandemic: Opportunities and Challenges

Pokhrel and Chhetri (2021) and Yang (2020) offered observations on the overall benefit of online education. They observed that although there have been overwhelming challenges for educational institutes in providing online education, the pandemic allowed implementing an entirely online-based learning system and evaluating the technical preparedness of the universities in challenging times like COVID-19. Pokhrel and Chhetri (2021) further discussed that the different online platforms used to deliver online teaching, such as Google meet, Zoom, are likely to retain their usefulness even after face-to-face teaching resumes. These platforms are expected to provide additional resources for teaching in the future. Yang (2020) commented on online education during the pandemic in China and discussed that the frequency of student–teacher interaction increased in online education mode. In addition, lecturers based outside China who could not return due to the sudden closure of borders continued teaching from their home countries, and students could learn from anywhere in the world.

Hodges et al. (2020), Adedoyin and Soykan (2020) discussed the drawbacks of online education. Hodges et al. (2020) argued that there is a difference between a meticulously planned online learning programme and courses offered in a crisis, which is the case with most universities during this pandemic. The sudden online migration of LTA is more of a crisis response by the universities without prior training. For Adedoyin and Soykan (2020), the major drawback of online LTA is the complete dependency on digital technology and electronic devices. This dependency restricted the learners without sufficient access from taking full benefit and thus excluded many students from the developing countries in accessing higher education. Another pertinent observation by Adedoyin and Soykan (2020) was that although reasonably compatible with social science and humanities, online learning is not effective with those disciplines requiring hands-on practical experiences, such as medicine, engineering or sports. Similarly, in social work education, fieldwork experience is a 'signature pedagogy', and an essential course component. The pandemic posed significant challenges in finding suitable field placements for practical experience in compliance with mandatory social distancing measures (Morris et al., 2020).

Further, seven studies from five countries are reviewed to evaluate the challenges and the benefits of online education for students during the pandemic, and are discussed below. More details of the studies such as the sample size, methodology and findings, are summarised in Table 1.

The Online Migration of LTA and Experience of Students

Studies in Australia (TEQSA, 2020), the USA (Patricia Aguilera–Hermida, 2020), the UK (Cambridge Centre for Learning and Teaching, 2021; Hewitt, 2020), Romania (Radu et al., 2020) and India (Chaturvedi et al., 2021; Naik et al., 2021) examined the benefits and challenges experienced by students in online education. The typical methodology adopted in these studies was 'online survey with self-administered questionnaires'. The studies conducted by Patricia Aguilera–Hermida, Cambridge Centre for Learning and Teaching (CCLT), Hewitt (2020), Radu et al. (2020), Naik et al. (2021) were single centre studies. CCLT (2020) studied students in three undergraduate courses at the University of Cambridge. TEQSA (2020) summarised reports from 118 higher education providers assessing the impact of remote teaching on students during the pandemic in Australia. The survey by Chaturvedi et al. (2021) drew a sample of students from different educational institutions in the National Capital Region (NCR) of India. The findings from these studies show that online education during the pandemic presented more challenges than opportunities to the students and the students unanimously expressed a strong preference for face-to-face teaching than online teaching. The drawbacks of online education discussed earlier (Adedoyin & Soykan, 2020; Hodges et al., 2020) proved to be significant impediments to compelling learning experiences.

Access to appropriate digital technology, the primary requirement in online learning, posed significant difficulty to the students in varying degrees. In countries including the UK, USA, Australia or Poland, the key problems were sub-optimum access or slow Internet connectivity. In a developing country like India (Naik et al., 2021), the technological impediments were so profound that the students suggested face-to-face revision of the courses once the universities reopen. In the remote areas of India, students experienced major learning disruptions due to very poor to zero internet connectivity, inaccessibility to online learning equipment, and inconsistent

Table 1 Students' experience of online higher education in the COVID-19 pandemic

Country	Author	Sample size	Methodology	Results
United States	Patricia Aguilera—Hermida (2020)	N = 270	Online survey with self-administered questionnaire	A majority preferred face-to-face teaching than online **Challenges**: (1) Struggle with adaptation to online learning (2) Lack of supporting academic resources, unfamiliar online technology, and increased workload. (3) Lack of optimum accessibility to digital technology. (4) A decrease in self-efficacy (the ability to perform scholastic activities), and cognitive engagement. (5) Struggle to sustain motivation due to lack of social interaction with classmates and teachers, lack of access to library and other activities in the campus. (6) Concentration difficulties due to distraction at home, exhaustion due to increased screen time (7) Difficulty in balancing home responsibilities and academic work. (8) Financial Hardship. (9) Sudden life changes (such as getting infected, death in family or being pregnant)

(continued)

Table 1 (continued)

Country	Author	Sample size	Methodology	Results
				Benefits: Increased time with family, engaging in new activities, more up to date with responding to online communication like emails
United Kingdom	Hewitt (2020)	N = 1075	Online survey with self-administered questionnaire	A majority of the students were satisfied with online learning arrangements **Challenges:** (1) Limited interaction with peers (2) Limited access to campus facilities such as libraries, independent study space, sports facilities, and student union buildings
	Cambridge Centre for Learning and Teaching (2021)	N = 149	Online survey with self-administered questionnaire	A majority of the students felt online teaching met their expectations **Challenges**: (1) Low or inconsistent internet connectivity. (2) Difficulty in accessing learning due to problems with information and guidance. (3) Disparity of teaching modes, formats and platforms. (4) Social isolation
				Benefits: Autonomy and flexibility in accessing lectures and course material. The students could rewind and watch the lectures according to their convenience

(continued)

Table 1 (continued)

Country	Author	Sample size	Methodology	Results
Australia	TEQSA (2020)	N = 118	Online survey with self-administered questionnaire	The students appreciated the effort of the higher education institutions to make the *transition to online learning* as effective as possible **Challenges**: (1) Reduced interaction with teachers and peers (2) Difficulties with digital technology and variation in staff expertise in its use (3) Increased workload. (4) Assessment changes (5) Isolation, lack of engagement and reduced motivation (6) Difficulty with the translation of some subject areas to an online mode of delivery. (7) Loss of quiet study space due to lockdown. (8) Mental health challenges

(continued)

Table 1 (continued)

Country	Author	Sample size	Methodology	Results
				Benefits (1) Flexibility in accessing study materials including early availability of lecture and tutorial questions; (2) Adequate access to online academic help and advice, with many staff making extra 'online' time for discussion groups or answering individual students' questions; (3) Use of appropriate technology to facilitate student learning. (4) Flexibility in managing their own time; (5) Better learning outcome; (6) Flexibility with types and outcomes of assessment conducted online

(continued)

Table 1 (continued)

Country	Author	Sample size	Methodology	Results
Romania	Radu et al., (2020)	N = 135	Online survey with self-administered questionnaire	A majority of the respondents were satisfied with online learning arrangements **Challenges**: (1) Lack of optimum access to digital infrastructure for all. (2) The communication with teachers was not so effective. (3) The absence of opportunity to perform practical experiments. (4) Reduced motivation for learning. (5) Ineffective online examination. (6) A lack of face-to-face interaction with peers and teachers. (7) Prolonged screen time. (8) Potential adverse impact on mental and physical health
				Benefits: (1) Greater flexibility in the teaching–learning process. (2) Improved digital skills. (3) Innovative teaching–learning tools

(continued)

Table 1 (continued)

Country	Author	Sample size	Methodology	Results
India	Chaturvedi et al. (2021)	N = 694	Online survey with self-administered questionnaire	A majority expressed negative view about online learning **Challenges**: (1) Limited interaction with teachers during classes. (2) An absence of social interaction decreased learning motivation. (3) A lack of optimum digital proficiency in both students and teachers
				Benefits: Investing time in different activities
	Naik et al. (2021)	N = 742	Online survey with self-administered questionnaire	A majority preferred in-person teaching and suggested face-to-face revision of topics once the pandemic recedes, and the colleges reopen **Challenges**: (1) Lack of access to appropriate digital infrastructure especially for students in rural areas. The screen shared by faculties during online sessions was not clearly visible on smart phones (2) Disruption in power supply in rural areas (3) Ineffective in disciplines requiring laboratory/practical experiments and difficulty in understanding subjects like mathematics and other analytical subjects. (4) Lecture recordings were not uploaded which affected learning outcome

(continued)

Table 1 (continued)

Country	Author	Sample size	Methodology	Results
				Benefits: Investing time in activities for personal growth

electricity supply. These technical challenges significantly affected the efficacy of the entire teaching–learning process during the pandemic.

Patricia Aguilera–Hermida (2020) discussed that the sudden onset and the rapid implementation of the pandemic containment measures entailed that students quickly moved onto the online system without prior training or preparation, and that had affected successful adoption and navigation through different online platforms. Similarly, different levels of staff expertise and disparity of teaching modes, formats and platforms adversely influenced the learning process (Cambridge Centre for Learning and Teaching, 2021; Naik et al., 2021; TEQSA, 2020). The disciplines requiring practical experiments particularly suffered in the online learning mode (Naik et al., 2021; Radu et al., 2020; TEQSA, 2020). A major limitation of online learning during the pandemic is the absence of face-to-face interaction of students with teachers and peers and direct accessibility to campus facilities such as libraries and other places of social interaction. The prolonged absence of social interaction adversely affected learning motivation (TEQSA, 2020; Patricia Aguilera–Hermida, 2020; Cambridge Centre for Learning and Teaching, 2021; Hewitt, 2020; Radu et al., 2020; Chaturvedi et al., 2021; Naik et al., 2021). Furthermore, the prolonged screen time and LTA being limited to one-on-one with a computer screen resulted in concentration difficulty and exhaustion in students (Patricia Aguilera–Hermida, 2020; Radu et al., 2020, TEQA,). In addition, the students were also concerned about the effectiveness of online examinations and assessments (Radu et al., 2020; TEQA, 2020). Mental health challenges during the pandemic also affected learning outcomes (Radu et al., 2020, TEQA, 2020).

The primary advantage of online education perceived by students is the flexibility in accessing study materials without time and space constraints. Both domestic and international students could access the lecture recordings before the classes and repeatedly watched them for clarity (Cambridge Centre for Learning and Teaching, 2021; Radu et al., 2020; TEQSA, 2020). Further, online education improved digital skills among students and provided with more time to spend with their families. In addition, online education increased opportunities to engage in activities for self-growth and relaxation such as listening to music, reading, cooking, physical exercise, painting or gardening (Chaturvedi et al., 2021; Naik et al., 2021; Patricia Aguilera–Hermida, 2020).

Thus, the above discussion and Table 1 demonstrate that the pandemic has changed the face of higher education and enforced an altered lifestyle for students. Fu et al. (2021) discussed that long-term home confinement and online education could lead to undesirable mental health consequences for students, discussed in detail in Section "The Mental Well-Being of Students in Higher Education".

The Mental Well-Being of Students in Higher Education

Holmes et al. (2020) discussed that a pandemic is likely to trigger a sense of uncertainty and apprehensions for most and can also cause significant psychological distress for some. Holmes et al. (2020) further predicted that pandemic-related mental health issues would interact with pre-existing mental health challenges in children and young people and exacerbate the symptoms. In addition, the closure of educational institutions would restrict accessibility to mental health support and participation in mental well-being promoting activities. Further, the level of psychological distress (stress, anxiety and depression levels) could intensify as the period of lockdown progresses (Brooks et al., 2020; Sha et al., 2020) but is likely to improve once lockdown ends (Pellerin & Raufaste, 2020). Brooks et al. (2020) drew attention to the adverse psychological effect of the quarantine period. With a loss of freedom, quarantine can barely be a pleasant experience. Separation from the loved ones, uncertainty over the infection status, and monotony cast a collective and long-lasting psychological impact. After quarantine, many participants continue to engage in avoidance behaviour.

Thus, lockdowns, quarantines and social distancing more than ever brought back the focus on the mental well-being of the affected population. The following section discusses the mental health impact of the pandemic on university students.

Impact of the Pandemic on the Mental Health of Students in Higher Education

Entering university life usually brings a sense of excitement and enthusiasm among students, accompanied by new stressors. Stressors of different kinds could trigger or accentuate mental health problems among students. This can further affect students' motivation, concentration and social interactions—some key contributing factors to students' academic performance and excellence in higher education (Son et al., 2020). Acharya et al. (2018) discussed that mental health problems are increasing among college students, and depression is a recurrent problem among college students in the USA and identified different stressors among the students. Furthermore, in a study involving two large universities in Australia, Stallman (2011) estimated a prevalence of 19.2% mental health problems, with 67.4% reporting subsyndromal symptoms. Therefore, internationally, the mental health of university students is recognised as an important public health issue.

With the onset of the pandemic, the challenges of this population were exacerbated. Consistent academic pressure in an increasingly competitive and altered academic environment increased students' mental health challenges (Burns et al., 2020). Studies across the world endeavoured to capture these challenges. In this section, seven studies are reviewed to analyse the overall effect of the pandemic on students, five and two studies are reviewed to analyse the impact of lockdown and quarantine, respectively. The results of the studies are discussed below to understand the likely mental health challenges of students and the potential risk factors generating them. Further details of the studies, i.e. the sample size, methodology and specifics of the findings, are summarised in Table 2.

Table 2 The COVID-19 pandemic impact on the mental health of students in higher education

Country	Author	Sample size	Methodology	Mental health problems	Risk factors	Coping mechanisms
Overall impact of the pandemic on mental health of students						
China	Ma et al. (2020)	N = 746,217	Online survey with a self-administered questionnaire	Mental health problems (45%), acute stress (34.9%), symptoms of depression (21.1%), anxiety (11%)	Relatives or friends being infected, increased exposure to media coverage on COVID-19, low perceived social support, senior year in college and prior mental health problems	Seeking social support
	Fu et al. (2021)	N = 89,588	Online survey with Generalised Anxiety Disorder 7-Item Scale (GAD-7)	Anxiety symptoms (41%)	Age (26–30), senior year in college, low economic status and low perceived social support	
India	Kochuvilayil et al., (2020	N = 113	Online survey with Six-Item State-Trait Anxiety Inventory (STAI)	Anxiety about own health (48%), and loved ones (91%), difficulty in sleeping (4.4%), eating (1.8%), and concentrating in studies (6.2%)	Online learning, fear of getting COVID-19 during clinical placements especially senior students, fear of infection in loved ones, financial hardships	Exercise, engaging in different activities, sharing concern with friends and confidants
Australia	Kochuvilayil et al., (2020	N = 99	Online survey with Six-Item State-Trait Anxiety Inventory (STAI)	Anxiety about own health (44.4%), anxiety about the health of loved ones (80.8%), difficulty in sleeping (46.4%), eating (20.4%) and concentrating in studies (68.7%)	Online learning, fear of getting COVID-19 during clinical placements, financial hardships	Reducing screen time to pandemic related news, reading or listening to news stories, social media, exercise

(continued)

Table 2 (continued)

Country	Author	Sample size	Methodology	Mental health problems	Risk factors	Coping mechanisms
	Dodd et al., (2021	N = 787	Online survey with Well-being (WHO), Sense of Coherence, Subjective Social Status (SSS) and Future Anxiety Scales	Low to very low psychological well-being (65%)	Age (21–23), negative online learning experience, lack of social contact with peers, junior year in college, being female, low subjective social status, low sense of coherence, high future anxiety, financial hardship	Accessing support offered by universities—such as assistance with postponing studies, well-being and counselling services, and/or financial support
United Kingdom	NUS (2020)	N = 4000	Online survey with a self-administered questionnaire	Low mental well-being with symptoms of anxiety, stress and depression (52%)	Online learning, lack of social contact, loneliness, home confinement	Seeking professional mental health support including online university counselling services
United States	Son et al. (2020)	N = 195	Online interviews with semi-structured interview guide	Increased stress and anxiety (71%), difficulty in concentration (89%) and sleeping (86%), depressive thoughts (44%), loneliness (33%), hopelessness (10%), insecurity (12%), mild to moderate suicidal thoughts (8%), disruption in eating patterns (70%)	Fear and worry about own health and health of loved ones, decreased social interactions and academic performance concerns	Seeking social support from friends and relatives, adopting either negative or positive coping mechanisms
Turkey	Akdeniz et al., (2020)	N = 3040	Online survey with a self-administered questionnaire and Beck Anxiety Inventory	Moderate level of anxiety and worry (38%)	Fear and worry about own health and health of loved ones, online education and social isolation	Not discussed

(continued)

Table 2 (continued)

Country	Author	Sample size	Methodology	Mental health problems	Risk factors	Coping mechanisms
Impact of Lockdown						
United Kingdom	Evans et al., (2021)	N = 254	Online longitudinal survey with Hospital Anxiety and Depression Scale (HADS), Pittsburgh Sleep Quality Index (PSQI), Warwick Edinburgh Mental Well-being scale (WEMWBS)	Negative impact on mental health due to lockdown (52%), symptoms of clinical depression (34.3%)	Fear of contracting the viruses themselves and family members, and poor sleep quality, poor adaptation to isolation and social distancing	Not discussed
	Savage et al., (2020)	N = 214	Online longitudinal survey with Warwick Edinburgh Mental Well-being scale (WEMWBS), Perceived Stress Scale (PSS)	Negative impact on mental well-being, increased sense of perceived stress and increased sedentary behaviour due to lockdown	Fear of infection and transmission, social distancing, social isolation from university campus and social networks, online assessment, being female	Not discussed
Italy	Meda et al., (2020)	N = 358	Online longitudinal survey with Beck Depression Inventory-2, Beck Anxiety Inventory, the Obsessive–Compulsive Inventory-Revised the Eating Habits Questionnaire (EHQ) and the Eating Disorder Inventory	6% of students experienced a clinically significant worsening of depressive symptoms during lockdown. Symptoms improved after lockdown was lifted	Lockdown-related difficulties	Not discussed

(continued)

Table 2 (continued)

Country	Author	Sample size	Methodology	Mental health problems	Risk factors	Coping mechanisms
	Villani et al., (2021)	N = 501	Online survey with self-administered scales	Anxiety (35.33%) and depression (72.93%)	Fear of contracting infection and death, Being female, social isolation from university campus, peers and partners, impact on academic performance, uncertainty about returning to university and future career, no outdoor sports	Physical activity and exercise
France	Bourion-Bédès et al., (2021)	N = 3926	Online Survey with Generalised Anxiety Disorder Scale and Scale of Perceived Social Support (MSPSS)	Mild to severe anxiety (61%)	COVID infection in the household, Being female, online learning conditions, tensions and conflicts with family or occupants of the dwelling, difficulties in isolating, noise, no private access to outside spaces, and increased tobacco consumption	Support of friends and family, accessing entertainment media, physical exercise, reading

(continued)

Table 2 (continued)

Country	Author	Sample size	Methodology	Mental health problems	Risk factors	Coping mechanisms
Impact of quarantine						
Riyadh	Meo et al., (2020)	N = 530	Online survey with a self-administered questionnaire	Depression (47.45%), Hopelessness, exhaustion or emotional unresponsiveness (76%), reduced sense of awareness and confusion (71.5%), anxiety dealing with patients (64.24), a sense of being emotionally detached from family and friends (88.5%), anxiety and insomnia (77%), poor concentration (79%), lack of motor coordination (50%), slowness in the execution of movement (54%), deterioration in study and work performance (99%)	Confinement an unpleasant experience, isolation from friends and family, losing freedom of movement, inadequate information and fear about the spread of infection, and financial hardship	Not discussed
Albania	Mechili et al. (2021)	N = 863	Online survey with a self-administered questionnaire	Depression (Mild- 75%, moderate to severe- 25%)	Dissatisfaction with COVID-19 preventive measures and isolation	Not discussed

Overall Impact of the Pandemic on the Mental Health of Students

As shown in Table 2, studies conducted in China (Fu et al., 2021; Ma et al., 2020), India (Kochuvilayil et al., 2020), Australia (Dodd et al., 2021; Kochuvilayil et al., 2020), UK (NUS, 2020,) and the USA (Son et al., 2020) Turkey (Akdeniz et al, 2020) are reviewed to understand the overall impact of the pandemic. All of the studies except the one by Son et al. (2020) adopted online survey with self-administered questionnaires or standardised scales as the data collection procedure. Son et al. (2020) utilised online Zoom interviews to assess the mental health of students in the USA. Further, all of the studies except Kochuvilayil et al. (2020) study examined the mental well-being of students of a particular university or region of a single country. The survey by Kochuvilayil et al. (2020) compared the mental health impact of undergraduate nursing students in India and Australia.

The Mental Health Impact

Broadly, the pandemic adversely affected the mental well-being of the students in higher education. Dodd et al. (2021) assessed the overall psychological well-being of students in Australia (N = 787), and 65% of the respondents reported low to very low psychological well-being. The other studies discussed the specific symptoms of the mental health impact of the pandemic. Increased stress, anxiety and worry associated with depressive thoughts are some of the common symptoms experienced by students in China (Fu et al., 2021; Ma et al., 2020), Turkey (Akdeniz et al, 2020), the UK (NUS, 2020), the USA (Son et al., 2020), India (Kochuvilayil et al., 2020) and Australia (Kochuvilayil et al., 2020). Students also experienced trouble in concentrating, sleeping and eating (Kochuvilayil et al., 2020; Son et al., 2020).

The comparative study by Kochuvilayil et al. (2020) revealed that the mean anxiety score for the Australian nursing student cohort was significantly higher than the score of the Indian cohort. In addition, Australian students reported significantly more difficulties in sleeping, concentrating and eating than Indian students did.

The Risk Factors

The studies discuss a wide range of pandemic-related risk factors to cause a negative impact on the mental well-being of students. *Fear of contracting COVID-19* generated significant anxiety among students (Akdenizet al., 2020; Kochuvilayil et al., 2020; Ma et al., 2020, Son et al., 2020). The undergraduate nursing students (Kochuvilayil et al., 2020) felt more at risk of infection due to the mandatory clinical placement required to complete their degree. Relatives, friends and family members contracting the infection also added to their anxiety (Akdeniz et al, 2020; Kochuvilayil et al., 2020; Ma et al., 2020). In some cases, students were more anxious about their loved ones contracting the infection than themselves. The comparative study by Kochuvilayil et al. (2020) showed that 48% of the Indian students and 44% of Australian students were anxious about their health. However, almost double the percentage of students were anxious about the health of their loved ones. A greater number of Indian nursing students (91%) experienced anxiety about the health of their loved ones than the Australian students (81%). Ma et al. (2020), Fu et al. (2021) discussed the negative impact of news reports and social media on increasing Chinese students' anxiety. News of increased infection rates and deaths due to COVID-19 triggered negative emotions and further added to depression, anxiety and stress. The study by Ma et al. (2020) revealed that more than three hours exposure to media coverage of the COVID-19 each day was associated with increased risk of acute stress. Chinese students with prior mental health issues were found more at risk of mental health problems.

As discussed in Section "Higher Education Arrangements in the COVID-19 Pandemic", the *unanticipated challenges of online learning*, i.e. difficulty in adapting to different modes of online learning, social isolation from peers and campus facilities, contributed to the anxiety and stress of students (Akdeniz et al., 2020; Dodd et al., 2021; Kochuvilayil et al., 2020; NUS, 2020; Son et al., 2020). Dodd et al. (2021) discussed that the online learning experience was negative for a majority of the Australian students in their study and affected their mental well-being. *Age and seniority of the students* were significantly associated with the mental well-being of Australian students. Younger students ($\leq$23 years old), those with lower subjective social status and speaking a language other than English at home, reported COVID-19 having a significant impact on their studies compared to students aged over 24 years. Psychological well-being was better in postgraduate students than undergraduate students. Undergraduate students and those enrolled for a graduate certificate or diploma course experienced lower mental well-being, reported greater anxiety for future and overall life orientation than postgraduate students did. Uncertainty about the future affected the academic progress of Australian students (Dodd et al., 2021). Concerns about academic performance also increased anxiety level of the American students (Son et al., 2020). Conversely, the studies in China showed (Fu et al., 2021; Ma et al., 2020) an increased vulnerability of senior college students (26–30 years) towards anxiety symptoms. The academic pressure, uncertainty about the future and increased tobacco consumption contributed to a higher anxiety level.

The study by Dodd et al. (2021) also projected *gender difference* in psychological well-being. Female students, particularly those with a negative experience of online learning, lower subjective social status, lower sense of coherence, reported significantly lower well-being and higher anxiety levels.

Financial vulnerability exacerbated the anxiety among college students (Dodd et al., 2021; Fu et al., 2021; Kochuvilayil et al., 2020; Ma et al., 2020). The Chinese students reporting low economic status experienced increased anxiety symptoms than those reporting higher status. Fu et al. (2021) discussed that COVID-19 negatively affected economic conditions of several families in China and that further affected students' mental well-being. The Australian students experienced financial hardship in paying for student accommodation to keep their place while not living at the university premises. Employment was one of the main ways students financially supported themselves while they were studying. However, the pandemic adversely affected students' employment, including reduced hours and job losses (Dodd et al., 2021).

Ma et al. (2020), Fu et al. (2021) discussed a significant association between *students' social support* and mental well-being. Lower levels of social support were associated with an increased risk of anxiety symptoms among Chinese students.

Impact of Lockdown on the Mental Health of Students

Lockdown, ease and lockdown again—the affected population has gone through a cycle of hope and despair. Many higher education students found themselves in a unique situation in lockdown, such as isolating in a household with others they do not know well (Office for National Statistics, 2020a, b). 'Young Minds' (2021) discussed the impact of lockdown on young people with mental health needs in the UK: isolation, loss of routine, and challenges accessing emotional, social and medical support, including mental health support. Learning in the confinement of home was akin to 'school without the fun bits' and exerted additional pressure on mental well-being. The second lockdown in the UK (January-March 2021) was even more challenging to cope with than the first one. The sense of isolation intensified, and the enthusiasm of video calls to connect with friends and families diminished. There was uncertainty about the future (no end in sight), combined with freezing winter weather, darker days and nights that disrupted basic routines.

Five studies from three countries, i.e. the UK (Evans et al., 2021; Savage et al., 2020), Italy (Meda et al., 2020; Villani et al., 2021) and France (Bourion-B´ed'es et al., 2021), are reviewed to discuss the impact of lockdown on the mental health of students. Online survey with self-administered questionnaires or standardised scales was the standard method adopted by these studies to examine the impact of lockdown. The studies by Evans et al. (2021), Meda et al. (2020) are longitudinal, measuring mental well-being before and after the lockdown. The remaining studies measured mental well-being during the lockdown period.

The Mental Health Impact

Results show a negative impact on mental health due to lockdown confinement (Evans et al., 2021; Savage et al., 2020). Anxiety and depression were the consistent mental health symptoms during lockdown (Bourion-B´ed'es et al., 2021; Evans et al., 2021; Meda et al., 2020; Villani et al., 2021). The before–after longitudinal studies further characterised the impact of lockdown on mental health. A significant increase in the self-reported level of depression symptoms was measured during 1–2 months into the UK lockdown compared to the baseline level of symptoms of seven months before lockdown. The increase in depression symptoms was also significantly associated with increased anxiety, reduced well-being, and worsened sleep quality among the UK students. Over a third of the sample was classed clinically depressed (Evans et al., 2021). In Italy (Meda et al., 2020), 6% of the sample experienced clinically significant depressive symptoms approximately seven weeks into lockdown. However, once the lockdown was lifted, the mental health condition of the students significantly improved in this study.

The Risk Factors

Fear of contracting COVID-19 both for the students and their loved ones (Bourion-B´ed'es et al., 2021; Evans et al., 2021; Savage et al., 2020; Villani et al., 2021) and poor adaptation to COVID-19 containment measures such as isolation and social distancing negatively affected mental well-being (Evans et al., 2021; Meda et al., 2020). *Online learning* adversely affected mental well-being (Bourion-B´ed'es et al., 2021; Savage et al., 2020; Villani et al., 2021) for similar reasons discussed in Section "Higher Education Arrangements in the COVID-19 Pandemic". Bourion-Bédès et al. (2021) discussed risk factors related to *the living conditions* of students during the lockdown. Students without private outside access (terrace, garden or balcony) and without space to isolate are more at risk to anxiety. Other risk factors included domestic tensions, noise disturbances, excessive snacking and increased tobacco consumption. In a prolonged lockdown, social and entertainment media use or engaging in other activities like reading ceased to be effective and this further increased risk to mental health problems. Further, *gender*, i.e., being a female student, is discussed as a risk factor to an alleviated mental health symptoms such as anxiety. Female students developed greater anxiety symptoms than male students in reaction to imposed confinement (Bourion-Bédès et al., 2021; Savage et al., 2020; Villani et al, 2021,). Villani et al (2021) discussed that gender specific results cannot be generalised as this is not the case in other studies across the globe.

Impact of Quarantine on the Mental Health of Students

Studies on quarantine-related mental health challenges are limited. Therefore, studies from two countries, i.e. Riyadh (Meo et al., 2020) and Albania (Mechili et al., 2021), are reviewed to understand the impact of two weeks of quarantine on students' mental health. Meo et al. (2020) studied mental health symptoms in the medical students of Riyadh, and Mechili et al. (2021) examined the students undertaking a course in public health in Albania. Self-administered scales are utilised in these studies.

The Mental Health Impact

In both of the studies (Mechili et al., 2021; Meo et al., 2020), symptoms of depression were the common mental health problem among the students. In addition, the medical students of Riyadh experienced feelings of hopelessness, reduced sense of awareness, slowness, and exhaustion, anxiety dealing with patients, deterioration in their study and work performance.

The Risk Factors

The participants of these two studies felt *quarantine is an unpleasant experience*. The loss of freedom, isolation from friends and family were the significant risk factors in quarantine. In addition, inadequate information and confusion about the spread of disease added to their anxiety.

The above discussion and Table 2 elucidate that the students in higher education experienced considerable mental health challenges during the COVID-19 pandemic. The coping strategies attempted by them to deal with those challenges are discussed further.

Coping Mechanisms of Students

Coping with mental health challenges is a broad area of discussion, and no deliberation on mental health challenges is conclusive enough without explaining the coping mechanisms. For the purpose of this chapter, the coping mechanisms adopted by the students in the fourteen studies reviewed above are discussed below and summarised in Table 2.

The studies in the UK (NUS, 2020), China (Fu et al., 2021; Ma et al., 2020), India (Kochuvilayil et al., 2020), Australia (Dodd et al., 2021; Kochuvilayil et al., 2020), the USA (Son et al., 2020), Italy (Villani et al., 2021) and France (Bourion-Bédès et al., 2021) discussed the coping mechanisms of students. Most of the studies did not mention students seeking professional help to cope with mental health crises during the pandemic. Only two studies, NUS (2020) and Dodd et al. (2021) discussed the students accessing mental health and other support services available in their colleges or universities. In the UK (NUS, 2020), the students primarily sought 'access to a counsellor' and 'someone to talk to' during the pandemic. In Australia (Dodd et al., 2021), the students sought university counselling services and financial support.

Furthermore, the studies discussed different positive or negative coping mechanisms adopted by the students. Positive coping mechanisms encompassed seeking social support from relatives and friends (Bourion-B´ed'es et al., 2021; Fu et al., 2021; Kochuvilayil et al., 2020; Ma et al., 2020; Son et al., 2020), engaging in different activities such as physical exercise (Bourion-Bédès et al., 2021; Kochuvilayil et al., 2020; Son et al., 2020; Villani et al., 2021), reading, accessing entertainment and social media (Bourion-B´ed‘es et al., 2021; Kochuvilayil et al., 2020; Son et al., 2020), meditation, playing with pets, listening to music, drawing (Son et al., 2020) and reducing exposure to COVID-19-related news (Dodd et al., 2021; Kochuvilayil et al., 2020). The negative coping methods included sleeping longer, drinking or smoking, and snacking between meals (Ma et al., 2020; Fu et al., 2021; Son et al., 2020; Bourion-Bédès et al., 2021).

Conclusion

This chapter analysed students' learning experience in higher education during the pandemic and the pandemic impact on the mental health of students. The COVID-19 pandemic forced closed the educational institutions, and all LTA moved online. Seven studies from five countries were reviewed to analyse the impact of online learning on students. The key benefit of online education included autonomy and flexibility of learning, i.e. the students could learn positioning anywhere in the world and access the recorded lectures repeatedly from any time zone. However, for a majority of students, the disadvantages of online learning outweighed the benefits. For example, the complete dependence on digital technology, disruption in learning or assessments on instances of malfunctioning technology (such as Wi-Fi or Zoom disconnection), the absence of social interaction with teachers and peers and campus facilities and prolonged screen time adversely affected the whole learning experience with potential mental health implications. Therefore, despite some benefits of online learning, the students would prefer traditional in-person teaching. To make online learning more effective, Patricia Aguilera-Hermida (2020) recommended providing appropriate training to the users and suggested the educational institutions adapt to the needs of the learners constantly. Naik et al. (2021) suggested that a developing country like India should develop infrastructure like open Wi-Fi areas with high-speed internet access in remote areas and ensure an uninterrupted power supply to improve accessibility to online learning.

The impact of the pandemic on the mental health and well-being of students in higher education was also examined in this chapter. Fourteen studies conducted in ten countries were reviewed to understand the overall mental health impact and specific impacts of lockdown and quarantine. The overall mental health impact on the pandemic included low psychological well-being with symptoms of depression, anxiety, and stress and associated impacts on sleep, concentration and eating. The students of disciplines requiring mandatory clinical or practical experience, such as medical and nursing sciences, experienced alleviated anxiety and fear of contracting COVID-19 in course experimental settings. Prolonged or repeated lockdowns proved to be detrimental to mental well-being. The longitudinal studies showed that the anxiety levels amplified, and symptoms of depression and sleep quality worsened during the lockdown. Mental well-being improved after the lockdown was lifted. The two-week quarantine was an unpleasant experience for students. In addition to anxiety and depression, quarantined students experienced a sense of hopelessness, and their work and study performance suffered. However, there are limited studies on the impact of quarantine on students; more studies are required to advance understanding in this area.

The common pandemic-related risk factors generating negative mental health consequences included an increased sense of worry about contracting COVID-19 infection for both the students and their loved ones, followed by challenges related to online LTA. The challenges associated with online learning caused significant mental health difficulties. Further, the age and seniority of the students, increased tobacco and alcohol consumption, financial vulnerability, and absence of social support added to the risk factors. Lockdown increased risk factors linked to living conditions. During consistent home confinement, the escalated domestic tensions, a lack of privacy and outdoor access for physical exercise increased stress and anxiety. The most debilitating impact on students' mental health during COVID-19 pandemic was the loss of face-to-face social interaction with friends, families, teachers and mental health service providers.

Furthermore, studies in China, Australia, France, the UK and the USA discussed an increased risk of female students to mental distress during the pandemic. However, additional empirical evidence, especially from countries with wider gender disparity, is required to generalise this evidence.

Student coping strategies involved accessing professional support available at the universities and adopting a range of positive and negative coping mechanisms. The positive coping strategies included seeking social support and engaging in a range of constructive activities, such as physical exercise, reading, drawing and accessing social media. The negative coping strategies were increased levels of snacking, tobacco and alcohol consumption and prolonged sleeping.

Shah et al. (2020), Evans et al. (2021) suggested proactive steps to limit the adverse effect on mental health during a pandemic like COVID-19. Targeted interventions to at-risk students to prevent further mental health problems were also recommended (Rossi et al., 2020). To restrict the impact on students' mental health during self-isolation and quarantine periods, Holmes et al. (2020), Brooks et al. (2020) suggested the following: providing appropriate services to at-risk people in consultation with people with lived experiences; providing sufficient and transparent information on the condition of the outbreak; engaging people in meaningful activities to reduce boredom; assisting to maintain a consistent connection with others; and ensuring basic supplies.

China has been implementing emergency psychological crisis interventions to reduce the negative psychosocial impact on public mental health, but challenges persist due to resource scarcity (Dong and Bouey, 2020). As other developing countries are also likely to encounter similar difficulties, Dong and Bouey (2020) suggested focussing on telemedicine to better access quality mental health care and integrate public mental health interventions into public health preparedness and emergency response plans.

Above all, investing in resources to build a network of family, friends, community and educational institutions to provide adequate support during a pandemic would go a long way in maintaining individuals' mental well-being (Zhai & Du, 2020). For that to be effective, the NUS (2020) suggested increased investment in mental health services for optimum provision and wider access to mental health care for students.

References

Adedoyin, B. O., & Soykan, E. (2020). Covid-19 pandemic and online learning: the challenges and opportunities. *Interactive Learning Environments*, 1–13 https://doi.org/10.1080/10494820.2020.1813180

Akdeniz, G. et al. (2020). A survey of attitudes, anxiety status, and protective behaviors of the university students during the COVID-19 outbreak in Turkey. *Frontiers in Psychiatry, 11*, 695.1–9. https://doi.org/10.3389/fpsyt.2020.00695

Acharya, L., Jin, L., & Collins, W. (2018). College life is stressful today—Emerging stressors and depressive symptoms in college students. *Journal of American College Health., 66*(7), 655–664. https://doi.org/10.1080/07448481.2018.1451869

Bedford, J., Enria, D., Giesecke, J. et al. (2020). COVID-19: towards controlling of a pandemic. *Lancet* (Epub ahead of print). https://doi.org/10.1016/S0140-6736(20)30673-5

Brooks, K. S., et al. (2020). The psychological impact of quarantine and how to reduce it: Rapid review of the evidence. *The Lancet, 395*, 912–920. https://doi.org/10.1016/S0140-6736(20)30460-8

Burns, D., Dagnall, D., & Holt, M. (2020). Assessing the impact of the COVID-19 pandemic on student wellbeing at universities in the United Kingdom: A conceptual analysis. *Frontiers of Education., 5*(582882), 1–10. https://doi.org/10.3389/feduc.2020.582882

Bourion-Bédès, S., et al. (2021). Psychological impact of the COVID-19 outbreak on students in a French region severely affected by the disease: Results of the PIMS-CoV 19 study. *Psychiatry Research*, 1–7. https://doi.org/10.1016/j.psychres.2020.113559

Cambridge Centre for Teaching and Learning. (2021). Department of psychology: Online learning survey results. https://www.cctl.cam.ac.uk/teaching-2020-21/cambridge-examples-practice

Chaturvedi, et al. (2021). COVID-19 and its impact on education, social life and mental health of students: A survey. *Children and Youth Services Review, 121*(105866), 1–6.

Department of Education (2020). *Higher education coronavirus (COVID-19) operational guidance.* https://www.gov.uk/government/publications/higher-education-reopening-buildings-and-campuses/higher-education-coronavirus-covid-19-operational-guidance

Dodd, R. H., et al. (2021). Psychological wellbeing and academic experience of university students in Australia during COVID-19. *International Journal of Environmental Research and Public Health., 18*(866), 2–12. https://doi.org/10.3390/ijerph18030866

Dong, L., & Bouey, J. (2020). Public mental health crisis during COVID-19 Pandemic, China. *Emerging Infectious Diseases, 26*, 7. www.cdc.gov/eid

Evans, S., et al. (2021). Effects of the COVID-19 lockdown on mental health, wellbeing, sleep, and alcohol use in a UK student sample. *Psychiatry Research, 28*, 1–7. https://doi.org/10.1016/j.psychres.2021.113819

Fu, W., et al. (2021). Mental health of college students during the COVID-19 epidemic in China. *Journal of Affective Disorders., 280*, 7–10. https://doi.org/10.1016/j.jad.2020.11.032

GOV.UK (2020, 2021). Coronavirus (COVID-19). https://www.gov.uk/coronavirus

Hewitt, R. (2020). Students' views on the impact of Coronavirus on their higher education experience in 2020/21. Higher Education Policy Institute. https://www.hepi.ac.uk/wp-content/uploads/2020/12/HEPI-Policy-Note-27-Students-views-on-the-impact-of-Coronavirus-on-their-higher-education-experience-in-2020-21-FINAL.pdf

Hodges, C., et al. (2020). The difference between emergency remote teaching and online learning. *Educause Review*. https://er.educause.edu/articles/2020/3/the-difference-between-emergency-remote-teaching-and-online-learning

Holmes, A. E., et al. (2020). Multidisciplinary research priorities for the COVID-19 pandemic: A call for action for mental health science. *Lancet Psychiatry, 7*, 547–560. https://doi.org/10.1016/S2215-0366(20)30168-1

Institute for Government. (2020). Timeline of UK coronavirus lockdowns, March 2020–March 2021. https://www.instituteforgovernment.org.uk/sites/default/files/timeline-lockdown-web.pdf

Kochuvilayil, et al. (2020). COVID-19: Knowledge, anxiety, academic concerns and preventative behaviours among Australian and Indian undergraduate nursing students: A cross-sectional study. *Journal of Clinical Nursing, 00*, 1–10. https://doi.org/10.1111/jocn.1563

Ma, Z. et al. (2020). Mental health problems and correlates among 746 217 college students during the coronavirus disease 2019 outbreak in China. *Epidemiology and Psychiatric Sciences, 29*, E181.1–10. https://doi.org/10.1017/S2045796020000931

Mechili, A. E. et al. (2021). Is the mental health of young students and their family members affected during the quarantine period? Evidence from the COVID-19 pandemic in Albania. *Journal of Psychiatric and Mental Health Nursing, 8*, 317–325. https://doi.org/10.1111/jpm.12672

Meda, N., et al. (2020). Students' mental health problems before, during, and after COVID-19 lockdown in Italy. *Journal of Psychiatric Research, 134*(2021), 69–77. https://doi.org/10.1016/j.jpsychires.2020.12.045

Mental Health Foundation. (2021). Mental health in the COVID-19 Pandemic: Recommendations for prevention. https://www.mentalhealth.org.uk/sites/default/files/MHF%20Mental%20Health%20in%20the%20COVID-19%20Pandemic.pdf

Meo, A. S., et al. (2020). COVID-19 pandemic: Impact of quarantine on medical students' mental wellbeing and learning behaviours. *Pakistan Journal of Medical Sciences, 36* (COVID19-S4), S43–S48. https://doi.org/10.12669/pjms.36.COVID19-S4.2809

Morris, A. Z., et al. (2020). *Isolation in the midst of a Pandemic: Social Work Students Rapidly Respond to Community and Fieldwork Needs., 39*(8), 1127–1136. https://doi.org/10.1080/02615479.2020.1809649

Naik, L. G., et al. (2021). Online teaching and learning of higher education in India during COVID-19 emergency lockdown. *Pedagogical Research, 6* (1), em0090, 2–14. https://doi.org/10.29333/pr/9665

NUS. (2020). *Coronavirus student survey phase III November 2020 mental health and well-being*. https://www.nusconnect.org.uk/resources/coronavirus-and-students-phase-3-study-mental-health-with-demographics-nov-2020

Office for the National Statistics. (2020a). *Coronavirus and the impact on students in higher education in England: September–December 2020*. https://www.ons.gov.uk/peoplepopulationandcommunity/educationandchildcare/articles/coronavirusandtheimpactonstudentsinhighereducationinenglandseptembertodecember2020/2020-12-21

Office for National Statistics. (2020b). *Coronavirus and the impact on students in higher education in England: September–December 2020*. Office for National Statistics. https://www.ons.gov.uk/peoplepopulationandcommunity/educationandchildcare/articles/coronavirusandtheimpactonstudentsinhighereducationinenglandseptembertodecember2020/2020-12-21

Patricia Aguilera-Hermida, A. (2020). College students' use and acceptance of emergency online learning due to COVID-19. *International Journal of Educational Research Open, 1*, 100011. https://doi.org/10.1016/j.ijedro.2020.100011.2020

Pellerin, N., & Raufaste, E. (2020). Psychological resources protect well-being during the COVID-19 pandemic: A longitudinal study during the French lockdown. *Frontiers in Psychology, 11*(590276), 1–7. https://doi.org/10.3389/fpsyg.2020.590276

Pokhrel, S., & Chhetri, R. (2021). A literature review on impact of COVID-19 pandemic on teaching and learning. *Higher Education for the Future., 8*(1), 133–141. https://doi.org/10.1177/2347631120983481

Radu, M. C., et al. (2020). The impact of the COVID-19 pandemic on the quality of educational process: A student survey. *International Journal of Environmental Research and Public Health, 17*(7770), 1–15. https://doi.org/10.3390/ijerph17217770

Rossi, R. et al. (2020). COVID-19 pandemic and lockdown measures impact on mental health among the general population in Italy. *Frontiers in Psychiatry, 11*, 790. https://doi.org/10.3389/fpsyt.2020.00790

Santos, D. F. C., et al. (2020). Covid-19 and mental health-what do we know so far? *Frontiers in Psychiatry., 11*(565698), 1–6. https://doi.org/10.3389/fpsyt.2020.565698

Sahu, P. (2020). Closure of universities due to Coronavirus disease 2019 (COVID-19): Impact on education and mental health of students and academic staff. *Cureus, 12* (40, e7541. 1–6. https://doi.org/10.7759/cureus.7541

Shah, K., et al. (2020). Focus on mental health during the Coronavirus (COVID-19) pandemic: Applying learnings from the past outbreaks. *Cureus, 12*(3), e7405. https://doi.org/10.7759/cureus.7405

Savage, et al. (2020). Mental health and movement behaviour during the COVID-19 pandemic in UK university students: Prospective cohort study. *Mental Health and Physical Activity, 19*(100357), 1–6. https://doi.org/10.1016/j.mhpa.2020.100357

Son, C., et al. (2020). Effects of COVID-19 on college students' mental health in the United States: Interview survey study. *Journal of Medical Internet Research, 22* (9), e21279. 1–14. https://doi.org/10.2196/21279

Stallman, H. (2011). Psychological distress in university students: A comparison with general population data. *Australian Psychological Society, 45*(4), 249–257. https://doi.org/10.1080/00050067.2010.482109

TEQSA. (2020). Foundations for good practice: The student experience of online learning in Australian higher education during the COVID-19 pandemic. https://www.teqsa.gov.au/latest-news/publications/foundations-good-practice-student-experience-online-learning-australian

United Nations. (2020). Policy brief: Education during COVID-19 and beyond. https://www.un.org/development/desa/dspd/wp-content/uploads/sites/22/2020/08/sg_policy_brief_covid-19_and_education_august_2020.pdf

Universities Australia. (2020). The crucial role of universities in a coronavirus recovery. https://www.universitiesaustralia.edu.au/media-item/the-crucial-role-of-universities-in-a-coronavirus-recovery/

Universities UK. (2015). Student mental wellbeing in higher education: Good practice guide. https://www.universitiesuk.ac.uk/policy-and-analysis/reports/Documents/2015/student-mental-wellbeing-in-he.pdf

Villani, L., et al. (2021). Impact of the COVID-19 pandemic on psychological well-being of students in an Italian university: A web-based cross-sectional survey. *Globalization and Health, 17*(39), 1–14. https://doi.org/10.1186/s12992-021-00680-w

Weeden, K. A., & Cornwell, B. (2020). The small-world network of college classes: Implications for epidemic spread on a university campus. *Sociological Science, 7*, 222–241. https://doi.org/10.15195/v7.a9

Watermeyer, R., et al. (2020). COVID-19 and digital disruption in UK universities: afflictions and affordances of emergency online migration. *Higher Education*, 1–19. https://doi.org/10.1007/s10734-020-00561-y

WHO. (2020a). *Timeline. WHO's COVID-19 response*. https://www.who.int/emergencies/diseases/novel-coronavirus-2019/interactive-timeline

WHO. (2020b November 4). *Critical preparedness, readiness and response actions for COVID-19*. https://www.who.int/publications/i/item/critical-preparedness-readiness-and-response-actions-for-covid-19.

WHO. (2020c). *Impact of COVID-19 on people's livelihoods, their health and our food systems*. https://www.who.int/news/item/13-10-2020-impact-of-covid-19-on-people's-livelihoods-their-health-and-our-food-systems

Yang, R. (2020). China's higher education during the COVID-19 pandemic: Some preliminary observations. *Higher Education Research & Development, 39*(7), 1317–1321. https://doi.org/10.1080/07294360.2020.1824212
Young Minds. (2021). Coronavirus: Impact on young people with mental health needs. youngminds.org.uk
Zhai, Y., & Du, X. (2020). Mental health care for international Chinese students affected by the COVID-19 outbreak. *Lancet Psychiatry, 7*, e22. PubMed.
Zhu, N. (2020). A novel Coronavirus from patients with pneumonia in China, 2019. *The New England Journal of Medicine., 382*(8), 727–733.

Saradamoyee Chatterjee is a Bye-Fellow and Director of Studies in Land Economy at Lucy Cavendish College, University of Cambridge. She is also an Affiliated Lecturer at the Centre of Development Studies, University of Cambridge. At the Centre, Saradamoyee co-ordinates and lectures a paper on migration and human trafficking to the MPhil students. She also teaches a similar course at the Cambridge Centre for International Research (CCIR) in Cambridge. She is a Senior Research Fellow at the Cambridge Centre for Applied Research in Human Trafficking (CCARHT). Prior to this, she was a post-doctoral researcher at the Von Hügel Institute (VHI), St. Edmund's College, University of Cambridge. Her research focused on the illegal trade in organs in India. Before coming to Cambridge, Saradamoyee completed her PhD in Social Work from the University of Delhi, studying the social adjustment of the parents of children with cerebral palsy in India. Further, as an Assistant Professor at the University of Delhi, she taught Social Work to undergraduate and graduate students. Saradamoyee also worked in the development sector in India. She was a consultant at the UNDP India and managed programmes both at the state and national level on issues related to human trafficking and HIV/AIDS. Her research interests include organ trafficking, human trafficking, gender, capability and disability related issues.

Community Initiatives, Responses and Ways Forward

The Impact of Relationship Issues on the Mental Health of Students in Higher Education

Raquel Peel and Natalie Ward

Abstract Relationship difficulties are at the core of why most people seek counselling. The same is true in the context of higher education. Many students who seek counselling at university report experiencing issues in their intimate relationships. Transitioning to university is a major life milestone. This is a time filled with possibilities, when individuals evaluate and make important life and career choices. Also, for some, this time represents the beginning of new relationships with romantic partners. While these intimate connections can be a source of security and foster well-being, some individuals experience relationship issues that interfere with their academic performance, life satisfaction, and future success. Evidence shows that both negative relationship quality and relationship break-ups are strongly associated with poor mental health outcomes contributing to academic failure, and sometimes leading to, university attrition, and economic burden. More specifically, relationship difficulties are a significant contributor to anxiety, depression, and suicidality. This chapter will present a theoretical discussion of the literature to highlight the importance of understanding intimate relationships in the context of higher education and the effect of relationship issues (including conflict, lack of relationship skills, self-handicapping and self-sabotage, and personality traits) on the mental health of individuals, with implications for research and practice.

Introduction

Relationship difficulties are at the core of why most people seek counselling. The same is true in the context of higher education. Many students who seek counselling at university report experiencing issues in their romantic relationships. This is not surprising considering that transitioning to university is a major life milestone.

R. Peel (✉) · N. Ward
School of Psychology & Counselling, University of Southern Queensland, Ipswich, Australia
e-mail: Raquel.Peel@usq.edu.au

N. Ward
e-mail: Natalie.Ward@usq.edu.au

A. P. Francis and M. A. Carter (eds.), *Mental Health and Higher Education in Australia*,
https://doi.org/10.1007/978-981-16-8040-3_14

Starting a university degree is a time filled with possibilities when individuals evaluate and make important life and career choices. Also, for some, this time represents the beginning of new relationships with romantic partners. These intimate connections can be a source of security and foster well-being. However, some individuals experience relationship issues that interfere with their academic performance, life satisfaction, and future success. Altogether, evidence shows that negative relationship quality and relationship dissolution are strongly associated with poor mental health outcomes contributing to academic failure, and sometimes leading to, university attrition, and economic burden. More specifically, relationship difficulties are a significant contributor to anxiety, depression, and suicidality. This chapter will present a theoretical discussion of the literature to highlight the importance of understanding relationships (especially those of romantic nature) in the context of higher education and the effect of relationship issues (including conflict, lack of relationship skills, self-handicapping and self-sabotage, and personality traits) on the mental health of individuals, with implications for research and practice.

Relationships in Higher Education

Difficulties in romantic relationships are within the top five most prominent reasons for seeking counselling, and this is no different in higher education. Reports by the Australian and New Zealand Student Services Association (ANZSSA) Heads of Counselling Services conducted in 2010 and 2018 examined service delivery in university counselling centres across 38 Australian and New Zealand institutions (29 from Australia, 7 from New Zealand, and 2 identified as located in both Australia and New Zealand). These reports showed that relationship difficulties were the third most common issue (83% and 72%, respectively) reported as the reason for seeking counselling. Relationship concerns specified, within 55–93% of the cases, were interpersonal conflict, inadequate interpersonal skills to establish significant relationships, and domestic violence. Further, sexual assault and/or rape was identified within 44–50% of the cases. Lastly, although relationship issues largely refer to issues in intimate relationships (of romantic nature), these can also relate to parent–child relationships, sibling relationships, peer relationships, close friendships, work relationships, and student–supervisor relationships.

Overall, the literature strongly suggests that the main components of a students' lives are their education, their families, and their romantic partners. In accordance, a Turkish study by Üner et al. (2008) asked students about the most distressing events in their lives in the past year. Results showed that nearly half of them reported educational problems such as failing a class or failure to study in a faculty of their preference (15.6%), loss of a family member (15.3%), or breaking up with their partner because of an infidelity or a quarrel (13.5%). Contrastingly, most of the students reported educational achievements such as passing a class or success in the university entrance exams (34.5%), a happy event in the family such as birth or marriage (15.4%), or positive progress in their romantic relationship (20.0%), as the happiest events in their lives the past year.

Altogether, the impact of romantic relationships on the mental health of higher education students is dichotomous (Le & Wilkinson, 2018). Intimate relationships can be a protective factor, supporting and allowing young people to grow, develop, and succeed. Factors which can lower the risk of mental health issues in students are high levels of connectedness and interrelatedness with an intimate partner and/or children. These factors have also shown to lower psychological stress. Specifically, for those who had moved to attend university, being in a romantic relationship was associated with lower risk of depression and anxiety (Farrer et al., 2016). In accordance, a study conducted by Arriaga (2001) showed that students in romantic relationships experience greater well-being than single students. Additionally, some studies (e.g., Dennis, 2011) suggest that intimate relationships might also help motivate and inspire students in higher education, and reduce the propensity for risky behaviours, such as drug and alcohol use and abuse.

On the other hand, loss of social support (e.g., being widowed, separated, divorced, or breaking up with a romantic partner) is associated with increased risk for mental health difficulties (Blanco et al., 2008) such as anxiety, depression, suicidality (First et al., 2002), and weakened immune system (Arriaga, 2001). Altogether, broken relationships can be a catalyst for destructive behaviours and a determinate for mental health issues (Stallman, 2008, 2010; Stallman & Shochet, 2009). Further, a study by Schmidt and Lockwood (2015) showed that being in a romantic relationship is a significant contributor to class absence. In particular, this finding suggests that intimate relationships can impact students' focus and concentration.

Comorbidity Between Relationship Difficulties and Mental Health Issues

Mental health and relationship difficulties are frequently comorbid, as evidence shows (Fincham et al., 1997; Mead, 2002; Rogers et al., 2018; Whisman, 2001). However, the bidirectionality of cause and effect means that interpretation of determinates of a client presentation is often difficult. Some research cites relationship difficulties as a predictor of depression (Gibb et al., 2011; La Greca & Harrison, 2005; Mirsu-Paun & Oliver, 2017; Rick et al., 2017; Seiffge-Krenke, 2006). Others discuss mental health difficulties as barriers to starting and maintaining relationships (Hewitt et al., 2003; Meyer et al., 2005). For instance, reports conducted by ANZSSA in 2010 and 2018 showed that stress, depression, and anxiety were diagnosed in clients 100% of the time. Also, a study conducted by Farrer et al. (2016) examined the responses of 611 Australian university students to ascertain the rates of mental disorders and their risk factors. Results were 7.9% for major depression and 17.5% for generalised anxiety disorder (GAD) and indicated that students in their first year of undergraduate study were at greatest risk of depression. Additionally, female students, who were living away from home to study, and those students feeling financial pressure were at greatest risk of GAD. Contributors to major depression included experience of body image issues and lack of confidence, while factors such as pressure to achieve, lack of confidence, and difficulty managing study responsibilities were discussed as being related to the prevalence of GAD among respondents. Interestingly, domestic students presented with higher rates of depression and GAD than their international counterparts (Farrer et al., 2016).

Although relationships issues were not explicitly listed as a cause for mental health disorders in Farrer et al.'s (2020) review, these were considered a common issue experienced by university students. It was identified that the prevalence of relationship issues can lead to insomnia, self-harm and suicide, financial issues, loneliness and social isolation, homesickness, adjustment to university (with specific focus on international students), grief and loss, concerns with career and life after university, perfectionism, stress, physical health (e.g., nutrition and exercise), poor time management and procrastination, learning disabilities, concerns with living arrangements, sexual and gender identity issues, and exam anxiety. Additionally, Auerbach et al. (2018) identified that irregular sleep, increased interpersonal stress (caused by changes in romantic status and interaction with peer groups), experimental substance use, and the reduced social support of living away from home, in conjunction with pressure to perform well academically and make smart career choices, contribute to an increased risk of mental health disorders in university students.

Overall, young adults attending university face increased risks for developing mental health issues. While this can be a peak period for mental health concerns, the financial burden of academic failure can significantly impact individuals lives for a prolonged period of time; well past the duration of university studies (Auerbach et al., 2018). In accordance, Farrer et al. (2020) reported that 30–50% of university students meet criteria for a mental health diagnosis. Also, it is known that the prevalence of severe psychological distress is significantly higher in tertiary students (19–48%), compared to their age-matched peers not undertaking tertiary education (3–11%). Reasons for this may be varied but are certainly exacerbated by competing commitments. These include academic workload (which may involve time intensive demands), work or financial responsibilities, and family obligations. Also, these commitments minimise available time for social activities and relaxation (Leahy et al., 2010).

Despite the prevalence of mental health concerns in higher education, very few students seek and therefore receive timely and suitable mental health care. As with their non-tertiary peers, young adults are more likely to first approach friends, family, or other non-clinical and non-evidenced-based services for support. And, although these informal sources may be a useful starting point, they do little to aid more serious mental health issues. Altogether, Farrer et al. (2020) reported that the most commonly listed reasons for university students not seeking help are unavailability, cost, and concerns with confidentiality and stigma associated with mental health diagnosis and care.

Students seeking therapy often present with complex comorbid symptoms. However, these are not always easily identified. An interview study conducted by Peel et al. (2018) discussed that although clients usually present to therapy with reported stress, anxiety, and depression, these are not usually what they end-up working on. Usually, therapy focusses on the root-end issues, such as relationship difficulties and break-ups. For some, it is their lack of relationship skills that can affect other areas of their life. For instance, students answering a study by Peel and Caltabiano (2021) reported a tendency to 'overtend' to their partners as a protective behaviour to avoid relationship break-up, which in turn affected other areas of their personal life (e.g., education). Thus, given the numbers of students attending university are increasing in Australia and internationally, Farrer et al. (2016) proposed, and we agree, that addressing mental health issues in this vulnerable group in a timely and effective manner should be a priority.

Early Theoretical Underpinnings to Relationship Difficulty

It is non-surprising that relationships have been identified as a major source of distress among tertiary education students. As originally proposed by Bowlby (1969, 1973, 1980), humans are intrinsically motivated to form close affectional bonds. These close bonds are first attained by attracting proximity and avoiding separation between an infant and caregiver. However, attachment is a continuous and persistent process that serves as a protective mechanism through human development and in the face of threat or danger. Thus, the central idea of this theory is that development involves the continual construction, revision, integration, and abstraction of mental models of attachment with others to provide individuals with guidelines for coping with different forms of stress.

The issue arises when the individual cannot rely on those close to them in times of stress. In accordance, Rusk and Rothbaum (2010) developed a model encompassing attachment and goal-orientation theories to understand how individuals' responses to stressful situations in romantic relationships can be shaped by their attachment styles and consequently trigger goals for the maintenance or dissolution of the relationship. Similarly to what is observed in infancy, in adulthood, the attachment figure can aid the individual to cope with stressful situations. Accordingly, Rusk and Rothbaum (2010) proposed two learning pathways developed in synchrony with adult attachment styles: (1) an adaptive pathway leading to constructive strategies and (2) a contrasting pathway leading to defensive strategies. Learning and self-validation goals can be formed based on whether the individual's view is changeable (incremental views) or fixed (entity views). Learning goals are adaptive goals motivated by the desire to succeed, while self-validation goals are maladaptive goals motivated by the desire to validate self-worth. In the company of a responsive significant other, the individual can expect support and care when dealing with stressful situations, which in turn results in secure views, potentially leading to learning goals filled with constructive strategies (e.g., 'to improve communication to deal with relationship stressors'). However, if the attachment figure is not responsive, the individual resorts to insecure views, leading to self-validation goals and defensive strategies (e.g., 'to avoid new relationships to prevent from getting hurt'). These defensive strategies will often lead to conflict in relationships.

Conflict and Lack of Relationships Skills

As identified in the 2018 ANZSSA survey, barriers to relationships are most often attributed to conflict and lack of relationships skills. Early work in this area conducted by Gottman (1993) refers to relationship conflict as a result of four main behaviours: criticism, contempt, defensiveness, and stonewalling. These behaviours have been described as the 'four horsemen of the apocalypse' because they are proposed to lead to divorce on an average of 5.6 years after marriage. Further, it is estimated that these behaviours are 90% accurate in predicting relationship dissolution if not addressed (Lisitsa, 2013). Gottman's (1993) original research detailed the process leading to relationship dissolution as a structural model cascading to show a sequence of interactions, with criticism the first horseman, successively leading to contempt, defensiveness, and stonewalling (Gottman, 2013).

Conflict happens as a result of communication dominated by mismatched emotional expressions. In relationships, individuals will often experience layers of vulnerable core (or primary) emotions, such as sadness and fear. In principle, these emotional expressions can help individuals understand and communicate their needs and goals, and in a healthy interaction, these expressions will serve as a basis for collaboration to be formed. However, in relationships dominated by conflict, these emotions will often be hidden beneath a defensive surface (or secondary) emotions, such as anger, and in turn drive partners further apart (Johnson, 2004). Emotions are layered to protect the individual in their pursuit to meet attachment needs (Greenberg & Johnson, 1998). Therefore, if the individual is not feeling secure in their relationships, they will most likely not be able to express vulnerable emotions and will communicate with secondary emotions.

Altogether, extensive research (e.g., Cavallo et al., 2010; Mikulincer et al., 2003; Murray et al., 2006; Rom & Mikulincer, 2003; Rusk & Rothbaum, 2010) shows that motivation to self-protect is a powerful reinforcer of maladaptive behaviours in relationships. Also, De Castella et al. (2013) showed that motivation to self-protect goes beyond cultural differences. In a study comparing Australian and Japanese students regarding academic motivation, the results indicated that self-protectors are typically high in defensive pessimism and self-handicapping and low in helplessness. We suggest this is the same in the context of romantic relationships. Overall, it is well established that adult relationship interactions are strongly guided by a specific set of goals linked to attachment (Johnson et al., 1999), meaning that secure attachment would possibly encourage goals of connection and insecure attachment would encourage goals of self-protection.

Self-defeating Attitudes and Behaviours in Education and Relationships

Self-handicapping is a cognitive strategy employed with the overall aim of self-protection. This phenomenon has been extensively studied in the context of education and sports, yet the same is not true in other contexts. The literature on self-handicapping suggests that this terminology is better used to describe physical barriers employed to explicitly hinder performance-driven activities (e.g. excessive alcohol consumption, high level of stress, lack of sleep, and sickness). However, it does not fully encompass the complex intrinsic behaviours commonly observed in the dissolution of romantic engagements (i.e. defensiveness, trust difficulty, and lack of relationship skills), Thus, a new operationalised definition was offered to explain self-defeating attitudes and behaviours in romantic relationships.

In romantic relationships, the term 'self-sabotage' better fits the description of self-defeating attitudes and behaviours that can lead to relationship difficulties and dissolution. Originally, Post (1988) proposed that self-sabotage can be used in the organisational context to explain maladaptive behavioural expressions of individuals dealing with intrapersonal struggles. Accordingly, there is an abundance of empirical evidence to suggests that patterns of behaviours characteristic of insecure attachment lead to the dissolution of romantic engagements (Harper et al., 2006; Hazan & Shaver, 1987) and forms the bases for self-sabotage in relationships. Thus, two studies conducted by Peel and colleagues (2019; 2021) offered a novel definition for the phenomenon. Similarly, to how self-handicapping is understood, relationship sabotage was defined as a pattern of self-defeating attitudes and behaviours in (and out) of relationships employed to impede success or withdraw effort and justify failure. However, this description is not exhaustive. Individuals who display these attitudes and behaviours also appear to hold insecure views of romantic relationships, and although they might be doing all they can to start and maintain the relationship (Ayduk et al., 2001), failure is an expected outcome in the short- or long-term future (Rusk & Rothbaum, 2010). Further, those who present self-sabotage tendencies are equally committed to portraying a win–win outcome. In the context of romantic relationships, the individual guarantees a win if the engagement survives despite the employed defensive strategies, or if the engagement fails and their insecure beliefs are validated (Peel et al., 2019). In other words, individuals under stress (and facing the risk of getting hurt) will often respond by behaving in ways that validate their fears and insecurities.

Personality Traits Responsible for Issues in Education and Relationships

Traits which are linked to negative self-concept and self-defeating attitudes and behaviours in education and relationships are locus of control, self-efficacy, and perfectionism (Arazzini Stewart and De George-Walker, 2014).

Being able to take responsibility for one's action is often referred to as internal locus of control. Individuals with an internal locus of control will tend to take responsibility for events in their lives. In contrast, individuals with an external locus of control will tend to assign others responsibility for events in their lives (Akin, 2011; Kovaleva, 2012; Rotter & Mulry, 1965). In the context of education, locus of control is a relevant way for individuals to assess their own abilities. In accordance, Akin (2011) found that academic locus of control is a significant contributor to self-handicapping. An earlier study conducted by Prager (1986) also showed that locus of control could be linked with an individual's ability to be in a romantic relationship. In this study and other studies (e.g. Luerssen et al., 2017), intimacy was measured as the ability to self-disclose and express affection. Prager (1986) found that females in romantic relationships have a higher internal locus of control than do females not in an intimate relationship. Overall, the evidence suggests that the willingness to accept responsibility for events in one's life also makes it possible for intimacy with others to be formed.

Relationship skills aid individuals in learning how to be in a relationship, as well as achieving personal growth by strengthening core beliefs about the self and others. This inference is in accordance with early teachings by Bandura (1997), which highlighted the importance of experiences in the process of forming schemas of expectations of a romantic partner. Additionally, Shaver and Mikulincer (2002) and Riggio et al. (2013) proposed that relationship skills aid in facing stressors, which are unavoidable in romantic relationships, with resilience and persistence to stay together. Thus, focus of research and practice should shift from defensive strategies to improving the skills of people in relationships to increase their understanding of how to be in an intimate engagement and the expectations of a romantic partnership.

Similarly to what is seen in the education context, relationship skills can be built by focusing on improving individuals' self-efficacy. Self-efficacy is defined as the belief that one can perform certain actions and these actions will in turn achieve desired outcomes (Bandura, 1977, 1997). A noteworthy distinction in this definition is that beliefs are not the same as expected outcomes. Therefore, self-efficacy requires the belief that one can both perform and achieve. Further, Maddux and Gosselin (2012) proposed that people build self-efficacy by using knowledge gathered from previous experiences of success and failure. This premise is similar to how self-handicapping is theorised. Consequently, self-efficacy is also commonly studied in the educational and sports contexts. Overall, it is proposed that self-efficacy is a predictor of self-handicapping (Arazzini Stewart and De George-Walker, 2014; Martin & Brawley, 2002). However, a recent study did not support this finding. A possible explanation for this result is that self-confidence, as opposed to self-efficacy, is a more stable predictor of self-handicapping. Self-efficacy is often also linked to self-esteem; however, Coudevylle et al. (2011) proposed that lack of self-confidence, as opposed to low self-esteem, offers a better explanation for self-handicapping. Investigations have also been conducted in romantic relationships (e.g. Byl & Naydenova, 2016; Futris et al., 2017; Riggio et al., 2013) which further support this.

In the context of romantic engagements, self-efficacy is understood as the ability to persist with the relationship in the face of difficulties and deal with stress in the relationship. An important prediction made by Riggio et al. (2013) suggests that the ability to be a partner in an intimate engagement is predictive of romantic relationship satisfaction. In line with this prediction, Byl and Naydenova (2016) compared females' relationship and sport self-efficacy and found that females with high sport self-efficacy also showed high relationship efficacy, thereby suggesting that self-efficacy is a transcendent trait. In accordance with Riggio et al.'s (2013) prediction, a positive correlation was found between self-efficacy and relationship satisfaction in males, yet not females. Nevertheless, females did report higher relationship satisfaction overall. Therefore, the difference in gender may be a result of the fact that males generally report higher self-efficacy than do females (Byl & Naydenova, 2016). This could also be explained by females showing higher internal locus of control in relationships compared to males. Similarly, a recent study conducted by Futris et al. (2017) to examine romantic self-efficacy in young people found that participants enrolled in a youth-focused relationship education program had better relationship skills than did those who were not enrolled. Specifically, individuals who attended the educational program reported increased confidence and intention to engage the skills learnt in romantic relationships. Further, this result suggests that educational programs designed to teach relationship skills have the potential to increase overall satisfaction and maintenance. Conclusively, self-efficacy is often linked with motivation, effort, and persistence (Byl & Naydenova, 2016).

Motivation is often studied in the context of education to better understand students' presentation and predict academic success. For instance, Deci and Ryan (1985) investigated the difference between intrinsic and extrinsic motivation. Intrinsic motivation is seen when an individual finds an activity interesting and satisfying. This differs from extrinsic motivation, which occurs when the activity is performed only for the purpose of receiving a reward or obtaining an external goal. Further, Auerbach et al. (2019) noted examples of why students might have different motivations to pursue a certain area of study of career and the impact of these choices on their mental health. Extrinsic reasons include 'my family wanted me to', 'my friends were going', 'teachers advised me to', and 'I did not want to get a job right away'. On the other hand, intrinsic reasons include 'to achieve a degree', 'I enjoy learning and studying', 'to study a subject that really interests me', 'to improve job prospects generally', and 'to train for specific type of job'. Altogether, research found that extrinsically motivated individuals are more likely to present with mental health issues.

Another trait of interest is perfectionism. This trait is defined as setting high standards that cannot be met (Karner-Huţuleac, 2014; Pacht, 1984). Hewitt et al.

(2003) proposed that perfectionistic self-promotion and non-display of imperfection are motivated intrapersonally by the desire for self-esteem maintenance and enhancement and interpersonally by the desire to please an audience or avoid negative social outcomes. Similarly, Karner-Huţuleac (2014) found that perfectionism among students with high academic expectations is driven from anticipatory anxiety and fear of failure. Self-handicapping behaviours in this context include procrastination and compulsive behaviours. In accordance with previous research, these maladaptive behaviours were first adopted by students as coping mechanisms; however, over time, the same behaviours become self-defensive and led to low self-esteem and depression.

In the context of romantic relationships, maladaptive perfectionism has been linked with fear of intimacy (Martin & Ashby, 2004). Shea et al. (2006) explained that this link is expressed differently in males and females. Within the dimension of adult insecure attachment, females will often express fear of closeness when avoidant and a high concern for the possibility of rejection when anxious. For males, fear of intimacy is often expressed as a discomfort with close relationships. Further, Haring et al. (2003) found that maladaptive coping strategies—such as conflict, self-blame, avoidance, and self-interest—mediate the relationship between perfectionism and poor marital functioning. Again, a gender difference exists, with females seen to adopt all listed coping mechanisms, while males often resort to conflict. This finding suggests that the expectation of perfection in the relationship leads both partners to experience maladjustment—while one partner feels constantly disappointed at unmet expectations, the other resorts to maladaptive coping mechanisms to avoid feeling inadequate against unrealistic standards. In accordance, Fletcher and colleagues (Fletcher & Simpson, 2000; Fletcher et al., 2000, 2004) explained that unmet relationship standards in romantic engagements are a significant contributor to relationship dissolution.

A Way Forward

Altogether, it is evident that negative relationship quality and relationship dissolution pose a risk to the mental health of students in higher education; it heightens the risk of anxiety, depression, and suicidality; and it can lead to academic failure, university attrition, and economic burden. Nevertheless, scholars in this space have recognised that taking responsibility for issues in a relationship (Shaver & Mikulincer, 2002), insight, and relationships skills (Peel & Caltabiano, 2021) can be a protective factor to mental health issues arising from relationship breakdowns. Also, when aiming to improve anxiety symptoms in university populations, reviews have found that computer, internet, and telephone-based mental health interventions are promising because of their accessibility and affordability (Farrer et al., 2020). Thus, these findings mean that the focus of research and practice needs to shift from identifying and treating defensive behaviours to improving the skills of people in relationships, so as to increase their understanding of what it entails to be in an intimate engagement, and the expectations of a romantic partnership.

Conclusion

Relationship difficulties are one of the most prominent reasons why individuals seek counselling and a significant contributor to anxiety, depression, and suicidality (First et al., 2002). While all forms of love are a source of security and can foster well-being, some relationships fail repeatedly without the opportunity for individuals to learn relationship skills. Research indicates that understanding how self-defeating attitudes and behaviours are presented in relationships can aid in the development of a model for researchers and practitioners to address issues and improve individuals' intimate engagements (Peel et al., 2019). In addition, an awareness of which personality traits might be helping versus hindering relationships may offer avenues of personal development. This is no different for university students.

Relationships formed by young adults are predictors of current and future mental health and well-being. Considering that university is a time when young adults often embark on their first romantic relationship, support around developing relationship skills could prevent unnecessary heartache, or in the least offer a chance for self-reflection and development, preparing them for future relationships. Because of the dichotomy that romantic relationships pose (i.e., being a source of stress and support), particularly in a university setting, being able to harness students' potential while reducing their emotional burden has academic, financial, and most importantly, mental health benefits. Also, healthy and positive connections act as buffers to life's stresses while also reducing instances of risky behaviours. Altogether, romantic relationships can be a protective factor, supporting and allowing young people to grow, develop, and succeed while reducing psychological stress, and preparing young adults for happier, more successful futures.

Overall, research into the impact that relationship issues have on the mental of students in higher education has highlighted the prevalence of mental health difficulties among this cohort and the low levels of seeking help. Thus, increasing the availability, accessibility, and affordability of mental health support systems can serve to normalise help seeking, affect change, and improve mental health outcomes. This is not just a clinical issue; improving the quality of relationships and increasing help seeking behaviours, is relevant to the entire population, and thus, a public health issue.

References

Akin, A. (2011). Academic locus of control and self-handicapping. *Procedia—Social and Behavioral Sciences, 30*, 812–816. https://doi.org/10.1016/j.sbspro.2011.10.157

Arazzini Stewart, M., & De George-Walker, L. (2014). Self-handicapping, perfectionism, locus of control and self-efficacy: A path model. *Personality and Individual Differences, 66*, 160–164. https://doi.org/10.1016/j.paid.2014.03.038

Arriaga, X. B. (2001). The ups and downs of dating: Fluctuations in satisfaction in newly formed romantic relationships. 754–765. https://doi.org/10.1037/0022-3514.80.5.754

Auerbach, R. P., Mortier, P., Bruffaerts, R., Alonso, J., Benjet, C., Cuijpers, P., Demyttenaere, K., Ebert, D. D., Green, J. G., Hasking, P., Murray, E., Nock, M. K., Pinder-Amaker, S., Sampson, N. A., Stein, D. J., Vilagut, G., Zaslavsky, A. M., Kessler, R. C., & Collaborators, W.H.O.W.M.H.-I.C.S. (2018). WHO World mental health surveys international college student project: Prevalence and distribution of mental disorders. *Journal of Abnormal Psychology, 127*(7), 623–638. https://doi.org/10.1037/abn0000362

Australian and New Zealand Student Services Association Heads of Counselling Services. (2010). *Benchmarking pilot survey*. Retrieved from https://static1.1.sqspcdn.com

Australian and New Zealand Student Services Association Heads of Counselling Services. (2018). ANZSSA Heads of Counselling Services HOCS Benchmarking Survey 2018 Summary Report. *Journal of the Australian and New Zealand Student Services Association, 27*(1).

Ayduk, O., Downey, G., & Kim, M. (2001). Rejection sensitivity and depressive symptoms in women. *Personality and Social Psychology Bulletin, 27*(7), 868–877. https://doi.org/10.1177/0146167201277009

Bandura, A. (1977). Self-efficacy: Toward a unifying theory of behavioral change. *Psychological Review, 84*(2), 191–215. https://doi.org/10.1037/0033-295X.84.2.191

Bandura, A. (1997). *Self-efficacy: The exercise of control*. Times Books.

Blanco, C., Okuda, M., Wright, C., Hasin, D. S., Grant, B. F., Liu, S. M., & Olfson, M. (2008). Mental health of college students and their non-college-attending peers: Results from the National Epidemiologic Study on Alcohol and Related Conditions. *Archives in General Psychiatry, 65*(12), 1429–1437. https://doi.org/10.1001/archpsyc.65.12.1429

Bowlby, J. (1969). *Attachment and loss* (2nd Ed., Vol. I, Attachment). Basic Books.

Bowlby, J. (1973). *Attachment and loss* (Vol. II, Separation Anxiety and Anger). Basic Books.

Bowlby, J. (1980). *Attachment and loss* (Vol. III, Loss Sadness and Depression). Basic Books.

Byl, M., & Naydenova, I. (2016). The association between romantic relationships, self-efficacy and sports self-efficacy in female athletes as measured by salivary cortisol. *Journal of Counseling and Psychology, 1*(2), Article 2. Retrieved from http://digitalcommons.gardner-webb.edu/jcp/vol1/iss2/2

Cavallo, J. V., Fitzsimons, G. M., & Holmes, J. G. (2010). When self-protection overreaches: Relationship-specific threat activates domain-general avoidance motivation. *Journal of Experimental Social Psychology, 46*(1), 1–8. https://doi.org/10.1016/j.jesp.2009.07.007

Coudevylle, G. R., Gernigon, C., & Martin Ginis, K. A. (2011). Self-esteem, self-confidence, anxiety and claimed self-handicapping: A mediational analysis. *Psychology of Sport & Exercise, 12*(6), 670–675. https://doi.org/10.1016/j.psychsport.2011.05.008

De Castella, K., Byrne, D., & Covington, M. (2013). Unmotivated or motivated to fail? A cross-cultural study of achievement motivation, fear of failure, and student disengagement. *Journal of Educational Psychology, 105*(3), 861–880. https://doi.org/10.1037/a0032464

Deci, E. L., & Ryan, R. M. (1985). *Intrinsic motivation and self-determination in human behavior*. Plenum. https://doi.org/10.1007/978-1-4899-2271-7

Dennis, M. R. (2011). Social control of healthy behavior between intimate college students. *Journal of American College Health, 59*(8), 728–735. https://doi.org/10.1080/07448481.2010.537419

Farrer, L. M., Gulliver, A., Bennett, K., Fassnacht, D. B., & Griffiths, K. M. (2016). Demographic and psychosocial predictors of major depression and generalised anxiety disorder in Australian university students. *BMC Psychiatry, 16*, 241–241. https://doi.org/10.1186/s12888-016-0961-z

Farrer, L. M., Gulliver, A., Katruss, N., Bennett, K., Bennett, A., Ali, K., & Griffiths, K. M. (2020). Development of the uni virtual clinic: An online programme for improving the mental health of university students. *British Journal of Guidance & Counselling, 48*(3), 333–346. https://doi.org/10.1080/03069885.2020.1729341

Fincham, F. D., Beach, S. R. H., Harold, G. T., & Osborne, L. N. (1997). Marital satisfaction and depression: Different causal relationships for men and women? *Psychological Science, 8*(5), 351–356. https://doi.org/10.1111/j.1467-9280.1997.tb00424.x

First, M. B., Bell, C. C., Cuthbert, B., Krystal, J. H., Malison, R., Offord, D. R., et al. (2002). Personality disorders and relational disorders: A research agenda for addressing crucial gaps in DSM. In D. J. Kupfer, M. B. First, & D. A. Regier (Eds.), *A research agenda for DSM—V* (pp. 123–199).

Fletcher, G. J. O., & Simpson, J. A. (2000). Ideal standards in close relationships: Their structure and functions. *Current Directions in Psychological Science, 9*(3), 102–105. https://doi.org/10.1111/1467-8721.00070

Fletcher, G. J. O., Simpson, J. A., & Thomas, G. (2000). The measurement of perceived relationship quality components: A confirmatory factor analytic approach. *Personality and Social Psychology Bulletin, 26*(3), 340–354. https://doi.org/10.1177/0146167200265007

Fletcher, G. J. O., Tither, J. M., O'Loughlin, C., Friesen, M., & Overall, N. (2004). Warm and homely or cold and beautiful? Sex differences in trading off traits in mate selection. *Personality and Social Psychology Bulletin, 30*(6), 659–672. https://doi.org/10.1177/0146167203262847

Futris, T. G., Sutton, T. E., & Duncan, J. C. (2017). Factors associated with romantic relationship self-efficacy following youth-focused relationship education. *Family Relations, 66*(5), 777–793. https://doi.org/10.1111/fare.12288

Gibb, S. J., Fergusson, D. M., & Horwood, L. J. (2011). Relationship separation and mental health problems: Findings from a 30-year longitudinal study. *Australian and New Zealand Journal of Psychiatry, 45*(2), 163–169. https://doi.org/10.3109/00048674.2010.529603

Gottman, J. M. (1993). A theory of marital dissolution and stability. *Journal of Family Psychology, 7*(1), 57–75. https://doi.org/10.1037/0893-3200.7.1.57

Gottman, J. M. (2013). *Marital interaction: Experimental investigations*. Academic.

Greenberg, L. S., & Johnson, S. M. (1998). *Emotionally focused therapy for couples*. Guilford Press.

Haring, M., Hewitt, P. L., & Flett, G. L. (2003). Perfectionism, coping, and quality of intimate relationships. *Journal of Marriage and Family, 65*(1), 143–158. https://doi.org/10.1111/j.1741-3737.2003.00143.x

Harper, M. S., Dickson, J. W., & Welsh, D. P. (2006). Self-silencing and rejection sensitivity in adolescent romantic relationships. *Journal of Youth and Adolescence, 35*(3), 435–443. https://doi.org/10.1007/s10964-006-9048-3

Hazan, C., & Shaver, P. (1987). Romantic love conceptualized as an attachment process. *Journal of Personality and Social Psychology, 52*(3), 511–524. https://doi.org/10.1037//0022-3514.52.3.511

Hewitt, P. L., Flett, G. L., Sherry, S. B., Habke, M., Parkin, M., Lam, R. W., et al. (2003). The interpersonal expression of perfection: Perfectionistic self-presentation and psychological distress. *Journal of Personality and Social Psychology, 84*(6), 1303–1325. https://doi.org/10.1037/0022-3514.84.6.1303

Johnson, S. M. (2004). *The practice of emotionally focused couple therapy: Creating connection* (2nd ed.). Brunner-Routledge.

Johnson, S. M., Hunsley, J., Greenberg, L., & Schindler, D. (1999). Emotionally focused couples therapy: Status and challenges. *Clinical Psychology, 6*(1), 67–79. https://doi.org/10.1093/clipsy.6.1.67

Karner-Huţuleac, A. (2014). Perfectionism and self-handicapping in adult education. *Procedia—Social and Behavioral Sciences, 142*, 434–438. https://doi.org/10.1016/j.sbspro.2014.07.699

Kovaleva, A. (2012). *The IE-4: Construction and validation of a short scale for the assessment of locus of control*. GESIS - Leibniz Institut für Sozialwissenschaften, Mannheim, Germany. Retrieved from http://nbn-resolving.de/urn:nbn:de:0168-ssoar-371199

La Greca, A. M., & Harrison, H. M. (2005). Adolescent peer relations, friendships, and romantic relationships: Do they predict social anxiety and depression? *Journal of Clinical Child & Adolescent Psychology, 34*(1), 49–61. https://doi.org/10.1207/s15374424jccp3401_5

Le, D. T. H., & Wilkinson, R. B. (2018). *Students' mental health during university transition across the cultures: An attachment perspective* Paper presented at the Role of School Psychology in Promoting Well-being of Students and Families, Hanoi National University of Education, Hanoi, Vietnam.

Leahy, C. M., Peterson, R. F., Wilson, I. G., Newbury, J. W., Tonkin, A. L., & Turnbull, D. (2010). Distress levels and self-reported treatment rates for medicine, law, psychology and mechanical engineering tertiary students: Cross-sectional study. *Australian & New Zeland Journal of Psychiatry, 44*(7), 608–615. https://doi.org/10.3109/00048671003649052 PMID: 20560848.

Lisitsa, E. (2013). *The Four Horsemen: Criticism, contempt, defensiveness, and stonewalling [Blog post]*. Retrieved from https://www.gottman.com/blog/the-four-horsemen-recognizing-criticism-contempt-defensiveness-and-stonewalling/

Luerssen, A., Jhita, G. J., & Ayduk, O. (2017). Putting yourself on the line: Self-esteem and expressing affection in romantic relationships. *Personality and Social Psychology Bulletin, 43*(7), 940–956. https://doi.org/10.1177/0146167217702374

Maddux, J., & Gosselin, J. (2012). Self-efficacy. In M. R. Leary & J. P. Tangney (Eds.), *Handbook of self and identity* (pp. 218–225). Guilford Press.

Martin, J. L., & Ashby, J. S. (2004). Perfectionism and fear of intimacy: Implications for relationships. *The Family Journal, 12*(4), 368–374. https://doi.org/10.1177/1066480704267279

Martin, K. A., & Brawley, L. R. (2002). Self-handicapping in physical achievement settings: The contributions of self-esteem and self-efficacy. *Self and Identity, 1*(4), 337–351. https://doi.org/10.1080/15298860290106814

Mead, D. E. (2002). Marital distress, co-occurring depression, and marital therapy: A review. *Journal of Marital and Family Therapy, 28*(3), 299–314. https://doi.org/10.1111/j.1752-0606.2002.tb01188.x

Meyer, B., Olivier, L., & Roth, D. A. (2005). Please don't leave me! BIS/BAS, attachment styles, and responses to a relationship threat. *Personality and Individual Differences, 38*(1), 151–162. https://doi.org/10.1016/j.paid.2004.03.016

Mikulincer, M., Shaver, P. R., & Pereg, D. (2003). Attachment theory and affect regulation: The dynamics, development, and cognitive consequences of attachment-related strategies. *Motivation and Emotion, 27*(2), 77–102. https://doi.org/10.1023/a:1024515519160

Mirsu-Paun, A., & Oliver, J. A. (2017). How much does dove really hurt? A meta-analysis of the association between romantic relationship quality, breakups and mental health outcomes in adolescents and young adults. *Journal of Relationships Research, 8*, e5. https://doi.org/10.1017/jrr.2017.6

Murray, S. L., Holmes, J. G., & Collins, N. L. (2006). Optimizing assurance: The risk regulation system in relationships. *Psychological Bulletin, 132*(5), 641–666. https://doi.org/10.1037/0033-2909.132.5.641

Pacht, A. R. (1984). Reflections on perfection. *American Psychologist, 39*(4), 386–390. https://doi.org/10.1037/0003-066X.39.4.386

Peel, R., & Caltabiano, N. (2021). Why do we sabotage love? A thematic analysis of lived experiences of relationship breakdown and maintenance. *Journal of Couple & Relationship Therapy, 20*(2), 99–131. https://doi.org/10.1080/15332691.2020.1795039

Peel, R., Caltabiano, N., Buckby, B., & McBain, K. A. (2018). Mental health diagnoses and relationship breakdown: Which is the chicken and which the egg? *International Journal of Innovation, Creativity and Change, 4*(3), 98–116. Retrieved from http://www.ijicc.net/images/Vol4_iss3_spec_ed_nov_2018/Raquel_Peel_et_al.pdf

Peel, R., Caltabiano, N., Buckby, B., & McBain, K. A. (2019). Defining romantic self-sabotage: A thematic analysis of interviews with practicing psychologists. *Journal of Relationship Research, 10*(e16), 1–9. https://doi.org/10.1017/jrr.2019.7

Post, R. D. (1988). Self-sabotage among successful women. *Psychotherapy in Private Practice, 6*(3), 191–205. https://doi.org/10.1300/J294v06n03_29

Prager, K. J. (1986). Intimacy status: Its relationship to locus of control, self-disclosure, and anxiety in adults. *Personality and Social Psychology Bulletin, 12*(1), 91–109. https://doi.org/10.1177/0146167286121010

Rick, J. L., Falconier, M. K., & Wittenborn, A. K. (2017). Emotion regulation dimensions and relationship satisfaction in clinical couples. *Personal Relationships, 24*(4), 790–803. https://doi.org/10.1111/pere.12213

Riggio, H. R., Weiser, D. A., Valenzuela, A. M., Lui, P. P., Montes, R., & Heuer, J. (2013). Self-efficacy in romantic relationships: Prediction of relationship attitudes and outcomes. *The Journal of Social Psychology, 153*(6), 629–650. https://doi.org/10.1080/00224545.2013.801826

Rogers, A. A., Ha, T., Updegraff, K. A., & Iida, M. (2018). Adolescents' daily romantic experiences and negative mood: A dyadic, intensive longitudinal study. *Journal of Youth and Adolescence, 47*(7), 1517–1530. https://doi.org/10.1007/s10964-017-0797-y

Rom, E., & Mikulincer. (2003). Attachment theory and group processes: The association between attachment style and group-related representations, goals, memories, and functioning. *Journal of Personality and Social Psychology, 84*(6), 1220. https://doi.org/10.1037/0022-3514.84.6.1220

Rotter, J. B., & Mulry, R. C. (1965). Internal versus external control of reinforcement and decision time. *Journal of Personality and Social Psychology, 2*(4), 598–604. https://doi.org/10.1037/h0022473

Rusk, N., & Rothbaum, F. (2010). From stress to learning: Attachment theory meets goal orientation theory. *Review of General Psychology, 14*(1), 31–43. https://doi.org/10.1037/a0018123

Schmidt, J., & Lockwood, B. (2015). Love and other grades: A study of the effects of romantic relationship status on the academic performance of university students. *Journal of College Student Retention: Research, Theory & Practice, 19*(1), 81–97. https://doi.org/10.1177/1521025115611614

Seiffge-Krenke, I. (2006). Coping with relationship stressors: The impact of different working models of attachment and links to adaptation. *Journal of Youth and Adolescence, 35*(1), 24. https://doi.org/10.1007/s10964-005-9015-4

Shaver, P. R., & Mikulincer, M. (2002). Attachment-related psychodynamics. *Attachment & Human Development, 4*(2), 133–161. https://doi.org/10.1080/14616730210154171

Shea, A. J., Slaney, R. B., & Rice, K. G. (2006). Perfectionism in intimate relationships. *Measurement and Evaluation in Counseling and Development, 39*(2), 107–125. https://doi.org/10.1080/07481756.2006.11909793

Stallman, H. M. (2008). Prevalence of mental health problems in a university health service sample. *Australian Family Physician, 37*(8), 673. Retrieved from https://www.racgp.org.au/afpbackissues/2008/200808/200808stallman.pdf

Stallman, H. M. (2010). Psychological distress in university students: A comparison with general population data. *Australian Psychologist, 45*(4), 249–257. https://doi.org/10.1080/00050067.2010.482109

Stallman, H. M., & Shochet, I. (2009). Prevalence of mental health problems in Australian university health services. *Australian Psychologist, 44*(2), 122–127. https://doi.org/10.1080/00050060902733727

Üner, S., Özcebe, H., Telatar, G., & Tezcan, S. (2008). Assessment of mental health of universitystudents with GHQ-12. *Turkish Journal Medical Sciences, 38*(5), 437–46. Retrieved from https://journals.tubitak.gov.tr/medical/issues/sag-08-38-5/sag-38-5-10-0709-14.pdf

Whisman, M. A. (2001). The association between depression and marital dissatisfaction. In S. R. H. Beach (Ed.), *Marital and family processes in depression: A scientific foundation for clinical practice* (pp. 3–24). American Psychological Association.

Raquel Peel is an internationally recognised TEDx speaker, an emerging researcher, and passionate lecturer. She is interested in researching relationships, suicide, bullying, stigma, and medical education. Her TEDx Talk titled 'Why do We Sabotage Love?' is featured in the TED series titled 'How to Be a Better Human' and in the TEDx Shorts series. She enjoys promoting scientific research to engage both academics and members of the general public alike. As an educator, she is passionate about raising awareness of mental health in higher education. She has experience teaching a diverse range of psychology and counselling subjects across all undergraduate year levels. Also, she has been recognised with prestigious awards, including the Excellence Award for Early Career Educator granted by the University of Southern Queensland (2020) and the Inclusive Practice Teaching Award granted by James Cook University (2018). For a complete portfolio, please visit: www.RaquelPeel.com

Natalie Ward has a Bachelor of Arts (Honours) (Politics) from James Cook University and a Master of Business Communications from Queensland University of Technology. After working for 20 years in sales and marketing, she underwent a career change to study psychology while working in the field of education. She completed a Bachelor of Psychology (Honours) at the University of Southern Queensland in 2020. Her honours thesis, under the supervision of Dr Raquel Peel, was titled 'The Relationship between Flirting Styles and the Cycle of Relationship Sabotage within Intimate Relationships'. As a mother of 5, she is passionate about supporting adolescents in their social and emotional journey and strongly believes in empowering young people while endorsing a positive, proactive approach to mental health. She commenced a Ph.D. through the University of Southern Queensland in 2021 pursuant in this field.

Detoxing University Through Creative Engagement

Ross W. Prior

Abstract This chapter outlines a philosophy of higher education practice that includes emphasis on using creativity to engage students, both in and outside of formal classes, to improve wellbeing. In an age of increasing discourse preoccupied with division and difference, individuals' feelings of isolation and loneliness, increased student debt, lack of job opportunities and societal destabilisation, there is urgent need for a philosophy of 'togetherness'. In developing this ideal of coming together, the benefits to mental health and wellbeing are many. Further, the way we conduct research in the academy is something to consider more carefully too. The choice of our research methodologies may not be as benign as we might think and can shift perceptions and distort values over time. The past decade has revealed an unhealthy preoccupation with measurement and performance rankings which has been pervasive amongst the neoliberalist higher education sector. However, lived experience, feelings and creative endeavour resist numerical reduction. Running alongside this issue has been growing calls across those working in wellbeing and education to increase usage of art-based approaches in understanding and evidencing the benefits of expressive art practice. To these ends, this chapter offers hope in how creative activity might bring about essential change to combat a corporate hardening that has in recent times ruthlessly hijacked the love of learning and indeed the love of enabling others. Reporting on an initiative where artistic processes have been used as an antidote to the 'toxic university', the chapter explores what we can do to bring about positive change for both students and staff.

Keywords Creative engagement · Mental health · Creativity

> Only by being suspended aloft, by dangling my mind in the heavens and mingling my rare thought with the ethereal air, could I ever achieve strict scientific accuracy in my survey of the vast empyrean. Had I pursued my inquiries from down there on the ground, my data would be worthless. The earth, you see, pulls down the delicate essence of thought to its own gross level. –ARISTOPHANES, *the Clouds*.

R. W. Prior (✉)
Faculty of Arts, Business and Social Sciences, University of Wolverhampton, Wolverhampton, United Kingdom
e-mail: r.prior@wlv.ac.uk

A. P. Francis and M. A. Carter (eds.), *Mental Health and Higher Education in Australia*,
https://doi.org/10.1007/978-981-16-8040-3_15

Introduction

The year is 423BC at the City Dionysia, an important festival in Athens during the spring. The audience sit watching a new play, *The Clouds* by the playwright Aristophanes (1973). The audience laugh and mock the characters as the play ridicules the absurdities of the Sophists' school of higher education. The play traces the journey of Strepsiades, a once rich but not so bright countryman of advanced years, who has found himself deeply in debt through the extravagant tastes of his trendy son, Pheidippides. The 'bank of mum and dad' is now emptied and in ruin. Seeking a solution, Strepsiades hears of the benefits of a powerful new method of argument taught by the Sophists (at some financial cost), making successful litigation possible through the clever use of words and thought. Lured by the prospect that education of this type would provide dividends for his life circumstances, he enters the 'Phrontisterion' or 'The Thinkery' of Socrates, known to be the 'best' of the teachers, with the aim to learn how to outsmart his creditors and avoid paying his debts. Not so incidentally, Socrates is presented in *The Clouds* as a petty thief and a fraud. However, Strepsiades subsequently joins the 'life-changing' school, but he is soon considered too old and stupid to benefit by the lessons. He then sends his son Pheidippides in his place, hoping he might make a more promising student. As hoped, Pheidippides proves to be a successful pupil of 'new thinking'. However, in an ironic twist, Pheidippides becomes so adept at this new method of argument that in a show of intellectual prowess, he physically beats his father and demonstrates that he is justified by all the laws, divine and human, in the right of what he is doing to his father. The play concludes with the old Strepsiades realising the immorality of this type of 'progressive' education, and he revengefully sets fire to the Phrontisterion, burning the wretched place to the ground.

Fast-forward almost 2,500 years and we reflect on the poignancy of the issues in Aristophanes' play, contemplating the state of our own neoliberalist higher education system and how the commercial nature of the 'education business' is serving society today. Students are being encouraged in unprecedented numbers to enrol in degree programmes with the lure of financial gain in the world of work, arguably resulting in a growing loss of interest in an education embedded in the classics, philosophy, history, arts and humanities. We find ourselves in a situation where a deep intellectual education in what makes us human and indeed civil, has given way to a rhetoric of 'better' jobs, greater wealth and university as a somehow driver of future enterprise. However, perhaps ironically, this rapidly changing higher education sector is now struggling to maintain its once prestigious position. In the wake of the COVID-19 pandemic, economic pressure, social change agendas and ready access to information and technical application via digital technology, the value of higher education is becoming somewhat challenged. Whilst there is still an expectation that more and more young people should at least possess an entry-level degree, this norm is coming under increasing question in relation to value for money, skills shortages and real-world need. Aristophanes through his play *The Clouds* intends us to see the Thinkery as ridiculous and not a place in which we should place our faith—indeed the satire provokes us to question the very drivers of why we might seek to engage in higher education in the first place.

The pressure to academise has not been without its problems, and the mental health of those involved has raised growing concern (Carter & Goldie, 2018; Prior, 2018; Erickson et al., 2020). The politics of what has been labelled the 'toxic university' (Smyth, 2017) is complex. However, Carter and Goldie, 2018: 6) underline the responsibility of universities to respond to wellbeing issues evident in Australia and beyond: 'With universities having a duty of care to their staff, there is scope for a better understanding of potential enablers of mental health in higher education settings'. This chapter, within its limited scope, aims to address some of the highlighted issues in relation to higher education wellbeing and importantly, propose how artistic and creative engagement initiatives may provide an effective antidote to the pressures of the 'toxic university'. Described later in the chapter is an original mindfulness project working with university students and staff alike, highlighting growing understanding of how as academics we may become enablers in our practice and to contribute more widely and effectively to improving wellbeing within contemporary higher education.

A Discourse of Dissonance

To more fully appreciate the current mental health concerns within higher education, it is necessary to briefly contextualise the fragmentary times in which this situation exists. 'The fundamental big issue in current discussion is that increasingly, universities are being corporatised and economised' (Prior, 2018: 129) into what is now known as neoliberalist higher education. Further, the sector is currently immersed in a fractious period in history where identity politics has gained significant traction and has also taken its place within the wider community propelled by the mass media. Although well-intentioned, many of these political agendas are creating a discourse of dissonance and fracturing of collective community. Narratives are driven by profiling individual characteristics such as race and gender to promote the concepts of 'equality and diversity', and in the UK, 'widening participation' also—a political initiative to put more people from what is being termed as 'under-represented groups' into higher education. In the UK, many of the narratives and agendas are framed by legislated 'protected characteristics' which include age, disability, gender reassignment, race, religion or belief, sex, sexual orientation, marriage and civil partnership and pregnancy and maternity. However, the public debates which have subsequently ensued challenge the definitions of identities with some resistance to accept fixed definitions altogether as in the case of 'gender fluidity'. Further to these agendas has been a resurgence in civil unrest in response to actual and perceived social or racial injustice.

Undoubtedly many educationalists are influenced by academic trends seen in poststructuralism, all the other *isms* and the work of French philosopher and political activist Michel Foucault (1978). Critical theorists have considerably influenced formal education for almost 100 years, with the most notable being Carl Marx (1818—1883). These critical theorists all aim to critique and change established social order. Paulo Freire is generally credited as the first to apply critical theory in learning and teaching with his seminal text *Pedagogy of the Oppressed* (1970), which in itself was influenced heavily by Marxist ideology. Amongst many challenging ideas, Freire argues that pedagogy should treat the learner as a co-creator of knowledge—although this concept has been slow to gain discernible traction.

A great deal of contemporary research and scholarship has also been framed by Marxism and critical theory, whether or not the authors of contemporary work realise it or not. These approaches in education have resulted in the proliferation of discourses of dissonance, difference and individual identity. Arguably this rise in individualism has perhaps unintentionally worked in adverse proportion to the value of community and collective community service. In Australia and the UK, for example, traditional places of belonging such as churches, service or social clubs and sporting/hobbyist clubs currently do not enjoy the same levels of community engagement as they once did. Diminishing cohesive social structures are also played out in our universities where student (and staff) experience of campus life has greatly diminished. Even pre-pandemic, the time spent on campus was noticeably diminishing and a physical scholarly community, as we once knew, evaporating. In relation to the corporatised modern university, I have previously written:

> With the rise in individualism, neoliberalism and consumerism, the student has been repositioned, quite uncomfortably, as a 'customer' replete with customer satisfaction surveys, entitlement and a 'value for money' ethos. This shift in mindset moves the student away from asking 'why is it so' to questions of 'what for', 'when' and 'how much' (Prior, 2018: 130).

Not only is learning being economised and commercialised but along with this is the increasing need for students to take employment, working long hours in order to cover escalating tuition and living costs. This shift has had a major effect in removing students from campuses. Further, as already acknowledged above, we are increasingly experiencing a fractious society littered with multiple polarising opinions being given prominence through both the mainstream media and social media. Undoubtedly this has a collective effect in pervading the social mindset and destabilises the young—a further stress on mental health. According to Carter and Goldie (2017) universities are well placed 'to support students' positive educational and social media experiences' (p. 78) and these authors call for 'academics to better design, develop and lead-manage inclusive and sustainable online teaching and learning environments conducive to students' digital identity, mental health and wellness' (p. 78). Undoubtedly the online space is taking over from the physical, and universities must respond accordingly.

Understanding Lived Experience in Higher Education

Mental health and wellbeing in higher education are at a critical point in history, as reflected in the need for this book as a whole. University staff are subjected to unprecedented pressure through the imposition of regulations, agendas, shrinking funding, responding to a raft of performance metrics, pressure to recruit, and particularly since COVID-19, to develop extensive online learning materials. As mentioned above, the overarching drivers come from an economised approach to higher education with increased numbers of universities aggressively competing against one another for student numbers. Increasingly the voice of the academic is diminished in an environment of brutal university administrations. This is born out in the lived experience of academics who perhaps once felt in control of their own destinies who no longer feel able to raise the issues that concern them most. The now widespread use (and arguably misuse) of audits and various statistical performance metrics and league tables that privilege certain kinds of knowing and judgement—which ironically decontextualise and simplify the very things they seek to measure. The weakness of statistically produced forms of knowledge is that it distracts from understanding the more vital lived experience and discourages individuals from noticing how such audit quantifications are inevitably generative (Espeland & Sauder, 2007), which do in time shift priorities and values.

By way of example to reflect the severity of concern, recent findings of a leaked report based on a staff survey from one UK university were made public, reporting high levels of staff unhappiness disclosing that '[m]any complain of unhealthy workloads and unreasonable hours. Some report bullying, discrimination and harassment' (Deacon, 2020: n.pag). It was reported that some of the most negative responses concerned staff not being able to take proper breaks and feeling they could not do their job properly without 'regularly working unreasonable hours'—a situation which can only have been further exacerbated by the effects of the COVID-19 pandemic.

The case above does not seem an isolated experience by any means, which is further borne out in a recent research study that focuses on higher education staff members' perception of their working conditions, managerial practices and personal wellbeing. This project sought to build on the central premises of 'statactivist' approaches to knowledge development and activism to address what Lynch and Ivancheva (2015) describe as the failure of academics as individuals, and universities as corporate bodies, to challenge the spread of market values and new managerialism in higher education (Erickson et al., 2020). The research surveyed a total of 5,888 academic staff self-selected from 78 universities across the UK in 2017. The qualitative data collected reveal 'an acute situation of endemic bullying and harassment, chronic overwork, high levels of mental health problems, general health and wellbeing problems, and catastrophically high levels of demoralisation and dissatisfaction across the UK HE sector' and was grimly summed up by the report's authors that the sector is 'on the edge of potential disaster' (Erickson et al., 2020: 15).

The report identifies a range of issues such as the perception of misuse of student fees to embark on over-ambitious building works or 'vanity projects' leading to a lack of funding for more basic aspects of university functioning. For example, one participant suggested:

> Senior Management at my university is appalling. In order to support a vanity project at my university staff are put under unbearable pressure. SM are driving staff to resign, take voluntary severance, or seek other posts because there is no support for research, or to deliver good quality teaching (p. 11).

The report also states that senior management at universities appears to be imposing a system more akin to a dictatorship enforcing compliance rather than critique, as the following study's participant articulately stated:

> People keep disappearing in a most macabre way. It is like living through Stalin's purges. I think this university is going to have a severe problem recruiting given the way it treats its existing faculty (p. 12).

The same research report also finds that a toxic environment under this 'new management' ethos often results in a range of health and wellbeing issues for staff such as anxiety disorder (e.g. struggling to sleep and breathe), difficultly to 'switch off' from work due to modern working contexts and technologies, factors which have previously been identified by Sonnentag and Bayer (2005). In addition to the allocation of resources and change at work resulting in negative wellbeing impacts for staff, others in the same report highlighted how this 'links to the ever-increasing silencing of academics' (Erickson et al., 2020: 13).

Sadly, for most people working in higher education, none of the above would be the least bit surprising and does not actually need this research to illuminate the issues evidenced in their own lived experience. However, what the research usefully provides is a sense of scale and that academics might take some solace that these issues are not entirely peculiar to their institution alone. Clearly, there seems little external will being currently exerted, either by governments or universities themselves, to combat the systemic failures of the neoliberalist university system. This may, in part, be because the very drivers that have caused these calamities have in fact become so deeply engrained in popularist and political rhetoric that there seems no immediate way out. Yet if there is hope, it resides within the academy itself to take action and turn to new ways of appraising and conducting research, moving away from the clouding bias of performance metrics in attempting to provide a closer understanding of the lived experience therein. Understanding personal experience may indeed be more of an art than a science.

Finding Alternative Ways of Knowing

Part of the conundrum resides in the situation that education research has tended to privilege social science-based inquiry in an attempt to qualify and quantify 'data', yet as an educationalist myself, I know how difficult it is to pin down and measure knowledge and knowledge construction. The unease of not complying with a belief in being able to measure everything has shoehorned many educationalists into thinking that empirical research has to be accompanied by narrow definitions of data and that data be subjected to some type of statistical measurement in order to demonstrate validity. Whilst I do not wish to advocate that these approaches are not without merit for answering certain questions where this methodology might be appropriate, however, I wish to highlight the particular deficiency in applying this to creative acts and various types of knowing. Consequently, the positioning of art-based research to investigate questions of practice has tended to be marginalised in the field of education. Curiously this situation exists despite the poignant and influential writings of John Dewey in 1934 who considerably advanced educational thought from the twentieth century. Dewey clearly identified the benefits of artistic engagement and addressed the essential qualities of art. This is particularly evidenced in his highly distinguished book *Art as Experience* ([1934] 2004) in which he expressed the central idea that art functions as experience itself, which justifies the broadening in the understanding of 'empirical' to mean 'observable'. Indeed, the word 'empirical' comes directly from the Greek and Latin. The term derives from the Latin *empiricus,* which is derived from the Greek *empeirikos* ('experienced') and earlier to the verb *peiran,* meaning 'to try, attempt or experiment'.

Dewey places great value on the actual processes of inquiry: looking and finding meaning. He highly values the various components of artistry that involves hard to pin-down qualities such as intuition, impulse, invocation and spontaneity—all concepts valued in today's push to become 'innovative', 'clever', 'personalised' and progress the 'pace of change'. Some current commentators have gone so far as to claim that these trends present 'critical challenges for the sector but also tremendous opportunities for those who understand the changes under way and how to convert them into positive momentum for their institution' (Spies, 2019: n.pag). The idea of another way of knowing might seem complex and may even be new to some, yet in 1934 Dewey understood precisely that these are found in the entwined and embodied nature of meaning contained within the aesthetic medium:

> As long as 'meaning' is a matter of association and suggestion, it falls apart from the qualities of the sensuous medium and form is disturbed. Sense qualities are the carriers of meanings, not as vehicles carry goods but as a mother carries a baby when the baby is part of her own organism. Works of art, like words, are literally pregnant with meaning Dewey ([1934] 2005: 122–23).

In making these distinctions, Shaun McNiff (2018), arguably the father of art-based research, makes the position clear in how artistic research differs from other research methodologies. He also points to the current distortion of research approaches within the applied arts that have not served artists particularly well:

> The common tendency since the beginning of applied arts research has been to examine art-related questions and issues through the methods, concepts and languages of psychology and social science, resulting in the general use of art as 'data' or raw material for a very different academic discipline. Many assume that this is what we are doing when we talk about art-based research. I define art-based research as the use of artistic expression by the researcher, either alone or with others, as a primary mode of inquiry (p. xi).

The complexity within artistic research is a result of artists calling upon multiple ways of knowing which are embedded *in* and *through* practice. Broadening understanding within the academy to recognise that knowledge within artistic practice becomes embodied and highly connected to both the form and the artefact. *The result of artistic expression is the artefact.* Responding to artworks of any type can also be through the artistic mode and not exclusively through the written word. For example, a response to a painting might be through movement or a piece of music through drawing. There are many artforms that resist the reduction of practice to words. Even those artforms that do use words such as poetry, song or drama, words are chosen for particular aesthetic effect. McNiff (2018) pertinently asks:

> *If we advocate for art as a way of knowing that engages realms inaccessible to linear and logical thought, then why is it that we do not use it as a primary mode of inquiry when researching how the arts might enhance human experience?* (p. xi, original emphasis).

What we indeed learn from artistic research is that it does not need to be quantified or qualified according to data sets. Art does not need additional 'data' to prove itself—the *art* is what we use to provide evidence. Moreover, art is actually empirical as it is verifiable through observation and experience (Prior, 2020). Artistic research extends beyond theory or pure logic alone and takes us to feelings (key for mental health), through what we term 'aesthetics'. Art and art processes are felt and are entirely observable, and therefore undeniably researchable by nature. Mitchell Kossak (2012), an active art-based researcher in the area of expressive therapies, supports the view by asserting: 'in art-based research, the phenomenological experience is represented through the creative act itself' (p. 22). Dewey ([1934] 2005) summarises that the potential limits in aesthetics are determined experientially and by what the artists make of it in practice. He states that: 'the *medium* of expression is neither subjective nor objective but is an experience in which they are integrated in a *new* object' (p. 299, original emphasis).

By finding these alternative ways of knowing, we can shift the dialectic away from a metrics-based approach to one that is engaged more directly with the whole person and the creative self. We can allow for person-centred generative understanding to inform what we know. There is tremendous potential for student engagement in creative acts and the employment of art-based research can help realign education and offers a way of thoughtful knowing through creative practice.

Art Heals

McNiff (2004) advocates for art's traditional healing function as a force for transformation, contemplation and an opportunity for solace or communal participation in group work. This healing quality for the mind offers significant opportunity in contemporary higher education where we are witnessing growing concerns for both students and the staff within them.

Returning to antiquity as this chapter began, the therapeutic benefits of creative activity have a long history stemming from the Ancient world itself. I recall that whilst on a trip to Greece in 2008 to speak at a conference of drama educators, I took time to explore the country beyond Athens itself. Indeed, I was brought face-to-face with the origins of arts for health in Epidurus, and upon reflection of my experience wrote:

> I was reminded of the long-standing acknowledgement of the therapeutic value of the arts. The sanctuary of Asclepius at Epidaurus is a spiritual place visited by the ancient Greeks in order to pay tribute to Asclepius (the god of medicine and healing in ancient Greek mythology) and to ask the gods for remedies for their physical ailments. Epidaurus was built around the third century BC and it is adorned with a multitude of buildings, most famous of which is the ancient acoustic marvel the 'Theatre of Epidaurus'. Epidaurus was a healing centre as well as a cultural centre—the two purposes closely entwined in ancient times (Prior, 2010: 3).

Whilst standing in this ancient healing place I realised quite powerfully that these art-based healing traditions had an integrated function and that this was precisely why applying art forms to health offers great potential for wellbeing. However, over time the world lost sight of this vital connection, and chemical treatments for emotional and psychological states became de rigueur within health care. A disassociation between human activity and wellbeing became an accepted societal norm. However, since the early 2000s there has been growing academic and community reinterest in the use of art—all artforms—for health and wellbeing benefits. During this period, I founded the *Journal of Applied Arts and Health* with Intellect Publishers in 2010 in order to capture and evidence work within the field. Now in its second decade, the Journal has been committed to serving the greater arts in health community around the world, 'publishing some of the most ground-breaking research and indicators of what is happening in the field today' (Kossak, 2018: 3). Through the efforts of many like-minds, the profile has been raised internationally of the benefits of creative and expressive activity. Interest in this work was stirred at the highest levels of government with the House of Lords in the British Parliament instituting an All-Party Parliamentary Group inquiry on Arts, Health and Wellbeing (2017). The inquiry concluded that the arts play a vital aspect in the health and wellbeing of communities across the spectrum and that resources spent on art-based projects would help relieve pressure on the National Health Service (NHS) and build a more cohesive society.

I was invited to the House of Lords to be part of the advisory group to discuss implementation strategies of the report, and for my part was able to advise on the need for higher education to take a greater lead in developing programmes of study and to include increased awareness amongst educators, trainee physicians and healthcare workers. However, against this backdrop of positive activity, as mentioned earlier, we have witnessed growing social problems of increased isolation and loneliness as traditional notions of cohesive community breakdown in favour of pluralist, diverse and individualist ideologies. Arguably these conditions have been exponentially exacerbated with the rise in digital technology and the complex stressors this creates for people and the most vulnerable in society (Prior, 2018). Yamamoto and Kushin (2014) suggest that 'engaging in polarised online environments, or being the recipient of criticism could have negative effects on self-image as well as impeding actualisation of intrinsic and extrinsic awards' (p. 434). The online world that is now an embedded part of many peoples' existence, especially the young, and the many issues this raises, will continue to become something of an interest to researchers. What needs to be foremost in educators' minds is what we can do to harness the conditions under which we can improve students as whole beings and how we can counter the negative and isolating effects of technology. In short, we must realise that art heals.

Art-Based 'Togetherness' for Wellbeing

All of us can be creators of art (of all art forms) and use this as a vehicle for bringing people together—ideally in person, but otherwise via video conferencing where necessary. The context prompting the urgent need for 'togetherness' is the growing numbers of under-18s who are suffering from anxiety, depression, eating disorders and other conditions. In addition, tragically, more are self-harming and attempting suicide. School stress, social media, troubled family life and pressures to 'succeed' are among the key reasons behind this rise, popularly reported. Consequently, the UK's National Health Service (NHS) is struggling to cope with the growing increase in young people needing psychological and psychiatric support. Globally, mental health is also a priority for the health agenda (WHO, 2017). Staff and students of universities are not exempt from the growing mental health issues experienced across society and as illustrated above.

An example of a novel project my colleagues and I introduced into one UK university gives some insights into how the use of art can offer a mindful approach to addressing the stressors of personal and academic life and brings both staff and students together. The project aimed to demonstrate one way in which universities can take seriously the mental health of their staff and students and the role that art can play in providing plausible answers in realigning the culture of contemporary higher education. The intention of this project was to jointly pay attention to the wellbeing of staff and students. I have previously argued that we are far too focussed on behavioural well-doing with an array of political and social agendas and not sufficiently focussed on experiential wellbeing (Prior, 2018). The project focussed on offering preventative measures through the use of art to facilitate experiential opportunities for 'togetherness' (Prior, 2018) and the desire to realign higher education through acknowledging the fundamental importance of 'communitas'—defined as 'inspired fellowship' (Turner, 2012) to enable and enhance human, personal, spiritual and social wellbeing.

The title of the project was 'pARTicipate: take a break with art'. As an important aside, the project paused due to the lockdown measures first introduced to combat COVID-19 in March 2020. However, this initial reporting over the first several months of the project gives a sense of a proactive exemplar initiative suitable for higher education. The project piloted a weekly lunchtime series of art-led participative workshops using art as a vehicle for promoting mindful wellbeing. The workshops attracted small groups of up to 10 participants at a time and lasted around one hour each, taking place within several campus locations such as a communal meeting area and the main library at the University of Wolverhampton in the UK. The workshops were open to any person regardless of ability and were intended to explore the effect of using participative art-based activities in the promotion of mental wellbeing. All art materials were supplied free-of-charge to the participants, with the most popular media being paper, sharpies/markers and pastels. The modality of the art form is not as important as the thoughtful, purposeful way it responds to and works in tandem with the needs of the participants.

In researching this project, the key question was: 'What evidence emerges from a voluntary project using art-making for wellbeing amongst university staff and students?' The team principally employed an established art-based methodology where art itself provides the evidence (McNiff, 1998, 2013, 2018; Kossak, 2012; Prior, 2017, 2020) and was intended to be supported by reflective interviews from a sample of participants. Informal early responses by the participants were noted, such as:

This is relaxing.

I've got an assignment due, but this is clearing my mind.

I don't think I'm a good drawer, but I know I'm having fun.

I'm going to schedule my lunchbreak for this time each week...it's so therapeutic.

I like drawing with others. There's no competition but I like seeing what others do.

I'm so busy but this feels like time well-spent.

It's been years since I did any art...I've missed it...I feel good.

This is really de-stressing me. Thanks guys.

Enjoying the chats.

However, the strongest evidence of effectiveness is not in what people said but in what was *observable*, or in research terms, 'empirical'. The mindful focus and creative flow exhibited by the participants were entirely observable and represented in the creative works themselves (Fig. 1). The artworks allow for greater transparency of tacit knowledge—knowledge that is richly embedded by experience but not necessarily something readily communicable in words. My earlier research on actors and those who train them demonstrates that 'knowledge is generated through direct, personal and experientially derived meaning' (Prior, 2012: 193). This view values the importance of knowledge that is incrementally gained through the act of doing and being. The artworks hold true as the evidence of engagement and of the expression created in and through the artistic/expressive process. Overall, the initial results of the project indicate the positive effect on the participants in taking time out to create in mindful ways. Whilst this approach is certainly not new, what was novel is that we applied this to a higher education setting and brought staff and students together for mindful wellbeing.

Fig. 1 'pARTicipate: take a break with art' 2020

Conclusion

The chapter has reflected upon the situation of the past decade or more that has revealed an unhealthy preoccupation with measurement and performance rankings which has been pervasive amongst the neoliberalist higher education sector. Undeniably higher education has changed from places where pace could be slowed in order to consider, read in depth, research at a careful pace, spend unhurried time with colleagues or students and allow oneself to be fully immersed in scholarship and academic development. These once-valued conditions have given way to the fast pace of life propelled by digital technology and the commercialisation of universities. A toxic culture driven by measurement and ranking has shifted emphasis from what it is that academics do, to how well they measure-up against artificially derived determinants. The lived experience has become pressurised for both staff and students alike.

However, lived experience, feelings, creative endeavour and in fact 'being human' all resist numerical reduction. Those of us working in wellbeing and education see the steady deterioration of the mental health of those who work and study within it. Greater inclusivity of artistic/expressive opportunities for staff and students offers real potential to enhance the on-campus experience. By adopting creative research methodologies that resist narrow scientised definitions of 'evidence', the field has potential to move away from the dehumanising effects playing out across the higher education sector. Art-based inquiry, therefore, includes affective, sensory, creative, observational and intuitional ways of knowing. In addition, the use of experimentation, risk-taking, discovery and meaning-making are all important attributes to research through the process of making art and contemplating feelings. Armed with the knowledge of artistic research methodology, educators at all levels can meaningfully embed art-based activity and research processes into learning and teaching and thus give greater confidence in artistic research and its results. To these ends, this chapter offers hope in how creative activity might bring about essential change to combat a corporate hardening that has in recent times ruthlessly hijacked the love of learning and indeed the love of enabling others. Predominantly, 'good mental health is essential for students to achieve their potential' (Carter et al., 2017: 18).

To return to 423BC and Aristophanes' *The Clouds* (1973), it is pertinent to remember that the character of Strepsiades, who early in the play puts his own self-interest ahead of all else and his neighbours whom he owes considerable sums of money (and had promised to repay them) by seeking an education in order to argue his way out of repaying those debts. Then there is the son, Pheidippides, who armed with his newly found cleverness physically beats his father and argues that he is fully justified in his actions by all the laws, divine and human. What defence is there against the son who wants to beat his parents when using the same system of 'education'? If there is to be a healthier future in higher education, then maybe we need to learn from the truisms of antiquity and get our heads out of the clouds and reconsider our education systems. We certainly must pause, as the pandemic made us do, and re-evaluate our priorities for promoting greater mental wellbeing in happier and healthier places.

Acknowledgements The 'pARTicipate: take a break with art' project team comprised Dr. Jane Booth, Dr. Rich Hall, Dr. Metka Potocnik and led by Professor Ross W. Prior. The project was made possible through funding from the Arts Learning and Teaching Research (ALTR) group at the University of Wolverhampton, UK.

References

All-Party Parliamentary Group (APPG). (2017). *Creative health: The arts for health and wellbeing* (2nd ed.). All party parliamentary group, unpaginated. Accessed May 1, 2020. https://www.culturehealthandwellbeing.org.uk/appg-inquiry/

Aristophanes. (1973). *Lysistrata, The Acharnians, The Clouds* (A. Sommerstein, Trans.). Penguin Classics.

Carter, M., & Goldie, D. (2018). 'Potential enablers of mental health and wellness for those teaching in tertiary education'. *International Journal of Innovation, Creativity and Change,* special edition: 'Ways forward in mental health innovation, prevention and promotion: Voices from the field', 4:3, pp. 3–20. Available online at: https://www.ijicc.net/images/vol4iss3/Margaret-Anne_Carter_and_Donna_Goldie.pdf

Carter, M. A., Pagliano, P., Francis, A., & Thorne, M. (2017). 'Australian university students and mental health: Viewpoints from the literature'. *International Journal of Innovation, Creativity and Change*, 3:3 special edition: Mental health, pp. 1–25. Available online at: https://www.ijicc.net/images/vol3iss3/1CarterPaglianoFrancisThorne.pdf

Carter, M. A., & Goldie, D. (2017). Educational Media: Potential impacts on tertiary students. *International Journal of Innovation, Creativity and Change, 3*(3), 61–88.

Deacon, T. (2020). 'The worrying findings of a report that shows the depth of unhappiness of Cardiff University staff', WalesOnline. Accessed July 29, 2020. Available: https://www.walesonline.co.uk/news/education/cardiff-university-staff-working-unhappy-17972757

Dewey, J. ([1934] 2005). *Art as experience*. Penguin.

Erickson, M., Hanna, P., & Walker, C. (2020). 'The UK higher education senior management survey: A statactivist response to managerialist governance'. *Studies in Higher Education*. Taylor and Francis Online: January 14, 2020.

Espeland, W. N., & Sauder, M. (2007). Rankings and reactivity: How public measures recreate social worlds. *American Journal of Sociology, 113*(1), 1–40.

Foucault, M. (1978). *The history of sexuality, translated by R.* Penguin Books.

Freire, P. (1970). *Pedagogy of the oppressed*. Continuum.

Kossak, M. (2012). Art-based enquiry: It is what we do! *Journal of Applied Arts and Health, 3*(1), 21–29.

Kossak, M. (2018). Editorial. *Journal of Applied Arts and Health, 9*(1), 3–7.

Lynch, K., & Ivancheva, M. (2015). Academic freedom and the commercialisation of universities: A critical ethical analysis. *Ethics in Science and Environmental Politics, 15*(1), 71–85.

McNiff, S. (1998). *Art-based research*. Jessica Kingsley Publishers.

McNiff, S. (2004). *Arts heals: How creativity cures the soul*. Shambhala.

McNiff, S. (Ed.) (2013). *Art as research*. Intellect.

McNiff, S. (2018). 'Foreword'. In R. W. Prior (Ed.), *Using art as research in learning and teaching: Multidisciplinary approaches across the arts* (pp. xi–xv). Intellect.

Prior, R. W. (2010). Editorial. *Journal of Applied Arts and Health, 1*(1), 3–6.

Prior, R. W. (2012). *Teaching actors: Knowledge transfer in actor training*. Intellect/The University of Chicago Press.

Prior, R. W. (2017). 'Afterword: Confidence in art as evidence'. In N. Rowe, & M. Reason (Eds). *Applied practice: Evidence and impact in theatre, music and art* (pp. 262–67). Bloomsbury Methuen.

Prior, R. W. (2018). 'Art-led communitas for developing improved mental health in higher education in a time of rapid change'. *International Journal of Innovation, Creativity and Change,* special edition: 'Ways forward in mental health innovation, prevention and promotion: Voices from the field', 4:3, pp. 125–41. Available online at: https://www.ijicc.net/images/vol4iss3/Ross_W_Prior_et_al.pdf

Prior, R. W. (2020). 'Embedding art as a research methodology within educational processes'. In *INTED 2020 proceedings, 14th annual international technology, education and development conference* (pp. 534–40). INTED.

Smyth, J. (2017). *The toxic university: Zombie leadership, academic rock stars, and neoliberal ideology*. Palgrave Macmillan.

Sonnentag, S., & Bayer, U.-V. (2005). Switching off mentally: Predictors and consequences of psychological detachment from work during off-job time. *Journal of Occupational Health Psychology, 10*(4), 393–414.

Spies, M. (2019). 'What are the drivers and innovations shaping tomorrow's higher education landscape?' *FutureLearn* on July 10, 2019. Accessed July 16, 2020. Available from: https://www.futurelearn.com/info/research-insights/what-are-the-drivers-and-innovations-shaping-tomorrows-higher-education-landscape

Turner, E. (2012). *Communitas: The anthropology of collective joy*. Palgrave Macmillan.

WHO—World Health Organization. (2017). Depression and other common mental disorders: global health estimates, pp. 1–22. Available online at: http://apps.who.int/iris/bitstream/10665/254610/1/WHO-MSD-MER-2017.2-eng.pdf.

Yamamoto, M., & Kushin, M. J. (2014). More harm than good? Online media use and political disaffection among college students in the 2008 election. *Journal of Computer-Mediated Communication, 19*, 430–445.

Ross W. Prior isProfessor of Learning and Teaching in the Arts in Higher Education at the University of Wolverhampton, UK. He is the founding principal editor of the *Journal of Applied Arts and Health*, established in 2010 and published by Intellect. He is author of numerous publications including his books *Teaching Actors: Knowledge Transfer in Actor Training* and more recently, *Using Art as Research in Learning and Teaching: Multidisciplinary Approaches Across the Arts*. Professor Prior is a member of the Arts and Humanities Research Council [AHRC] Peer Review College, Fellow of the Royal Society for Public Health, Member of the Australian College of Educators, and in 2018 he was made Principal Fellow of the Higher Education Academy in recognition of his strategic influence in the sector.

Art, Truth and Beauty in the Classroom: Individual Creativity, Knowledge and the Natural Emergent Properties of a Self-organising System

Richard Hill

Abstract The existence of mental health issues in education, for both students and teachers, requires a response. This chapter explores the potential benefits of approaching education and learning from perspectives that seem outside the practical and pragmatic constructs of the current education system. The lenses of *art truth* and *beauty* are used to reveal how methods of teaching and learning can emerge that are individually and/or context driven. These incorporate subjective considerations including the art of creativity and the subjectivity of personal feeling of what is effective and what is not. The chapter looks at historic and current expressions of these qualities and then looks to the scientific basis, and especially the neuroscience, that underpins why these diversions from the generalised implementation of education towards a universally flexible and/or individually relevant process often proves to be more effective and successful.

Keywords Mental health · Creativity · Art · Truth and beauty

Introduction

Teaching in formal institutions is supported, protected and, in some ways, limited by the same parameters – it is necessary to provide an equivalent education for each student. Equivalence of education is established by: creating standard requirements; universal curriculums designed to achieve those standards; and maximum and minimum levels of prior education to qualify for higher study. Variations between students can then be monitored and calculated by various forms of testing, which include written exams, presentations and verbal Q&A. The theoretical principle is that this provides a level playing field for all involved. Equivalent standards, applied in an equivalent format, are intended to produce equivalent opportunities to all students. Is that true in practice? The answer lies in another question. Why do some students manage and yet others not only have difficulty, but also struggle with mental health

R. Hill (✉)
The Science of Psychotherapy, Brisbane, Australia
e-mail: richardhill@tpg.com.au

A. P. Francis and M. A. Carter (eds.), *Mental Health and Higher Education in Australia*,
https://doi.org/10.1007/978-981-16-8040-3_16

issues? Some of these issues may already exist, what some people call the "invisible disability" (Venville et al., 2016, p. 571), but can also be *because of* the education process (Ibrahim et al., 2013). Teachers, too, suffer mental health issues under the stresses and pressures of providing education (Lever et al., 2017).

Many of the difficulties lie in the lack of equivalence between the interacting components of an "education system". The most obvious variables are the human elements, both students and teachers. There are many other variables which include the educational institution, institutional policies, socioeconomic demands and career requirements and opportunities. Educators have been overtly addressing the issue of diversity in the student body for most of this century with particular motivation and focus on students with disabilities. The term "universal design learning" was the subject of the book by Rose et al. (2002) where they discussed numerous topics including the neuroscience of learner differences; how those differences could inform flexibility in curricula; how to utilise digital media; and determine appropriate goals and assessment for every student. Burgstahler and Cory (2008) edited a book that presented the perspectives of forty-one scholars, practitioners and students, describing the principles and practice of "universal design": "Instead of creating courses, services, information technology and physical spaces for the 'typical' student and then making modifications… This approach leads to educational products and environments… that address all aspects of diversity including disability" (p. ii).

It may be that various structures and programs based on the principles of universal design are becoming accepted in the mainstream, but the persistence of mental health problems, especially from stress and distress, that continue to be evident in response to education practices in both students and teachers, indicates that more has yet to be done. The title of this chapter proposes a fundamental orientation, or organisational context, that could lead to a shift in how educational programs and institutions are developed: "Art" represents a creative quality, what might be figuratively described as a "heartfelt" or emotionally satisfying criterion of evaluation; "Truth" represents the reliable information that forms a "knowledge base" that informs, inspires and catalyses creative activity; and "Beauty" represents an intrinsic quality that enables people to not only see that a program satisfies technical requirements, but also "looks" and "feels" right. These subjective qualities are, of course, difficult to include from the practical and pragmatic construct perspective of educational practice, but subjectivity is beginning to be seen, by some, as a reliable criterion.

Murray Gell-Mann, the noted astrophysicist, made remarks in relation to one of his famous equations during a TEDtalk in 2007, *Beauty and Truth in Physics*.

> The main thing I want to talk about is this: we have this remarkable experience in this field of fundamental physics that beauty is a very successful criterion for choosing the right theory. Why on earth can that be so? … I think there are laws out there and we, of course, don't understand them… but even if we don't come across them in our lifetimes… we can believe that there *is* one out there and we're just trying to get closer and closer to it.

In the context of that framework this chapter will seek to show how the qualities of art, truth and beauty can be successfully incorporated into educational programming and teaching. We begin with an exploration of how these elements have been utilised in the past. Then we will examine how and where science is able to back up the principles and then how this experience and knowledge can be, and has been, integrated to construct practical methods and protocols that are altering the shape of modern education systems.

Can We Learn from the Past?

There is a history of unorthodox teaching methods that have not only managed to enable students with disadvantages and personal difficulties to express their potential but have also helped the teachers as they struggle against the restrictions of standard forms of teaching. Many of these stories have been written about and even filmed as docu-dramas for cinema release.

Freedom Writers (DeVito, 2007) is a dramatisation of the experiences of teacher, Erin Gruwell. In 1994 she took up a teaching position at the Woodrow Wilson Classical High School in Long Beach, California. Students were bussed in from disadvantaged neighbourhoods. Gruwell floundered as she tried to find a way to connect with and engage the students. She did two things that transformed the students from people who were uncertain whether they would be shot in the streets, to students that embraced their future and, in the end, proved their academic abilities. She utilised art and truth when she asked them to write something about themselves, about their lives, hoping this might personalise their education. In an attempt to inspire, she assigned them the book *The Diary of a Young Girl* by Anne Frank (who perished during the *Holocaust*). Intuitively she sensed that the students needed to see something of struggle, oppression and danger outside of their own limited existence. This did have a positive effect and students began to write and submit their stories and, in doing so, found their identity which enables them to choose a better quality of life. From this personal breakthrough, all the students graduated and went on to college. Their stories were eventually published as a book, *The Freedom Writers Diary*, a title that was in recognition of the "Freedom Riders" who were civil rights activists in 1961 (Arsenault, 2006). This is not to say every teacher has to deal with drive-by shootings, drugs and poverty in the classroom, but it is an example of how a teacher needed to move well beyond the standard practices and be "artful" in order to release the potential of her students.

Even further back was the social and educational experiment in England known as *The Peckham Experiment* (Stallibrass, 1989). The main objective was an investigation into the nature of health. It ran from 1926–1950 in Peckham, South London, operating from the Pioneer Health Centre which was a purpose-built centre predominantly made of glass to maximise the ability to observe. The experimenters, principally doctors, observed families interacting in a social setting. The facility was allowed to operate as a self-organising system where the members of the community were not directed towards any outcomes. Although often described as an experiment in personal freedom, it was more oriented towards what would emerge when resources and facilities were readily available. Experimenters would respond to needs and interests, providing necessary resources as required. In some laboratory experiments with animals, this might be referred to as an *enriched environment*. A swimming pool was constructed in the middle of the building. The experimenters were interested in how people, who were not generally able to access swimming, would manage. Over time, swimming groups began to form with non-swimmers being taught by those who could swim. Surprisingly, some group "teachers" were young children and "students" were adults. The groups formed in response to need and capacity. Education operated in a similar fashion. Materials were supplied and people were attracted to what interested them. Over time, those trying to learn found they needed assistance or needed to expand their learning towards subjects that they would ordinarily have no interest in. Their degree of interest changed when they *needed* the learning to help them moved forward with the material that did interest them.

A surprising quality that emerged without interference, regulation or enforcement by the experimenters was the absence of interest in competition. Alison Stallibrass explains in her book (1989), *Being Me and Also Us: Lessons from the Peckham Experiment*, that,

> The Biologists were surprised at the Centre children's complete lack of competitiveness. Below the age of 13 or 14 they never organised competitions or races among themselves or asked anyone to do so for them. They seemed to have no desire to prove that they could do better than the next child or to compare their skill with that of others. Sometimes they played games that entailed winning or losing and to that extent they enjoyed competition with others but it was evident that their pleasure lay mainly in the acquisition of a skill to their own satisfaction or in solving a problem or meeting a challenge that they had chosen for themselves (p. 215).

Equally surprising was that,

> With very few exceptions, they did not seem to be subject to destructive or anti-social impulses (p. 212)

and

> At the Centre no instance of bullying was ever observed by any member of staff (p.214),

despite nearly 2000 families being watched almost continually over 15 years.

These examples, and especially the Peckham Experiment, indicate that although there are benefits in creating an *organised system* of education (or society), when given the opportunity and the appropriate circumstances it is possible for groups to allow the elements of the system to *self-organise* (another common term used is *create organically*) and achieve not only what is required of them, but also in a way that is satisfying and personally pleasing.

> At the Centre, it was observed that when a child had worked—sometimes every day for weeks—at mastering a particular skill, he would revel for a while in his newly acquired power and then move on to the mastery of something else, even if it meant changing his play-fellows. It appeared that between the age of five and eleven...choice of activity was more important to the children than choice of companions... the children ...were satisfying their own instinctive needs rather than emulating their elders (p. 203).

The question is whether there are lessons in those examples that can be applied to the larger educational experience, the broader population and the structural institutions. What is the opportunity and how do we create the appropriate circumstances for education to be an experience without the side effect of mental health issues for students and teachers?

How Does Science Inform Us?

Stress and anxiety are not, in themselves, terrible things to experience. It can be beneficial for drive and motivation, but the stress needs to be about something that can be resolved or overcome. Stress is actually a response to a demand, and it is the natural response for a short period, after which there is a natural recovery. This is how we avoid chronic problems. It is not necessarily the demand, but the ability to satisfy the demand before being overwhelmed or *dis*-stressed. Stress, or at least the demands that cause stress, can come from many sources: lower socioeconomic situations; violence in the home and/or community; being an "outsider", especially for those in minority or disadvantaged groups; being controlled or repressed by a rigid system; and prior mental health issues. Impossible pressures on time also create demand and stress: to have to work whilst studying; family obligations; multiple assignments due at the same time; and overwhelming exam timetables.

Neuroscience confirms that the brain's ability to process information is altered by the conditions of the inner and outer environment (McEwen & Gianaros, 2010). Daniel Siegel puts it simply—*where the attention goes, neural firing flows* (2018, p.19). Stress levels (Porcelli et al., 2008), state of health (Dantzer, 2004), sense of safety (Porges, 2011), environmental conditions (Schmidt, 2007), cultural stereotypes (Steele & Aronson, 1995) and other social systems such as poverty (Hanson et al., 2011), the economy (Fehr & Camerer, 2007) and political activity (Kato et al., 2009), can all impact on the way the brain functions. Even more damaging to the brain, in relation to learning, is the presence of physical threat and danger. The problem of bullying and the impacts of fearfulness due to dangers in the social environment are pervasive in modern life. Recent life stress has similar neurochemical effects as more severe trauma (Bevans et al., 2008) and chronic stress is known to affect brain plasticity and the activity of the hippocampus (Schwabe & Wollfe, 2009; Gilabert-Juan et al., 2016). Increases in stress hormones due to activation of the HPA axis affect the functionality of the polyvagal complex which can cause ongoing disruptions in the heart, lungs and digestive system (Guzmán et al. 2019; Porges, 2007).

The *Polyvagal Theory,* championed by Stephen Porges, establishes a connection between the mind, the brain and the body. The theory suggests that humans behave in a hierarchy of behaviours that are dependent upon the degree of perceived safety in the environment. When in a safe and unthreatening environment people "turn on" a socially engaged state of being that affects functions throughout the brain and body.

Most importantly, this socially engaged state has a direct impact on the nerves of the neck and face.

When socially engaged the face becomes more muscularly active around the cheek and jaw, the eyes, the vocal cords and, most importantly, the middle ear. When socially engaged, the stapedius muscle will tighten to attenuate the ear to the frequency of human speech. When the environment is believed to be dangerous the stapedius will not be activated, and the ear attenuates to the lower frequencies that are associated with potential predators moving and the deep sounds of growling.

When fearful, people will lose activity in the face muscles, diminish their capacity to hear speech, diminish their capacity to speak, heart-rate and breathing can speed up, the gut may shut down causing nausea and the muscles prepare for fight or flight. When the danger is perceived as overwhelming and/or life threatening, a third level takes over which sends the body into a state of collapse. This is a last resort to try and make a predator give up or reject what appears to be a corpse. At worst, it lifts the body's pain threshold so that succumbing to the predator will not be painful. In short, when there is a perception of danger the body begins to shut down expansive processes such as thinking, learning and social interaction and turns on more fundamental functions for the purpose of survival (Porges, 2001, 2011).

When we are overwhelmed with demands and chronically stressed, our whole biological system can become dysfunctional. Our brain is part of our biological system. Understanding how brains react on a day-to-day basis and how different areas of the brain are turned "on" and "off" during teaching and learning will help us understand how these processes can best be utilised in the practice of teaching and in the experience of learning.

Are We Responding to Current Research?

In response to the growth of neurobiological understandings and other breakthroughs in pedagogical research, the way in which education is delivered has developed radically over the past 2–3 decades (Garcia-Huidobro et al., 2017). Many of these developments in understanding and practice are not, however, universal and much continues to be experimental. Educator Sir Ken Robinson argues that the entire system has to be revolutionised for real change to occur (Robinson, 2011). Early education practice has been likened to systems used in factories:

> In the early 1900s, the challenge of providing mass education was seen by many as analogous to mass production in factories... Children were regarded as raw materials to be efficiently processed by technical workers (teachers) to reach the end product. (NRC, 2000, p.132)

Various alternative forms of education have found a place within the educational process. Montessori Schools began in the early 1900s which utilise a more tactile, student participatory teaching system. Research has shown that it can produce better academic and social results than standard elementary school students (Lillard & Else-Quest, 2006). The Hawn Foundation has developed a program, the *MindUp*

Program, which incorporates teaching neuroscience and utilising mindfulness practices to produce improved academic performance and greater personal development (Schonert-Reichl & Lawlor, 2010). *Whole Brain Teaching* seeks to incorporate a wide range of processes that stimulate various areas of the brain, especially the aspects of movement and gesture (University of Rochester, 2007).

These programs show that there are a number of strong advocates for change and development within education practices. The resistance to wide-ranging implementation of innovative methods of teaching that are based in modern theory and postulation is a complex question. It is, however, still apparent that there are a number of pressures, stresses and social difficulties that interfere with equally beneficial, universal education of young people. The answers have either not yet been found, not yet understood or not yet incorporated. Most likely it is a combination.

There is an international awareness and encouragement of thriving environments in education. Dr Karla Hylton (2017) writes in the *Jamaican Observer*,

> … as educators we need to consider methods of fostering or of improving a positive learning environment. In my almost two decades of teaching, I have come to recognise the value of the educational climate in deepening student learning. It is not just about the content we teach; other elements of teaching matter too.

London South Bank's new Pro-Vice Chancellor Shân Wareing wrote about her plans for the higher education program at University Business (Oakman, 2015).

> I like universities as communities where people cluster to think and learn, and collectively solve problems to improve the world. Changes in funding, policy, pedagogy, technology, employability and students' expectations could be seen as challenges but if instead you see strategic opportunities and the possibility of doing things better, it's a very exciting time for higher education… I'll be working… to integrate students' voices into course planning and design and other university decisions, increase work-related and work-based learning, and make sure courses are relevant, exciting and engaging, and that teaching is informed by research.

The Gallup organisation conducted an extensive survey (2017) to explore the conditions and principles of wellness in education. They considered five elements of wellbeing that applied to general living as well as education. It is surprising that it is necessary sometimes to conflate the activities of our lives into the scope of "living". We have a colloquial expression *work/life balance* which implies that "work" and "life" are somehow separate things. The word "life" is most likely meaning "personal life" and/or "family life", but these colloquialisms can readily become assumptions that embed in our implicit thinking: the idea that work—and it is easy for school to be swept up in this parameter—is something that we do in a different way to normal living. The complication is that in some ways there is a separation between "life" at work and "life" outside of work. Managers and teachers may sometimes wish that employees and students would just get on with the task without adding the complexity of their unique dispositions, needs and wants and personal issues, but that has an unpleasant echo of the horrendous work and education condition of the 1900s. That history is still a source of the socio-educational problems we are trying to now resolve. There are three especially relevant elements in the Gallup research:

wellbeing fundamentals; principles for avoiding burnout; and the top six experiences that improve higher education.

Fundamentals of wellbeing:

- Purpose: Liking what you do each day and being motivated to achieve your goals; engagement is your ability to create excitement for learning and development and for students, being aligned to their learning or major.
- Social: Having supportive relationships and love in your life, including strong relationships with classmates, faculty and staff.
- Financial: Managing your economic life to reduce stress and increase security including student loans, college tuition and financial aid and also your, or a parent's, ability to put food on the table, buy school supplies or keep their employment.
- Community: Liking where you live, feeling safe and having pride in your community, including pride in the campus or school and having a sense of belonging.
- Physical: Having good health and enough energy to get things done daily; nutritious meals, exercise, sufficient sleep and healthy mechanisms for dealing with stress.

In the context of these fundamentals the research determined that these principles were important to avoid burnout and to have a quality educational experience.

Principles to avoid burnout (education and business).

- Listen to work-related problems: Good leaders know employees as individuals, celebrate achievements, have performance conversations, conduct formal reviews and, above all, respect their employees.
- Encourage teamwork: Co-workers provide an essential line of emotional support for educators who are struggling; creating an environment where teamwork thrives, people help one another, and everyone has someone at work who is willing to listen.
- Make everyone's opinion count: Actively seek the opinions and ideas because when people believe their opinions are welcome and make a difference, they feel important and included, and they begin taking more responsibility for their performance. This gives people a feeling of control over their work—rather than feeling like work is something that happens to them.
- Make work purposeful: Educators are less inclined to want to work just for a paycheck and want to find meaning in what they do. Leaders must help people discover how their role and daily tasks contribute to fulfilling that meaning.

Six student experiences for better higher education.

1. My professors care about me as a person.
2. I have at least one professor who makes me excited about learning.
3. I have a mentor who encourages me to pursue my goals and dreams.
4. Having an internship or job that allows you to apply what you're learning in the classroom.

5. Working on a project that took a semester or more to complete.
6. Being active in extracurricular activities and organisations.

The value of the Gallup study is that they explore what people are thinking and feeling in order to gauge sentiment. It is, in some ways, helpful that many of the sentiments that emerged seem obvious and unremarkable. Discovering that a student has a better educational experience when they feel cared about or a teacher is less likely to burnout if their work has purpose are reminding us that the needs of students and teachers are not radical or surprising. That the educational systems have had difficulty satisfying these basic needs is more of a comment about the way education systems have been developed. Now, there is a call for universal approaches, innovative teaching techniques and radical shifts in the approach of administrators.

That opens the door for radical change in the ways academic performance is tested and measured. Formal exams where all students sit at a desk with a time limit to answer a set of questions have been increasingly expanded to include coursework, presentations, demonstrations and teacher assessments. Carnegie Mellon University in Pittsburgh, USA openly encourages a broad scope of testing students' knowledge (CMU, 2020). They emphasise that, "Learning takes place in students' heads where it is invisible to others. This means that learning must be assessed through performance: what students can *do* with their learning. Assessing students' performance can involve assessments that are formal or informal, high- or low-stakes, anonymous or public, individual or collective". Australian primary schools chose to implement a national testing program to assess literacy and numeracy, NAPLAN, which has received a wide spectrum of comment both for its benefits and deficits (Dulfer et al., 2012). Individual capacities to manage the examination format is one of the contentious issues. The degree to which it causes distress, anxiety and depression in some students is concerning (Rogers et al., 2016). The way in which the results affect future opportunities and administrative decisions is another (Rogers et al., 2018).

The quest is to have confidence that the battle between generalised and universal approaches is resolvable. One of the most encouraging theories comes from the studies on Positive Psychology. It gives us confidence that we are not doomed to suffer the damaging effects of this discord, but we can benefit when we engage in our natural capacity to find a way towards potential and possibility. Barbara Fredrickson examined the nature of positive emotions. She found that positive emotions generated an expansive state that she called "broaden and build", (Fredrickson, 2013). Broaden and Build theory posits that "experiences of positive emotions broaden people's momentary thought action repertoires, which in turn serves to improve their enduring personal resources, ranging from physical and intellectual resources to social and psychological resources". (Fredrickson, 2001, p. 218) The possibility of an individual to flourish is enhanced when in an environment of positive emotions such as joy, contentment, pride and love. Part of this positive process is to create an environment where the brain is more able to be attentive, more able to notice and more able to activate neural processes for memory and learning.

Implementation

The question of how to implement such individually relevant and self-organising systems into education practice is far from easy or obvious. There is still considerable philosophical argument about the purpose and required outcome of education that is provided by government. It is unquestioned that human beings arrive in the world with both the need to and the capacity to learn. We need to learn survival skills and a very complex set of social skills. Many other species are also not born with all the survival skills required. Orangutans, for example, require education to learn what might be thought of as basic survival skills including climbing and bed making (Preuschoft et al., 2021). Human beings have been learning the necessary skills for survival for millennia, but our modern education system goes well beyond just survival and social management. Many students wonder how or whether they will ever apply some of things they learn in school to their usual daily life. Others not only utilise what they learn but go on to discover more things that then get added to the learning repository.

The evidence provided here indicates that individualised, creative and elegant educational practices are usually engaged when the standard generalised practices are either unsuccessful or an entity is created that steps outside the conservative system, such as Montessori and Steiner, although they still have to comply in ways that satisfy government requirements. The employment market is also looking for people who can provide the services required to maintain business productivity. These "outcome needs" by entities that are seeking to benefit from an "educated person" provide both a personal pressure to achieve what is desired and a competitive drive to become educated within specific parameters. This is not to say that teachers and students do not have a degree of latitude to practice individualised education practices. The discussion now turns towards the flexibility that exists within specific institutions, which will, no doubt, vary.

The key is for changes in educational practices by the teacher and for the student to become mainstream. Changes can be seen, especially over the past decade (Garcia-Huidobro et al., 2017), and for change to become embedded, activity needs to persist. So, it is what is *done* in education, what is *persistently done* and what becomes embraced as "normal" and "unremarkable". This also applies to policies and attitudes of government and to employers. Ironically, all those seemingly fixed mindsets in institutional bodies require education in order to change.

Conclusion

It is, clearly, not easy, nor always practical, or organisationally convenient to implement approaches that incorporate the individual as the orienting context of curriculum development and classroom presentation. The individuality of "universal design" can be very hard to implement in large educational institutions. Individual needs can be disruptive when the primary purpose is to produce people whose education prepares them to meet the needs of the socioeconomic environment. On the other side of the pendulum swing, it is equally disruptive when the primary purpose of education is to only learn what is easy in order to enjoy a stress-free passage through school. The ideals of art, truth and beauty as an orienting lens for teaching and learning are not to create either experience devoid of the other, but to create something that integrates those things and more.

Individual creativity and utilisation of knowledge are ingredients of a complex system. Throughout this chapter numerous other elements, influences and conditions have been discussed. The rigid implementation of linear mechanisms in order to achieve pre-determined goals is known to be a problem that causes difficulty for teachers and students alike. Sweetening linear programs with things that are deemed as more satisfying is also not the answer. Different approaches are required if we wish to continue to produce novel, more effective, educational formats. The elements of the system need to be allowed to interact and we need to have confidence that the outcome will be a movement towards a positive and productively integrated system. The key to such blind trust is to have confidence that a positive outcome will emerge from a system that is given the opportunity and the appropriate circumstances. Is our excessive reliance on predictive cognitive rationality the quality that restricts our ability to see the beauty, as Gell-Mann describes? I suggest that the principle of "art, truth and beauty" is a naturalistic foundation from which to create "appropriate circumstances" because it is founded not in our obligation or our sense of service, but in the "opportunity" to discover things that are not yet known which is, surely, the essential basis of education.

References

Arsenault, R. (2006). *The freedom riders: 1961 and the struggle for racial justice*. Oxford University Press.

Bevans, K., Cerbone, A., & Overstreet, S. (2008). Relations between recurrent trauma exposure and recent life stress and salivary cortisol among children. *Development and psychopathology, 20*(1), 257–272. https://doi.org/10.1017/S0954579408000126

Burgstahler, S. E. & Cory, R. C. (Eds). (2008). *Universal design in higher education: From principles to practice*. Harvard Education Press.

CMU, (2020). *How to assess student's learning and performance. Eberly Centre—Teaching excellence and educational innovation. Carnegie Mellon University*, online. https://www.cmu.edu/teaching/assessment/assesslearning/index.html. September 2020.

Dantzer, R. (2004). Cytokine-induced sickness behaviour: A neuroimmune response to activation of innate immunity. *European Journal of Pharmacology, 500*(1–3), 399–411.

DeVito, D. (producer), LaGravenese, R. (director). (2007). *Freedom writers* [Motion Picture] Paramount Pictures.

Dulfer, N., Polesel, J., & Rice, S. (2012). The *Experience of education: The impacts of high stakes testing on school students and their families*. An Educator's Perspective (The effectiveness of the National Assessment Program—Literacy and Numeracy, Submission 26—Attachment 1), The Whitlam Institute, University of Western Sydney. Retrieved from: https://www.aph.gov.au/DocumentStore.ashx?id=214ba798-d9ff-4352-af6a-f698cfc7c082&subId=11560. September 2020.

Fehr, E., & Camerer, C. F. (2007). Social neuroeconomics: The neural circuitry of social preferences. *Trends in Cognitive Science, 11*, 419–427.

Fredrickson B. L. (2001). The role of positive emotions in positive psychology. The broaden-and-build theory of positive emotions. *The American psychologist*, *56*(3), 218–226. https://doi.org/10.1037//0003-066x.56.3.218

Fredrickson, B. (2013). Chapter one—Positive emotions broaden and build. *Advances in Experimental Social Psychology, 47*, 1–53.

Gallup. (2017). *Education survey (USA)—How to improve wellbeing in education.* Retrieved from: https://www.gallup.com/education/316709/how-to-improve-wellbeing-in-education.aspx. September 2020.

Garcia-Huidobro, J., Nannemann, A., Bacon, C., & Thompson, K. (2017). Evolution in educational change: A literature review of the historical core of the Journal of Educational Change. *Journal of Educational Change, 18*(3), 263–293. https://doi.org/10.1007/s10833-017-9298-8

Gell-Mann, M. (2007) Beauty and truth in physics. *TEDtalks* online. https://www.ted.com/talks/murray_gell_mann_beauty_truth_and_physics

Gilabert-Juan, J., Bueno-Fernandez, C., Castillo-Gomez, E., & Nacher, J. (2016). Reduced interneuronal dendritic arborization in CA1 but not in CA3 region of mice subjected to chronic mild stress. *Brain and behavior, 7*(2), e00534. https://doi.org/10.1002/brb3.534

Guzmán, A., Jaime, V., Beatriz, R., Pedro, M., & Ángel, M. M. (2019). The relationship between heart rate variability and electroencephalography functional connectivity variability is associated with cognitive flexibility. *Frontiers in Human Neuroscience, 13*, 64. https://doi.org/10.3389/fnhum.2019.00064

Hylton, K. (2017). How to build a thriving classroom environment. *Jamaica Observer*, online issue, August 27, 2017. http://www.jamaicaobserver.com/career-education/how-to-build-a-thriving-classroom-environment_108986, September 2020.

Ibrahim, A. K., Kelly, S. J., Adams, C. E., & Glazebrook, C. (2013). A systematic review of studies of depression prevalence in university students. *Journal of Psychiatric Research, 47*(3), 391–400. https://doi.org/10.1016/j.jpsychires.2012.11.015

Kato, J., Ide, H., Kabashima, I., Kadota, H., Takano, K., & Kansaku, K. (2009). Neural correlates of attitude change following positive and negative advertisements. *Frontiers in Behavioral Neuroscience, 3*(6), 1–13.

Lever, N., Mathis, E., & Mayworm, A. (2017). school mental health is not just for students: Why Teacher and school staff wellness matters. *Report on Emotional & Behavioral Disorders in Youth, 17*(1), 6–12.

Lillard, A., & Else-Quest, N. (2006). The early years: Evaluating Montessori education. *Science, 313*, 1893–1894.

McEwen, B. S., & Gianaros, P. J. (2010). Central role of the brain in stress and adaptation: Links to socioeconomic status, health, and disease. *Annals of the New York Academy of Sciences, 1186*, 190–222. https://doi.org/10.1111/j.1749-6632.2009.05331.x

NRC (National Research Council), (2000). *How people learn: Brain, mind, experience and school.* National Academy Press.

Oakman, H. (2015). Creating a thriving learning environment. *University Business News*, online April 24, 2015. https://universitybusiness.co.uk/news/creating-a-thriving-learning-environment/, September 2020.

Porcelli, A. J., Cruz, D., Wenberg, K., Patterson, M. D., Biswal, B. B., & Rypma, B. (2008). The effects of acute stress on human prefrontal working memory systems. *Physiology & Behavior, 95*(3), 282–289.

Porges, S. W. (2007). The polyvagal perspective. *Biological Psychology, 74*, 116–143.

Porges, S. W. (2011). *The polyvagal theory: Neurophysiological foundations of emotions attachment communication self-regulation.* Norton.

Preuschoft, S., Yassir, I., Putri, A. I., Aoliya, N., Yuliani, E., Badriyah, S. N., Corbi, P., Sugianto, Y., Sitepu, B. S., Mukhlisi; & Kalcher-Sommersguter, E. (2021). Learning to be an Orangutan—Implications of life history for Orangutan Rehabilitation. *Animals, 11*(3), 767. https://doi.org/10.3390/ani11030767

Robinson, K. (2011) Out of our minds: Learning to be creative. Presented at *Learning Without Frontiers*, Recorded March 16, 2011. Retrieved from http://www.youtube.com/watch?v=9X0CESnGQ8U&feature=related. May 2020.

Rogers, S. L., Barblett, L., & Robinson, K. (2016). Investigating the impact of NAPLAN on student, parent and teacher emotional distress in independent schools. *The Australian Educational Researcher, 43*(3), 327–343.

Rogers, S. L., Barblett, L., & Robinson, K. (2018). Parent and teacher perceptions of NAPLAN in a sample of Independent schools in Western Australia. *Australian Educactional Researcher, 45*, 493–513. https://doi.org/10.1007/s13384-018-0270-2

Rose, D., Meyer, A., Strangman, N., & Rappolt, G. (2002). *Teaching every student in the digital age: Universal design for learning*. Association for Supervision and Curriculum Development.

Schmidt, C. W. (2007). Environmental connections: A deeper look into mental illness. *Environmental Health Perspectives, 115*(8), A404–A410.

Schonert-Reichl, K. A., & Lawlor, M. S. (2010). The effects of a mindfulness-based education program on pre- and early adolescents' well-being and social and emotional competence. *Mindfulness, 1*(3), 137–151.

Schwabe, L., & Wolf, O. T. (2009). Stress prompts habit behavior in humans. *The Journal of neuroscience : the official journal of the Society for Neuroscience, 29*(22), 7191–7198. https://doi.org/10.1523/JNEUROSCI.0979-09.2009

Siegel, D. J. (2018). *Aware: The science and practice of presence—The groundbreaking meditation practice*. Tarcher-Perigee

Stallibrass, A. (1989). Being me and also us: Lessons from the Peckham Experiment. Scottish Academic Press

Steele, C. M., & Aronson, J. (1995). Stereotype threat and the intellectual test performance of African Americans. *Journal of Personality and Social Psychology, 69*(5), 797–811.

University of Rochester. (2007). Hand gestures dramatically improve learning. *Science Daily*. Retrieved October 25, 2011, from http://www.sciencedaily.com/releases/2007/07/070725105957.htm

Venville, A., Mealings, M., Ennals, P., Oates, J., Fossey, E., Douglas, J., & Bigby, C. (2016). Supporting students with invisible disabilities: A scoping review of postsecondary education for students with mental illness or an acquired brain injury. *International Journal of Disability, Development and Education, 63*(6), 571–592. https://doi.org/10.1080/1034912X.2016.1153050

Richard Hill presents internationally on the topics of human dynamics, communications, the brain and the mind, and his specialty: Curiosity & Possibility. His work with the eminent Ernest Rossi, PhD, has led to the publication of *The Practitioner's Guide to Mirroring Hands*, which is a complete approach to therapeutic practice. He is currently Education Director of *The Science of Psychotherapy*, Managing Editor of *The Science of Psychotherapy* monthly magazine, Science Director for CIPPS in Salerno, Italy, and Director of the *Mindscience Institute*. His other books include, *Choose Hope* and *How the 'real world' Is Driving Us Crazy!* as well as numerous articles, journal papers and book chapters. www.richardhill.com.au

Australian International Border Closures: Impact on International Student Well-Being

Venkat Pulla, Elizabeth Carter, and Abraham Francis

Abstract This chapter is an exploration of some of the issues that interface international students studying in Australian institutions. From the advent of COVID-19, the corresponding author raised concerns and responded to the critical issues that overwhelmed the international student community that entered a week before the Australian international border closures. The chapter also utilises the debate that ensued amongst the academic commentators around the impacts of border closure restrictions and the response of the Australian universities, the federal and the state governments, and the larger Australian society. The COVID-19 pandemic resulted in major issues not only for academic institutions but also for international students who needed to adapt to border closures, loss of jobs and income to pay bills, lockdown rules and for many an overnight shift to distance education, something for which they need not have to come into Australia.

Keywords International students in Australia · COVID-19 · ESOS Act Australia

Introduction

International students have provided $18.5 billion funds in the last five years alone, and universities in Australia use such funds for recruiting teaching and support personnel, research funding and expansion of infrastructure. On 1 February 2020, when COVID-19 travel restrictions were declared for travellers a bulk of Australian students that come from China obviously couldn't arrive on Australian shores. The effect began to be felt by student visa holders and the higher education providers in Australia. The few that arrived a week before from India, China and other countries

V. Pulla (✉)
Senior Research Fellow, (Adjunct) ILWS, Charles Sturt University, Wagga Wagga, Australia

E. Carter
Research Associate, Brisbane Institute of Strengths Based Practice, Brisbane, Australia

A. Francis
James Cook University, Townsville, Australia
e-mail: Abraham.framcis@jcu.edu.au

A. P. Francis and M. A. Carter (eds.), *Mental Health and Higher Education in Australia*,
https://doi.org/10.1007/978-981-16-8040-3_17

were literally inducted into a shock during the very popular 'orientation weeks' across all universities. There were to be no classroom-based teaching anymore, something that the international student was unprepared for and did not come to Australia for. Their narratives expressed sadness and helplessness/frustration. We offer a critique of the response by the universities and the government in relation to mitigating the concerns of the new arrivals that landed onshore prior to closure of borders due to COVID-19 and briefly narrate the larger community response and its rescuing efforts for the new entrants.

These students lacked the local family and social security support that domestic students have. It puts them in a particularly vulnerable position as large segments of the labour market collapse (Maley, 2020). There were some who believed that if international students and temporary workers were left high and dry, word would quickly spread through their personal networks about how Australia treated them when the financial crisis hit. As a result, people may be discouraged from studying or working here in future. And this could be especially damaging in higher education, where Australia could attract the best and brightest of the international market for a few years if it plays its cards right: people who, seeing how poorly the coronavirus has been handled in Europe, the UK and the USA, would prefer to come to a country that has its act together (Maley, 2020).

It was clear that in the early days of the COVID-19 crisis that if international students were forced to return home or were unable to pay their tuition, that it would most likely trigger a broader higher education sector crisis. At best, thousands of higher education employees will be laid off. At worst, many universities will require government assistance to survive. Critics understood that we have a duty of care as a nation (Norton, 2020; Pulla, 2020a, 2020b). Referring to Indian students, who comprise the second-largest student cohort in Australian universities, the principal author, a higher education commentator, wrote that the Prime Minister of Australia has a responsibility to these students:

> Many international students enrolled into our postgraduate courses scrupulously study our manpower forecasts for the future of Australia. Many of them have genuine desire to make Australia their home in future using ethical and legal means. These are skilled here as per our systems, and it would be a shame if they must return to their countries on charity flights provided by the Indian High Commission. Mr. Prime Minister, we appreciate what you do with our citizens. But it is also the time for you to tell the universities that the fat accrued from these 'cash cows'- at least some of it be returned to the bleeding cows- Time for you to ask universities to pitch in. (Pulla, 2020a, 2020b)

On 4th April 2020, the federal government issued a summary about the international students during the COVID-19 disruption. This sent a distressing message that international students and other temporary visa holders can return to their home countries if they were unable to support themselves. Many international students couldn't return to their home countries due to border closures and had signed rental contracts in Australia. In March and April 2020, universities were considering different options, including offering hotel quarantine in a couple of countries, before bringing back non-COVID—uncompromised Chinese students into Australia (Pulla, 2020a, 2020b).

However, in April 2020, we saw the second largest group, of Indian origin, a great majority of them that come from middle-income households in India not comparable to lower-income Australian taxation bracket, beginning their struggle in Australia. Many students arrive on the Australian shores after borrowing money from banks, extended family and money lenders. In addition, there are dubious recruitment agents in many countries world that allude to international students about part-time job opportunities in a range of occupations in Australia. Prospective students put much faith in this misinformation and unfortunately land themselves into serious difficulties to supplement their living here let alone pay for full tuition in Australia or do remittances for the borrowed money (Pulla, 2020a, 2020b).

International students working in nursing and aged care have had their 40-h-per-fortnight work limit lifted since May 2020, as have students working in supermarkets. More than 40% of international students who have been in Australia for less than a year report wages as their primary source of income. As they stay longer, the proportion of them who rely on wages rises (Norton, 2020).

Why Do International Students Study in Australia?

It is important to understand why Australia seems to be attracting overseas students. Often this question is raised on campus and off campus here in Australia and overseas. The sentiment utilised in recruitment and marketing of international students is that Australia can boast of high-quality academic programmes in most areas including research focus. There are also some limited opportunities where students may be able to apply for scholarships to assist with their study. Students can work part-time while studying and can apply for a post-study work visa to stay and work after graduation. The spouse/partner of the student may be able to work full time. Often there are postgraduate programmes that can assist them to gain permanent residency. The cultural diversity within the nation is also advertised a lot. Most students come from China, India, Nepal, Philippines, South and East Asia, East Africa and some Latin American countries. The Department of Home Affairs, which handles immigration in Australia, has less complicated access to student visas than in some other countries that take international students. The outdoors, the vast countryside, the quality of life that comes with it and even the laid-back attitude are not spared in the advertising.

Literature Review

Australian legislation has long recognised the insecurity of overseas students, Education Services for Overseas Students Act 2000 (the ESOS Act). The pandemic has produced many difficulties for these students, including casual job losses and economic hardships. Anecdotally, it appeared that the overnight switch to distance education mode for which academia and the students were unprepared was also unwelcome and many international students coming from south Asian countries students were resentful as they did not come overseas to receive distance education.

According to the International Education Association in Australia (IEAA), up until the end of 2019 education was Australia's fourth-largest export and was a significant contributor to economic growth (IEAA, 2019). Australia has promoted itself as a leader in providing education to overseas students. Offering students an experience that includes living in a multicultural society, a large choice of subjects in top-rated institutions, cities that are affordable and provide job opportunities, and opportunities to work in Australia once they have finished their study (Austrade, 2018). As a result, international student numbers have been increasing every year, with a large percentage of those students enrolling in our universities and vocational education and training (VET) sector (Dept. of Education and Training, 2018a).

The education industry found itself in trouble with the appearance of COVID-19 in 2020 as it resulted in border closures that restricted the movement of international students, leading to decreasing numbers of fee-paying international students. During this time, the Australian government also decided to change the fee structure for domestic students which has also impacted the university sectors income. Although this change does not alter the fees international students pay, it is important to understand that it may reduce university resources and have an impact on the international student experience of studying in Australia.

While studying in Australia, international students are protected by the Education Services for Overseas Students 2000 ESOS Act, ensuring that they are provided a high standard of education, facilities and support services (Dept. of Education and Training, 2018b). The ESOS Act recognises that for international students' studying in a foreign country can present many challenges and have an impact on their study. Standard six of the ESOS Act states that educational institutions must provide support services to assist the student to meet learning goals and maintain satisfactory progress in their chosen course (Dept. of Education and Training, 2018b). The ESOS Act states that support services should meet the specific needs of international students; the question is if institutions are not meeting these needs why are they not being held accountable for this? Brydon and Liddell (2012) have concluded that education has now been conceptualised as an export industry, both government and educational institutions see international students as consumers and a revenue source rather than individuals who require support to complete courses. COVID-19 highlighted the problem with this approach as international students found themselves unsupported and unable to find work when the borders closed, and jobs disappeared because of COVID-19 lockdowns. This leads to a question: Do international students think if Australia is still a safe and secure place to study? This chapter examines the challenges international students face when studying in Australia and explores the institutional response to these challenges.

The Cash Cow Phenomenon

In Australia, international students are referred to as 'cash cows'. They account for slightly more than a quarter of all students on Australian university campuses. No one can deny that international students bring in billions of dollars to Australia's universities. In Queensland, for instance, students from China, India, Brazil, South Korea and Taiwan are seen in large proportions. Visa grants for Indian students increased to 42% in 2017–2018 and a further 35% in 2018–2019. In 2018, 38.3% (152,591) of students were from China, 18.0% (71,857) were from India, with Nepal coming in third, followed by other Asian countries (Pulla, 2020a, 2020b).

In Australia, international student's fees bolster university revenue and significantly contribute to the local community (Martin, 2020). During the pandemic, it became obvious that the government was not going to protect one of Australia's largest export industries (IEAA, 2019). Universities were blocked from getting JobKeeper, which was designed to assist employers to keep workers, leading to mass layoffs in the university sector (Ross, 2020a, 2020b; Karp, 2020). Students that were stranded in Australia struggled financially without income from casual work and were excluded from federal safety nets (Norton, 2020).

The government treated international students as a commodity, 'cash cows' (ABC, 2020) prioritising profits over their needs, which became glaringly obvious when the Australian prime minister told international students who could not support themselves to return home. The criticism has been that the students are welcome when it is advantageous to Australia's economy but when a crisis hits a clear signal has been given that they are unwelcome at this time. It is necessary for the federal government recognises the important role international students play in the Australian economy, not only student fees and funding our educational institutions, but also taxes, and as consumers of goods and services (McCauley & Chung, 2020; Gibson & Moran, 2020; Ross, 2020a, 2020b).

International students have invested a lot of their own personal resources to study in Australia with the assurance that Australia offered students a safe and high-quality education experience so the governments' response telling students to go home and locking them out of the federal governments COVID-19 response was a shock to the students but we are sure even the educational institutions to which we belong were in a shock as well. On top of this, assistance provided by the state governments and universities for international students was poorly advertised and difficult to access (Decobert & Lamb, 2020).

For many international students, Australia has become home, with years of study, graduation close and the promise of being able to apply for citizenship only a couple of years away leaving would mean lives that they have built here, invested in and worked hard for will be lost (Olmos, 2020). COVID-19 and the lockdowns resulted in increased stress and an increase in mental health issues for international students (Olmos, 2020). The move to online teaching during lockdown made continuing with studies difficult or impossible as many international students did not have access to computers or reliable internet services where they were in lockdown, and they seem to rely on saying that many international students only use university computers and Internet (Decobert & Lamb, 2020). During the early days of the pandemic, the following questions were looming large without any seriously deliberated answers:

- Would students be refunded fees paid upfront?
- Will visas be extended?
- Was any forecasting undertaken of the impacts on life and education for international students?
- What would happen to those students who had no means to return home as many borders closing and the cost of and lack of flights home?
- Were students' overseas family's financial distresses ever part of consideration?
- What would happen to the students that couldn't go from here to at all as countries from where they came were in deeper pandemic conditions?

Many international students found themselves isolated in small one-roomed accommodation during the lockdown which added to mental health problems and many students were unaware of increased counselling services being provided by universities or they were concerned about the stigma of accessing such services (Decobert & Lamb, 2020).

The international border closing in March 2020 and COVID-19 restrictions blocking travel resulted in a reduction of international students which has led to funding shortfalls for universities impacting higher education jobs. COVID-19 has resulted in universities shedding thousands of jobs. Australian stimulus packages did not protect higher education jobs or the university sector as the system is considered publicly funded. This along with recent government reforms to funding domestic students has the higher education industry concerned over how this reduction in resources is going to impact the sector and how they will continue to provide quality education and services for all students.

It is expected that there will be an increase in university enrolments because of COVID-19 as school leavers are unable to find employment and due to older Australians needing to retrain to find a new job. The reforms to higher education funding announced in 2020 are not expected to impact international student fees. The government has decided to discount fees, for domestic students, to degrees that have been identified as those that will be in demand in future. The restructure will result in some degrees costing more for domestic students but overall government contributions per enrolment have decreased, leaving universities worse off. A plus for domestic students studying stem degrees but the result is increased fees for humanities students. Some thought is that this will have little impact on student choices. As the ability to defer fees reduces the need to pay now, so students may choose by what they are interested in or what will lead to a higher paying job on completion. According to a Melbourne University discussion paper

> The deteriorating economic circumstances in most countries and growing unemployment affect decisions about what to study and whether it will provide financial benefit and employment security in the future. (While recession often means that study is an attractive option for those unemployed or underemployed, it also means students are more likely to select

courses perceived to lead to professional entry or to enhance their employment prospects. (Croucher, & Locke, 2020).

The Melbourne discussion paper also suggests that the international student market may recover somewhat, but only slowly, and that the incentive to study abroad will be greatly reduced due to perceived risks. This will most likely have the greatest impact on laboratory and practice-based disciplines, which have a high proportion of international students. The impact could be especially severe for business and commerce disciplines, which have the most international students and are typically in the higher-margin range of offerings (Croucher & Locke, 2020).

There is concern that reducing university funding will put Australia's reputation for high-quality teaching and innovative research at risk. It follows that if universities have reduced income that can only lead to a reduction in resources to teach and to continue quality research. Putting Australia's leading academic programmes at risk. Reduced funding will incentivise increased class sizes, move to non-individualised teaching strategies and cost-cutting for practical components of courses. Resulting in lower quality degrees. It may also result in the cancellation of courses, intakes for courses underfunded or with low enrolment numbers. It has the potential to leave students without a university place. Decreased funding will see universities cut back on non-core areas, such as student support. This is a concern because student support is an important aspect in helping international students have a positive educational experience. In the final analysis, all Australian higher education organisations have been adversely affected by the COVID-19 pandemic and in some cases resulting in changes to fee structures for domestic students. Even though this does not affect international students directly, indirectly there is concern that it will reduce resources available to international students.

Marketing Australia Higher Education

To market Australian education services, the government and universities promote the fact that they are amongst the top universities and vocational education and training providers in the world. To maintain this standard, it would follow that they should support international students in reaching their learning goals through the provision of services that meet the needs of the student (Austrade, 2018; Brydon & Liddell, 2012).

Absence of Specialist Supports

International students pay much higher fees than the domestic students, but it has been observed that many institutions have not put a priority on catering for this cohort. Unfortunately, many institutions have not designed specialist supports, but expect international students to use services that were designed for and staffed by those trained to support domestic students (Brydon & Liddell, 2012). Brydon and Liddell (2012) believe that if institutions are to succeed at creating a sort after product, they need to strengthen a student's ability to succeed by the internationalisation of curriculum and support services. Internationalisation involves adapting curriculum and services that cater for and support the needs of international students. These adaptions should be the result of careful consideration of the research involving this cohort. One of the ways that universities and vocational education and training providers can gauge if student supports are successful in meeting the needs of students is by monitoring the retention rate of students, recruitment of international students is only the first step but making sure they are able to complete their studies successfully should be the institutions goal (Brydon & Liddell, 2012).

Poor Transitioning

One of the main issues that can impact many areas of a student's daily life and contribute to poor transitioning is mental health problems. It has been identified that there is an increase in mental health problems for young people in Australia with a greater prevalence in students at university and in particular international students (Kambouropoulos, 2014; Forbes-Mewett & Sawyer, 2016). Studies have shown that the peak period for the onset of mental health problems is between 12 and 25 years of age, this not only affects domestic but also international students who are also facing many challenges without traditional supports (Huixian et al., 2014). For international students' cultural integration and academic pressures can increase the possibility of mental health problems at a time when a young person is trying to establish a sense of identity and direction (Forbes-Mewett & Sawyer, 2016). Unfortunately, many students are reluctant to seek help and studies have identified several reasons for their reluctance. In many countries, mental health treatment and counselling is an underdeveloped service so mental health problems go undiagnosed or untreated (Pham & Tran, 2015). A reluctance to access professional mental help could be a result of cultural practices and traditional beliefs—shame and negative attitudes to needing professional help (Pham & Tran, 2015). Students may also fail to disclose existing psychiatric disorders due to visa requirements and a belief that it will mean that they will not be able to obtain a visa or permanent residency after study completion as they believe they may not be able to meet Australia's health requirements (Forbes-Mewett & Sawyer, 2016).

Poor Mental Health

The quality of the international education experience being provided should be of importance to universities (Brydon & Liddell, 2012). The period of transition requires supports. It is important that students should be assisted in their adjustment to these new circumstances and institutions should provide conditions for successful transition as it is critical to a student's general well-being and academic success (Roberts and Dunsworth, 2012; Forbes-Mewett & Sawyer, 2016). For many international students, transition issues generally occurred in the first 12 months of study (Kambouropoulos, 2014) and admitting students to education system without appropriate support may result in these issues impacting on a student's ability to cope with the many changes occurring for them (Khawaja & Stallman, 2011; Roberts & Dunworth, 2012). Prerequisite skills, support structures, role models and cultural capital are essential for success when studying. Studies have shown that it is not uncommon that individuals to enter higher education without the skills and resources to successfully navigate through their study requirements and to transition to a new country (Hoyne & McNaught, 2013). This lack of skills and resources can lead to many issues that international students experience when transitioning to academic study in a new country (Kambouropoulos, 2014; Khawaja & Stallman, 2011; Forbes-Mewett & Sawyer, 2016; Huixian et al., 2014). The following diagram created by the authors summarises several findings from the above studies.

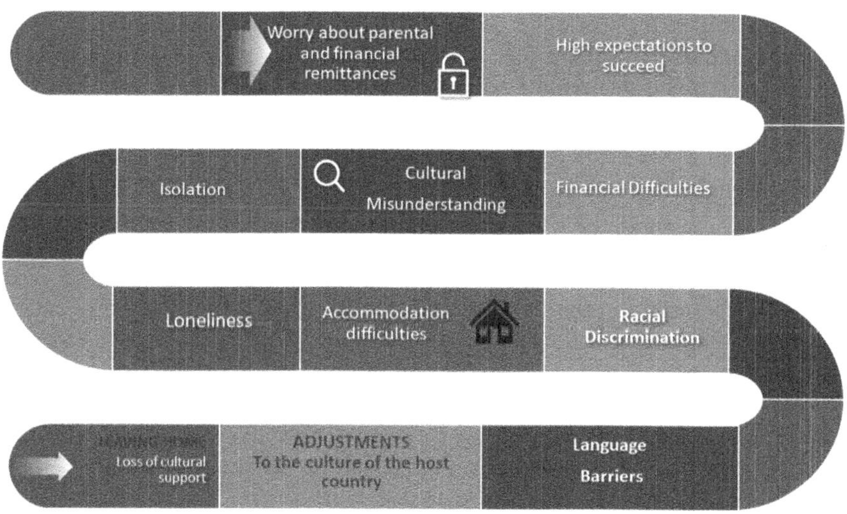

Forbes-Mewett and Sawyer found the presence of mental health concerns to be a major concern (2016). In their study, they presented three sets of factors that impacted the mental health of international students, namely

- Unfamiliar academic setting, English language difficulties, and modes of teacher/student interaction
- Living off-campus when coming from a restrictive background and unaccustomed to independence; daily practices such as cooking, budgeting, cleaning, managing house and relationships, and trying to find part-time work to support their living expenses

- International students avoid using counselling services for a variety of reasons, including a reluctance to seek help due to cultural perceptions, help-seeking delays associated with stigma, fear of 'losing face' or reputation, or disclosing personal information (Forbes-Mewett & Sawyer, 2016).

Suggested Supports

Studies have identified three forms of support that are commonly required by international students to address these issues: cognitive support which involves addressing learning needs and issues; affective support which involves addressing a student's emotional needs; and systemic support which involves information and administration that supports a student's administrative and physical needs (Kambouropoulos, 2014; Roberts & Dunworth, 2012). Institutions must realise that when providing these supports to international students that differences in coping styles have been identified between cultures, so it is important that services are person-centred (Khawaja & Stallman, 2011). For this reason, there is a need to understand the nature of international student challenges so that support can be tailored to their needs (Brydon & Liddell, 2012).

It has been observed that social and structural conditions within institutions value and reward students that master Anglo-Australian values (Pham & Tran, 2015). If international students have difficulty with mastering these values or the values do not align with the student's values, they may feel disconnected or as if they do not belong. Pham and Tran (2015) believe that a feeling of belonging shapes international students well-being, success and adaption, so if this need is not addressed it can lead to loneliness, lower motivation and disengagement. Pham and Tran (2015) also argues that there is an overemphasis on language barriers and cultural differences when examining the issue of transition problems for international students, they believe that there should be an increased emphasis on how social and academic structures can also be barriers to successful transition to studying in Australia.

When creating supports for international students' institutions have implemented interventions that mainly focus on language barriers and cultural differences (Pham & Tran, 2015). It has been observed that in general international students have been seen from a deficit perspective; international students have reported that it is the opinion of institutions, supervisors and domestic students that it is the international student's responsibility to adjust and not the host university (Pham & Tran, 2015). In this context, institutions and those working with international students assume that transition and study issues stem from an international students deficiencies and success is graded against their ability to adjust to the host country (Marginson, 2014; Pham & Tran, 2015).

Most educational institutions provide a range of student supports but research shows that there is a disparity between student and staff perceptions of needs and how to address them. Students and staff often agreed on what needs to be done but consensus could not be found on the best way to help (Roberts & Dunworth, 2012). If supervisors or staff use a Eurocentric deficit approach when dealing with international students then this can result in mis-matched beliefs on individual responsibility, a lack of a supervisors ability to approach student issues in a culturally appropriate way, and service delivery that is not student-centred (Roberts & Dunworth, 2012; Forbes-Mewett & Sawyer, 2016). To improve student outcomes, educational institutions should be actively working to improve staff/student culture. Being able to build strong respectful relationships between students and staff would only be possible if an institution actively explores and understands the different perceptions students and staff have on problematic issues so that they can be addressed (Roberts & Dunworth, 2012).

The way international students approach learning has been identified as an issue which should be of concern to institutions and considered when creating curriculum and when training staff. Students can be confronted by major differences in teaching styles, and in the way that they are expected to approach their learning experience. For students to be successful in their studies, staff need to be aware of the cultural differences in learning and address this issue when creating curriculum for international students (Brydon & Liddell, 2012). It has been observed that many international students come from a culture that seeks expert wisdom, learning by rote, which can look like plagiarism as opposed to the Australian approach of synthesising information (Forbes-Brydon & Liddell, 2012; Mewett & Sawyer, 2016). If language barriers are then added to the mix, this can affect the student–supervisor relationship as students may be reluctant to speak to supervisor, the student may not understand feedback from supervisor, or fear of being found not proficient in English. This is a serious issue as this relationship is important to a student's academic success (Baohua & Wright, 2016).

When academic institutions are reviewing their support, services attention needs to be given to the promotion of services. International students have reported that the way promotional material and documentation was written was not in a way they could relate it to themselves. This is where cultural differences must be taken into consideration when designing promotional material (Roberts & Dunworth, 2012). Research has shown that many international students are unaware of university support services or may not comprehend the full range of services available (Ling & Tran, 2015; Roberts & Dunworth, 2012). The introduction of these services to students generally happens during orientation, unfortunately with so much important information being given over a short period of time information overload can result in students disengaging with service information. It has been observed that service promotion and information provision are more effective if available at time of need (Roberts & Dunworth, 2012). For this reason, it would be advisable that institutions find ways of bringing services to student's attention as soon as it has been identified that they are struggling. Studies have also shown that many students struggle with written and spoken English, this not only impacts their ability to succeed in studies but also to navigate their way around issues as they arise (Baohua & Wright, 2016; Kambouropoulos, 2014). To address this issue, it would be helpful if information is available in other languages as students' have reported that information is easier to understand in their own language when they are stressed (Roberts & Dunworth, 2012).

Discussion

Although international students report having issues with transitioning to studying in Australia, many do not utilise the support systems provided. It has been observed that many students especially those from Asian cultures are less inclined to seek help and will use maladaptive coping strategies—repression, avoidance, or other passive coping strategies (Khawaja & Stallman, 2011). Instead of accessing formal support services, students often prefer to use informal sources of help (Huixian et al., 2014). This form of help-seeking in first instance is from fellow students generally from same ethnic or cultural background. This may lead to professional help if assisting students have had positive experiences with support services (Forbes-Mewett & Sawyer, 2016). The use of informal supports such as peer support allows students to share their experiences and knowledge to assist new students with transition. Research has shown that international students' have identified the following strategies they feel have been successful in their own transition. It is important to prepare before departure by researching the institution where they will be studying, course information, education system, campus information, the local city and the culture of host country. It is also important before leaving home to prepare for an independent life by learning day-to-day living skills such as cooking, shopping, finances. Make attending orientation activities a priority so that students can take advantage of information and planned activities designed for them. Take all opportunities to improve English proficiency by joining social organisations and groups which can also help students to practice social skills. If students are unsure or have a problem seek help from support services (Khawaja & Stallman, 2011). Unfortunately, research has shown that international students generally resort to accessing services when the student is in crisis or due to academic referral. This reluctance to access support services and waiting until the situation is in crisis may result in irreversible consequences for the student, e.g. failing a subject (Kambouropoulos, 2014; Forbes-Mewett & Sawyer, 2016). It is important that educational institutions are aware of international students help-seeking behaviour and look for ways to encourage them to engage with support services, if they are to provide an environment that promotes successful transition to study in Australia.

Evidence suggests that international students who are struggling are least likely to engage with support services (Hoyne & McNaught, 2013). Students have identified that they are less willing to access face-to-face support services due to embarrassment, anxiety over confidentiality and a perception that services provided are for those not coping or failing (Pham & Tran, 2015; Roberts & Dunworth, 2012). Help-seeking behaviour can be inhibited by fear, a belief they are beyond help, shame, previous negative experiences or denial of the need that exists (Hoyne & McNaught, 2013; Forbes-Mewett & Sawyer, 2016). Specifically, mental health is an area of concern; mental health problems can impact a student's daily life and is an area in which students commonly seem reluctant to seek help. Research has identified several factors which contribute to this reluctance, they are cultural constructs of personal distress, counselling not readily accepted at home, mental health is often interpreted through physical health problems, stigma and fear of revealing personal or family information (Forbes-Mewett & Sawyer, 2016). For these reasons, educational institutions cannot rely on an international student to actively seek out support so must implement ways of identifying students that would benefit from obtaining support (Hoyne & McNaught, 2013).

Studies have shown that implementing a compulsory support programme for students that are identified as at risk has led to a significant improvement in engagement with support services and improved academic performance (Hoyne & McNaught, 2013). For international students, a compulsory support programme could be a compulsory unit and/or peer mentoring that teaches and supports positive coping behaviours. Research has shown that the following positive coping behaviours can have a positive effect on transitioning to studying and living in Australia; self-knowledge, understanding of others, expanded world view, help-seeking behaviour and building a support network (Khawaja & Stallman, 2011). This type of support programme not only addresses the issue of students avoiding support services, can assist with identifying students at risk and informing students about available services.

There is no doubt that support services are an important service to assist students in transition to study and living in Australia, to make sure students are successful educational institutions need to consider the importance of making these services relevant and accessible to all international students.

References

Austrade, (2018), Adaptation and satisfaction of international higher degree research students in Australia, (Australian Trade and Investment Commission), Future Unlimited: Why study in Australia? Study in Australia web site. Retrieved from https://www.studyinaustralia.gov.au/english/why-australia

Brydon, K., & Liddell, M. (2012). Supporting International students undertaking Australian university studies. *Social Work Education, 31*(8), 995–1011.

Croucher, G., & Locke, W. (2020). *A post-coronavirus pandemic world: Some possible trends and their implications for Australian higher education*. The University of Melbourne.

Decobert, A., & Lamb, V. (2020, December 2). Australia's future as a destination for international students. Pursuit, The University of Melbourne.

Forbes-Mewett, H., & Sawyer, A.-M. (2016). International students and mental health. *Journal of International Students, 6*(3), 661–677. https://doi.org/10.32674/jis.v6i3.348

Forbes-Mewett, H. (2019). Mental health and international students: issues, challenges and effective practice. Research digest 15, International Education Association of Australia (IEAA). Retrieved from www.ieaa.org.au

Gibson, J., & Moran, A. (2020, April 3). As coronavirus spreads, 'Its time to go home' Scott Morrison tells visitors and international students. *ABC News* https://www.abc.net.au/news/2020-04-03/coronavirus-pm-tells-international-students-time-to-go-to-home/12119568

Hoyne, G., & McNaught, K. (2013). Understanding the psychology of seeking support to increase Health Science student engagement in academic support services. A Practice Report. *The International Journal of the First Year in Higher Education, 4*(1). 109–106. https://doi.org/10.5204/intjfyhe.v4i1.149

https://andrewnorton.net.au/2020/04/04/international-students-and-the-covid-19-recession/

https://www.thehansindia.com/hans/opinion/news-analysis/indian-students-in-australia-may-return-616798

Huixian Lu, S., Farran-Dear, B., Johnston, L., Wootton, B., & Titov, N. (2014). An internet survey of emotional health, treatment seeking and barriers to accessing mental health treatment among Chinese-speaking international students in Australia. *Counselling Psychology Quarterly, 27*(1), 96–108. https://doi.org/10.1080/09515070.2013.824408

International Education Association of Australia (IEAA), Document, undated https://www.ieaa.org.au/documents/item/1151

Kambouropoulos, A. (2014). An examination of the adjustment journey of international students studying in Australia. *Australian Education Research, 41*, 349–363. https://doi.org/10.1007/s13384-013-0130-z

Karp, P. (2020, May 4) Australian universities angry at 'final twist of the knife' excluding them from jobkeeper. *The Guardian*. https://www.theguardian.com/australia-news/2020/may/04/australian-universities-angry-at-final-twist-of-the-knife-excluding-them-from-jobkeeper

Khawaja, N., & Stallman, H. (2011). Understanding the coping strategies of international students: A qualitative approach. *Australian Journal of Guidance and Counselling, 21*(2), 203–224. https://doi.org/10.1375/ajgc.21.2.203

Ling, C., & Tran, L. T. (2015). Chinese international students in Australia: an insight into their help and information-seeking manners. *International education journal: comparative perspectives, 14*(1), 42–56.

Maley, M. (2020, April 5). One might also add that if international students and temporary workers are left high and dry. [Comment on the post "How many jobs are there in higher education?"]. Andrew Norton. https://andrewnorton.net.au/2020/04/04/international-students-and-the-covid-19-recession/

Marginson, S. (2014). Student self-formation in international education. *Journal of Studies in International Education, 18*(1), 6–22. https://doi.org/10.1177/1028315313513036

Martin, F. (2020, June 10). time to reset Australian international education. East Asia Forum—Economics, politics and public policy in East Asia and the pacific. https://www.eastasiaforum.org/2020/06/10/time-to-reset-australian-international-education/

McCauley, D., & Chung, L. (2020, April 3). Go home, Morrison tells international visitors. *The Sydney morning herald*, https://www.smh.com.au/politics/federal/go-home-scott-morrison-tells-international-visitors-20200403-p54gu2.html

Norton, A. (2020, April 5). International students and the COVID-19 recession. https://andrewnorton.net.au/2020/04/04/international-students-and-the-covid-19-recession/

Olmos, D. (2020, December 14) Australia wants international students to study here, but abandoned them during the covid crisis. *The Guardian*. https://www.theguardian.com/commentisfree/2020/dec/14/australia-wants-international-students-to-study-here-but-abandoned-them-during-the-covid-crisis

Pulla, V. (2020, April 11). Indian students in Australia may return. *The Hans India*. https://www.thehansindia.com/hans/opinion/news-analysis/indian-students-in-australia-may-return-616798

Pulla, V. (2020, April 7). Thanks for picking up this area and strongly advocating for international students. [Comment on the post "How many jobs are there in higher education?"]. *Andrew Norton*. https://andrewnorton.net.au/2020/04/04/international-students-and-the-covid-19-recession/

Roberts, P., & Dunworth, K. (2012). Staff and student perceptions of support services for international students in higher education: A case study. *Journal of Higher Education Policy and Management, 34*(5), 517–528.

Ross, J. (2020, April 3). 'Time to go home', Australian PM tells foreign students: vice-chancellors stress support for students stranded in crisis. *The World university rankings*. https://www.timeshighereducation.com/news/time-go-home-australian-pm-tells-foreign-students
Ross, J. (2020, May 3). Australian government moves again to exclude universities from bailout. *The world university rankings*. https://www.timeshighereducation.com/news/australian-government-moves-again-exclude-universities-bailout
Tran, L. T., & Pham, L. (2015). International students in transnational mobility: Intercultural Connectedness with domestic and international peers, institutions and the wider community. *Compare: A Journal of Comparative and International Education*. https://doi.org/10.1080/03057925.2015.1057479
Yu, B., & Wright, E. (2016). Socio-cultural adaptation, academic adaptation and satisfaction of international higher degree research students in Australia. *Tertiary Education and Management, 22*(1), 49–64. https://doi.org/10.1080/13583883.2015.1127405

Venkat Pulla (MA, Ph.D. (Member, AASW, Accredited), Member, APASWE) is an Alumnus of the prestigious Tata Institute of Social Sciences, India, and a Tata Dorabji Scholar. He has made significant contributions to social work education in SAARC countries and continues to offer strengths-based practice, grounded theory and research writing Master Classes globally. He has been the foundation Head of the School of Social Work, Northern Territory University, now Charles Darwin University. He has co-edited volumes on strengths-based practice, 2012; perspectives on coping and resilience, 2013; theories, experiences, and challenges in community work, 2014; advancing social work in mental health through strengths-based practice, 2014; some aspects of community empowerment and resilience, 2015; and the Lhotsampa People of Bhutan-Resilience and Survival, 2016, and is the Principal author of the new title 'Discrimination, Challenge and Response', September 2020 with Palgrave Macmillan. He is on the editorial board of Springer Nature, Social Sciences, International Journal of Innovation, Creativity and Change, UK, and Space and Culture, India, also published from the UK. He has published with Sage, Routledge, Macmillan, Palgrave and Wilfred Laurier Press, Canada; Primrose Hall, UK and Australia; Fernwood, California; and others in Asia. He is a recipient of NAPSWI, India, Life Time Achievement Award 2015, and Karma veer Puraskar, Global Indian Social Worker Award 2008. And he is currently a Foundation Professor at the Brisbane Institute of Strengths-based practice and Senior Research Fellow (Adjunct), at the Institute of Land, Water and Society at the Charles Sturt University, Australia. He is an active accredited member of the Australian Association of Social Work and Asia Pacific Association of Social Work Education. https://orcid.org/0000-0003-0395-9973.

Elizabeth Carter, MSW, BA (Social Sciences), with Postgraduate Study in Gerontology and Aboriginal culture, is a Research Associate with the Brisbane Institute of Strengths-Based Practice and a peer reviewer for a number of international journals. Her research has resulted in several published articles and book chapters on racism, research theory, diversional therapy and international students. Her work experience is varied having worked in disability and aged care, administration, finance and social work with international students and in community. She has an interest in social justice, research practices, multicultural society, community work and disability.

Abraham Francis is an Associate Professor and currently the Head of Academic Group in Social Work and Human Services at James Cook University, Australia. He has worked with government, non-government and corporate sector and has developed many international partnerships. He taught social work at the Delhi University in India and worked as a senior mental health social worker with Country Health South Australia before moving to Townsville to join James Cook University. Dr. Francis has established many international partnerships and research collaborations with universities and non-government organisations.

He has extensively contributed to the literature on social work practice in mental health through his publications, convening conferences, establishing research networks and by developing consortiums. His other research interests are in the field of communities, criminal justice, international social work and gerontological social work. His excellence in teaching has been recognised on a number of occasions. For example, in 2010, he was a recipient of James Cook University's Inclusive Practice Award for his 'exceptional support for students with a disability'. In 2016, he received the university's '***Citation for Outstanding Contributions to Student Learning***' for his 'leadership and expertise in social work education in mental health that inspires and nurtures students to be competent, confident and compassionate practitioners'.

Dr. Francis was one of the finalists at the 2018 India ***Australia Business and Community Awards*** in the category of Community Services Excellence Award and Business Leader/ Professional of the Year. In 2018, Dr. Francis received the NAPSWI (National Association of Professional Association Social Workers in India) Life Time Achievement Award for his outstanding contribution to social work education.

For more details—https://research.jcu.edu.au/portfolio/abraham.francis/.

COVID-19 and Mental Health and Well-Being of Higher Education International Students

Hyacinth Udah and Abraham Francis

Abstract This chapter examines the impacts of COVID-19 on higher education international students, highlighting their experiences and the importance of promoting mental health and well-being. The authors argue that student's mental health and well-being strongly correlate with their academic performance and general experience. Drawing on findings from their research project into the experiences of international students in North Queensland, Australia, during the COVID-19 pandemic, the authors highlight the necessity to support higher education international students with a focus on quality and equity in order to improve their well-being and educational outcomes. Suggestions are made on actions for higher education institutions in relation to providing nurturing, supportive, responsive and needs-orientated environments to ameliorate services offered and address international students' challenges, and the mental health needs posed by the pandemic and beyond.

Keywords COVID-19 · Higher education · International students · Mental health · Well-being

Introduction

The number of international students studying in higher education worldwide is increasing. Over five million students study abroad (United Nations Educational, Scientific and Cultural Organisation (UNESCO), 2019). With increasing internationalisation of education, it is more likely that the number of higher education international students would continue to increase for years to come. English-speaking Western countries like Australia, UK and USA are the top and most common and popular study destinations for international students (International Student, 2021).

H. Udah (✉) · A. Francis
James Cook University, Townsville, Australia
e-mail: hyacinth.udah@jcu.edu.au

A. Francis
e-mail: abraham.francis@jcu.edu.au

A. P. Francis and M. A. Carter (eds.), *Mental Health and Higher Education in Australia*,
https://doi.org/10.1007/978-981-16-8040-3_18

Various scholars use the push–pull theoretical framework to explain factors influencing decisions of students to cross national and cultural boundaries or territories of origin to study abroad (Bista & Dagley, 2015; Shafaei et al., 2018). Some students are pushed by unfavourable conditions (such as political instability, lack of educational and employment opportunities) in their home countries. Others are pulled by better opportunities (such as quality research and education, scholarships, economic and employment opportunities) and possible immigration prospects in the host countries.

International students represent one of the most relevant and biggest sojourner groups (Ambrósio et al., 2017; Neto, 2020). As Neto (2020) describes, sojourners are "people who travel internationally to achieve a particular goal or objective with the expectation that they will return to their country of origin after the purpose of their travel has been achieved" (p. 457). For many international students, who have either been pushed or pulled to study abroad, their destination/host countries are lands of opportunity, where they can further their education, study at a world-class institution, gain globally recognised credentials and qualifications (Udah, 2021). For many of these students, studying abroad also allows them to explore a different culture, broaden their worldviews, enhance their cross-cultural and professional knowledge, and skills, learn new ways of thinking and behaving, make new friends, better their life and solidify their status on return to their countries of origin (Sherry et al., 2010). While the majority gain international educational experiences, and a degree abroad, it is important to emphasise that many international students, as student sojourners, tend to face and encounter several challenges and setbacks that many universities fail to recognise (Carter et al., 2017; Gautam et al., 2016; Huang et al., 2020; Udah, 2021).

Research demonstrates that studying abroad implies many challenges and adjustment problems (Altinyelken et al., 2020; Ambrósio et al., 2017; Firang, 2020; Gautam et al., 2016; Shafaei et al., 2018; Soong, 2020; Wu et al., 2015). In their study destinations, international students face several unique hardships (Soong, 2020) and experience more difficulties, either academically or socially, than domestic students (Ambrósio et al., 2017; Firang, 2020). Despite their eagerness to study abroad, international students must adjust to a new (unfamiliar) culture and social environment, and educational system (Ahrari et al., 2019; Altinyelken et al., 2020; Khawaja & Dempsey, 2007). They must also deal with language barriers, most of the time, in their study destinations, and learn different cultural norms (Ambrósio et al., 2017). In addition, international students, often, experience challenges and setbacks such as social isolation, loneliness, and homesickness, loss of interpersonal contacts, financial difficulties, discrimination and prejudice (Ambrósio et al., 2017; Firang, 2020; Gautam et al., 2016; Soong, 2020; Wu et al., 2015).

These challenges and setbacks can trigger feelings of uneasiness, insecurity, inferiority, depression, anxiety, loss and other mental health conditions (Carter et al., 2017; Wu et al., 2015). These challenges have significant implications for student success, retention, completion and achievement (van Agteren et al., 2019). Consequently, there has been an increasing focus on the importance of supporting and promoting the mental health and well-being of students across the higher education sector (Baik et al., 2019). This is because (1) the mental health of students is an important public health issue (Barkham et al., 2019); (2) mental health and well-being strongly correlate with a student's academic performance and general experience (Huang et al., 2020).

Therefore, to improve outcomes for international students, there is a need to best support them as they experience challenges and cope with psychological distress and mental health problems (Carter et al., 2017). As various scholars indicate, higher education students have a higher incidence of mental health problems, experiencing high levels of psychological distress, severe depressive symptoms and other mental health difficulties (Browne et al., 2017; Carter et al., 2017). Even before the COVID-19 pandemic, higher education international students are at even higher risk for mental ill health (Huang et al., 2020; Orygen, 2017). A range of demographic and psychosocial demands influences their stress and psychological distress (Khawaja & Dempsey, 2007). Compared to their local peers (domestic students), international students face more difficulties (Shafaei et al., 2018) and are at greater risk for poor adjustment (Ahrari et al., 2019; Huang et al., 2020). The added stress of high tuition fees may compound their pre-existing stress (Carter et al., 2017). In addition, in times of crises and public health emergencies such as the COVID-19 pandemic, higher education international students are, particularly, a vulnerable group (Altinyelken et al., 2020; Firang, 2020). They experience additional challenges due to risk factors such as immigrant and student status, discrimination, othering, exclusion, isolation, social distancing, financial uncertainties, work visa restrictions, fear of infection and transmission of COVID-19, and excessive exposure to COVID-19 news in social and mass media (Khan et al., 2020; Udah, 2021; Zhai & Du, 2020). The COVID-19 pandemic has the potential to make their challenges worse (Soong, 2020).

This chapter examines the experiences of higher education international students during the COVID-19 pandemic. As non-Western and immigrant social work researchers and academics interested in international students' well-being, the authors are keen to highlight the importance of supporting and promoting the mental health and well-being of international students across the higher education sector. Drawing on findings from our research project in North Queensland (NQ), Australia, during the COVID-19 pandemic, this chapter sheds insights into the experiences, challenges and impacts of the COVID-19 pandemic on higher education international students. It indicates the need to support higher education international students during a pandemic and beyond with a focus on quality and equity to improve their educational outcomes and well-being. The chapter also discusses how higher education institutions and interested parties can implement programmes, policies and interventions aimed at addressing international students' disadvantage, and improving their interactions, engagement, performance and retention. By indicating the multiple stressors and risk factors exacerbated by the COVID-19 pandemic that contribute to psychological distress among higher education international students, the authors outline suggestions on how higher education institutions can provide nurturing, supportive, responsive and needs-orientated environments, ameliorate services offered and address international students' challenges, and the mental health needs posed by the pandemic and beyond.

COVID-19 and Mental Health

Mental health is a state of mental well-being in which people can cope well with the life stresses, realise their potential, function productively and fruitfully at work and in their private life and are able to contribute to their communities and the wider society (World Health Organisation (WHO), 2018). Globally, having good mental health is important and a priority for the health agenda. Having good mental health has a huge impact on every aspect of our lives as individuals. It "affects behaviour, physical health, work and relationships, as well as the people around" us (Commonwealth of Australia, 2021). Mental well-being goes beyond the absence of mental illness and encompasses a range of positive mental, emotional, physical, social and motivational states, relating to feeling resilient, functioning well and being able to connect with others (van Agteren et al., 2019). Thus, improving students' cognitive, emotional and behavioural status, that is their mental well-being, can lower their risk of mental illness, and increase productivity, which can translate to better personal, social, economic and academic outcomes (van Agteren et al., 2019). However, unexpected events and emergencies such as the COVID-19 pandemic can make people, including students feel anxious, stressed, isolated and worried, producing significant emotional effects that are detrimental to mental health and well-being (Commonwealth of Australia, 2021; Paredes et al., 2020).

The COVID-19 crisis was first reported in Wuhan, Hubei, a city in China, in December 2019 (Cao et al., 2020). Due to its rapid spread across the globe, the WHO characterised it, officially, as a pandemic on 11 March 2020. By a pandemic, COVID-19 is seen as "an epidemic occurring worldwide", crossing international boundaries and affecting many people (Last, 2001). The pandemic is not just a public health emergency, but also an economic and social crises of both national and international concerns. As Francis and Udah (2020) explain, "it is a health crisis with huge impact on social and economic welfare. It is also a welfare issue with huge impact on public health. It is a crisis like no other in modern human history, disrupting almost every aspect of our lives and society" (p. 167). The virus brought not only an urgent medical crisis but also exposed larger structural inequalities and challenges that have always existed and persisted in our societies (Udah & Francis, 2021). It is one of the greatest challenging crises not seen in the last 100 years that is so far-reaching, generating fear and leading to a spectrum of psychological, psychosocial and economic consequences (Montemurro, 2020; Zhai & Du, 2020). It has significantly transformed relationships among individuals, families, students and communities (Paredes et al., 2020), posing a threat to the welfare, physical and mental health of people.

The pandemic has taken a toll on most people: Families have been affected socially and economically. Millions have lost their income and means of livelihood. Some have lost their homes, and their loved ones. Some have also skipped meals to feed their children. As a result of the pandemic, some people have been discriminated, denied of natural justice and duty of care due to their citizenship, nationality or country of origin (Francis & Udah, 2020). As COVID-19 hit many countries, many restrictions were put in place. As part of the national and global efforts to contain the spread and protect vulnerable populations, governments in various countries worldwide responded by introducing and implementing quarantines, lockdowns, physical distancing practices, self-isolation and travel restrictions. Schools, businesses and borders were also closed. Some of these containment strategies and public health measures were enforced with controls ranging from recommendations to on-the-spot fines and arrests of individuals who fail to comply with directions. With the measures and restrictions to reduce person-to-person transmission of COVID-19, many people, including international students, could not leave their homes except for shopping for essential supplies, attending medical or care needs, exercise, including work or study if they cannot be done remotely.

The loss of personal autonomy and social connectedness afforded by COVID-19 restrictions and the stress caused by unemployment or loss of income adversely impacted people's mental health and well-being (Berger & Reupert, 2020). Shekhar Saxena, Professor of the practice of global mental health at Harvard University argues that COVID-19 is affecting people's mental health and well-being in three ways: psychological impact, feeling of loss, and feeling of hopelessness and helplessness. First, there is the *psychological impact*, which comes from fear and uncertainty, associated with the virus. During this pandemic, many people have developed fear of getting infected or dying, and fear of the virus striking their own family members or city or country. Second, there is the *feeling of loss*. In this pandemic, many people have lost their freedom to socialise and do what they want, leaving many people more distressed, disrupted and with a persistent feeling of something missing. In addition, there is the *feeling of hopelessness and helplessness*, which are characteristic signs of depression. While not everyone will have anxiety and depression as an illness, many people have experienced stress and distress during this pandemic (Saxena as cited in Bhargava, 2020). For some international students, it has become symptomatic and even evolved into a mental health disorder, impairing normal functioning and requiring help (Cao et al., 2020).

Studies have shown that some of the measures adopted to control COVID-19 spread as well as the emotive reactions to the pandemic itself have had significant effects on people's mental health and well-being in both short and long terms (Berger & Reupert, 2020; Kumar & Nayar, 2020; Montemurro, 2020). For example, disruptions to daily routines caused by some of the control measures affected usual activities and livelihoods of people. The disruptions led to an increase in, and experiences of, loneliness, fears of infection, panic attacks, frustration, high levels of stress, anxiety, and depression, insomnia, self-harm or suicidal behaviour, and harmful alcohol and drug use (Berger & Reupert, 2020; Kumar & Nayar, 2020; Montemurro, 2020; Zhai & Du, 2020). Also, the lockdown measures contributed to poor lifestyle behaviours and reduced physical activity (Pierce et al., 2020) and led to an increase in domestic violence and intimate partner abuse, where women and children who live with domestic violence have no escape from their abusers (Graham-Harrison et al., 2020). In addition, some of the measures adopted increased the severity of pre-existing mental illness and caused new symptoms to emerge during the lockdown in individuals with no previous disorders (Paredes et al., 2020).

While mental health problems are believed to exist along a continuum from mild, time-limited distress to severe mental health conditions (Patel et al., 2018), the COVID-19 pandemic has influenced where people are situated on that continuum (United Nations, 2020). Many higher education international students, who coped well before the pandemic, are now less able to cope because of the multiple stressors generated by the pandemic (Zhai & Du, 2020). Importantly research shows that higher education international students, who had few experiences of anxiety, depression and distress before the pandemic, now experience an increase, with some developing a mental health condition (Cao et al., 2020). Furthermore, higher education international students, who previously had a mental health condition, experience, now, a worsening of their condition and reduced functioning, suffering from poor mental health and well-being (Firang, 2020). This means that the psychological and psychosocial effects of the pandemic on higher education international students can be significant (Zhai & Du, 2020).

COVID-19 and International Students

The COVID-19 pandemic brought unprecedented changes to higher education institutions worldwide, resulting in significant pressure and challenges for international students. It forced higher education institutions to shut their campuses and suspend in-person class attendance, which had potential consequences on day-to-day life, mental health and well-being of students (Soong, 2020). The suspension of in-person classes and on-campus social events affected over 80% of the world's student population (Sahu, 2020). For many higher education international students with pre-existing mental health needs, the closure of campuses or suspension of on-campus learning means a lack of access to resources and exacerbated triggers of poor mental health (Cao et al., 2020).

The changes implemented by higher education institutions to cope with the pandemic and meet government regulations impacted international students' mental well-being (Sahu, 2020). For example, as universities transitioned to online education and learning during the lockdowns, many international students felt alone and disconnected (Firang, 2020). More higher education international students than domestic students reported significant distress (Zhai & Du, 2020) and compounded negative emotions (Montemurro, 2020; Paredes et al., 2020), including experiences of shock, stress, isolation, frustration, trauma, depression, anxiety, fears of contracting COVID-19, betrayal, grief and confusion (Cao et al., 2020; Khan et al., 2020; Sahu, 2020), which are risk factors for mental illness. As one of the vulnerable student population (Firang, 2020), many international students faced exclusion, marginalisation and neglect during the pandemic, which created psychological distress (Soong, 2020).

International students studying in Australia, most of whom are on temporary visas, account for approximately 30% of higher education enrolments in Australia (Australian Institute of Health and Welfare (AIHW), 2019). As of September 2021, there were over 356,143 international students in the higher education sector, representing 52 per cent of the total population of all student visa holders studying in Australia (Department of Education, Skills and Employment (DESE), 2021). These students see Australia as a place to achieve their study abroad dreams and aspirations (Udah, 2021). However, as non-citizens and temporary residents or visa holders, they could not receive unemployment benefits or benefits from the stimulus packages. They were excluded from government emergency COVID-19 relief packages and assistance measures, told to return to their home countries and left to stay with no money for basic necessities[1] (O'Sullivan et al., 2020; Soong, 2020). The Australian federal government did not consider them eligible for federal government subsidies and income support packages like the JobKeeper wage subsidies, which violated their basic rights (Firang, 2020) and heightened their anxieties and stress, increasing risks to mental health (Soong, 2020). Not only were international students stranded (in Australia and other comparable countries) and unable to leave their homelands during the COVID-19 lockdowns, but many of them lost their jobs and had little or no support from family or close friends during COVID-19 (Soong, 2020).

Research over the decade has shown a strong correlation between stressful life events and the incidence of mental illness (Caron et al., 2012). International students experiencing social and psychological distress due to COVID-19 are at an increased risk of suffering poor mental health and well-being (Firang, 2020), which can have detrimental effects on physical health and academic success (van Agteren et al., 2019). Psychological distress impact negatively on student success, academic performance and learning experience (Baik et al., 2019). It is, therefore, important for higher education institutions as well as the wider communities to step up and understand international students' unique experiences, vulnerabilities and challenges. There is a need to become more aware of, and response to, what can be done to effectively support international students' mental health and well-being and prevent psychological distress.

Methods and Procedures

The research objective is to examine the impact of COVID-19 on international students' mental health, well-being and learning experience in North Queensland

[1] Many international students are facing hardship due to COVID-19. While various Australian states and territories released funds to support international students facing hardship due to COVID-19, the federal government excluded them from the government's $130 billion stimulus package. The Prime Minister Scott Morrison even suggested that international students unable to support themselves could return to their home countries. The state of Victoria committed $45 million, co-contributed by Victorian universities, to support international students for one-off relief payment of up to $1100. The ACT committed A$450,000 to support vulnerable people on temporary visas and international students without income due to COVID-19. In addition, New South Wales committed $20 million, Northern Territory $5 million, Queensland $15 million, South Australia $13.8 million, Tasmania $790,000 and Western Australia $402 m to help temporary residents and international students—whether it be one-off payments, free mental health support or help with food and shelter.

Australia. This research received ethical approval from James Cook University Research Ethics Committee in 2020. It is a mixed-method study, utilising both qualitative and quantitative research methods. The quantitative component involved a questionnaire survey to collect descriptive generic data while the qualitative component involved in-depth face-to-face semi-structured interviews to best capture detailed information and critically explore the participants' subjective experiences of being international students in NQ during the COVID-19 pandemic. Given the issues being investigated, it was important that participants met specific criteria—(1) participants are international students aged 18 years and over and (2) attending a recognised university in the northern region of Queensland, Australia.

A survey (online questionnaire) was first conducted to reach a wider sample of international students in North Queensland. The survey link was emailed out to the international student population via noticeboards of universities, university offices of international students, email and community organisations. Permission/approval was sought from organisations and universities where sites are moderated at which survey links were disseminated. The questionnaire survey consisted of sixty questions. The quantitative survey, a multidimensional instrument, collected data in different domains, including identity, ethnicity, education level, pandemic impacts and coping, social needs, socioeconomic status and life priorities. There were fifty-eight (58) students who attempted and completed the survey. The survey respondents varied in terms of gender, type of degree, employment and status.

To enhance understanding of international students' experiences, open-ended interview questions were used to further investigate the initial quantitative survey findings (Creswell & Creswell, 2018). After an examination of the initial survey responses, the researchers decided on the themes that emerged from the responses provided. The key themes, emerging from the survey data such as the impacts of pandemic, challenges, mental well-being and satisfaction, were explored in more depth with a sample of international students residing in North Queensland.

A purposive snowball strategy was used to recruit participants (Patton, 2015). The participants ($N = 20$) consisted of international students (13 females and 7 males), between the ages of 22 and 40 years. Informed consent for participation was sought and obtained from each participant. Participation in the study was voluntary. Participants were assured of their privacy and confidentiality.

In-depth semi-structured interviews (40–60 min) were conducted with the participants, allowing the researchers to examine in detail and gain a rich understanding of participants' experiences and challenges during the COVID-19 pandemic from their perspectives and perceptions (Patton, 2015; Udah & Singh, 2019). The interviews were exploratory and stimulated the narration of experiences that would remain unexpressed within a questionnaire format (Udah, 2016). The interview questions focused on participants' migration and study experiences, personal and socioeconomic conditions, satisfaction and well-being. Most interviews were conducted and recorded via zoom and a few face-to-face at the researchers' office, while maintaining social distancing guidelines. The interview data were recorded with the permission of participants and transcribed verbatim. The transcription was time-consuming but helpful. It allowed familiarity with the data, which added a depth to the analysis as well as increasing the validity and utility of the findings.

Thematic analysis was used to analyse the interview data—to identify, interpret and report common thematic elements across the participants' transcribed interview data (Braun & Clarke, 2006; Cresswell & Cresswell, 2018). The transcribed interview data were coded using NVivo. During the coding, the researchers searched for keywords, buzzwords and metaphors to support analysis and interpretation (Udah et al., 2019). The coding process helped to identify and produce a concise matrix of key emerging themes.

While the research sample is much larger, in this chapter, we briefly present questionnaire survey findings and draw on interview data extracted from six participants to establish and provide important insights into the experiences of international students during the pandemic in NQ. What their interviews reveal is relevant and practical. Participants have been given pseudonyms to protect their identity. The quotes that are used, in the section that follows, are direct quotations and excerpts from the transcriptions of the qualitative interviews.

Research Findings

The results of the survey study prepared the ground for the selection of participants to be interviewed for a more detailed exploration of international students' lived experiences during the pandemic. The following findings beginning with the demographic characteristics of respondents are identified during the quantitative descriptive statistical analysis of the survey data.

The gender distribution is unequal. It is not a 50–50 split. Of the fifty-eight respondents, fifteen (25.9%) are males and forty-three (74.1%) are females. The ages of the respondents vary. Among the respondents, more than half, that is thirty-four (58.6%) are between 25 and 34 years of age. Another fourteen (24.1%) respondents are between 18–24 years of age and ten (17.2%) respondents are between 34 and 45 years old. Among the respondents, twenty-eight (48.3%) are married, two (3.5%) are engaged, twenty-seven (46.6%) are never married, and one (1.7%) is in a de facto relationship.

More than half 42(72.4%) of respondents say that paying tuition fee is the most important challenge facing international students. While most respondents are satisfied (72.4%) or very satisfied (10.3%) with life in Australia, twenty-one (36.2%) respondents feel anxious, fourteen (24.1%) feel frustrated, seven (12.1%) feel helpless, seven (12.1%) feel lost, two (3.4%) respondents feel abandoned and six (10.3%) feel supported during the pandemic. These findings are explored in more detail via the qualitative interviews.

In the analysis of the interviews, some of the important themes that emerged, based on participants' accounts, involve themes that related to COVID-19 impacts, mental health, financial difficulties, including adjustment challenges, isolation and discrimination. Participants' accounts indicate that many international students are experiencing significant social, emotional, financial and mental health challenges because of the disruptions, psychological pressure and restrictions the virus brought. For example, Dorcas, a doctoral student from India, describes herself as a studious person, but suggested that the COVID-19 pandemic has impacted her study and personal life. According to Dorcas:

> I think this COVID-19 has affected my mental health a lot because I have not been able to see my family for two years. So, it affected my study because if I am not feeling happy here, how can I focus on my work…I am emotionally down because I cannot meet my people, my family again and I am not getting enthusiasm or motivation to continue my work. So, it is impacting my study and personal life a lot. I am emotionally very weak…If I would have gone to India and come back like meet them, refresh my mind, and come back, I would be more energetic or more motivated for my work... I think a lot of dropping out of my PhD because I am more concerned about my mental health and for my well-being.

The comments above suggest that the pandemic is affecting not only on Dorcas' work productivity but also her mental health and emotional stability. As an international student, Dorcas feels isolated and believes that visiting her family in India will re-energise her. Given the border closures, she is not able to travel home. One of her biggest challenges in Australia is socialising and connecting with people. As she states:

> As an international student, one of the biggest challenges I feel is connecting with people. You are from a different cultural background, different language, and worldviews but they are different. So, it has happened to me with socialising with people and I think, sometimes, I am isolated …. So, this is the main problem. I like to make friends here, local, and the main causes maybe language or cultural difference. I do not know but yeah or it could be because we are living the way we lived in our countries. The way people here live is quite different and our mentality is also different that might be a reason I could not make some friends here.

Isolation is always a challenge for international students (Sherry et al., 2010; Soong, 2020), which COVID-19 pandemic restrictions have compounded. Many international students feel isolated and disconnected because they are far away from their family and close friends, cultural and social environment (Ambrósio et al., 2017). Explaining how the COVID-19 pandemic has affected her, another participant, Arabella from Ecuador, comments:

> As an international student, it was very hard…I lost my job, and I was not entitled to the support the university was providing… I felt more disconnected. It affected me financially and emotionally…It was a huge thing. The COVID-19 thing affected me.

The lack of support—emotional and financial—is a risk factor for poor mental well-being among international students (Soong, 2020). Not having enough support system can be a serious challenge for international students, requiring higher education institutions to support them emotionally right from the start of their study (Sherry et al., 2010). Other challenges reported by participants apart from the lack of support, cultural, communication and language barriers include unemployment and financial hardships. For example, Rosita, a female Master of Social Work Student from Kenya, talks about her financial challenges during the pandemic. When COVID-19 hit, everything she was expecting crashed. She was expecting to receive support from her husband and mother, but it never happened. According to Rosita:

> I think right now with the pandemic and everything, I am unable to get the fees. It has been a challenge for me. It is really a challenge because before, you can get somebody to assist you. Right now, everybody's life is really tight and so yeah, I am thinking fee is what makes it so difficult...

Similar to Rosita's experiences, many other participants worry about how to raise money for their tuition fees during the pandemic. Financial hardship is reported as the biggest challenge, and, is noted as a significant stressor and risk factor for poor mental health and well-being. This financial stress is linked to their loss or lack of part-time or casual jobs. As a participant, Ann, said, "*It was a very stressful time. I did not have a job because of COVID-19, and I cannot live on my parents all the time*".

Given that many of the participants (19 out of 20) lost their part-time jobs, they could not meet their daily needs. Financial hardship meant that some of them could not afford basic necessities such as buying food and paying rents, impacting them academically, socially and psychologically. For example, speaking on what life has been for him as an international student in NQ, Australia since the COVID-19 pandemic, Paul from India, a Master of Social Work student who loves swimming, hiking as well as providing fitness training, says:

> Being an international student coming from India, times have really been hard ... It has been a depressing experience. After spending so much money, taking education loan, hoping to study at university and experience the campus life, COVID-19 shattered my dreams... Financial stress is one of my biggest challenges since COVID-19. I do not really make a lot of money at my workplace. Sometimes, I split my money, eat less just to survive, and live a cheaper life. Back in India, I was living lavishly and eating whatever I want.

Echoing Paul's experiences, other participants suggest that they were unable to support themselves financially during the pandemic. For many of these participants, lack of employment added to their worries, stress and anxiety. However, one thing that most participants indicated is that the pandemic did not jeopardise their study plans. Despite the confusion and anxiety brought by the pandemic, online classes meant no participant stopped his or her studies. Nonetheless, participants suggest that their learning and engagement were impacted by their financial and emotional distress. As one participant, Sean, summarises, "*They* [international students] *were basically struggling due to hopelessness*" during the pandemic. Indeed, more international students than ever are at risk of poor mental health, well-being and outcomes.

Discussion and Conclusion

This chapter has examined the impact of COVID-19 on international students' mental health, well-being and learning experience. While the pandemic has laid bare the vulnerabilities and structural challenges that many international students still experience when studying abroad (Gallagher et al., 2020; Soong, 2020), this chapter highlights the importance of supporting international students across the higher education sector. As our participants' accounts indicate the emotional, social and structural challenges that higher education international students experience and encounter before and during the pandemic have the potential to adversely impact on their mental health and well-being.

With good mental well-being, higher education international students are more likely to reach their full potential, achieve academic success and live a meaningful life in their host countries (Baik et al., 2019). However, it is more likely that the pandemic-related stresses will persist as long-term stressors, affecting international students' physical, cognitive, emotional and interpersonal functioning, performance (Huang et al., 2020), leading to learning difficulties and course attrition (Baik et al., 2019). Therefore, to counter the looming crisis and improve international students' mental health, academic success and retention, higher education institutions, governments and policymakers should respond to the needs of these students exacerbated by the COVID-19 pandemic. There is a need to prioritise and consider steps towards addressing and promoting their mental health and well-being.

Higher education institutions can play a crucial role in mitigating the effects of the pandemic on international students, thereby fulfilling their core mission of providing high-quality learning experiences and positive graduate outcomes (Baik et al., 2019). Higher education institutions need to be aware of, and understand, the pandemic-related stresses and other potential sources of stress and challenges in the lives of international students. A better understanding of the ways to mitigate experiences of distress, respond to structural challenges and discrimination, and foster closer relationships would help higher education institutions and their academics to improve structures and services for supporting international students (Gallagher et al., 2020; Wu et al., 2015). Thus, it is important to recognise international students' needs presented by the pandemic and effectively focus on ways to foster well-being and improve their overall outcomes.

The pandemic generated uncertainty, anxiety and fear, including increased stress among international students, which, in turn, have detrimental impact on mental well-being (Paredes et al., 2020; Zhai & Du, 2020). In our research, many participants reported experiences of COVID-19 related stress, anxiety and isolation. Given the psychological impacts of the pandemic, it is important for higher education institutions to offer supportive resources and services with multifaceted strategies to address international students' challenges and enable them to achieve their goals. There is a need, therefore, for the development and implementation of interventions, and intentional outreach to international students with special circumstances, to improve their access to services offered. Many participants see the latter as very important to supporting students' mental health and well-being. Reaching out to students intentionally can help improve access to service and manage students to control their feelings and stay away from the misfortunes brought about by emergencies such as COVID-19 (Zhai & Du, 2020).

Based on our participants' accounts, our findings highlight areas that deserve attention in mitigating the impact of COVID-19 on international students' mental health. For many participants, higher education institutions should focus on financial and emotional support. Consistent with existing studies (Dodd et al., 2021; Firang,

2020; Gallagher et al., 2020; Huang et al., 2020), the employment of many participants was affected by COVID-19. While many of them lost their jobs, some skipped meals due to the lack of finance. As non-permanent residents, participants were excluded from Australian government's financial support programmes. To help ease international students' financial problems, it is important that higher education institutions consider providing more access to scholarships for international students, especially for those students who are unable to get support from both their home and host countries. However, this financial support through scholarships to ease international students' burden must be paralleled with culturally competent and easily accessible support and services (Soong, 2020).

As emotional support is vital for student well-being, sense of belonging and continued learning (Dodd et al., 2021), it would help also to provide nurturing and supportive environments that ensure higher education international students are critically engaged in learning that is of high quality, meaningful, genuinely relevant and potentially transformative (Udah, 2021). Providing supportive environments can help enhance their mental health and well-being (Zhai & Du, 2020). As COVID-19 pandemic is having a huge emotional and psychological impact on everyone, there is also a need to recognise international students' risk factors. This recognition will help to plan and provide interventions, with improved access for international students, to better address the negative emotional and mental health issues caused by the COVID-19 pandemic.

While higher education institutions' free counselling services play important role in supporting international students with academic, adjustment and mental health needs, unfortunately, many higher education international students, experiencing difficulties or psychological distress, are less likely to seek professional help (Friedli, 2009; Gallagher et al., 2020; Huang et al., 2020). Thus, there is a need to identify the barriers to seeking professional help among international students. Due to the stigma associated with mental health, many international students feel embarrassed to discuss their problems. There is also among international students, the fear of lack of privacy and confidentiality, the fear of ruining reputation, the fear of revealing personal information, including unfamiliarity of western therapeutic approaches and lack of awareness of available counselling and mental health support services (Barkham et al., 2019; Friedli, 2009; Gallagher et al., 2020; Huang et al., 2020). For this reason, a more targeted effort is needed to encourage and ensure information about counselling, safety and support services for international students are reflected everywhere at institutional levels and beyond.

Good mental health is critical to the physical, cognitive, emotional and interpersonal functioning, performance and success of international students. It is important that higher education institutions take the time to educate international students on mental health issues in order to develop mental health knowledge and self-regulatory skills, promote resilience and reduce mental distress and vulnerability. Thus, higher education institutions need to focus on developing and improving mental health literacy among international students. This is because promoting mental health and well-being is more likely to advance students' well-being and quality of life, and prevent psychological distress (Appleby & Bourke, 2014). Similarly, educating students on mental health issues can increase their awareness and understanding of mental health problems, enhance their ability to cope with daily life challenges, participate meaningfully in society and encourage them on how to seek professional help when needed (Barkham et al., 2019; Friedli, 2009). It is important, therefore, to help international students identify symptoms, practice self-care (such as engaging in physical activity) and know where to seek support to change their attitudes towards seeking care (Gorczynski, 2018). Hence, there is a need for mental health literacy and stress management training, provided by lecturers, to form part of the study plan and core curriculum of all higher education international students (Appleby & Bourke, 2014). Providing mental health literacy and stress management training would be appropriate and should underpin interventions, for supporting student well-being (Dias et al., 2018).

While experiences of international students may differ, it is important, from a practical standpoint, that higher education institutions take a holistic—a whole-of-institution—approach to creating a supportive environment and address the risk factors common among them (Wright & Winslade, 2018). This requires introducing a range of programmes such as free mental health training programmes, and services to target not only students with greater adjustment difficulties (Ahrari et al., 2019) but create a healthy working and learning environment for everyone. This also calls for developing a model of care that is more creative, responsive and needs-orientated for students' satisfaction (Dodd et al., 2021). Policies and programmes that prevent international students from feeling a worsening sense of entrapment or being boxed-in by their circumstances (Soong, 2020) should inform such a model of care. To effectively support international students, models of care need to be sensitive to cultural differences instead of being primarily rooted in Western methodologies, which, often, focus on treatment and insensitive to cultural differences (Huang et al., 2020). It is not sufficient to simply improve existing services, but greater understanding of how international students think about and talk about issues is essential and needed to better meet their needs (Huang et al., 2020). Hence, higher educational institutions need to incorporate and strengthen, if needed, teaching practice that is respectful, inclusive and relevant to the mental health beliefs, practices, culture and linguistic needs of international students (Cunningham, 2019). It is, therefore, important that higher education institutions take the time to listen to, and understand, their international students' needs and challenges, and provide supportive social, physical and culturally responsive services and needs-orientated environments that promote their sense of belonging, and support their well-being. While the COVID-19 pandemic is having a differential impact on higher education international students, it also presents an opportunity to work closely with them. The pandemic presents opportunity to foster engaging curricula and learning experiences; targeted interventions and programmes and strengthening of resources and effective services that improve mental health knowledge, educate self-regulatory skills, promote resilience and reduce vulnerability.

References

Appleby, M., & Bourke, J. (2014). Promoting law student mental health literacy and wellbeing: A case study from the college of law, Australia. *International Journal of Clinical Legal Education, 20*(1), 461–498.

Ahrari, S., Krauss, S. E., Suandi, T., Abdullah, H., Sahimi, A. H. A., Olutokunbo, A. S., & Dahalan, D. (2019). A stranger in a strange land: Experiences of adjustment among international postgraduate students in Malaysia. *Issues in Educational Research, 29*(3), 611–632.

Altinyelken, H., Hoek, L., & Jiang, L. (2020). Improving the psychosocial wellbeing of international students: The relevance of mindfulness. *British Journal of Guidance & Counselling, 48*(4), 524–536.

Ambrósio, S., Marques, J., Santos, L., & Doutor, C. (2017). Higher education institutions and international students' hindrances: A case of students from the African Portuguese-speaking countries at two European Portuguese universities. *Journal of International Students, 7*(2), 367–394.

Australian Institute of Health and Welfare. (2019). *Higher education and vocational education.* https://www.aihw.gov.au/reports/australias-welfare/higher-education-and-vocational-education

Baik, C., Larcombe, W., & Brooker, A. (2019). How universities can enhance student mental wellbeing: The student perspective. *Higher Education Research & Development, 38*(4), 674–687.

Barkham, M., Broglia, E., Dufour, G., Fudge, M., Knowles, L., Percy, A., Turner, A., & Williams, C. (2019). Towards an evidence base for student wellbeing and mental health: Definitions, developmental transitions, and data sets. *Counselling and Psychotherapy Research, 19*(4), 351–357.

Bhargava, M. (2020, May 6). Mental health issues have always been poorly understood: Shekhar Saxena. *The Hindu BusinessLine.* Retrieved from https://www.thehindubusinessline.com/news/mental-health-issues-have-always-been-poorly-understood-shekhar-saxena/article31516705.ece

Bista, K., & Dagley, A. (2015). Higher education preparation and decision-making trends among international students. *College and University, 90*(3), 2–11.

Braun, V., & Clarke, V. (2006). Using thematic analysis in psychology. *Qualitative Research in Psychology, 3*(2), 77–101.

Browne, V., Munro, J., & Cass, J. (2017). Under the radar: The mental health of Australian university students. *Journal of the Australian and New Zealand Student Services Association, 25*(2), 51 62.

Berger, E., & Reupert, A. (2020). The COVID-19 pandemic in Australia: Lessons learnt. *Psychological Trauma: Theory, Research, Practice, and Policy, 12*(5), 494–496.

Cao, W., Fang, Z., Hou, G., Han, M., Xu, X., Dong, J., & Zheng, J. (2020). The psychological impact of the COVID-19 epidemic on college students in China. *Psychiatry Research, 287*, 112934.

Carter, M., Pagliano, P., Francis, A., & Thorne, M. (2017). Australian university students and mental health: Viewpoints from the literature. *International Journal of Innovation, Creativity and Change, 3*(2), 1–25.

Caron, J., Fleury, M., Perreault, M., Crocker, A., Tremblay, J., Tousignant, M., Kestens, Y., Cargo, M., & Daniel, M. (2012). Prevalence of psychological distress and mental disorders and use of mental health services in the epidemiological catchment area of Montreal South-West. *BMC Psychiatry, 12*, 183.

Commonwealth of Australia. (2021). *About mental health.* https://www.health.gov.au/health-topics/mental-health-and-suicide-prevention/about-mental-health

Creswell, J., & Creswell, J. (2018). *Research design: Qualitative, quantitative, and mixed methods approaches.* Sage.

Cunningham, H. (2019). Responding to what we notice: International student teaching as a pathway to cultural responsiveness. *Urban Education, 54*(9), 1262–1289.

Department of Education, Skills and Employment. (2021). *International student data*. https://internationaleducation.gov.au/research/international-student-data/Documents/MONTHLY%20SUMMARIES/2021/Sep%202021%20MonthlyInfographic.pdf

Dias, P., Campos, L., Almeida, H., & Palha, F. (2018). Mental health literacy in young adults: Adaptation and psychometric properties of the mental health literacy questionnaire. *International Journal of Environmental Research and Public Health, 15*(7), 1318.

Dodd, R., Dadaczynski, K., Okan, O., McCaffery, K., & Pickles, K. (2021). Psychological wellbeing and academic experience of university students in Australia during COVID-19. *International Journal of Environmental Research and Public Health, 18*, 866.

Firang, D. (2020). The impact of COVID-19 pandemic on international students in Canada. *International Social Work, 63*(6), 820–824.

Francis, A., & Udah, H. (2020). Coronavirus and Ruby Princess crew in Australia: A call for increased macro level social work. *International Journal of Innovation, Creativity and Change, 14*(6), 166–181.

Friedli, L. (2009). *Mental health, resilience, and inequalities*. WHO Regional Office for Europe.

Gallagher, H., Doherty, A., & Obonyo, M. (2020). International student experiences in Queensland during COVID-19. *International Social Work, 63*(6), 815–819.

Gautam, C., Lowery, C., Mays, C., & Durant, D. (2016). Challenges for global learners: A qualitative study of the concerns and difficulties of international students. *Journal of International Students, 6*(2), 501–526.

Gorczynski, P. (2018, February 22). More academics and students have mental health problems than ever before. The Conversation. Retrieved from https://theconversation.com/more-academics-and-students-have-mental-health-problems-than-ever-before-90339

Graham-Harrison, E., Giuffrida, A., Smith, H., & Ford, L. (2020, March 28). Lockdowns around the world bring rise in domestic violence. *The Guardian*. Retrieved from https://www.theguardian.com/society/2020/mar/28/lockdowns-world-rise-domestic-violence

Huang, L., Kern, M., & Oades, L. (2020). Strengthening university student wellbeing: Language and perceptions of Chinese international students. *International Journal of Environmental Research and Public Health, 17*(15), 5538.

International Student. (2021). *Growing destination*. https://www.internationalstudent.com/study_australia/why_study_australia/growing-destination/

Khan, A., Sultana, S., Hossain, S., Hasan, M., Ahmed, H., & Sikder, T. (2020). The impact of COVID-19 pandemic on mental health & wellbeing among home-quarantined Bangladeshi students: A cross-sectional pilot study. *Journal of Affective Disorders, 277*, 121–128.

Khawaja, N., & Dempsey, J. (2007). Psychological distress in international university students: An Australian Study. *Australian Journal of Guidance and Counselling, 17*(1), 13–27.

Kumar, A., & Nayar, K. (2020). COVID 19 and its mental health consequences. *Journal of Mental Health, 30*(1), 1–2.

Last, J. (2001). *A dictionary of epidemiology*. Oxford University Press.

Montemurro, N. (2020). The emotional impact of COVID-19: From medical staff to common people. *Brain, Behavior, and Immunity, 87*, 23–24.

Neto, F. (2020). Subjective well-being of Angolan students in Portugal. *Journal of Studies in International Education, 24*(4), 456–473.

Orygen. (2017). *Under the radar. The mental health of Australian university students*. Orygen, The National Centre of Excellence in Youth Mental Health.

O'Sullivan, D., Rahamathulla, M., & Pawar, M. (2020). The impact and implications of COVID-19: An Australian perspective. *The International Journal of Community and Social Development, 2*(2), 134–151.

Paredes, M., Apaolaza, V., Fernandez-Robin, C., Hartmann, P., & Yañez-Martinez, D. (2020). The impact of the COVID-19 pandemic on subjective mental well-being: The interplay of perceived threat, future anxiety, and resilience. *Personality and Individual Differences, 170*, 110455.

Patel, V., Saxena, S., Lund, C., Thornicroft, G., Baingana, F., Bolton, P., Chisholm, D., Collins, P., Cooper, J., Eaton, J., Herrman, H., Herzallah, M., Huang, Y., Jordans, M., Kleinman, A., Medina-Mora, M., Morgan, E., Niaz, U., …, UnÜtzer, J.(2018). The Lancet commission on global mental health and sustainable development. *Lancet, 392*(10157), 1553–1598.

Patton, M. (2015). *Qualitative research & evaluation methods: Integrating theory and practice.* Sage.

Pierce, M., Hope, H., Ford, T., Hatch, S., Hotopf, M., John, A., Kontopantelis, E., Webb, R., Wessely, S., McManus, S., & Abel, K. (2020). Mental health before and during the COVID-19 pandemic: A longitudinal probability sample survey of the UK population. *The Lancet Psychiatry, 7*(10), 883–892.

Sahu, P. (2020). Closure of universities due to coronavirus disease 2019 (COVID-19): Impact on education and mental health of students and academic staff. *Cureus, 12*(4), e7541.

Shafaei, A., Nejati, M., & Abd Razak, N. (2018). A model of psychological well-being among international students. *Educational Psychology, 38*(1), 17–37.

Sherry, M., Thomas, P., & Chui, W. (2010). International students: A vulnerable student population. *Higher Education, 60*, 33–46.

Soong, H. (2020, May 4). COVID-19 increases risk to international students' mental health. Australia urgently needs to step up. *The Conversation.* Retrieved from https://theconversation.com/covid-19-increases-risk-to-international-students-mental-health-australia-urgently-needs-to-step-up-137596

Udah, H. (2021). Coloniality of power and international students experience: What are the ethical responsibilities of social work and human service educators? *Ethics and Social Welfare, 15*(1), 84–99.

Udah, H. (2016). *Understanding African immigrant experiences in South East Queensland.* (Unpublished doctoral dissertation). Griffith University.

Udah, H., & Francis, A. (2021). COVID-19: Challenges, opportunities, and the future of Social Work. *International Journal of Innovation, Creativity and Change, 15*(1), 54–74.

Udah, H., & Singh, P. (2019). Identity, othering and belonging: Toward an understanding of difference and the experiences of African immigrants to Australia. *Social Identities, 25*(6), 843–859.

Udah, H., Singh, P., Holscher, D., & Cartmel, J. (2019). Experiences of vulnerability and sources of resilience among immigrants and refugees. *The Australasian Review of African Studies, 40*(1), 81–100.

United Nations. (2020). *Policy brief: COVID-19 and the need for action on mental health.* https://www.un.org/sites/un2.un.org/files/un_policy_brief-covid_and_mental_health_final.pdf

United Nations Educational, Scientific and Cultural Organisation. (2019). *Education: Outbound internationally mobile students by host region.* http://data.uis.unesco.org/

van Agteren, J., Woodyatt, L., Iasiello, M., Rayner, J., & Kyrios, M. (2019). Make it measurable: Assessing psychological distress, wellbeing, and resilience at scale in higher education. *Student Success, 10*(3), 1–13.

World Health Organisation. (2018). *Mental health: Strengthening our response.* https://www.who.int/news-room/fact-sheets/detail/mental-health-strengthening-our-response

World Health Organisation. (2020). *Coronavirus.* https://www.who.int/health-topics/coronavirus#tab=tab_1

Wright, B., & Winslade, M. (2018, August 21). University staff and students are at high risk of ill health. Here's how to make sure they can cope. *The Conversation.* Retrieved from https://theconversation.com/university-staff-and-students-are-at-high-risk-of-ill-health-heres-how-to-make-sure-they-can-cope-101070

Wu, H., Garza, E., & Guzman, N. (2015). International student's challenge and adjustment to college. *Education Research International*, 202753.

Zhai, Y., & Du, X. (2020). Addressing collegiate mental health amid COVID-19 pandemic. *Psychiatry Research, 288*, 113003.

Hyacinth Udah is a Senior Lecturer in Social Work and Human Services at the James Cook University. He holds Doctorate and Master's degrees in Social Work from Griffith University, and the Australian Catholic University, respectively. He also has a First-Class Honours degree in Theology and Philosophy. His doctoral study explored the African immigrant experiences, and his recent research publications are extending his interests in immigrant experiences, coloniality and decoloniality, community development, mental health and wellbeing, social work ethics, values, education, research and practice.

Abraham Francis is an Associate Professor and currently the Head of Academic Group in Social Work and Human Services at James Cook University, Australia. He has worked with government, non-government and corporate sector and has developed many international partnerships. He taught social work at the Delhi University in India and worked as a senior mental health social worker with Country Health South Australia before moving to Townsville to join James Cook University. Dr. Francis has established many international partnerships and research collaborations with universities and non-government organisations.

He has extensively contributed to the literature on social work practice in mental health through his publications, convening conferences, establishing research networks and by developing consortiums. His other research interests are in the field of communities, criminal justice, international social work and gerontological social work. His excellence in teaching has been recognised on a number of occasions. For example, in 2010, he was a recipient of James Cook University's Inclusive Practice Award for his 'exceptional support for students with a disability'. In 2016, he received the university's '***Citation for Outstanding Contributions to Student Learning***' for his 'leadership and expertise in social work education in mental health that inspires and nurtures students to be competent, confident and compassionate practitioners'.

Dr. Francis was one of the finalists at the 2018 India ***Australia Business and Community Awards*** in the category of Community Services Excellence Award and Business Leader/Professional of the Year. In 2018, Dr. Francis received the NAPSWI (National Association of Professional Association Social Workers in India) Life Time Achievement Award for his outstanding contribution to social work education.

For more details—https://research.jcu.edu.au/portfolio/abraham.francis/.

Mental Health in Higher Education and the Community—Building Capability, Sharing Experience

Jeremy Audas

Abstract Higher education providers operate within local, state, national, and international communities and share many of the issues and concerns about mental health and wellbeing. Collaboration between communities and universities benefits both and contributes to better outcomes for staff, students, community service providers, and community members. Local examples illustrate how this can occur in a range of community service settings. The key to success is the resilience of communities, organisations, and individuals. Within this content the contribution of lived experience in building resilience must be recognised as this contribution will support a collaborative approach to work across the higher education and community service sectors.

Keywords Community · Mental health · Capacity building

Background

Higher education has long been a place where research, teaching, and discovery have played a strong role in identifying new trends and approaches to a wide range of human and community service endeavours. As a leader of contemporary discourse about mental health, higher education is uniquely positioned to influence mental health theory and practice.

Current community service provision is informed by work being done by researchers, students, and academic staff as they reflect their communities' desire to improve wellbeing and mental health programs and services. It is vital though that such work also focusses on what is occurring inside higher education institutions. We must consider the mental health and wellbeing of students and staff across all levels of university life. Just as there is a general trend in Australia towards addressing the impacts of poor mental health in community organisations, local government areas,

J. Audas (✉)
Richmond Fellowship Queensland (RFQ), Annerley, Brisbane, Australia
e-mail: Jeremy.audas@rfq.com.au

A. P. Francis and M. A. Carter (eds.), *Mental Health and Higher Education in Australia*,
https://doi.org/10.1007/978-981-16-8040-3_19

workplaces, sporting bodies, and other sites the higher education sector must reflect on how these changes can also be embedded in universities.

Research into mental ill health has been occurring for centuries in one form or another and from the eighteenth and nineteenth centuries the foundations of our current mental health practices were laid with the rise of the moral treatment movement in Europe in the late eighteenth century. This is essentially a journey from a custodial framework where people with psychosocial disorders were often isolated from their communities to a recovery-oriented framework where people are encouraged to become agents in their own pathways to a better life. As a result of historical and contemporary research there is a growing body of knowledge about the impacts of poor mental health on individuals, institutions and communities as societal conditions change.

The current COVID pandemic is a case in point. This pandemic has revealed just how important it is to ensure structures and systems are in place to support people impacted not just by Covid19 itself but the mental health and wellbeing of individuals, families, and communities that the disruption to our daily lives has wrought. It is interesting to observe just how quickly research organisations across the world swung into action to research the effects of and responses to the virus, including vaccine development. It is research, including into lived experience of mental illness, that underpins the discourses and approaches to mental health and wellbeing that now drive contemporary practice.

Community organisations adopt best practice in mental health and wellbeing service delivery through mandated frameworks such as the National Standards for Mental Health Services which have been developed through consultation with stakeholders, including people with a lived experience of mental illness as well as their family members and carers. The standards are also underpinned by extensive reference to contemporary research.

Today we have increasing government investment into mental health research however not all this work is undertaken directly by universities. Organisations such as Beyond Blue for example, are heavily invested in research through its annual Partnership Grants Scheme with research teams on National Health and Medical Research Council Partnership Grants and Australian Research Council Linkage Grants. Naturally, universities play a major role in these endeavours by partnering with other organisations to support mental health and wellbeing research and evaluation.

To date much mental health research has been ad hoc and driven by one interest group or another or based on the needs of the research funding body. What is urgently needed is a national mental health research strategy. To this end and based on the findings of its Contributing Lives Review, the Australian National Mental Health Commission has been tasked under the Commonwealth's Fifth National Mental Health and Suicide Prevention Plan with developing a research strategy to drive better outcomes across the mental health sector in Australia. The Fifth National Mental Health and Suicide Prevention Plan was endorsed by the Council of Australian Governments (COAG) Health Council in August 2017. The Fifth Plan represents commitment from all governments to work together to achieve integrated planning and service delivery of mental health and suicide prevention related services.

The Commission is working in collaboration with consumers and carers, states and territories, research funding bodies and prominent researchers to develop the strategy which is due to be completed in 2021. An overarching strategy for mental health research has long been called for by people working in the mental health and wellbeing sector in Australia. Peak bodies, mental health leaders, and advocates have been instrumental in driving this approach.

In 2013, Obsessive Hope Disorder, Reflections on 30 Years of Mental Health Reform in Australia and Visions for the Future, was published by ConNetica (Mendoza et al., 2013). The paper asserts that much mental health reform has taken place without the strong foundations that reform needs, including comprehensive national research. The title of this report refers to both the notion of hope as a driver of personal recovery from mental illness and the fact that the mental health service system has been advocating for major reform with little result, that is, we live in hope of positive responses to the scores of government sponsored reports, inquiries, and investigations into mental health over the last 30 years. In the report's foreword David Richmond AO (Chair of the Richmond Inquiry into Health Services for the Psychiatrically Ill and Developmentally Disabled, 1983) states that: *The ability, however, to analyse and synthesise the economic, political, social, scientific and systems knowledge and experience we possess and then to mobilise reform through advocacy appears currently beyond our fragmented system of mental health services.*

This is a major problem the implications of which are only now being realised as increasing levels of anxiety, depression, and other psychosocial impacts of societal stressors—unemployment, disengagement, financial disadvantage, discrimination, family breakdown, uncertainty about the future, and natural and anthropogenic induced disasters.

Mental Health in Higher Education

The Australasian Mental Health in Higher Education (AMHHEC) Conferences and webinars have attracted a great deal of interest nationally and internationally amply demonstrated by the range of speakers, workshop conveners, topics, and proceedings. The efforts to connect with the local community and bring together the interests of communities and higher education is a prominent feature of the AMHHEC initiative. Clearly issues around mental health and wellbeing are not solely the province of one sector or another or one industry or another. Neither is it a matter for health providers only. In fact, health providers should be the last line of defence when it comes to responding to growing levels of mental illness and psychological distress. With a paucity of early intervention services and the bulk of government funding going to hospitals and clinical services the community mental health sector struggles to meet demand for essential early intervention and prevention services.

Good mental health and wellbeing is the responsibility of all of us. From individual responsibility to take care of oneself to workplaces and national strategies Australia has some wonderful examples of how to better manage mental health and wellbeing yet do we really do enough?

Certainly, within universities students and staff can find themselves in incredibly stressful situations, they remain vulnerable to external and internal stressors and are at risk of being impacted by poor mental health. This has been exacerbated by the impact of Covid19. For example, the plight of international students who have been stranded in Australia with little or no government support. The Australian government's decision not to bring universities into the Jobkeeper scheme means the highly casualised workforce is at risk. In the same way other sectors outside of higher education are exposed to stressors that impact wellbeing. The results might be the same—deteriorating mental health, the causes may be different, and the responses can be incredibly varied. With evidence-based prevention, intervention and postvention there is potential to manage mental health and wellbeing in a positive, practical, and cost-effective way.

But it is not just students in higher education whose wellbeing must be considered. It is also about academic, administrative, and ancillary staff. Universities are workplaces and as such need to consider the welfare of all staff and students. The purpose of Australian workplace health and safety laws is to eliminate or minimise risks to the health and safety of workers. "Health" is defined as meaning psychological as well as physical health. Employers have specific duties in relation to managing risks to psychological health and safety. There are multiple causes of workplace stress or injury and the benefits of managing these well are obvious. But how to do so is problematic and involves investments guided by a long-term view. There is no quick fix.

From Creating a Mentally Healthy Workplace Return on Investment analysis:

> Mental health conditions present substantial costs to organisations. However, through the successful implementation of an effective action to create a mentally healthy workplace, organisations, on average, can expect a positive return on investment (ROI) of 2.3. That is, for every dollar spent on successfully implementing an appropriate action, there is on average \$2.30 in benefits to be gained by the organisation. (page iv)

There are lessons to be learnt from outside the higher education sector. The Queensland Department of Education is acutely aware of the psychological risks to secondary students' mental health and wellbeing and has implemented some important strategies to support pupils, teachers, principals, and other staff. The approach it has employed includes policy and procedural responses that incorporate guidance officers, chaplains and welfare officers, community education counsellors (with a focus on aboriginal and Torres Strait Islander students), school-based youth health nurses, state school registered nurses and for students at risk of disengagement, youth support coordinators and alternative learning strategies.

It seems that access to these kinds of specific and targeted wellbeing and mental health supports and interventions might be lacking in the higher education sector. However, it must be acknowledged that universities generally employ a range of student support services including contact officers, mentoring programs, equity and access services, chaplains, and counselling as well as support for particular groups, disability, cultural and indigenous students. These are essential services but are they enough? Is there a need for a comprehensive overarching approach that incorporates these efforts into an inclusive strategy to support and enhance student wellbeing? Does the university have a mentally healthy workplace policy?

Resilience

Resilience is a protective factor and key to supporting people with various mental health conditions, such as depression and anxiety. Resilient individuals are better able to cope with what comes their way, to get back on their feet after a crisis and to support others. This applies to organisations too.

Organisational resilience is the ability to adjust quickly to events, expected or not. It allows an organisation to increase its chances of surviving its own mistakes and external events and thus reducing the impact on its clients, customers, students, and staff. Its premise is that to survive unforeseen events (e.g., a pandemic) an organisation needs to be pro-active through four elements: foresight, agility, robustness, and planned recovery. By using risk management tools to look ahead and predict potential issues then being agile enough to navigate the problem requires a robust organisation able to absorb unexpected shocks whilst at the same time having an underlying recovery strategy which should always be about people first. This approach is entirely appropriate and relatively easily implemented (From Achieving Organisational Resilience, 2011 Bob Dick and Brian Donaldson).

The University and Community

Universities, as places of higher learning, were once very much exclusive sites set apart from the communities in which they operated and not universally accessible. Over time this has changed remarkedly to the point where they are now, generally speaking, far more egalitarian, and accessible, albeit with financial consequences for students. New universities have emerged, and campuses can be accessed by people in many regional centres around Australia. This has led to greater interaction with local communities as well as business and industry. The ability for universities to reach into local communities and engage with external stakeholders appears to be growing. However scarce resources, government policies and the interests of business and professional bodies also have an impact. Increasingly governments see higher education as a tool in the hands of decision-makers that should be used to further national economic and employment agendas rather than a place where citizens can grow and develop as they follow their own interests and career paths.

In the major regional city of Townsville, North Queensland, the presence of James Cook University and Central Queensland University provide for many opportunities for locals and those studying as external students. It is where community members can further their studies, it supports employment for staff and graduates and local organisations such as the Australian Institute of Marine Science (AIMS), provides local community organisations, businesses, and industry with expertise through graduate recruitment. Townsville University Hospital has strong links with James Cook University through teaching and research programs. These and other partnerships, sponsorships and connections embed higher education in the local and regional communities.

On a smaller but no less important scale, local community-based organisations, mostly not for profit, benefit from the presence of a university. Various disciplines within the university provide an opportunity for collaboration in the local community.

Student placements are a critical part of higher education, and a thriving community service industry provides placement opportunities for students as well as potential opportunities for the community organisation to benefit from students' knowledge of current theory and practice. The university provides opportunities for evaluation and research of community service programs and initiatives, and this has been highly beneficial in terms of building the capability of both. If only funding for community service provision included a research or evaluation component! For the community sector this is the major issue because it hinders the development of new programs and services targeted at particular issues or populations. As well as thinking about evidence-based practice, we should also be looking at practice-based evidence where organisations innovate and create new ways of working that can lead to better outcomes.

Some Local Examples of Collaboration and Partnerships

Community Development

The Tropical Brain and Mind Foundation has partnered with Townsville City Council to deliver the Mentally Healthy Cities Project (www.mentallyhealthycitytownsville.com.au) The Foundation seeks and encourages research excellence in brain health, brain skills, and the economic benefits that come from such projects. This partnership has delivered workshops, programs, and interventions that support the good mental health and wellbeing of people in Townsville and is supported by the Qld Mental Health Commission and the Qld Alliance for Mental Health amongst others.

Law

Townsville Community Law partners with the Law School at James Cook University to provide opportunities for law students through its clinical programs and volunteer advice program that enables evening services to be provided to eligible community members. Law graduates are encouraged to apply for vacant positions and clinical support is provided to support students' professional development. The Queensland Law Society has developed a resilience and wellbeing portal, through which members can access all current mental health and wellbeing initiatives of the QLS and receive the information and support tools necessary to manage the pressures of work and life in the legal profession.

Medical Training

The organisation formerly known as the Mental Illness Fellowship of North Queensland provided Mental Health First Aid Training for students in the School of Medicine and Dentistry at James Cook University amongst others. This connection between expertise based in the community and higher education was beneficial and regular repeat sessions were delivered to various cohorts within the university.

Youth

Headspace National has oversight of the network of headspace centres around Australia that aim to address psychosocial issues for young people. Their model of service and its outcomes and impacts are constantly measured through research and partnerships with higher education providers. The provision of evidence-based data drives the development of the headspace model and is continually monitoring and evaluating all aspects of its work. It has a publicly accessible webpage with details about what research exists about reducing mental health issues in young people.

Migrants and Refugees

The Townsville Intercultural Centre held its inaugural Unity in Diversity Conference in Brisbane in 2019. This conference brought together community organisations, academics, advocates, and community leaders to discuss a wide range of issues to do with concepts of social justice, equity, inclusion, identity, cultural diversity, inclusive services, and community cohesion. The willingness of academics and others to engage in the conference topics enabled the sharing of ideas, information, issues, and concerns that in turn generated closer connections between agencies and individuals for the benefit of our communities. The Intercultural Centre has developed a range of initiatives to support clients with their mental health and wellbeing.

Suicide Prevention

The Townsville Suicide Prevention Network, a community initiative established by the Mental Illness Fellowship of North Queensland in partnership with Wesley Life Force has amongst its membership academic staff of James Cook University. This enables research-based activities to inform and evaluate the network's development and growth.

For both higher education and the community services sector there are obvious benefits to working more collaboratively in multiple ways, formal and informal relationships, fee for service activities, program research and evaluation, workshops and forums and other mechanisms that bring higher education and community together.

One of the often-heard criticisms of higher education, even from the employers of graduates, is that it does not prepare them for the "real world". This begs the question about the purpose of universities. Either way there is huge potential for the sharing of expertise, ideas and creative endeavour that would enrich both community services and higher education. It is wonderful to experience the contribution that is made by university students on placement in a community service organisation. That interface creates opportunities for the exchange of ideas, for reflective practice and for students to engage directly with the organisation's staff and clients, systems and processes, governance and service delivery models which enhance both the students' appreciation of what work in the community entails and the organisation's ability to identify and learn new ideas and approaches.

Community Mental Health

Many community service organisations, especially those working in mental health and wellbeing, have adopted strong governance models that incorporate mental health and wellbeing policies. Such policies focus on two groups, the organisation's clients and the organisation's staff. The former is generally supported and underpinned by clinical governance and accreditation frameworks that guide practitioners in their work. They are often developed out of a risk management framework and are in place to protect the rights, wellbeing, and health of clients. The latter are internal policies aimed at supporting staff rights, wellbeing, risk management, and health. Both sets of policies have elements that are mandated by workplace health and safety laws but may also incorporate specific components that are driven by best practice rather than statutory legal imperatives.

An organisational approach to improving responses to mental health and wellbeing challenges might incorporate a self-audit of policies and procedures to ensure that they support good mental health for staff and clients. Such an audit identifies shortcomings and risks and, with a continuous improvement approach can result in the development of better contemporary practices and strengthens workplace effectiveness and employee health.

It is useful to consider the meaning of the term "Community Mental Health" because its meaning varies depending on context and adds another layer of complexity to the mental health and wellbeing discourse. The following explanation is helpful and is from a submission from the peak body Community Mental Health Australia (CMHA) on the Productivity Commission Draft Report on Mental Health (Bill Gye CEO CMHA January 2020).

The phrase "Community Mental Health" has at least eight meanings depending upon context, these being:

1. The mental health of the community (where the "community" referred to also depends upon context—from the whole Australian community to small regional area communities to groups that identify by a common characteristic(s) such as the LGBTQIA + Community)
2. All mental health services delivered in the community (both public, private & not-for profit)
3. Mental health services that are to a considerable extent delivered by the community, that is by peers and/or people that identify with or are part of that local community.
4. Mental health services delivered by the non-government sector (both private and not-for-profit organisation)
5. Mental health service delivered by the not-for-profit sector (i.e., community managed organisations (CMOs), usually registered with ACNC)
6. Public mental health services delivered outside of hospital (i.e., "Specialist Community Mental Health Services", "Ambulatory Community Mental Health Services")
7. Of late, Psychosocial Support Services have sometimes been used as a substitute for the term community mental health, which is both helpful and unhelpful.
8. So called "Clinical" verses "non-Clinical" services.

For the not-for-profit mental health service sector these definitions are important because for people with a mental illness, their carers and family members the most pressing need is for quick access to appropriate services and supports when a crisis arises. The entire mental health system is fragmented, multi-layered, complex and at times confusing so taking the perspective of a community member who is having an episode of mental illness, maybe for the first time, and who is seeking help and whose family is worried, not knowing what to do, it's easy to see why people can struggle to gain the help they need when there is not even a common understanding of the term "community mental health".

People's experiences drive their behaviour and for people with a mental illness negative experiences when seeking help can be very damaging and result in social isolation, disengagement and can exacerbate their condition. People well on the way to recovery from mental illness and who have struggled against all odds to attain a mentally healthy state generally have many stories and learnings about their experiences. This might include their interface with clinicians in a hospital setting, with police and the criminal justice system, stigma, poor physical health, family and carer support, and most importantly what it is they have learned that has helped them move forward. These collective experiences when reflected on, absorbed, and transformed provide the underpinning attributes for turning these often-negative experiences into positive strategies to self-manage and build resilience.

Lived Experience

Over recent decades more and more evidence has emerged about the value of a lived experience of mental illness. This has resulted in the peer workforce movement which utilises the important and authentic voices of people impacted by mental illness to inform the development of programs, services, and models of service that best meet the needs of clients, including family members and carers.

Lived Experience Australia is an organisation that is based on the voices of people with a lived experience of mental illness and has a strong research function designed to provide support to advocate for improvements in the mental health system. It certainly makes a difference in systemic advocacy by being informed about the issues facing people with mental health issues, their families and carers and using this to influence mental health policy, planning and decision-making at local, state, and national levels.

Lived experience teaches us about the impact of various models of service delivery on individuals and has led to significant changes in approaches. De-institutionalisation, recovery-oriented practice, human rights, and issues with restrictive practices have all been informed by people with a lived experience. The results are that today someone with a mental illness can receive much better supports and services than in the past.

Lived experience also contributes strongly to the reduction of stigma. It was not so long ago that depression and PTSD were rarely talked about in the open and that there was an element of guilt and shame about such a diagnosis. Today we see a reduction in stigma around anxiety, depression, suicidality, and PTSD and certainly this has contributed to a better acceptance of people impacted by mental illness. On the other hand, other illnesses such as schizophrenia, for example, have not experienced such a decline in stigma and remain highly stigmatised and misunderstood.

Working Together for Mental Health

In one sense mental health services in the community use a collaborative approach in the relationship between the mental health worker and the client. Negotiated support outcomes and risk assessments, goal setting and recovery pathway development rely on the relationship between the worker and client. For both people this can be a liberating experience as it firmly puts the needs of the client at the forefront and enables them to become informed decision-makers in relation to their own lives.

Collaboration is evident at case management meetings where the client, family members, carers, clinicians, and support workers engage in discussions about how to move forward, what the person's needs and wants are and how these can be addressed in a way that enhances the individual's recovery pathway.

A multi-disciplinary approach to recovery is important with the involvement of psychologists, psychiatrists, mental health nurses, social workers, and occupational therapists all having a role. As important as these roles are it does not mean that is all that is required. Other complementary approaches carry equal weight; peer mentoring, recovery coaching, housing support, employment programs are important for some people. Others may benefit from ongoing counselling or meaningful voluntary work.

The approach must be led by the person's authentic expressed needs and must be tempered by a willingness to enable safe and supported risk taking. The challenge is to walk side by side with the person, guiding but not directing, supporting but not creating dependency and working out of a genuine commitment to the principles of recovery-oriented practice within a human rights framework.

The key to successful work in mental health and wellbeing is to have or develop positive relationships. This applies equally to relationships with clients, family members, and those directly impacted by mental distress as it does to relationships within and across human and community service sectors. These sector relationships can lead to collaboration around common issues and concerns and open the door for more formal relationships that in turn can lead to surprising discoveries.

Higher education and community services serve the same purpose, the betterment of the human condition. Together, employing respectful relationships, collaboration, and cooperation lead to far better outcomes for individuals and communities. That is why building capability and sharing experience through collaboration is so important to improving mental health and wellbeing.

References

Community Mental Health Australia. (2020). *Submission from Community Mental Health Australia (CMHA) on the productivity commission draft report mental health.* https://cmha.org.au/wp-content/uploads/2020/02/community-mental-health-Australia-submission-on-the-pc-draft-report.pdf

Lived Experience Australia. (n.d.). *The representative organisation for consumers and families in mental health.* https://www.livedexperienceaustralia.com.au/

Mendoza, J. A., Bresnan, A., Rosenberg, S., Elson, A., Gilbert, Y., Long, P., Wilson, K., & Hopkins, J. (2013). *Obsessive hope disorder: Reflections on 30 years of mental health reform in Australia and visions for the future.* ConNetica. https://static1.squarespace.com/static/540e6e4b0311c08079c4/t/54167eb6e4b00c34afd90922/1410760374509/

Jeremy Audas has worked in human and community services for over 40 years. Much of this time was as a schoolteacher and later as a TAFE teacher and program manager. For the last twenty years, he has held leadership roles in various state government departments in North Queensland and since 2011 has worked in the not-for-profit community service sector. As a former CEO of a medium-sized mental health organisation, he has wide experience in managing workplace and funding challenges including the introduction of the National Disability Insurance Scheme. He has been a member of the Queensland Mental Health Commission Advisory Council, is a board member of the Queensland Alliance for Mental Health as well as Chair of the board of the Townsville Intercultural Centre and President of Townsville Community Law. He is also a member of the North Queensland Primary Health Network Advisory Group. His interests are in community development, social justice, advocacy, the design and promotion of high-quality services for people with a mental illness and those who might have alcohol and other drug problems, including support for carers and family members. Whilst he is currently Executive Manager, North Queensland, for the Richmond Fellowship Queensland he is not representing the organisation in this paper.

Interprofessional Collaboration in Promoting Wellbeing in the Higher Education Sector: The AMHHEC Experience

Beryl Buckby

Abstract The Australasian Mental Health in Higher Education Conference brings together academics, students, practitioners, community organizations and interested members of the general public to collaboratively discuss and debate mental health wellbeing to inform and transform misconceptions of the university community and the general public. The interprofessional planning group drawn from diverse disciplines worked effectively together by adapting profession and discipline-specific terminologies to ensure clear and accurate communication.

Keywords Interprofessional collaboration · Mental health · Universities · Higher education

The Australasian Mental Health in Higher Education Conference reflected the WHO (2010, p. 7) definitions of interprofessional education and collaboration which are "necessary steps in preparing a collaborative practice-ready health and mental health workforce that is better prepared to respond to local health needs." In the AMHHEC context, the focus of two face-to-face conferences was primarily wellbeing of university students and staff, with significant participation from the university sector, community organizations and individuals from around Australia and visitors from overseas. Conference planning was collaborative from the outset with representation from the Colleges of James Cook University, as well as other Australian and international universities, local community organizations, individuals and invited guest speakers. Presenters were drawn mostly from universities across Australia, as well as health, mental health sectors and community organizations in two face-to-face conferences in 2018 and 2019 and then in response to COVID-19, in two online webinars.

Universities Australia (2008) advocated for collaborative engagement across governments, universities, community organizations and industry to enhance skills and employability of university graduates. While the AMHHEC conference did not

B. Buckby (✉)
James Cook University, Townsville, Australia
e-mail: beryl.buckby@jcu.edu.au

A. P. Francis and M. A. Carter (eds.), *Mental Health and Higher Education in Australia*,
https://doi.org/10.1007/978-981-16-8040-3_20

directly advocate for such goals, the participating attendees, organizations, presenters and presentations provided a diversity of thought-provoking ideas to promote wellbeing to carry forward into career goals and opportunities for students and others who attended. The approach and the obvious collegiality of presenters modeled interprofessional collaboration as a desirable goal for students and others in attendance establishing as well as informing their own careers and practice to avoid the harms of burn-out and other occupational hazards (Eaton, 2019).

Furthermore, interprofessional educational experiences for students learning together with students from other health, mental health and social care disciplines have consistently found positive attitude change following a multidisciplinary/interprofessional education programs (Fitzgerald et al., 2006; Kelly et al., 2020). In this respect, students, academics and others attending the conference had a significant interprofessional learning experience that exposed attendees to multiple professions, conceptualizations, methodologies of working and opportunities to meet, discuss and question information they had seen, heard about and learned from, to inform their understanding of mental health. Such opportunities, particularly for students, are difficult if not impossible to apply within university learning and teaching structures, whereas the tacit learning acquired in multidisciplinary environments such as the AMHHE Conference involving education and health/mental health tends to erode acquired stereotyped attitudes that inhibit effective collaborative practice in many workplaces.

At the same time, as JCU was initiating the establishment of Australasian Mental Health in Higher Education Conference, a network of universities was meeting to establish a network of health promoting universities.

Mentally Healthy Universities in Australia

"Representatives from 25 Australian universities have joined together to form the Australian Health Promoting Universities Network, which will see them work collaboratively to create healthier university campuses and communities" (Sydney University 15/3/2016).

> *"The network and its universities will also seek to sign the Okanagan Charter launched in October 2015 by the University of British Columbia. The Charter calls for universities to embed health into all aspects of campus culture and operations and to encourage health promotion activities in the wider community."*

The purpose of the Okanagan Charter is threefold:

1. Guide and inspire action by providing a framework that reflects the latest concepts, processes and principles relevant to the health promoting universities and colleges movement, building upon advances since the 2005 Edmonton Charter.
2. Generate dialog and research that expand local, regional, national and international networks and accelerate action on, off and between campuses.

3. Mobilize international, cross-sector action for the integration of health in all policies and practices, thus advancing the continued development of health promoting universities and colleges.

The Okanagan Charter has two calls to action for higher education institutions:

1. Embed health into all aspects of campus culture, across the administration, operations and academic mandates.
2. Lead health promotion action and collaboration locally and globally.

Australian universities (25) that joined the healthy universities network initiative in 2016 did not include James Cook University (JCU). This highlights the unique potential the AMHHE Conference plays in informing understanding and support for mental health and wellness in higher education, particularly at JCU where the conference originated, as well as promotion of the wellbeing of students, academics and other employees of the university and the broader communities in which JCU is embedded. Developing a short training aspect of the AMHHE Conference, for example, mental health wellbeing support, could be a productive future development initiative. As the often-quoted saying goes "suicide is everyone's business," in universities, mental health wellbeing is equally an imperative for students and staff to function optimally, suggesting that mental health is also everyone's business, yet seeking support is considered by some as a weakness and detrimental to future career prospects.

The relevance for the AMHHE Conference is that a selected few universities in Australia explicitly use the health promoting university approach. According to Taylor et al. (2019) while services are provided for students and staff, in Australia, it is infrequently used as a whole of university strategy as advocated by the Okanagan Charter. The obvious exceptions are the 25 universities that signed on to the Australian Health Promoting Universities Network (AHPUN) as reported in the Medical Journal of Australia in 2016.

What is known from empirical studies of Australian university students' use of mental health help-seeking support is instructive for planners of the AMHHE Conference. For example, Li et al. (2018) in their investigation of 611 Australian domestic students found that mental health knowledge and the services available, as well as perceived need and benefits of services, were influenced by stigma, other personal values, student knowledge and attitudes toward help seeking. However, Australian students, who may need mental health support, were found reluctant to use such services. It seems mental health stigma remains a barrier for students to seek help in a timely way.

One of the most interesting findings according to the authors (Li et al., 2018) was that "most participants had limited awareness of available services, and many had unfavorable attitudes and/or significant stigma concerns." In this respect, the AMHHE Conference has the potential to broadly inform students and academics about services available within universities and in the local community without the need to speak directly to a self-stigmatizing student who is far less likely to reveal their need for support.

Interprofessional Communication

Inevitably in coalitions of academics and practitioners with different professional training who come together in a collaborative endeavor such as conference planning, the potential for miscommunication increases. In conference planning as in practice, communication requires respect for the knowledge and skills of others and a deliberative attempt to modify professional terminologies into plain English for effective communication exchanges (IECEP, 2011). Effective interprofessional communications include:

- A teamwork environment of trust and openness within the group.
- Effective communication requires checking in to ensure there is common understanding.
- Trusting and respectful relationships within the group.
- Avoidance of discipline-specific terminologies.
- Active listening to other group members and open discussions of new ideas.
- Self-awareness that one's academic and professional history contributes most effectively when using plain English and limiting profession-specific terminologies.

Four themes relevant to interprofessional collaboration for the conference planning group were identified in Fernandez et al. (2020). These were: *the importance of a sense of belonging to a team, the imperative to meet face-to-face, the practice of soliciting the working hypotheses of colleagues and summarizing meeting discussions.*

The experience of working within the conference team drawn from colleges across the university and community sectors since 2016 is indicative of a team environment epitomizing effective goal directed collaboration. Observations of the planning group in action showed planning conversations were conducted within a Communication Accommodation Theory framework (Watson, Jones & Hewett, 2016) that ensured shared understandings across the group primarily through the willingness of members to adjust profession-specific terminologies into common inclusive wording easily understood by others (Table 1).

AMHHEC Leadership

In terms of leadership, the planning group tends to fall into a mixed model with contemporary and traditional elements defined by four dimensions (*structure, process, power and influence, responsibility within the planning group*).

The sharing of leadership sometimes involves supporting relationships and interconnectedness that values honesty, mutual respect, valuing what others offer and the ability to exercise personal choice. Shared AMHHEC leadership focused on facilitating the ability of the team to work to the shared vision for the conference. "Power"

Table 1 The AMHHEC Conference Leadership: A Contemporary model

Dimension	Traditional models	Contemporary models
Structure	Vertical The leader sits at the apex of the team	Horizontal/lateral Leader shifts from person to person depending on the specific expertise required
Process	Hierarchical The leader directs followers	Collective, shared, distributed "democratic"
Power and influence	Based on position, role, credentials	Based on knowledge and expertise
Responsibility for the team	Primarily the leader/s role	Distributed across the team

sat at the center of the team rather than as a top-down hierarchy. The valuing of, and respecting, individual differences contributed to a collective "ownership" of all planning decisions. Then, the COVID-19 tsunami came along and disrupted the business as usual of learning and teaching. Adaptations to teaching and learning quickly followed which were unsettling for students and teaching staff, yet with goodwill and creative planning ensured the AMHHEC group also adapted and delivered a short online series presentation.

As O'Grady (2021) succinctly states, "*Working and leading through turbulent times makes it nearly impossible to put your best professional foot forward, Monday through Friday. Sure, the work still needs to be done. You still need to hold teams accountable, ask for updates, and resolve problems. But if 2020 taught leaders anything, it is that our campuses won't succeed in the long term if we do not take care of the people we manage.*" However, what "taking care of" means is not particularly clear although it clearly points to the aims and objectives of the AMHHE Conference.

The issues identified in O'Grady provide some cues to potential conference inclusions going forward. Strolin-Goltzman et al. (2020) applied similar logic to the potential for interprofessional collaboration, leadership and competency to secondary traumatic stress in the child welfare and mental health sector, proposing that compassion fatigue (Figley, 1995) among service providers may be averted through the influence of community and organizational factors such as interprofessional collaboration. It may, however, professional structures differ significantly in mental health practice in which mental health wellbeing is the primary foci, whereas child welfare-related professions and practitioners prioritize child physical safety (p. 6) before mental health wellbeing, so it was not a foregone conclusion that the outcome would be beneficial to either the young persons or the practitioners. Consequently, drawing logical conclusions about what might work effectively was difficult to determine. However, interprofessional collaboration in Strolin-Goltzman et al. (0.58, $p < 0.01$ and 47, $p < 0.01$) had strong effects on secondary traumatic stress competency among child welfare workers and mental health providers indicating that there is some relevance to the saying "better together" in collaborative practice in the context of child welfare and secondary traumatic stress, (also known as compassion fatigue and burn-out).

Commitment and Acceptance

There is no doubt that university students' experience considerable stress when entering and during their period of enrollment and that many continue to subscribe to mental health stigma beliefs. Student support services are provided Australia-wide, yet engagement with support services may not occur, or attendance may be sporadic when the student, or staff member, self-stigmatize such struggles as being "weak." This is born out in research (Reavley et al., 2012), who conducted telephone interviews with 774 Australian students at a metropolitan university and 422 staff as a comparison group. Students expressed greater psychological distress than staff, however, staff were more likely to be proactive in dealing with their distress by seeking help from a GP and being more proactive in physical activity than students. Students, although being more psychologically distressed than staff, tended to describe their experiences similarly to the depression vignette used in the study and were reluctant to seek help from student counseling preferring to rely on friends who may or may not be well equipped to provide informed support.

Unrealistic expectations about becoming a university student (Christie et al., 2008) are likely to play a significant role for first in family or "non-traditional" students when "coming to know" a new community of practice that generates emotional responses including feelings of alienation and exclusion. Christie et al. argue that the emotional interaction between the student and the learning environment of the university is equally important. The process of adaptation for such students is very likely to involve commitment to adjust to the learning environment as well as an emotional adjustment for the student and their interaction with the learning environment. On the education provider side of the equation, support for such students to adjust to the new learning context and university environment is likely to support student wellbeing and possibly success in their chosen course.

The Zochil and Thorsteinsson (2018) study found similarly to Reavley et al. (2012) that even if symptoms of depression, anxiety and stress were present and students experienced poor sleep their intention to seek help was low. These studies provide sound evidence that the AMHHE Conference plays a significant role in de-stigmatizing mental health in the higher education sector and to the potential need to inform students about the signs and symptoms among colleagues experiencing mental health challenges. Similarly, Thompson (2019) advocates for staff to be better informed about mental health issues and how to recognize signs of psychological distress, e.g., erratic attendance, deteriorating quality of student output and then follow up by asking sensitively about the student's welfare and the pressures of university study.

One possibly undervalued pressure point for students of all ages is the transition phase into university with little or no experience of how universities function and an expectation that students will be self-directed and motivated (Meyer, 2019). However, the transition phase also significantly changes the context of life and learning for young persons and mature aged students attending university for the first time. Feelings of loss, uncertainty and adapting to a new learning environment can be psychologically challenging and generate feelings of disconnection and loneliness which were described vividly in Christie et al. (2008) as:

> *"An intrinsically emotional process and that feelings of loss and dislocation are inherent to the students' experiences of entering university, and that "coming to know" a new community of practice is an emotional process that can incorporate feelings of alienation and exclusion, as well as of excitement and exhilaration. A broader understanding of how students learn then depends not just upon the individual's emotional commitment to developing a new learning identity, but on the emotional interaction between the student and the learning environment of the university."*

Meyer (2019) describes three stages of transition (page 65):

(a) *Ending of the previous life stage that generates feelings of loss, grief, resistance, protest, doubt, homesickness and sometimes elation.*
(b) *A neutral zone between the two stages: letting go, sadness, uncertainty, disorientation, self-doubt, discomfort, worry about the future, excitement, feeling overwhelmed, anxiety, fear of failure.*
(c) *New beginning: acceptance, readiness, comfort, integration, clarity, commitment, ambition, celebration and probably ongoing fear, resistance or resignation.*

In some respects, Meyer (2019) reflects the intent of the Australian mentally healthy universities collective that aimed to sign and apply the Okanagan Charter.

Interprofessional Collaboration in the University Workplace

Interprofessional collaboration in mental health is at the heart of many roles in professional practice contexts. However, preparing students for working in interprofessional contexts can be challenging when it involves students collaborating with students from different colleges and disciplines. In this respect, Marcussen et al.'s (2019) study is instructive. In this case, Marcussen assessed interprofessional clinical training in a training ward with students from medicine, nursing, psychotherapy, pedagogy and social work. Two groups were formed: the interprofessional training group and a training as usual comparison group. The intervention group showed stronger and significantly higher scores on the post-measure of interprofessional learning and team collaborative practice than the comparison group. Students also reported feeling better prepared for practice.

While the Marcussen study had the data to evidence greater depth of knowledge and understanding through collaborative practice, the AMHHEC planning group developed in a similar way. The longevity of the AMHHEC planning group since 2016 is a testament to the group's commitment to the mental health of the university students and staff, as well as commitment to collaboration with community organizations and the university networks around Australia and our regional neighbors.

Closer to the university context, Caleb (2019) provides guidance for staff to support students who are troubled or distressed within a university policy framework using five guiding principles while remaining within one's boundaries of expertise:

1. Identifying a problem: know the student, observe behavior, e.g., weight changes, tearfulness, study problems.
2. Recognizing if the situation is urgent, and the student is considered at risk. Then, immediate action is necessary to keep the student safe.
3. Signposting: The guide should outline how to signpost, list the available services internal and external and what to do if the student is resistant to assistance.
4. Know who to contact: internally, external and emergency.
5. Remain mindful of one's own boundaries and act accordingly to refer the student to student welfare on site in the first instance.

Interprofessional education and collaboration are key elements of the design of the Australasian Mental Health in Higher Education Conference that draws together educators, practitioners across the spectrum of health and mental health professions, academics, students and community organizations providing services. The collaborative structure of the conference provided multiple perspectives and thought-provoking conceptualizations that informed and transformed ways of thinking and challenged one to reflect more deeply and critically. Universities as centers of learning also play a significant role more broadly in the communities in which they are located. The Australasian Mental Health in Higher Education Conference is one such initiative that draws together community and academia.

Appendix

Australian Health Promoting Universities Network as at 15 March 2016.

The network is a shared vision of the following Australian universities:

- Australian Catholic University
- Australian National University
- Curtin University
- Deakin University
- Federation University Australia
- La Trobe University
- Macquarie University
- Queensland University of Technology
- RMIT University
- Southern Cross University
- Swinburne University of Technology

- University of Adelaide
- University of Melbourne
- University of New England
- University of New South Wales
- University of Newcastle
- University of Notre Dame
- University of Queensland
- University of South Australia
- University of Sydney
- University of Tasmania
- University of Technology Sydney
- University of the Sunshine Coast
- University of Wollongong
- Western Sydney University

References

Caleb, R. (2019). From strategy to policy and procedure: Making mental health policies work. In N. Barden & R. Caleb (Eds.), *Student mental health & wellbeing in higher education: A practical guide*. Sage Publications.

Christie, H., Tett, L., Cree, V. E., Hounsell, J., & McCune, V. (2008). A real rollercoaster of confidence and emotions: Learning to be a university student. *Studies in Higher Education, 33*(5), 567–581. https://doi.org/10.1080/03075070802373040

Eaton, L. (2019). Health workforce burn-out. *Bulletin of the World Health Organization, 97*, 585–586. https://doi.org/10.2471/BLT.19.020919

Fernandez, N., Cyr, J., Perreault, I., & Brault, I. (2020). Revealing tacit knowledge used by experienced health professionals for interprofessional collaboration. *Journal of Interprofessional Care, 34*(4), 537–544. https://doi.org/10.1080/13561820.2020.1724901

Figley, C. R. (Ed.). (1995). Compassion fatigue as secondary traumatic stress disorder: An overview. In *Compassion fatigue: Coping with secondary traumatic stress disorder in those who treat the traumatized* (pp. 1–20). Brunner/Mazel., Inc.

Fitzgerald, J. T., Williams, B. C., Halter, J. B., Remington, T. L., Foulk, M. A., Persky, N. W., & Shay, B. R. (2006). Effects of a geriatrics interdisciplinary experience on learners' knowledge and attitudes. *Gerontology & Geriatrics Education, 26*(3), 17–28. https://doi.org/10.1300/J021v26n03_02

Interprofessional Education Collaborative Expert Panel. (IEPEC). (2011). *Core competencies for interprofessional collaborative practice: Report of an expert panel*. Interprofessional Education Collaborative.

Kelly, P. L., Heyman, J. C., Tice-Brown, D., & White-Ryan, L. (2020). Interprofessional practice: Social work students' perspectives on collaboration. *Social Work in Health Care, 59*(2), 108–121. https://doi.org/10.1080/00981389.2020.1719565

Li, W., Denson, L. A., & Dorstyn, D. S. (2018). Understanding Australian university students' mental health help-seeking: An empirical and theoretical investigation. *Australian Journal of Psychology, 70*, 30–40. https://doi.org/10.1111/ajpy.12157

Marcussen, M., Nørgaard, B., Borgnakke, K., & Arnfred, S. (2019). Interprofessional clinical training in mental health improves students' readiness for interprofessional collaboration: A

non randomized intervention study. *BMC Medical Education, 19*, 27. https://doi.org/10.1186/s12909-019-1465-6
Medical Journal of Australia Careers. (April 2016). *Network Committed to Healthy Unis*. 204(7), 18 https://doi.org/10.5694/mja16.1804C1
Meyer, D. (2019). The student lifecycle: Pressure points and transitions. In N. Barden, & R. Caleb (Eds.), *Student mental health and wellbeing in higher education: A practical guide*. Sage Publications.
O'Grady, K. L. (March 19, 2021). Careers: How to manage through emotional exhaustion. *The Chronicle of Higher Education*. 61–63.
Reavley, N. J., McCann, T. V., & Jorm, A. F. (2012). Actions taken to deal with mental health problems in Australian higher education students. *Early Intervention in Psychiatry, 6*, 159–165. https://doi.org/10.1111/j.1751-7893.2011.00294.x
Strolin-Goltzman, J., Breslend, N., Hemenway-Deaver, A., Wood, V., Woodside-Jiron, H., & Krompf, A. (2020). Moving beyond self-care: Exploring the protective influence of interprofessional collaboration, leadership, and competency on secondary traumatic stress. *Traumatology*. Advance online publication. https://doi.org/10.1037/trm0000244
Taylor, P., Saheb, R., & Howse, E. (2019). Creating healthier graduates, campuses and communities: Why Australia needs to invest in health promoting universities. *Health Promotion Journal of Australia,* 30, 285–289. https://doi.org/10.1002/hpja.175
Thompson, D. (2019). Student mental health and the developing mind. In N. Barden, & R. Caleb (Eds.), *Student mental health & wellbeing in higher education: A practical guide*. Sage Publications.
Universities Australia. (2008). *A National internship scheme: enhancing the skills and work readiness of Australian university graduates.*
Watson, B. M., Jones, L., & Hewett, D. G. (2016). Accommodating health. In H. Giles (Ed.), *Communication accommodation theory: Negotiating personal relationships and social identities across contexts* (pp. 152–168). Cambridge University Press.
World Health Organization. (2010). Framework for action on interprofessional education and collaborative practice.
Zochil, M. L., & Thorsteinsson, E. B. (2018). Exploring poor sleep, mental health, and help-seeking intention in university students. *Australian Journal of Psychology, 70*, 41–47. https://doi.org/10.1111/ajpy.12160

Web Links:

Okanagan-Charter. https://bp-net.ca/wp-content/uploads/2019/03/Okanagan-Charter.pdf
University of Sydney. Australian universities make health and wellbeing a priority. https://www.sydney.edu.au/news-opinion/news/2016/03/15/australian-universities-make-health-and-wellbeing-a-priority.html

Beryl Buckby is a Clinical Psychologist and Lecturer in the Undergraduate and Postgraduate Master of Psychology (Clinical) Programs at the Townsville campus of James Cook University. Her teaching and research encompasses Clinical supervision and psychopathology, Interprofessional Education and Practice, Young-age onset dementia, mental health particularly Interventions for PTSD, and secondary traumatic stress, as well as suicide and suicide prevention in North Queensland Communities. Her current focus is Interprofessional education and communication and the role Psychologists play in enhancing person-centred care. She was previously a researcher for three years in the National beyondblue Postnatal Depression Program screening 4600 mothers-to-be in antenatal clinics across Queensland with follow-up at six months post-partum.

Mentally Healthy City Townsville: Promoting Wellbeing in Communities

Sue McGinty, Catherine Day, Cathy O'Toole, Kathryn Montafia, Anneliese Young, and Zoltan Sarnyai

Abstract This is the story of the implementation and outcomes of the Mentally Healthy City Townsville project (MHCT) introduced in 2018 in a regional university city in northern Australia. The project supports the people of Townsville to flourish and thrive by heightening the focus on mental wellness and by assisting individuals and organisations to better support those who, from time to time, may be mentally unwell. Townsville has many clinical services on offer, as well as two universities that educate students in medical, social work, psychological and business disciplines. However, it is not enough to address just clinical intervention for mental illness without promoting informed mental wellbeing and prevention. Partnerships between community groups, businesses and higher education benefit both participants in these groups and the people they work with.

Keywords Mental Wellbeing · Communities · Mentally healthy city

Introduction

This chapter outlines the purpose, implementation and progress of the Mentally Healthy City Townsville project. Collaborative action for community wellbeing is a necessary step in improving the mental health of our community. However, the current clinical approach is not sufficient to address mental health concerns in Australia

---

S. McGinty (✉) · C. Day · C. O'Toole · K. Montafia · A. Young · Z. Sarnyai
Townsville, Australia
e-mail: smcginty@tbmf.com.au

C. Day
e-mail: cday@tbmf.com.au

C. O'Toole
e-mail: cotoole@tbmf.com.au

A. Young
e-mail: ayoung@tbmf.com.au

Z. Sarnyai
e-mail: zoltan.sarnyai@jcu.edu.au

A. P. Francis and M. A. Carter (eds.), *Mental Health and Higher Education in Australia*,
https://doi.org/10.1007/978-981-16-8040-3_21

and bring real and lasting change to the lives of Australians who experience poor mental health and, more distressingly, take their own lives. A mentally healthy city addresses mental health as a comprehensive, whole of life, health and wellbeing agenda involving individual citizens and the support of the broader community.

Mental health is a significant public health issue throughout Australia as it is in many other countries. In Australia, national statistics show that 45% of the population will live with mental distress in their lifetime and 20% of the population will live with mental distress in any twelve-month period (Mental health—Australian Institute of Health and Welfare aihw.gov.au, 2020). Nationally, Aboriginal and Torres Strait Islander communities have a mental distress rate three times the national average (Buckby et al., 2016). Townsville, with a population of 200,000, like similar locations across regional Australia, has rising mental health issues within the community and a suicide rate of 2.5 times the national average (https://www.townsvillebulletin.com.au/news/townsville/check-your-mates-now-is-the-time-to-look-after-each-other/news-story/4b035c0500d2dede48688b5a4d832f8b). In 2020, Townsville had nearly 10% of the Australia's Indigenous suicides (https://thestringer.com.au/highest-suicide-rate-health-inequality-is-discrimination-13114#.YNpxI-gzY2w). This acknowledges that mental ill health does not discriminate among members of our community; it is not us or them situation. A thriving community will deliver positive health outcomes in addition to economic, cultural, educational and sporting benefits.

Thus, addressing these growing statistics about the negative incidence of mental health and wellbeing must be everyone's business (Mental health is everybody's business—Black Dog Institute). The growing burden of mental ill health and the impact of suicide on the nation's future health budget, suggest that a valid analogy for what the MHCT does is, in the words of Pope Francis when speaking about the church, that it is a field hospital for the sick and that we are all in that field hospital together (https://www.ncronline.org/blogs/francis-chronicles/pope-s-quotes-field-hospital-church).

At a national level, the Productivity Commission Inquiry into Mental Health in Australia (2020) articulates a focus on a person-centred mental health system at the core of its reform; this requires some fundamental cultural shift in how mental healthcare is accessed and experienced. The report also calls for the Australian Government to provide once-off seed funding for a professional association for lived/living experience workers. It asks the Australian, State and Territory Governments to develop a programme for educating health professionals about the role and value of lived/living experience workers. The report also states that there is a great need for increased funding and action to be taken regarding prevention and early intervention.

The Mentally Healthy City Townsville

Townsville, in the State of Queensland, is the largest city in northern Australia. It was the first city in Australia to take up the Mentally Healthy City challenge to support population-wide wellbeing. Mentally Healthy City Townsville (MHCT) is auspiced by the Townsville-based Tropical Brain and Mind Foundation (TBMF) to take action to support the communities within the Townsville City Council area. The TBMF's commitment to MHCT is clearly stated in the Foundation's purpose: "*a community-based organisation that exists to promote and improve brain health and wellbeing through advocacy, education, and research* (https://www.tropicalbrainandmind.com.au/statement-of-strategic-intent/)". The Foundation's aspiration is to "create *flourishing communities with healthy minds, bodies and environments*". The MHCT takes a whole of community approach to achieve a level of mental health and wellbeing that nurtures the city to "*a state of wellbeing in which every individual realises his or her own potential, can cope with the normal stresses of life, can work productively and fruitfully, and is able to make a contribution to her or his community*".

To achieve this, the MHCT engages with the Townsville City Council (TCC), Townsville Health and Hospital Service (THHS), MHCT Champions, James Cook University, the corporate and business sectors, community mental health sector and broader community groups to build local wellbeing capacity to create, improve and grow community resources. Similar approaches have been successfully implemented in London and Philadelphia.

Introducing the idea of the MHCT to the TBMF as a project designed for the Townsville community was the brainchild of Professor Brett McDermott, a child and adolescent psychiatrist, previously Professor of Psychiatry at James Cook University who had spent time as a member of the national beyondblue Board where the Mentally Healthy City concept was first considered. Whilst initial efforts were made to introduce the idea in Geelong, Victoria, it was in Townsville in 2018 that the concept became a reality for the first time in Australia. From the outset, MHCT was designed to work with the wider community in building stronger awareness of how to maintain positive mental health and support those in the community who from time to time suffer mental ill health. The initial support from the Townsville City Council was a strong incentive to begin the project. The TBMF was grateful for the early support of beyondblue in building the foundation for the MHCT project, including the Chair of beyondblue, former Prime Minister Julia Gillard, who came to Townsville to launch the project in November 2018.

The Essence of the MHCT Approach

As stated above, Townsville, like other similar locations across Australia, has a rising rate of mental ill health within the community. To date, the people of Townsville, from a range of different cultures and backgrounds, have been vocal about the importance of supporting their fellow residents. Townsville has a strong community ethic based on sporting and cultural investment by the population, the largest Australian Army base in Australia, James Cook University which has a national and international leadership role in addressing critical challenges facing the tropics. CQUniversity also has a presence in the city, and it takes pride in providing training for a number of health professionals. This is a city that can lead the way for social and cultural change, and reduce the stigma in the understanding and primacy of positive mental health. The MHCT programme assists the people of Townsville by heightening the focus on mental wellness and assisting individuals and organisations to better support those who may be mentally unwell. Townsville has many clinical services on offer; however, it is not enough to address just intervention to mental illness without informed prevention.

Thus, the MHCT assists in building individual and community resilience and capacity to respond to mental health issues and self-care, reduce stigma and build social cohesion. The MHCT focusses on a grassroots level of service by educating and empowering the local community to understand and maintain positive mental health. MHCT is not replacing services already provided, but working alongside mental health service providers and other organisations to provide the resources for engagement, education and promotion of positive mental wellness in everyday lives in keeping with Level 1 in the Stepped Care Model currently utilised in the mental health system (https://www.connecttowellbeing.org.au/stepped-care).

The MHCT approach is based on two international programmes: the European Alliance Against Depression and the model adopted by the Mentally Healthy Cities Alliance, which exists in eight countries and is called I-CIRCLE. It includes cities such as Philadelphia, London and Stockholm.

The European Alliance Against Depression (EAAD) is an international not-for-profit organisation based in Leipzig, Germany (http://www.eaad.net/home). It has more than 100 regional network partners in Europe, Canada, Chile and Australia.

> The main aim of the European Alliance Against Depression is to improve care and optimise treatment for patients with depressive disorders and to prevent suicidal behaviour. It was established in 2008 by a number of mental health experts from different European research institutions in order to sustain the EU-funded EAAD projects (2004–2008). The EAAD is involved in several European research projects targeting depression and suicide prevention (http://www.eaad.net/home).

Founded in Philadelphia USA, the international city and urban regional collaborative (I-CIRCLE) emphasises building social capital by supporting mental health and wellbeing within urban settings and to "enable citizens to complement the formal mental health system (e.g. through forming strategic local partnerships with groups and organizations in the local communities)" (https://www.iimhl.com/icircle-homepage).

I-CIRCLE members share innovations that include:

- taking protective action to prevent future problems (e.g. addressing the social determinants of health, ensuring a healthy start, building resilience and strengthening social connectedness)
- enhancing early recognition and effectively responding to emerging issues (e.g. through classes and training that enable people to take the necessary action to respond and heal themselves, their families and neighbours and others they encounter at work and in their wider lives)

- ensuring a comprehensive range of behavioural health services that is appropriate for the population served (https://www.iimhl.com/icircle-about-us).

The work of MHCT is also aligned with the National Mental Health Commission's "Contributing lives, thriving communities" (https://www.mentalhealthcommission.gov.au/social-determinants/contributing-lives-thriving-communities) where people living with a mental health difficulty can expect the same rights, opportunities, and health as those without a mental illness. MHCT's work is aligned to The Contributing Life framework (https://www.flourishaustralia.org.au/mental-health-a-z/category/contributing-life) which is a whole-of-person, whole-of-system, whole-of-life approach to mental health and wellbeing.

For the MHCT, a contributing life is a fulfilling life enriched with close connections to family and friends; good health and wellbeing to allow those connections to be enjoyed; having something to do each day that provides hope, meaning and purpose—whether it be a job, supporting others or volunteering; and a home to live in, free from financial stress and uncertainty. In short, it means thriving, not just surviving. The MHCT's aim is to assist people in the broader community to take action themselves before experiencing mental distress. This approach aligns with the MHCT's commitment to Step 1 of the Stepped Care model.

'Stepped Care is an evidence-based, staged approach to the delivery of mental health services, comprising a hierarchy of interventions—from the least to the most intensive—matched to the individual's needs' (https://www.connecttowellbeing.org.au/stepped-care). Level 1 of the Stepped Care model, the focus for the MHCT programme, is for the general mentally well population who can use publicly available resources to ensure their continuing mental wellbeing. The health activation approach assists people and organisations to act and be responsible for their own mental wellbeing.

Part of assisting people to maintain or gain mental health is addressing the stigma that mental ill health can generate (https://www.healthdirect.gov.au/mental-health-stigma#what-is). Even with the MHCT's programmes at Level 1 of the Stepped Care model, the reality of stigma attached to mental ill health is a constant issue. To address the negativity that the general public sees in mental illness and to address the impact this negativity may make on their work and the perception of what the MHTC does, the organisation has used a range of strategies such as education in being conscious of the language used to combat the stigma.

MHCT Essentials

The MHCT has developed an "Essentials" document framed against the Australian recognised Stepped Care model for mental health and aligned to a Health Activation Approach. The basis for MHCT Essentials is to ensure there is a focus on overall wellness for the individual and the Townsville community in order to improve education and personal empowerment for self-care, whilst also reducing the stigma around mental health.

The essentials document that guides the MHCT has eight planks (https://www.mentallyhealthycitytownsville.com.au/about/):

- Brand Development and Marketing
  - The MHCT has been established within the Townsville community as a reputable, and relatable brand.
- Website and Resource Hub
  - The MHCT Website is the central repository for all information around the programme. The website will be updated throughout the life of the programme with databases containing wellbeing-related organisations and mental health service providers (https://www.mentallyhealthycitytownsville.com.au/services/mental-health-providers/).
- Community Programmes
  - MHCT assists in building the capacity of the Townsville Community through the sponsorship of hosted events and through the dissemination of the Wheel of Wellbeing (WoW). WoW is a framework of six themes that underpin mental and physical health and wellbeing: body; mind; spirit; people; place; planet (https://www.mentallyhealthycitytownsville.com.au/wheel-of-well-being).
- Events and Promotions
  - The MHCT is an event partner with large local community organisations to further support the advocation of mental health in North Queensland.
- Mental Health in the Workplace
  - MHCT delivers workshops for businesses and small operators in the Townsville community in partnership with State Government organisations. The workshops are based on the Mentally Healthy Workplace Toolkit (https://www.worksafe.qld.gov.au/safety-and-prevention/mental-health/mentally-healthy-workplaces-toolkit).
- Mental Health in Schools
  - MHCT supports existing frameworks, initiatives and objectives in State, Private and Catholic education systems in the delivery of wellbeing programmes. These programmes provide opportunities for wellbeing education in schools from Early Years centres, primary and secondary schools to tertiary institutions such as James Cook University.
- MHCT Pledges and Industry Alliances
  - Building on established industry partnerships, MHCT is continuing to encourage schools, organisations and workplaces to pledge to be Mentally

Healthy City Advocates, to help raise awareness about mental health and connect residents in need with available resources, tools and service providers.

- MHCT Champions and Advocates
  - MHCT Champions are high profile and influential members in the Townsville Community from various industries who raise awareness and encourage participation. The Advocates are individuals who help the MHCT get the word out on what mental health is, how it affects us all, and what resources and support are available to each of us.

Delivery Phases

The MHCT programme is currently in phase two of a three-phase agenda. Phase 1 (2018–2020) of the initiative, the establishment phase, focussed on stakeholder engagement, marketing and media, governance and development of relationships with mental wellness providers to train/conduct workshops for staff, organisations and individuals. Through strategic collaborations the programme has:

- delivered integrated communications and marketing campaigns to educate and raise awareness of the mental health continuum
- developed and engaged the community through innovative events to promote mental wellness
- supported Townsville-based mental health service providers, through the development of a web platform and resources
- assisted in the rollout of national campaigns to support businesses, schools, university staff and students, especially those in disciplines that deal with mental health, community organisations and individuals
- developed a Townsville specific stigma reduction campaign for mental health
- developed and promoted a Townsville-centric Wheel of Wellbeing programme
- promoted the integration and networking of existing services to assist individuals, university staff and health professionals in navigating the mental health service sector.

At the end of Phase 1, the following objectives were achieved:

- Townsville became the first Australian city to embrace a common understanding of the importance of holistic wellness.
- Townsville became a site for a stigma reduction campaign, strengthening the community by creating a common and positive approach to mental wellness.
- The development of mental health resilience became a high priority for the city agenda in supporting healthy children, adolescents and adults from all demographics.
- Townsville is a national leader in having one of the most developed and integrated mental health service sector.

Phase 2, the Collective Impact phase (2020–2023) has begun although extensive local flooding (February 2019) and COVID-19 has curtailed some initiatives and assessment. This phase is working to ensure, in addition to continuing the initiatives from Phase 1, that the programme is fully embedded in the community and that the establishment phase has been evaluated. To this end, a Charter of Actions has been developed and approved by the TBMF Board and is being revised with further community consultation. This is a very practical charter which outlines the focus of activities in the city. It will also provide funders with concrete actions so that KPIs can be measured against it (see Appendix at the end of the chapter).

Phase 3, from 2023 on, will focus on sustainable and enduring initiatives to ensure that long-term MHC programmes exist and the reach of project outcomes is expanded throughout the local population.

Future Directions for the MHCT

The MHCT works at Level 1 of the Stepped Care model where emphasis is on the general mentally well population. This population can use self-help or publicly available resources to ensure their continuing mental wellbeing. MHCT initiatives like the Wheel of Wellbeing and other workshops and promotions are useful for individuals, mental health professionals both in the community and those studying at university, community groups and businesses. Empowerment happens as people draw on their strengths and abilities both individually and collectively. Having power and control comes from identifying one's own needs, making choices and taking responsibility for finding solutions. But there is more than an individual benefit in this process. The results from the tools the MHCT use and teaches or when it auspices external speakers and programmes, can be further multiplied in a flow-on effect to family, workmates, other students as well as through random meetings and sharing by individuals.

To add to the benefits from wellness strategies, there is the opportunity of a further flow-on when the techniques and skills that the MHCT fosters are taught within organisations such as schools, universities, and the Australian Defence Force. Many schools in Townsville practice daily meditation at each educational level. This is a wellness technique in itself but it could be amplified by teaching students, and not just teachers, the Wheel of Wellbeing and other strategies to maintain physical and mental health. Members of the defence force, too, can also benefit from a knowledge of wellbeing strategies, both as individuals and as a team. Members work in a stressful and ordered environment where mental and physical wellbeing are paramount, the type of environment where MHCT resources would be useful and beneficial.

Similarly, at universities, wellbeing strategies are useful for the mental health of both staff and students as individuals. University teaching staff, as well as students, are under increasing pressures that impact their mental health (Morrish, 2019; Spalek, 2021; James Cook University Webinar 7 July 2021) and staff would benefit from the Step 1 activities given by the MHCT. In regard to university students, in 2017

Orygen released *Under the radar: the mental health of Australian university students* which identified a lack of guidance regarding the role of universities in supporting the mental health and wellbeing of students. Subsequently, Orygen has developed a University mental health framework (https://www.orygen.org.au/Policy/University-Mental-Health-Framework/Framework/) that supports university students' mental health and wellbeing. The MHCT, through education, advocacy, guidance to appropriate services and promotion of the Wheel of Wellbeing contributes to higher education wellbeing for both staff and students.

But, at a more empowering level, students in professions that deal with people in stressful or high energy situations may strengthen their professional work by using and passing on what they have learned about mental and physical wellbeing. We know that mental health can impact physical health and vice versa (https://www.mentalhealth.org.uk/a-to-z/p/physical-health-and-mental-health). Professions such as social work, education, psychology, nursing and medicine all work in situations where people's mental and physical health is vital for their functioning. Education at university level provides teaching guidelines that emphasise pathology and disease (see, e.g., AASW, July 2020). Students in these professions need to know and understand wellness and good mental health and how to speak about (Craig, 2010) and educate others about mental health to add to their knowledge of pathologies and mental diseases.

Level 1 of the Stepped Care model emphasises self-management and self-help strategies. Level 1 services are designed to prevent the onset of mental illness, prevent its escalation and focus on supporting both the well population as well as the vulnerable. This is what the MHCT does through public information, education and training.

Appendix: Mentally Healthy City Townsville—Charter of Actions

Townsville was the first city in Australia to take up the Mentally Healthy City challenge to support population-wide wellbeing. Mentally Health City Townsville (MHCT) is auspiced by the Tropical Brain and Mind Foundation (TBMF) to take action to support the communities within the Townsville City Council (TCC) Local Government Area (LGA). The aim is to achieve a balance of mental health and wellbeing that nurtures a city where "*a state of wellbeing in which every individual realises his or her own potential, can cope with the normal stresses of life, can work productively and fruitfully, and is able to make a contribution to her or his community*" (WHO | Mental Health).

The Mayor on behalf of the TCC has pledged to support and collaborate with MHCT to build local wellbeing capacity to create, improve, and grow community resources. The Townsville Hospital and Health Service (THHS) and Northern Queensland Primary Health Network (NQPHN) have also provided significant support to MHCT. MHCT acknowledges that our city thrives when the communities where we live, work, and play thrive because mental health and wellbeing are everyone's business.

To further develop Townsville's commitment to MHCT a formal endorsement for the MHCT Charter of Actions will be sought from the Mayor TCC, THHS Board, NQPHN, the Business Sector and the Mental Health Community Sector. The Charter of Actions aims to ensure that our city is "*one that is continually creating and improving those physical and social environments and expanding those community resources which enable people to mutually support each other in performing all the functions of life and developing to their maximum potential*" (Urban Insight https://www.swecourbaninsight.com).

MHCT in collaboration with key stakeholders, will work collaboratively to facilitate and support the following thirteen (13) Charter Actions to drive social changes that will deliver mental health and wellbeing, promote social inclusion, and reduce stigma in our local communities. MHCT will:

1. Work with local universities, TAFE, schools, and early childhood education centres to facilitate the development of and annually review of policies and/or leadership guidance documents such as but not limited to The Resilience Project, Be You and Wellbeing in Schools to encourage their community's wellbeing.
2. Work with local mental health community organisations including veteran organisations to facilitate the development of and annual review of policies and leadership documents to encourage community, inclusion, wellbeing, and support that is informed by lived experience.
3. Work with local.
4. Together a collective dedicated group to focus on community inclusion, wellbeing, and support.
5. Work with local older persons agencies and/or advocacy group/s, both community-based and in residential settings to establish access to and/or facilitate the development of community wellbeing programmes and activities to reduce loneliness and increase wellbeing.
6. Work with local art galleries to hold an annual exhibition focussing on the diversity of mental health and wellbeing lived experience journeys in our community.
7. Work with local stakeholders to host an annual mental health and wellbeing event during Mental Health Week to promote wellbeing, diversity, social connection, and stigma reduction.
8. Collaborate with the Mayor and TCC to create a Mayor's Award to highlight the most creative and innovative wellbeing event, including both individual and organisational participation, during Mental Health Week. Representation from the mental health sector, including lived experience will determine the winners of the Mayor's prizes.
9. Collaborate with key stakeholders including TCC, THHS and NQPHN to promote wellbeing community programmes to engage neighbourhoods in

social connection and wellbeing activities including partnerships with, but not limited to the Townsville Recovery Acceleration Project Committee (Social Working Group), GO1 (online learning management system for self-education) and Wheel of Wellbeing (WoW—online training/certification for wellbeing support managers).

10. Work with local social, print, and other media agencies to promote and showcase the lived experience of positive mental health and wellbeing activities and events.
11. Ensure that key stakeholder's mental health and wellbeing policies, supports and practices demonstrate an understanding of how First Nations and Culturally and Linguistically Diverse Peoples and other identified community groups shape the experience of mental health and wellbeing, through ethnic, religious, gendered, and sexual identity and through the social experience of poverty, inequality, and disenfranchisement.
12. Encourage and invite lived experience evidence from local agencies for the homeless and imprisoned regarding mental health and wellbeing support.
13. MHCT under the guidance of the Tropical Brain and Mind Foundation will establish a review and evaluation process regarding these social change activities/targets in the first two years with the intention to grow further community involvement into the future.

Reference
This document has been modelled on the Compassionate City Charter of Actions: Allan Kellehear—From K. Wegleitner, K Heimerl, A. Kellehear (2016). Compassionate Communities: Case Studies form Britain and Europe. Abingdon, Routledge, 2016 (80–82).

References

AASW. (2020). *Accredited mental health social workers qualifications, skills and experience*. Australian Association of Social Workers. https://www.aasw.asn.au/document/item/11704

Buckby, B., Stodden, A., & Lutkin, S. (2016). Preventing Suicide in the North: Developing capacity, local knowledge and skills. *A Report for the Townsville Suicide Prevention Network*. https://doi.org/10.13140/RG.2.2.24880.15369

Craig, N. (2010). Mental health issues and higher education psychology teaching. *Psychology Teaching Review, 16*(1), 16–23.

James Cook University Webinar. https://www.jcu.edu.au/events/2021/july/australasian-mental-health-and-higher-education-webinar

Mental Health—Australian Institute of Health and Welfare. (2020). aihw.gov.au.

Mental Health is Everyone's Business. https://www.blackdoginstitute.org.au/education-services/workplaces/workplace-programs/mental-health-is-everybodys-business/. Accessed May 25, 2021.

Morrish, L. (2019). *Pressure vessels: The epidemic of poor mental health among higher education staff*. Higher Education Policy Unit.

National Mental Health Commission. (2021). *Contributing lives, thriving communities*. https://www.mentalhealthcommission.gov.au/social-determinants/contributing-lives-thriving-communities. Accessed May 25, 2021.
Pope Francis, The Church as a Field Hospital. (2019). https://www.vaticannews.va/en/pope/news/2019-08/pope-francis-general-audience-church-cares-for-sick.html. Accessed May 25, 2021.
Qld Alliance for Mental Health Summary, Key Issues. (2020). *The productivity commission inquiry into mental health final report*. https://www.pc.gov.au/inquiries/completed/mental-health/report. Accessed May 25, 2021.
Spalek, B. (2021). The forgotten mental health crisis: pressures on staff. *University World News*, 16 January 2021. https://www.universityworldnews.com
Stepped Care. (2019). https://www1.health.gov.au/internet/main/publishing.nsf/Content/2126B045A8DA90FDCA257F6500018260/$File/1.%20PHN%20Guidance%20-%20Stepped%20Care%20-%202019.pdf. Accessed May 25, 2021.
Values_Framework_Peer_Working.pdf (scottishrecovery.net). https://www.scottishrecovery.net/wp-content/uploads/2020/12/Values_Framework_Peer_Working.pdf. Accessed May 25, 2021.
WHO Mental Health Report. https://www.who.int/research-observatory/analyses/mentalhealth/en/. Accessed May 25, 2021.

Sue McGinty loves walking pilgrimage routes: the longer the better. She has completed the Camino de Santiago twice, plus walking routes through England, Portugal, France and Switzerland. Sue's home-based interests and activities lie with the Tropical Brain and Mind Foundation of which she was a co-founder. Currently she is working with the Foundation to establish a Centre for Brain Health in the Tropics. Sue was Professor of Educational Psychology at James Cook University (JCU) before 'retiring' in 2015. She is now an Adjunct Professor at James Cook University.

Catherine Day Ph.D., Retired Executive Director, School Principal and Teacher. Chairperson Tropical Brain and Mind Foundation.

Cathy O'Toole has extensive experience in the mental health community sector at the national, state, and local levels. Cathy is a former Federal Member of Parliament, CEO in the Community Mental Health Sector for 15 years and small business owner for 30 years. She has recently undertaken consultancy work in First Nation Mental Health, Palliative Care and is currently consulting with the Tropical Brain and Mind Foundation. Cathy also has her own lived experience of managing her mental health and wellbeing, a young family and life in general. Cathy is currently serving on the following boards on a voluntary basis: Queensland Alliance for Mental Health, Community Mental Health Australia, Carers Australia, Glasser Australia, Townsville Multicultural Support Group, Townsville Region Committee of the Ageing, Connecting End of Life Care Steering and Working Groups (Palliative Care Qld) and Steering Committee for Brain Health in the Tropics.

Kathryn Montafia's career as a multimedia designer has spanned national and international design and advertising agencies. She has also worked in not-for-profit, and across multiple departments within State Government in traditional and digital platforms. Kathryn has a Bachelor of Nursing degree, and a Graduate Certificate in Digital Communications from Queensland University of Technology. Kathryn's healthcare knowledge has enabled her to combine both fields of academic study and past career experience to advance the awareness of mental health and well-being into the Townsville community through the Mentally Healthy City Townsville project. Kathryn worked for MHCT in Phase One of the project from February 2019 as the Digital and Marketing Manager.

Anneliese Young A domestic and international marketing and communications professional, Anneliese has worked overseas in London managing a nationwide women's active campaign, This Girl Can. Originally from Perth, Western Australia, Anneliese studied a Bachelor Degree in Marketing and Advertising at Curtin University and is in the midst of completing a Post Graduate Certificate in Communications (majoring Public Relations) at Deakin University. Anneliese has extensive experience working within WA Government, specifically the health sector, with over four years' experience in not-for-profit. Additionally, she has a Certificate 3 and 4 in Fitness, proving she is a true advocate for health, fitness, and mental health and well-being. Anneliese joined Phase One of the project in January 2020 and is a Project Officer at MHC.

Zoltan Sarnyai is a Professor of Neuroscience at James Cook University. He was previously University Lecturer in the Department of Pharmacology, University of Cambridge and a Fellow of Pembroke College, Cambridge where he was Director of Studies for Medicine. He trained at Harvard Medical School and at The Rockefeller University. He conducts research on the contribution of stress, energy metabolism, gut microbiota and immune activation to brain health. He has over a hundred publications (H index 38). His research has been recognised by awards and fellowships, including the Lady Davis Visiting Professorship at Technion-Israel Institute of Technology. He currently serves on the Executive Committee of the Biological Psychiatry Australia and of the International Society for Nutritional Psychiatry Research. He is Associate Editor for *Nutritional Neuroscience* and for *Frontiers in Neuroscience*, and member of the editorial board of the journals *Stress* and *International Journal of Environmental Research and Public Health.*

The manufacturer's authorised representative in the EU is Springer Nature Customer Service Centre GmbH, Europaplatz 3, 69115 Heidelberg, Germany. If you have any concerns regarding our products, please contact ProductSafety@springernature.com

Printed and bound by CPI Group (UK) Ltd, Croydon, CR0 4YY
30/09/2026
02225246-0018